Morocco

DREAM TRIP

JULIUS HONNOR

CONTENTS

THIS IS
MOROCCO

Come to Morocco for its elusive magic and exotic mystery and you will probably leave with more prosaic, yet intimate, human memories: kids playing football under the shade of a tree in a sunny square, or a blind man selling bunches of fresh mint.

The romance of its reputation is real enough, but it is also a viscerally lived-in place, a seething mass of humanity and inhumanity, of sounds and colour and none-too-pleasant smells.

Morocco is rewarding and remarkably good value as a destination for walking, surfing and yoga; for aimless exploring or for focused lazing. But whatever you're doing here, it's the nature of the place itself that gets deepest into the pores of your skin.

So close to Europe, yet so very different, it has dark, dank alleys as well as magnificent desert sand dunes; dirty tanneries as well as soaring mountains and secret valleys.

Aït Benhaddou

The depth of experience and the detail is part of the extraordinary attraction of Morocco. Any of the routes described in this book will give you a great introduction to the country and its dusty, spicy flavours. But they are mere frames on which to hang your experience, and not ones to which you should always stick too rigidly.

Once you leave the sumptuous luxury and dazzling intricacy of your riad behind, no guidebook can ever tell you about the mass of life around every medina corner or the views from every bend in the road. And the near impossibility of knowing it all just adds to the seduction of trying.

FIRST STEPS
PUTTING IT ALL TOGETHER

There's often a temptation to try to squeeze more into a shorter trip, but journeys that may look like short hops on a map can be deceptively long.

In three weeks, any of the four itineraries detailed in this book will give an excellent introduction to a sizeable part of the country. If you have longer than three weeks, all the routes could be extended, or you could factor in some longer walks, some extra side trips, or extended time hanging out on the beach.

You could also consider combining two or more of the suggested routes. For example, given five or six weeks, Dream Trip 1 in the mountains and out on the coast, or Dream Trip 2 around the south, could easily be added to the end of Dream Trip 3, the journey around the Atlas from Fès to Marrakech. You could even arrive in Tangier on a ferry, do Dream Trip 4 and then catch the train south to Marrakech for Dream Trip 1.

Double the time frame to 10 or 12 weeks and you could start in Fès with Dream Trip 3, head south with Dream Trip 2 and then up into the mountains and out to the coast with Dream Trip 1 before heading north to complete a grand tour of Morocco with Dream Trip 4.

Conversely, if you only have a fortnight, all the routes could be shortened. In Dream Trip 1 you could miss out the coast, or double back to Marrakech from Essaouira. Trip 2 could be cut short in Agadir, missing out Marrakech. Trip 3 covers big distances and is harder to shorten, though you could spend less time in the gorges and perhaps bypass Meknès and Er Rachidia. Dream Trip 4 could be shortened by skipping Rabat and heading back to Tangier from Chefchaouen.

There's often a temptation to try to squeeze more into a shorter trip, but journeys that may look like short hops on a map can be deceptively long. What with winding mountain roads and the uncertainty of when that last passenger will turn up to fill the grand taxi, we'd recommend not hurrying things. Besides, they cook those tagines slowly for a reason: it gives the flavours longer to soak in.

→ DOING IT ALL

Fès → Meknès → Moulay Idriss and Volubilis → Ifrane and Azrou → Midelt → Er Rachidia → Merzouga → Tineghir and Todra Gorge → Boumalne du Dadès and Dadès Gorge → Zagora and M'Hamid → Aït Benhaddou → Telouet → Taroudant → Agadir → Taghazoute → Immouzer → Tafroute → Tiznit → Mirleft → Sidi Ifni → Tin Mal → Toubkal National Park → Marrakech → Essaouira → Sidi Kaouki → Oualidia → El Jadida → Casablanca → Rabat → Larache and Lixus → Asilah → Tangier → Chefchaouen → Tetouan → Ceuta

---

1 Essaouira 2 Streets of Marrakech

Best time to visit
Marrakech can have rain in winter, when the medina turns into a mud bath. But in general, even in winter it's pleasantly warm and sunny, though with cool nights. In spring and autumn temperatures are warm, even hot, and summer can be unbearable. The mountains are cooler, with snow in winter. The coast is much more stable, with pleasant temperatures year-round.

Marrakech (page 35) is the hub of routes across the High Atlas mountains to the south and to the coast in the west. The sights are amazing but there are also plenty of lower-key pleasures to discover in the maze of the city's streets; it's not a place to hurry. Three nights will give you enough time to acclimatize, to soak up the atmosphere and to gaze at the looming mountains on the horizon.

You should try to spend at least one of those nights in a riad. Cool in summer and warm in winter, the spectacular rooms and quiet courtyards of the city's beautifully adapted old houses are a highlight of any visit.

At the centre of the city, the elegant 12th-century Koutoubia Mosque towers above Jemaâ el Fna, a misshapen 'square' famed for its seething mass of entertainments and open-air restaurants. Around them stretches the medina, a maze of narrow streets and minarets. North of Jemaâ el Fna are the souks, or markets, thronged with colourful carpets, pottery drums and carved wooden chests. Beyond is the Sidi Ben Youssef Mosque, the city's main mosque

Jemaâ el Fna: a misshapen 'square' famed for its seething mass of entertainments and open-air restaurants.

→ GOING FURTHER

Trek up the twin peaks of **Jbel Siroua**, an isolated region between the High Atlas to the north and the Anti-Atlas to the south. **→ page 80**

after the Koutoubia. Also here is the ancient Almoravid structure of the Koubba, the Medersa Ben Youssef, and the Museum of Marrakech. On the eastern side of the medina are the smelly but colourful tanneries at Bab Debbagh. South of Jemaâ el Fna, down Riad Zitoun el Kedime, is an area of palaces, the Saadian Tombs and an ethnographic museum, the Maison Tiskiwin. Around the edges of the medina are various lush gardens, including the artistically colourful Jardin Majorelle, the Menara, with a large square pool set in a vast olive grove, and the Agdal, an olive grove.

Rising out of the haze to the south of Marrakech, North Africa's highest mountains offer the scope for skiing in winter and walking and cooling off the rest of the year.

Two main routes from Marrakech cross the mountains. To the west, en route to Taroudant, the spectacular Tizi-n-Test (page 65) is just south of the ancient, semi-ruined mosque of Tin Mal (page 64), one of two in the country that can be visited by non-Muslims. To the east, heading to Ouarzazate, the road crosses the Tizi n'Tichka (page 69) pass near the Glaoui citadel of Telouet (page 69).

The Ourika Valley is rich in walking opportunities and the Toubkal National Park (page 65) centres on Jbel Toubkal (page 66), the highest peak and destination for many treks. Oukaïmeden (page 68) is the High Atlas ski resort and Setti Fatma (page 67) has waterfalls, spring blossom and riverside cafés. Four nights in the mountains allows for some good walking.

Rising out of the haze to the south of Marrakech, North Africa's highest mountains offer the scope for skiing in winter and walking and cooling off the rest of the year.

1 Night food stalls in Jemaâ el Fna, Marrakech 2 Jbel Siroua 3 Tizi n'Tichka in the High Atlas

Ouarzazate (page 71) is the centre of Morocco's film industry, the desert surroundings standing in as various parts of this and other planets. Nearby, Aït Benhaddou (page 70) is the biggest film star of all, a stunning sandcastle of a kasbah.

To the south there are alternative tastes of desert life to be enjoyed as you follow the Draâ Valley (page 73) through miles of lush oases and sleepy villages until the ribbon of tarmac finally stutters to a halt at M'Hamid el Ghizlane (page 75) and the Sahara beckons. Here, the dunes of Erg Chigaga (page 75) are the star attraction. Three nights here should include a camel trek and a couple of nights under the stars. After a stopover in the walled market town of Taroudant (page 78), the medina streets of the Atlantic port are the top attraction in Essaouira (page 82). Ramparts, the oldest of which are Portuguese-built, protect against the waves; a walk along them is a good way to appreciate the town. Seagulls wheel above the fishing boats in the port, from where the day's catch is taken to be sold in the central market. Nearby are plenty more shopping opportunities in streetside stalls and shops. Fishy menus dominate the town's restaurants, some of which are excellent. Sea breezes turn the beach into a wind- and kite-surfing playground. Camels are led up and down looking for riders, while the sky is filled with colourful sails.

Up the coast, the beaches, stunning lagoon and excellent seafood restaurants of Oualidia make it a good stopover.

Up the coast, the beaches, stunning lagoon and excellent seafood restaurants of Oualidia (page 90), famous for its oysters, make it a good stopover, and the crumbling old Portuguese bastion of El Jadida (page 91) has atmosphere in abundance.

Brash Casablanca (page 97), where the cars are faster and the lights are brighter, is a city dominated by business and money. The huge Hassan II Mosque is the city's biggest draw.

1 Erg Chigaga **2** Oasis with date palms **3** Kasbah in the Atlas mountains **4** Hassan II mosque, Casablanca

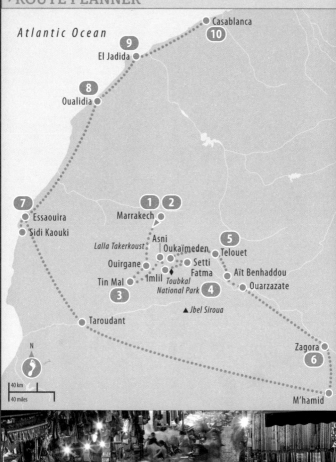

Atlantic Ocean

Casablanca **10**

9 El Jadida

8 Oualidia

7 Essaouira
Sidi Kaouki

Marrakech **1** **2**

Lalla Takerkoust

Asni
Oukaïmeden **5**
Telouet
Ouirgane
Setti Fatma
Aït Benhaddou
Tin Mal
Imlil
Ouarzazate
3 *Toubkal National Park* **4**

▲ *Jbel Siroua*

Taroudant

Zagora **6**

M'hamid

N

40 km
40 miles

1 The souks, Marrakech 2 Camel trekking 3 Medersa Ben Youssef, Marrakech

→ WISH LIST

1 Buy shoes and bags and almonds in the souks of Marrakech. **2** Contemplate the extraordinary beauty of the Medersa Ben Youssef. **3** Photograph the open-to-the-sky arches of Tin Mal. **4** Climb Toubkal, North Africa's highest peak. **5** Wander among the high ruins of Telouet. **6** Go camel trekking from Zagora. **7** Kite surf in Essaouira. **8** Eat oysters in Oualidia. **9** Skip over puddles in El Jadida's 16th-century cistern. **10** Drive along Casablanca's seafront in an open-topped car.

DREAM TRIP 2
AGADIR → ANTI-ATLAS → COAST → MARRAKECH

Best time to visit Warm in winter, Morocco's south soon heats up in spring and becomes an oven in summer, when the interior, at least, is best avoided. The coast, however, is kept fairly stable by sea breezes all year round. It can be misty through the winter though

Oceanside Agadir (page 113), Morocco's package holiday resort, has beach life and bar life, a long bustling promenade, a smart new marina and pizza restaurants. It's far from the country's most exciting destination, but it's a good place to let yourself in gently, and relax on the beach.

Just to the north are the surf beaches and surf schools around Taghazout (page 119) – a relaxed place to hang out for a few days and catch some of the best Atlantic waves around or at least start learning how to. Cafés, restaurants and lots of other surfers make it an especially social spot too. Winding mountain routes from here lead into the more remote interior, where the little market town of Immouzer des Ida Outanane (page 119), with its nearby waterfall, makes an excellent stopover for a night.

1 Surfing in Taghazout 2 Atlantic sunset 3 Immouzer des Ida Outanane 4 Berber horse fantasia 5 Landscape between Tafraoute and Akka

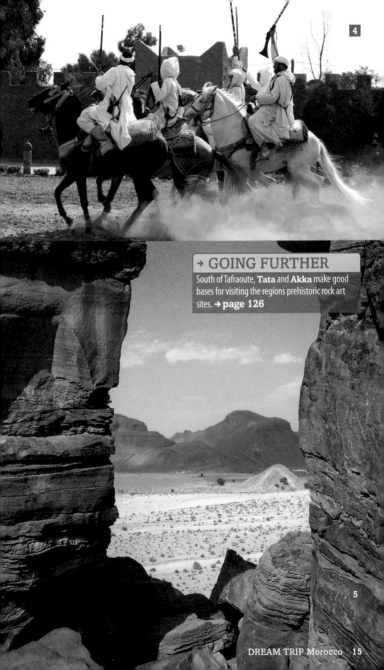

4

→ **GOING FURTHER**

South of Tafraoute, **Tata** and **Akka** make good bases for visiting the regions prehistoric rock art sites. → **page 126**

5

DREAM TRIP 2
AGADIR → ANTI-ATLAS → COAST → MARRAKECH

To the south, inland from Agadir, in the densely fertile agricultural Souss Valley, lies walled Taroudant (page 78), often compared to Marrakech. Two nights here gives time to explore its squares, higgledy-piggledy streets and to shop in its souks.

Moving inland, the great natural rock amphitheatre of Tafraoute (page 124), in the spectacular red landscape of the Anti-Atlas mountains, is an excellent centre for climbing, walking and trips to nearby canyons, where date palms grow, and to rocky outcrops beyond, where prehistoric art can be found. The neighbouring Ameln Valley (page 124) is carpeted with almond blossom in February.

Heading west, Tiznit (page 129), often unfairly overlooked by visitors, has plenty of colour in its dusty streets and rewards exploration. There are a couple of great accommodation options here too and nearby, a nature reserve known for its migrating birds.

Back on the coast, there are more good surfing waves and the hipsters of Mirleft (page 131) have turned a one-camel town into a celebration of Moroccan cool. Paths lead down rocky cliffs to sandy coves and three nights gives plenty of time for trying out the various excellent beaches in the area and the range of good restaurants

1 Taroudant **2** Bald Ibis (*Geronticus eremita*) **3** Legzira beach, near Mirleft **4** Ameln Valley **5** Village in the Anti-Atlas

too. Just to the south the whitewashed, one-time Spanish enclave of Sidi Ifni (page 131) has more beaches, as well as crumbling, colonial architecture, giving the town its own special atmosphere.

Another night in Agadir breaks up the journey to Marrakech (page 35), where three nights allow time for shopping, watching the entertainment in the city's electrically busy square Jemaâ el Fna and visiting the city's palaces and ancient monuments.

The Ameln Valley is carpeted with almond blossom in February.

N

30 km
30 miles

Atlantic Ocean

Marrakech

Immouzer des
Ida Outanane

3

2

Taghazoute

1 Agadir

4

Taroudant

*Oued Massa
Nature Reserve* ◆

5

6

Tiznit

9

Mirleft

8

Tafraoute

7

Tata

Sidi Ifni

10

Akka

1 Drink cocktails on the beach in Agadir. **2** Learn to surf in Taghazoute. **3** Buy honey from a beekeeper on the mountain road to Immouzer. **4** Walk around the city walls of Taroudant. **5** Explore Kasbah Tizourgane. **6** Find blue rocks and prehistoric art near Tafraoute. **7** Walk across the Anti-Atlas to the Ameln Valley. **8** Buy antique jewellery in Tiznit. **9** Hang out on the beach in Mirleft. **10** Tour the crumbling Spanish architecture of Sidi Ifni.

1 Aftas Plage, Mirleft   **2** Painted blue rocks, Tafraoute   **3** Kasbah Tizourgane

DREAM TRIP 3
FES → DESERT → GORGES → MARRAKECH

Best time to visit The high mountain passes in the centre of the country can be blocked with snow in winter and the gorges can flood. Conversely, camel trekking across Saharan sand in the height of summer is no fun, and Merzouga mostly shuts down until autumn. That leaves spring and summer as by far the best times to tackle this contrasting route.

The spiritual capital of Morocco, Fès (page 139) can seem a little closed, its attractions often hidden behind high walls. But it's worth persevering: once you find your feet, its streets reveal all sorts of treasure. In Fès El Bali, the old medina, and the best place to stay, ancient schools, grand, ornate, arched gates, pungent tanneries and buzzing souks will take two or three days of wandering. Fès is spectacularly sited in a huge bowl of a valley and you should take time to climb to one of the vantage points around the old city and look down on it. Spend a day wandering through Fès El Jedid too. The old Merinid capital has several palaces and the one-time Jewish district, where there's still a synagogue, cemetery and museum. The new town is light on sights, but you should try one of its excellent restaurants. If time permits, you could also take a day trip to a nearby town, such as Sefrou.

1 Tanneries of Fès **2** Riad interior, Fès **3** Nuts and dried fruit for sale, Fès **4** Roman ruins at Volubilis

Nearby Meknès (page 164) is Fès's smaller, more relaxed sibling. At one point the capital of Morocco, it has plenty of grand architecture as well as shopping opportunities in its souks. Meknès also makes a good base for an excellent excursion. Spend one day exploring the city before heading out to the impressive, crumbling Roman ruins of Volubilis (page 173) and holy pilgrimage site of Moulay Idriss (page 172).

Heading south, either Ifrane or Azrou would make a good stopping point in the Middle Atlas. Surrounded by cedar forest, Azrou (page 177) has an attractive market square and lots of Barbary apes living in the woods nearby. Smarter Ifrane (page 179) has the slightly surreal air of an Alpine ski resort and nearby limestone lakes, good for birdspotting.

Midelt (page 179) is a mining town high in the hills. There's a monastery but not much else to see other than the landscape. It's a laid-back place, though, and makes a good stopping point. If you have time, you could also do some mountain excursions from here.

Beyond Midelt, Morocco slopes down towards the Sahara, with gorges and valleys en route. Er Rachidia (page 184) makes a good base for exploring the Gorges du Ziz (page 181), just to the north, and, where the Ziz valley flattens out to the south, the fertile fig- and tamarind-growing area of the Tafilalet (page 185). Beyond, if time allows, are the mud constructions of the ksars of Rissani (page 187).

1 Rissani 2 Barbary apes in cedar trees, Atlas mountains 3 Todra Valley 4 Todra Gorge 5 Aït Benhaddou

Camel treks and a night or two sleeping at camps in the sand dunes are a great way to experience the desert.

Merzouga, almost on the Algerian border, is little more than a string of hotels set up to take advantage of the cinematic splendours of the sand dunes of Erg Chebbi (page 188). Camel treks and a night or two sleeping at camps in the sand dunes are a great way to experience the desert.

Heading west on the long drive to Marrakech, two huge gorges are cut into the slopes of the High Atlas. A couple of nights in each of the Todra Gorge (page 192) and the Dadès Gorge (page 193) will give time for walks along the verdantly green floors of the rocky red canyons and exploring the higher slopes.

Aït Benhaddou (page 70), a fairytale kasbah north of Oualidia, makes a great place to stop for a night before heading north again, over the high mountain pass of Tizi n'Tichka (page 69) and down to Marrakech.

Four nights in Marrakech (page 35) are a great way to finish off this trip, experiencing the many sights and sounds, smells and flavours of the beautiful Red City.

N

50 km
50 miles

Atlantic Ocean

RABAT ■

③ Moulay Idriss & Volubilis

④

① ②
Fès

Meknès

Ifrane

Azrou
⑤

Midelt

Er Rachidia

Marrakech

⑧ *Dadès Gorge*
Boumalne du Dadès

Todra Gorge ⑦
Tineghir

⑩
Tizi n'Tichka

⑨
Aït Benhaddou

Ouarzazate

Erfoud

Tafilalet
Rissani

Erg Chebbi ⑥

Merzouga

1 Fès **2** Dadès Gorge

→ WISH LIST

1 Walk all the way down Tala Kebira in Fès. 2 Have breakfast on a Fès riad rooftop overlooking the roofs and minarets. 3 Climb the streets to the top of Moulay Idriss. 4 Act like an emperor in the Roman ruins of Volubilis. 5 Stroll through cedar forests with Barbary apes. 6 Spend a night under canvas on the dunes of Erg Chebbi 7 Drive the switchback roads at the head of the Todra Gorge. 8 Stroll along the verdant valley floor of the Dadès Gorge. 9 Spend a night in a fairytale kasbah at Aït Benhaddou. 10 Survive to tell the tale of the Tizi n'Tichka pass over the High Atlas to Marrakech.

DREAM TRIP 4
TANGIER → RABAT → CHEFCHAOUEN → CEUTA

Best time to visit Northern Morocco can have distinctly European weather in winter with rain and grey days. Winters are short, however, and spring and autumn are excellent times to visit, with warm days and plenty of sunshine. In spring there is the added bonus of blooming flowers. Summer can get unpleasantly hot, especially in the city, but there are cooler hills and coast to escape to.

Morocco's north has huge European influences, from its Roman remains and the whitewashed houses of Chefchaouen to the listless men who stand on the Tangier seafront staring north across the narrow straits. There's plenty that is distinctively Moroccan here too. It's a fascinating junction of history and culture.

Arriving by boat is the best introduction to Tangier (page 199): its port is, after all, why it's here. It's also a little like being thrown in at the deep end: don't expect to be left in peace to find your own bearings. Three nights in the city gives plenty of time for exploring the oldest part of town: the medina and kasbah. Allow some time too for lazing on the beach, where you'll be entertained by acrobats and footballers, and for visiting the city's galleries and the Cinémathèque de Tanger, testament to its artistic and intellectual past and present. Set aside a day for a trip out of the city too, west along the coast to Cap Spartel and the Caves of Hercules or east to Ksar es Seghir.

1 Man playing *qarkabebs* (iron castanets), Tangier **2** Tangier beach **3** Asilah

To the southwest, Asilah (page 211) faces the Atlantic but has a Mediterranean feel. Whitewashed houses, immaculately clean streets, a large beach and some good seafood restaurants make it a popular spot. There are cultural enticements too: a summer festival combines music and art. Two nights will allow time for the top attractions: lazing, eating and people-watching.

Further south, Larache (page 214) has a much more Moroccan feel, with winding medina streets, and across the estuary, at Lixus (page 215), evocative Roman ruins.

Whitewashed houses, immaculately clean streets, a large beach and some good seafood restaurants make Asilah a popular spot.

Casablanca's status as the economic capital leaves Rabat to be a rather more refined city, its cafés full of civil servants and politicians drinking good coffee and eating fine pastries.

Rabat (page 225) is another version of Morocco again. Casablanca's status as the economic capital leaves Rabat to be a rather more refined city, its cafés full of civil servants and politicians drinking good coffee and eating fine pastries. Only the capital for 100 years, the city has an interesting past of pirates and battles that can be seen in its walls and gates and in the walled ruins of the Chellah, a 14th-century citadel. Take time to explore the medina and neighbouring Salé, and take advantage of the city's good restaurants.

Heading east, Meknès (page 164) is a previous incarnation of the country's capital and it retains vestiges of power such as palaces and grand gates as well as a manageable medina. Nearby are the country's most impressive Roman remains, at Volubilis (page 173).

Beyond Meknès, Fès (page 139) is a magical mix of religion and intellect in a stunning medieval setting.

After four nights in Fès, the relaxed, laid-back nature of the white-washed Chefchaouen (page 246), a one-time Andalucían town in the foothills of the Rif mountains, should be a pleasant counterpoint. Allow time for walks in the nearby hills, or even trips to the higher peaks, and for exploring the town's breathtakingly beautiful streets.

1 Sweet stall in Rabat 2 Chefchaouen 3 Al Hoceima

Tetouan (page 255) is markedly less laid-back, but it has a UNESCO-protected medina to make up for it as well as a Jewish quarter, some good souks and a couple of good museums. There's more Spanish architecture too and a mountainous backdrop. You could also use it as a base for a trip to a Mediterranean beach.

Ceuta (page 261) takes the Spanish influence in this part of Africa to a new level: it remains a part of Spain and you'll need to cross a chaotic international border to get in. Once there, it's a pleasant, if slightly incongruous, Spanish provincial town, with good museums and some impressive city walls; a taste of African Spain from where you can catch a ferry back to the European version.

→ GOING FURTHER

If you've got time head up to **Al Hoceïma**, which has one of the most beautiful settings on the Moroccan Mediterranean. → **page 250**

3

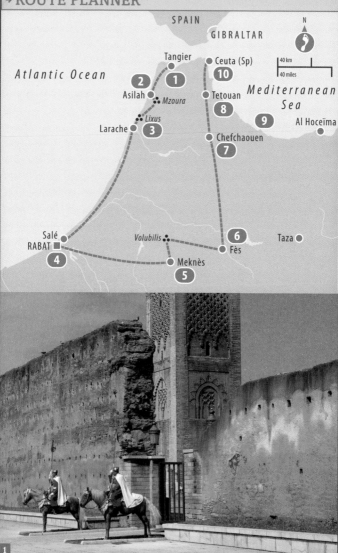

1 Royal mounted guard, Rabat 2 Chefchaouen 3 Camel ride on a Mediterranean beach

1 Find your way through the labyrinth of Tangier's medina to the top of the hill. **2** Eat exquisite seafood by the beach in Asilah. **3** Uncover Roman remains in Lixus. **4** Compare the ruling classes and the pirates in Rabat. **5** Visit the palaces of Meknès. **6** Smell the pungent tanneries in Fès. **7** Photograph Morocco's whitest walls in Chefchaouen. **8** Get lost in the UNESCO-listed medina of Tetouan. **9** Swim in the Mediterranean from a northern Moroccan beach. **10** Walk across the border into Spain at Ceuta.

High Atlas Mountains

DREAM TRIP 1
Marrakech→High Atlas→Essaouira→Casablanca
21 days

Marrakech 4 nights, page 35

Tin Mal 1 night (at Ouirgane or Lalla
Takerkoust), page 63
Car or shared taxi from Marrakech (3 hrs)

**Western High Atlas (Toubkal National
Park)** 2 nights, page 65
Car or shared taxi from Tin Mal to Asni, Imlil
or Setti Fatma (2 hrs)

Western High Atlas (Telouet) en route,
page 69
Car or shared taxi

Western High Atlas (Aït Benhaddou)
1 night, page 70
Car or shared taxi from Asni (5 hrs)

Western High Atlas (Ouarzazate)
en route, page 71
Car or shared taxi from Aït Benhaddou

Zagora and M'Hamid 3 nights,
pages 73 and 75
Car or shared taxi from Aït Benhaddou
(4 hrs)

Taroudant 1 night, page 78
Car or shared taxi from Zagora (6 hrs)

Essaouira 3 nights, page 82
Car or shared taxi from Taroudant (5 hrs)

Sidi Kaouki 1 night, page 86
Car or shared taxi from Essaouira (30 mins)

Oualidia 1 night, page 90
Car/taxi from Sidi Kaouki, or bus from
Essaouira (3 hrs)

El Jadida 1 night, page 91
Car, taxi or bus from Oualidia (1 hr)

Casablanca 2 nights, page 97
Car, taxi or bus from El Jadida (1 hr)

GOING FURTHER

Jbel Siroua page 80
5 hrs' walk from Taliouine (which is on the
N10) to Akhfamane, where many treks start

DREAM TRIP 1
Marrakech→High Atlas→Essaouira→Casablanca

Marrakech, the so-called Red City, is actually many shades of dusty terracotta, a complex crossroads of a place within reach of cool High Atlas valleys and windsurfing Atlantic beaches. One of the furthest western extremities of the Islamic world, it is a surprisingly open city, its many historical and social influences resulting in an air of tolerance and a sense of possibility.

To the north, the Atlas Mountains tower over the plains, snow-capped into spring, when blossom lights up their lower slopes. The peaks have panoramic views and the valleys plenty of opportunities for strolls and relaxed contemplation.

There is history in the hills too, with sites such as Telouet and the magical ruins of the Tin Mal mosque providing a reminder of the strategic importance of the Atlas and the routes across them.

Beyond, the mountain meltwaters fade into the parched ground of the Sahara. Zagora and M'Hamid, past the film studios of Ouarzazate, give a taste of the dunes and sun-bleached colours and big starry skies of Northern Africa's dry heartland.

Respite from the heat of the interior isn't far away: Morocco's Atlantic coast is kept temperate by year-round onshore breezes. Whitewashed Essaouira is the obvious draw, with its big beaches, photogenic streets and squares and a lively music festival. Wave-worn and whitewashed, the town retains a fishing fleet and has plenty of seaside character despite its increasing gentrification.

There are wilder, less frequented options in and around Sidi Kaouki just to the south, while to the north, Oualidia has oysters and beaches and El Jadida has a ragged, crumbling charm.

Casablanca is a world apart, a brasher, richer, higher-octane Morocco, sports cars and big architecture punctuating its Atlantic glamour.

MARRAKECH

Marrakech, Morocco's tourist capital, has most of the country's attractions in concentrated form, its markets, music and performers almost omnipresent accompaniments to its palaces, museums and gardens. The city's alleyways, tanneries and souks could keep explorers busy for months but can also create sensory overload; a side-trip out into the extraordinary landscapes of Marrakech's surroundings provides a counter-balance of relative calm.

A heaving mass of dust, noise and colour, the old centre of Marrakech is for many the enduring image of the country. The apparent chaos hides many cool, calm courtyards of luxurious riads, islands of relaxed and pampered sanctuary.

→ ARRIVING IN MARRAKECH

GETTING THERE

Accessible by air, road and rail, the city makes an excellent central point of arrival in Morocco, situated at the meeting point of routes for Essaouira (Atlantic coast), Ouarzazate (key to the gorges south of the Atlas and Sahara desert), and the northern imperial cities. **Airport Marrakech Menara** ① *T0524-447910, www.marrakech.airport-authority.com,* is 6 km west of the city, by the Menara Gardens. The **BMCE** and the **Banque Populaire** have bureaux de change, closed outside office hours, and there are ATMs. Euros may be acceptable to taxi drivers. A petit taxi (three passengers) or grand taxi (six passengers) from the airport should cost 100-150dh (more after 2000) to the medina or Guéliz, and takes 15 minutes. Although fares are fixed price, published on an airport noticeboard, taxi drivers still try to charge more. Agree the price first. Alternatively, there's a handy airport shuttle bus, No 19, which runs every 30 minutes to Jemaâ el Fna and stops at most hotels in Guéliz, Hivernage and the Palmeraie; 20dh single, 30dh return. For the quickest connection to the train or bus station, your best bet is to take a 15-minute taxi ride and agree the fare. If you're staying in a riad, it's normal practice to arrange a meeting point at the edge of the medina, from where someone will escort you; finding a riad on your own is difficult. You can also ask your riad to arrange airport transfer for about 200dh, which saves a lot of hassle.

From the **railway station** to the heart of the Ville Nouvelle is a 15-minute walk; Jemaâ el Fna and the old city is a further 20-minute walk. A taxi into the city from the station is around 15dh; alternatively, take bus No 3 or 8 from outside the station along Avenue Hassan II and Avenue Mohammed V, to the medina.

Inter-city public **buses** arrive at Bab Doukkala bus station or *gare routière*, a 15-minute walk from Jemaâ el Fna. Bus companies **CTM** and **Supratours** also stop at Bab Doukkala but have their main termini in Guéliz near the train station.

MOVING ON

For getting into and across the mountains a car is useful – there are car hire places at the airport or in the new town (see also page 270). Alternatively, a shared taxi will get you to Asni or Setti Fatma – get a city taxi to take you to the shared taxi departure spot at Bab Rob. Ouirgane (see page 63), Lalla Takerkoust (see page 63) and Tin Mal (see page 63) are harder to reach by public transport: get a group together or be prepared to pay for a few places in a shared taxi. Alternatively, for Tin Mal, find a Taroudant bus going via Tizi n-Test. Local buses are fairly frequent to Asni, from where you could get a taxi.

ON THE ROAD
Haggling

Part of the fun of shopping in the medina is the haggling that comes with every purchase. To buy in the souks you will have to engage in the theatre and the mind games of the haggle.

In order to come out of the process happy, there are some things to bear in mind. Don't get too hung up on the idea of 'a good price'. The best price is the one you are happy to pay. Have one in mind before you start and don't go above it. Be prepared to walk away if the price is too high – whatever you're buying, there will almost certainly be another stall around the corner selling the same thing.

Be friendly and polite but firm and don't suggest a price you would be prepared to pay for anything you're not sure you want. Once you start talking numbers, you are in negotiation and you may find it hard to extricate yourself. The price you are first quoted might be twice as much as the seller is prepared to accept, but there is absolutely no firm rule about this. A decent starting point from the buyer's point of view is to take about a half to a third off the amount you'd be prepared to pay and start by offering that.

As a very rough guide, and depending on quality, size, etc, expect to pay these sort of prices: *babouches* 50-150dh; leather bag 200-400dh; teapot 50-200dh (more for silver); spices 30-60dh per kg; pouffe 150-450; blanket 300-600dh.

Carpet-buying can be especially complex and has many potential pitfalls – don't be too swayed by offers of mint tea/declarations of antiquity/the years of hard toil the seller's elderly aunt spent making it.

GETTING AROUND

Marrakech is a spread-out city, built on a plain – hence the large number of mopeds and bicycles; rental of a two-wheeler is an option, though not without risk in the chaotic traffic. Short taxi journeys in Marrakech should not be more than 10 or 15dh – try to have change and insist on using the meter even though you may be told that it is broken. The most picturesque way to drive around is in a *calèche*, a horse-drawn carriage, but it is perfectly possible to explore the centre on foot.

TOURIST INFORMATION

Office du Tourisme ① *Pl Abd el Moumen Ben Ali (on Av Mohammed V opposite Café Negoçiants), T0524-436131, Mon-Fri 0830-1830.* Conseil Régional du Tourisme ① *Pl Youssef Ibn Tachfine, opposite Koutoubia, T0524-385261, Mon-Fri 0830-1830.*

SAFETY

The 'hassle' which deterred some visitors in the past has been reduced thanks to the unseen but ever-vigilant **Brigade Touristique** and the predominant atmosphere is relaxed. If you are robbed or hassled, the Brigade Touristique is based on the Mamounia side of the Koutoubia, near the CMH petrol station, in a small building on a public square with a few trees.

ORIENTATION

Central Marrakech is clearly divided into two parts: the large historic city, the **medina**, and the Ville Nouvelle, **Guéliz**. The focal point of the medina, and indeed of the whole city, is the **Jemaâ el Fna**, an open place full of street entertainers and food sellers, adjacent to which are the most important souks. Handily, it is located in the middle of the main areas of historic sights. North of Jemaâ el Fna are the **souks** and the **Sidi Ben Youssef Mosque**, the city's main mosque after the Koutoubia. On a walk in this neighbourhood, you can visit the **Almoravid Koubba**, the **Medersa Ben Youssef**, and the **Museum of Marrakech**. South of Jemaâ el Fna, down Riad Zitoun el Kedim, is an area of **palaces**, the **Saâdian Tombs** and a small ethnographic museum, the **Maison Tiskiwine**.

If you are staying in a riad, you may well be in the **Bab Doukkala** or **Leksour/Mouassine** neighbourhoods, the former on the Guéliz side of the medina. The latter is very central, just north of Jemaâ el Fna, and is one of the most chic enclaves, home to bijou places like the **Dar Cherifa** *café littéraire*. Bab Doukkala is handier for the bus station. For visitors with more time, the Thursday flea market at **Bab el Khemis** is ideal for those seeking gems amongst junk and second-hand treasures. Another point of interest are the **tanneries** at Bab Debbagh.

Marrakech's gardens can be a welcome respite from the cramped spaces and heat of the medina: the **Jardin Majorelle**, quite close to Bab Doukkala, the **Menara**, a large square pool set in a vast olive grove south of Guéliz, and the **Agdal**, another olive grove close to the Sidi Youssef Ben Ali neighbourhood. To the east and north of Marrakech, across the Oued Issil, is the **Palmeraie**. Close to the medina, the gardens between Koutoubia and Mamounia are planted with roses. Even once scruffy Arset Moulay Slimane, opposite the Municipality on your way to Jemaâ el Fna, has been spruced up.

Guéliz, the suburb laid out by the French in the 1920s is, despite all the new apartment buildings and traffic, worth a wander for its cafés, upmarket boutiques and art galleries, and it has many of the city's best restaurants. The main thoroughfare is Avenue Mohammed V and the evening promenade here is popular.

→ BACKGROUND

THE CITY

In some early European maps Marrakech appears as 'Morocco city', although 'Maraksh' is the Arabic name. The origins of the name are obscure: some see it as a corruption of 'aghmat-urika', the name of an early town. The city is surrounded by extensive palm groves, into which suburbs are gradually spreading. Yet there are also sandy, arid areas near and, even, within the city which give it a semi-Saharan character.

And then, there are the mountains. Arriving from Fès or Meknès you run alongside the bald arid Jebilet: 'the little mountains', or cross them at Sidi Bou Othmane as you come from Casablanca or Rabat. Perhaps the most beautiful approach to Marrakech is on the N7, from Casablanca and Sidi Bennour, which crosses the Plateau des Gantours and the end of the Jebilet. However, from most points in Marrakech, cloud and heat haze allowing, it is the High Atlas, the Adrar (literally 'the mountains'), which dominate. At times the optical illusion is such that the snow-covered mountain wall appears to rise from just behind the city.

Marrakech is Morocco's fourth largest city. The population is around 1.5 million, although nearer two million including the suburbs. Its people are a mix of Arab and Amazigh; many are recent migrants from surrounding rural regions and further south. For centuries an important regional market place, Marrakech now has a booming service economy and there is still a wide range of handicraft production and small-scale industry, particularly in the medina. Out in the western suburbs are new factories.

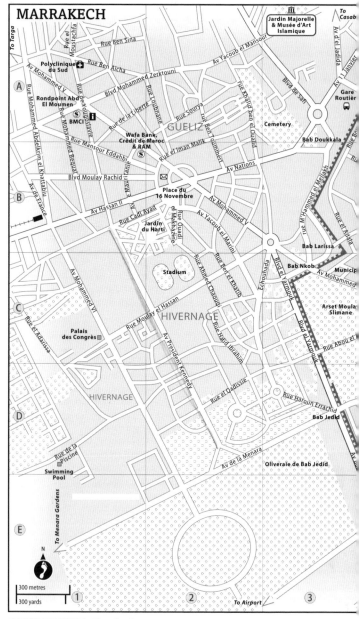

MARRAKECH

To Targa

To Casab

Jardin Majorelle
& Musée d'Art
Islamique

Av 11 Janvier

Av d/el Jadida

Rue el Moustachfa

Rue Ben Sina

Rue Ben Aïcha

Av Yacoub el Mansour

Blvd de Safi

Gare
Routièr

Polyclinique
du Sud

Av Mohammed V

Rue Ibn Zaglane

Rue de la Liberté

Rue Tournani

Rue Khalid ben el Ouaid

Rue Sourya

Blvd Mohammed Zerktouni

Rondpoint Abd
El Moumen

A

BMCI

Av Mohammed Abdelkrim el Khattabiu

Rue Mansour Eddahbi

GUELIZ

Rue Ben Toumert

Cemetery

Bab Doukkala

Wafa Bank,
Crédit de Maroc
& RAM

Rue el Iman Malik

Rue M'Hammed el Mesfioh

Rue el Adaa

Blvd Moulay Rachid

Av Nations

Av de France

Av Hassan II

Place du
16 Novembre

Av Mohammed V

B

Rue Cadi Ayad

Rue Ouadi
el Makhazine

Av Yacoub el Marini

Bab Larissa

Jardin
du Harti

Echouhada

Bab Nkob

Municip

Av Mohammed

Av Mohammed VI

Stadium

Rue Ahmed Chaoughi

Rue Ben el Khatib

Blvd el Yamour

Arset Moula
Slimane

C

Rue el Adarissa

Rue Moulay el Hassan

HIVERNAGE

Rue Hard Ibrahim

Blvd el Maimouk

Rue Abou el

Palais
des Congrès

Av Président Kennedy

Rue el Qadissie

Rue Haroun Errachid

D

HIVERNAGE

Bab Jedid

Rue de la
Piscine

Av de la Menara

Oliveraie de Bab Jedid

Av

Swimming
Pool

E

To Menara Gardens

N

300 metres

300 yards

1

2

To Airport

3

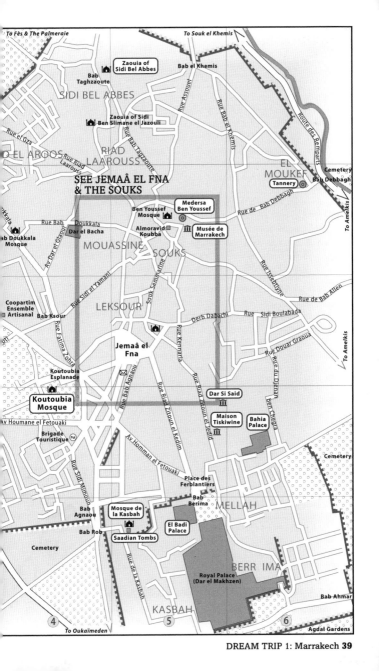

Increasingly, tourism is seen as the mainstay of the city's economy. Marrakech is one of the major tourist attractions of Morocco and many of the city's large number of unemployed or under-employed supplement their incomes by casual work with tourists.

ALMORAVID ORIGINS AND ROLE

Marrakech was first founded in 1062 by Youssef Ibn Tachfine, the Almoravid leader, as a base from which to control the High Atlas mountains. A kasbah, Dar al Hajar, was built close to the site of the Koutoubia Mosque. Under Youssef Ben Tachfine, Marrakech became the region's first major urban settlement. Within the walls were mosques, palaces and extensive orchards and market gardens, made possible by an elaborate water transfer and irrigation system. The population was probably a mixture of people of black-African descent from the Oued Draâ, Imazighen from the Souss Valley and the nearby Atlas, and Amazigh Jews. The city attracted leading medieval thinkers from outside Marrakech.

Marrakech was taken by the Almohads in 1147, who almost totally destroyed and then rebuilt the city, making it the capital of their extensive empire. Under the Almohad Sultan Abd el Moumen, the Koutoubia Mosque was built on the site of Almoravid buildings, with the minaret added by Ya'qub al Mansour. Under the latter, Marrakech gained palaces, gardens and irrigation works, and again became a centre for musicians, writers and academics, but on his death it declined and fell into disarray.

MERINID NEGLECT AND SAADIAN REVIVAL

While the Merinids added several *medersas* to Marrakech, Fès received much more of their attention and was preferred as the capital, although from 1374 to 1386 Marrakech was the centre of a separate principality. Marrakech was revitalized by the Saâdians from 1524, with the rebuilding of the Ben Youssef Mosque and the construction by Ahmed al Mansour Ad Dahbi of the El Badi Palace and the Saâdian Tombs. Marrakech also became an important trading post, due to its location between the Sahara and the Atlantic.

ALAOUITE MARRAKECH

The Alaouites took control of Marrakech in 1668. In the early 18th century the city suffered from Moulay Ismaïl's love of Meknès, with many of the major buildings, notably the El Badi Palace, stripped to glorify the new capital. The destructive effects of this period were compounded by the civil strife following his death. However, from 1873, under Alaouite Sultan Moulay Hassan I and his son, the city's prestige was re-established. A number of the city's fine palaces date from this time and are still open to visitors.

EARLY 20TH CENTURY: GLAOUI RULE

From 1898 until independence, Marrakech was the nerve-centre of southern Morocco, ruled practically as a personal fiefdom by the Glaoui family from the central High Atlas. The French took control of Marrakech and its region in 1912, crushing an insurrection by a claimant to the Sultanate. Their policy in the vast and rugged southern territories was to govern through local rulers, rather as the British worked with the Rajahs of India.

With French support, Pacha T'hami el Glaoui extended his control over all areas of the south. His autonomy from central authority was considerable, his cruelty notorious. And, of course, there were great advantages in this system, in the form of profits from the new French-developed mines. In the 1930s, Marrakech saw the development of a fine Ville Nouvelle, Guéliz, all wide avenues of jacarandas and simple, elegant bungalow houses

ON THE ROAD
The riad experience

The riad (*maison d'hôte* or guesthouse) gives you the experience of staying in a small but fine private medina house. Prices are high for Morocco, but you get service, style and luxury in bucketloads. The often painstakingly restored houses are managed either directly by their owners or via an agency which deals with everything from reservations to maintenance. There are hundreds of riads in the city, probably around 1000, though estimates vary wildly.

Guests are met either at the airport, or the edge of the medina. Prices vary enormously, and some are extremely luxurious. Reactions to this type of accommodation are generally very positive. The riads have created a lot of work for locals (and pushed property prices up), so many feel they have a stake in the guesthouse system. (With regard to tipping, err on the generous side.)

Most riads are available to rent in their entirety, making a great base for a group or family holiday. Staff are usually included and food and entertainment (acrobats, musicians, dancers) can often be arranged.

When booking a stay in a riad in winter, check for details of heating. All riads should provide breakfast, included as part of the price, and most will also cook an evening meal on request, though advance warning is usually required. Cooler, darker ground floor rooms are preferable in summer; lighter, warmer first floor rooms in winter. Note too that, in winter, it can rain heavily in Marrakech, turning streets in the old town to muddy tracks.

What riads consider to be high season varies but always includes Christmas and Easter holidays. Rates often fall substantially outside these times. Riads usually quote their fees in euros.

Riad rental agencies

It may pay to shop around and see what is offered by riad rental agencies – they usually add a commission to the price, but they can also have special offers available.
Hôtels & Ryads, 31 Bis, Rue Victor Massé, 75009 Paris, T+33-(0)1-42 08 18 33, www.riads. co.uk. With 64 riads in Marrakech on their books and one of the easiest to use websites, a good place to get an idea of what's available.
Riads au Maroc, 1 Rue Mahjoub Rmiza, Guéliz, T0524-431900, www.riadomaroc. com. A personalized service for both rooms in riads and whole riads from a range of 55 properties. Prices for a double room are from €45 up to €300, most are around the €70 mark.
Marrakech Riads, 8 Derb Charfa Lekbir, Mouassine, T0524-391609, www.marrakech-riads.net. Friendly and highly recommended agency with eight excellent riads, including the simple Dar Sara and the beautiful Al Jazira. The headquarters, the beautiful Dar Cherifa, a 17th-century house converted with gallery space on the ground floor, are worth a visit in their own right (see page 52).
Villas of Morocco, Immeuble Berdai, 1st floor, Guéliz, T0522-942525, www.villasof morocco.com. For the ultimate in luxury beyond the confines of the medina, this UK agency has a portfolio of magnificent private villas in the Palmeraie and elsewhere. All are fully staffed to cater for weddings, events and family deluxe holidays. On average from around €3600 per night for exclusivity.

and, on acquiring a railway line terminus, Marrakech reaffirmed its status as capital of the south. It was at this time, when travel for pleasure was still the preserve of the privileged of Europe, that Marrakech began to acquire its reputation as a retreat for the wealthy.

CAPITAL OF THE SOUTH

In recent decades Marrakech has grown enormously, its population swelled by civil servants and armed forces personnel. Migrants are attracted by the city's reputation as 'city of the poor', where even the least qualified can find work of some kind. For many rural people, the urban struggle is hard and, as the Tachelhit pun puts it, Marrakech is ma-ra-kish, 'the place where they'll eat you if they can'.

North of the medina, new neighbourhoods like Daoudiate and Issil have grown up next to the Université Cadi Ayyad and the mining school. South of the medina, Sidi Youssef Ben Ali, referred to as SYBA, is an extension of the old town and has a reputation for rebellion. West of Guéliz, north of the Essaouira road, are the vast new housing areas of Massira, part low-rise social housing, part villa developments. The most upmarket area is on the Circuit de la Palmeraie. Little by little, the original farmers are being bought out, and desirable homes with lawns and pools behind high walls are taking over from vegetable plots under the palm trees. East of the medina is the vast Amelkis development, a gated community complete with golf course and the discrete Amenjana 'resort'. Here the money and privilege are accommodated in an area equal to one third of the crowded medina.

FUTURE OF MARRAKECH

The early 21st century saw Marrakech in an upbeat mood. The Brigade Touristique, set up to reduce the hassling of tourists, has been reasonably successful. Tourist activity, property development and riad businesses were booming during the first decade of the new millennium, but, with the global economic recession post-2008, this progress has reached a plateau. The ongoing problem for the city is how to deal with the influx of visitors. Certain monuments have reached saturation point: the exquisite Saâdian tombs, for example, are home to a semi-permanent people jam. And, while being packed with people is an important part of the attraction of Jemaâ el Fna, there is the danger that the magic of the place will eventually be diluted by the massive numbers of visitors. The square is now closed to traffic for some of the time, but the roads around the edge of the medina are hellishly busy.

In April 2011 an explosion rocked the famed Café Argana in the main square of Jemaâ el Fna (see opposite). Though the **Café Argana** is being rebuilt at time of writing, and after a short hiatus where travellers avoided Marrakech, the city has recovered and there is no evidence of Islamist sympathies. Inhabitants of Marrakech will tell you emphatically that the attack was the work of 'outsiders'.

THE 'VENICE OF MOROCCO'?

Marrakech continues to draw the visitors in and to maintain its hold on the Western imagination. The setting is undeniably exotic, eccentricities are tolerated and (rather less honourably) domestic help is cheap. Features in international decoration magazines fuel the demand for property; major monuments are being restored. One-time resident the late Yves St Laurent even dubbed Marrakech 'the Venice of Morocco' – which might seem an appropriate description on a February day with torrential rain on Jemaâ el Fna.

Still, the Red City retains a sense of rawness, despite the creeping gentrification, and remains the closest Orient one can find within a few hours, flight of the grey north

European winter. Provided city authorities can keep vehicle pollution in check, it looks set to maintain its popularity.

→ JEMAÂ EL FNA AND THE NORTHERN MEDINA

Heaving with Moroccan humanity, Jemaâ el Fna, the sprawling square at Marrakech's core, is the city's most popular sight and, together with the neighbouring Koutoubia mosque, its most easily located landmark. The Jardins de la Koutoubia, the mosque's gardens, make a good viewing area for the minaret. North of the square are the souks, a huge labyrinth of narrow streets packed tightly with markets. Thread your way up Souk Semmarine and its continuations to reach a cluster of the city's most important Islamic monuments: the city's oldest structure, the Almoravid *koubba*, and its most beautiful, the Medersa Ben Youssef. Also here are two more fine examples of Moroccan architecture: the Museum of Marrakech and the arts foundation of Dar Belarj. Many visitors to the Marrakech medina concentrate on this central zone, but there is plenty of interest in the quieter, more residential streets further north and east. Out east towards the gate of Bab Debbagh are the pungent and colourful tanneries, while to the north the Zaouïa of Sidi Bel Abbes commemorates the holiest of Marrakech's seven saints. Further west, Avenue Mohamed V leads past the Cyber Parc Moulay Hassan, a green space with internet access just inside the city walls, to the Ville Nouvelle. The 16 km of city walls, originally Almoravid, are themselves an impressive sight.

JEMAÂ EL FNA

Special enough to be given UNESCO recognition, the central square of Jemaâ el Fna is both the city's greatest pull for tourists and a social area for Moroccans. Despite its fame, popularity and snake charmers, it remains an essentially Moroccan space, big and vibrant enough to absorb its visitors without bowing to them. It's also useful for navigation around a city that is remarkably easy to get lost in, a place that visitors return to again and again.

The atmosphere of 'La Place' changes through the day. Open to limited traffic during daylight hours, you can wander between sellers of orange juice, herbs and spices, clothes, shoes, alarm clocks and radios. There are snake charmers and monkey tamers, watersellers and wildly grinning gnaoua musicians with giant metal castanets, all too ready to pose for photographs, for which they proceed to charge a small fortune.

Sheltering from the sun under their umbrellas, fortune tellers and public scribes await their clients. As dusk falls it takes on an increasingly carnival atmosphere, with acrobats and musicians vying with storytellers for the attention of the crowds. Many tourists retreat to the rooftop cafés to watch the spectacle.

Watching the setting up of the food stalls in the early evening is another piece of theatre, as is walking between them and braving the food, be it sheep's heads, snails, fried fish or lentil soup. People have been known to fall ill after eating in the square, though in general hygiene is fairly good (see page 61).

Jemaâ el Fna means 'assembly of the dead', and, though there is disagreement over the origins of the name, it may refer to the traditional display of the heads of criminals, executed here until the 19th century. In 1956, the government attempted to close down the square by converting it into a corn market and car park, but soon reverted it to its traditional role. In the late 1980s, the bus station was moved out to Bab Doukkala. In 1994, the square was fully tarmacked for the GATT meeting. The food stands were reorganized, and the orange juice sellers issued with smart red fezzes and white gloves.

Jemaâ el Fna's storytellers have long been a part of its magic and they can still be seen working their magic on crowds of locals today. Even for non-Arabic speakers these are worth a look, as much for the rapt reactions of the crowd as for the skills of the storytellers. Thanks to campaigning by a team led by Spanish writer and Marrakech resident Juan Goytisolo, Jemaâ

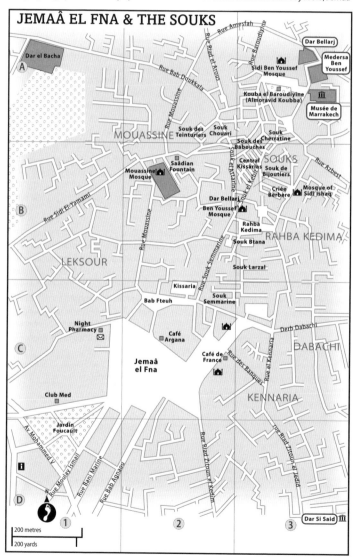

JEMAÂ EL FNA & THE SOUKS

Dar el Bacha

Dar Bellarj

Medersa Ben Youssef

Sidi Ben Youssef Mosque

Rue Amesfah

Rue Baroudiyine

Rue Bab Doukkala

Rue Riad el Arous

Kouba el Baroudiyine (Almoravid Koubba)

Musée de Marrakech

MOUASSINE

Souk des Teinturiers

Souk Chouari

Souk Cherratine

Souk de Babouches

SOUKS

Rue Azbest

Rue Mouassine

Mouassine Mosque

Saâdian Fountain

Central Kissarias

Souk de Bijoutiers

Souk el Attarine

Criée Berbère

Mosque of Sidi Ishaq

Dar Bellarj

Ben Youssef Mosque

Souk el Kebir

Rue Souk Semmarine

Rahba Kedima

Souk Btana

RAHBA KEDIMA

Rue Sidi El Yamami

LEKSOUR

Souk Larzal

Kissaria

Bab Fteuh

Souk Semmarine

Night Pharmacy

Café Argana

Jemaâ el Fna

Café de France

Derb Dabachi

DABACHI

Rue des Banques

Rue el Kennaria

KENNARIA

Club Med

Jardin Foucault

Av. Mohammed V

Rue Moulay Ismail

Rue Bani Marine

Rue Bab Agnaou

Rue Riad Zitoun el Kedim

Rue Riad Zitoun el Jedid

Dar Si Said

N

200 metres

200 yards

1

2

3

ON THE ROAD
Jemaâ el Juice

Ask people about their impressions of Jemaâ el Fna and they'll mention the snake charmers, the food, the acrobats, the swarming mass of humanity, but also the orange juice. Around the edges of the square, from dawn to dusk and beyond, are stalls piled high with immaculately stacked oranges; a 4dh glass of refreshing juice from the army of drink vendors is an important part of the Jemaâ el Fna experience. Depending on which stall you get it from, it may come slightly watered down with squash, and the locals complain when there's no sugar added, but it's invariably delicious and absurdly cheap. Expect to pay 10dh if it's freshly squeezed (and therefore entirely unadulterated) in front of you, or for grapefruit.

el Fna received UNESCO recognition for its place in humankind's oral heritage. Sheltering from the sun under their umbrellas, fortune tellers and public scribes await their clients.

More recent attractions include the *nakkachat*, women with syringes full of henna, ready to pipe a design onto your hands. 'Hook the ring over the coke bottle' is popular, and golf putters have recently appeared. You may find an astrologist-soothsayer tracing out his diagram of the future on the tarmac with a scrubby piece of chalk. A modern variation on the traditional *halka* or storyteller's circle touches harsh social reality: local people listen to a true tale told by the relatives of a victim of poverty or injustice. And should you need an aphrodisiac, there are stalls with tea urns selling cinnamon and ginseng tea and little dishes of black, powdery *slilou*, a spicy sweet paste.

Pickpockets are occasionally a problem on Jemaâ el Fna. Have plenty of change handy for entertainments and orange juice. The hassling of tourists by false guides which marred visiting Jemaâ el Fna in the 1980s and 1990s is largely a thing of the past: the plain clothes Brigade Touristique is watching, and the penalties are severe. You will, however, experience plenty of enthusiastic encouragement to buy orange juice, or to have a snake draped around your neck.

MOSQUEE DE LA KOUTOUBIA
ⓘ *Closed to non-Muslims.*

The 67-m high **minaret** of the Koutoubia Mosque is the city's tallest building and dominates the whole of Marrakech. Built in pale pink stone and lit up at night, it is visible from afar, and provided the focal point for urban planner Henri Prost when he laid out the modern neighbourhood of Guéliz. Legend says that as this structure once overlooked the harem, only a blind muezzin was allowed to climb to call the faithful to prayer. The name Koutoubia derives from the Arabic *kutub* (books) and means the 'Booksellers' Mosque', reflecting the fact that the trade of selling manuscripts was conducted in a souk close to the mosque.

Unusually, the Koutoubia is a **double mosque**, both parts dating from the reign of the second Almohad ruler, Abd El-Mumin (1130-1163). The ruins of the first Koutoubia, now behind railings, were first excavated in the late 1940s. The bases of the prayer hall's columns and the cisterns under the courtyard are clearly visible. The ground plan of the second Koutoubia, still standing, is the same as that of the ruined one, with 17 naves. The Almohad mosque at Tin Mal (see page 64), open to visits by non-Muslims, has a similar plan.

The site of the mosque is itself historic, originally being occupied by a late 11th-century kasbah, the Almoravid **Dar al-Hajar**.

The Almohads destroyed much of the previous Almoravid city, and in 1147 built their first huge mosque. Unfortunately, the orientation of the new Almohad mosque was not quite right – the focus point in a mosque is the direction of Mecca, indicated by the *mihrab* or prayer niche, and this one missed its target. The solution was to build a second mosque – the present Koutoubia.

The two mosques existed for some time side by side, the first probably functioning as an annexe. Given Almohad religious fervour, the congregations were large. Today, bricked-up spaces on the northwest wall of the Koutoubia Mosque indicate the doors which connected them. However, the double complex was excessively big and the older structure fell into disrepair and eventual ruin. The excavations of 1948 revealed a *maqsura*, or screen, in front of the *mihrab*, which could be wound up through the floor to protect the Sultan, and a *minbar*, or pulpit, which was moved into position on wooden rollers. Two cisterns in the centre may have been from a previous Almoravid structure. On the eastern flank of this mosque was an arcade of which a niche and the remnants of one arch remain.

The existing Koutoubia Mosque was built by Abd el-Mumin in 1162, soon after the building of the first mosque. The minaret is 12.5 m wide and 67.5 m to the tip of the cupola on the lantern, and is the mosque's principal feature, architecturally admired alongside later Almohad structures, the Hassan Tower in Rabat and the Giralda in Seville. A great feat of engineering in its day, it had a huge influence over subsequent building in Morocco. Holding 20,000 worshippers, the mosque's interior is made up of 17 horseshoe-arched aisles.

The minaret is composed of six rooms, one on top of the other. The cupola on top of the minaret is a symmetrical, square structure topped by a ribbed dome and three golden orbs. These are alleged to have been made from the melted down jewellery of Yaqoub al Mansour's wife, in penance for having eaten three grapes during Ramadan. The proportions of the minaret match the Almohad architectural principle of being five times as tall as it is wide. The cupola has two windows on each side, above which is a stone panel in the *darj w ktaf*, 'step-and-shoulder' motif. The main tower has a band of coloured tiles at the top.

The Koutoubia, a vast structure for 12th-century North Africa, had to be a mosque equal to the lofty ambitions of the western caliphate. It is held to be the high point of Almohad construction, a cathedral-mosque of classic simplicity. It is here that the innovations of Hispano-Moorish art – stalactite cupolas, painted wooden ceilings, sight-lines through horseshoe arches – reach their peak. The elaborate *minbar* (preacher's chair), set against this apparent simplicity, is all decoration and variety – and very much in keeping with the elaborate taste of Ummayad Spain. The original *minbar*, recently restored, can be viewed at the Badi Palace (see page 56). Both prayer hall and chair were to be a source of inspiration for later generations of builders and decorators.

To the west of the mosque, the floral **Jardins de la Koutoubia** are open to all and are a pretty spot from which to view the mosque.

SOUKS

Marrakech's huge network of colourful street markets, or souks, lies to the north of Jemaâ el Fna. With flickering slivers of sunshine filtering down through the slatted sunshades and donkeys and motorbikes pushing through the massed ranks of shoppers and sellers, a day perusing the treasures in the city's bazaar is one of the great Moroccan pleasures.

ON THE ROAD

The highlights of the city are less its museums and historic sites than the streets and souks of its medina, and you should allow plenty of time for wandering, stopping for mint tea, and, almost inevitably, getting lost.

Jemaâ el Fna makes a good place to start with a fresh orange juice. The long straight Rue Riad Zitoun el Jedid, to the southeast of the square, is an easily navigated introduction to the medina. Keeping the tall minaret of the Koutoubia Mosque behind you, head for the narrower northeastern arm of the square and turn right at the Marrakchi restaurant along Rue des Banques. Bear right at the end onto Rue Riad Zitoun el Jedid. Off to the left of this street is the riad museum of **Dar Si Said** (see page 54) and the fascinating **Maison Tiskiwin** (see page 54). At the end of the street, also on the left, is the beautiful **Palais de la Bahia** (see page 55).

Turn right at the end of Rue Riad Zitoun el Jedid and almost immediately you'll have the **jewellery market** straight in front of you – look for the finely carved Grand Bijouterie sign above the entrance. Opposite is the small and much earthier **Mellah** souk, with stalls selling everything from spices to footballs. Following the road around to the left will bring you to the **Place des Ferblantiers**, a traditional place for metalworkers – you can see them at work around the edge of the square making lanterns. On the corner of the square, **Kosybar** is a good place for a drink or a bite to eat.

Near here are two more sights you could make a detour to: the ornate **Tombeaux Saadiens** (see page 57) and the barren spaces of the ruined **Palais El Badi** (see page 56). Also here is the **marché couvert**, good for a taste of how the locals shop for fruit, veg and live chickens.

From Place des Ferblantiers, head northwest to find the end of Rue Riad Zitoun El Kedim. The parallel twin of Rue Riad Zitoun el Jedid, this is another long straight route with plenty of small shops along the way, heading back to Jemaâ el Fna.

To the north of the square, the **souks** are a tightly packed network of markets on narrow streets, many protected from the sun by rush matting overhead. Enter the souks by the medicine men on the square, opposite the Marrakchi, bending round to the right and crossing a junction to head north along Rue Semarine. Shopping in the souks can be overwhelming and disorientating, but this is a sort of souk high street – the straightest, widest route through.

On the right, about half way along is **Rahba Lakdima**, a pretty square with a good café. Continuing north along Rue Semarine will eventually bring you (with a little left-right necessary at the end) blinking out into the sunshine just south of another cluster of Marrakech's sights, the **Medersa Ben Youssef** (see page 49), **Musée de Marrakech** (see page 50), and the **Koubba El Baroudiyine** (see page 50).

Retracing your steps into the souks, take a sharp right at the main junction just before Rahba Lakdima. This is Souk Staila. Taking the first left off here will bring you past the Souk Sebbaghine, with freshly dyed wool hanging out to dry, to the Mouassine fountain and mosque. Keep the mosque on your left and turn down Rue Mouassine, which will take you to Place Bab Fteuh. Keep straight on across here to reach Jemaâ el Fna again, where you can grab a drink on one of the café terraces overlooking the square as it comes to life at sundown.

Nominally the souks are separated into distinct areas, each specializing in certain goods; in reality this isn't clearly observed: leather goods, for example, can be found just about everywhere. However, some areas do retain their original function.

Bab Fteuh is an open space just to the north of Jemaâ el Fna, usually filled with men resting in their handcarts, waiting for business. The central route through the souks is Rue Semarine; useful for orientation, it runs fairly straight north-south from the eastern end of Bab Fteuh up to the Medersa Ben Youssef. At the western end of Bab Fteuh, Rue Mouassine is another useful route, skirting the western edge of the souks. Finally, on the eastern side, Rue Rahba Kedima, starting near the Mosquee Quessabine arm of Jemaâ el Fna, is another possible route north to the medersa.

Souk Semmarine is a busy place, originally the textiles market, and although there are a number of large, expensive tourist shops, there are still some cloth sellers. To the left is a covered *kissaria* selling clothes. The first turning on the right leads past **Souk Larzal**, a wool market, and **Souk Btana**, a sheepskin market, to the attractive open space of **Rahba Kedima**, the old corn market, also known as the Place des Épices. There's a good café overlooking the square (see page 62) and stalls selling a range of hats, traditional cures and cosmetics, spices and cheap jewellery. Around the edge are some good carpet shops and other places piled high with cages containing chameleons and other assorted reptiles. Walk back onto the main souk past the bank machine in the corner of the square. Here the souk forks into **Souk Stailia** on the left and **Souk el Kebir** on the right.

To the right of Souk el Kebir is the **Criée Berbère**, where carpets and *jallabahs* are sold. This was where slaves – men, women and children – mainly from the Sahara, were auctioned until the French occupation in 1912. Further on is the **Souk des Bijoutiers**, with jewellery. To the left (west) of Souk el Kebir is a network of small alleys, the *kissarias*, selling various goods. Immediately north of the *kissarias* is the **Souk Cherratine**, with leather goods: a good place to bargain for camelskin bags, purses and belts.

To the west of the *kissarias* is the colourful **Souk Smata** (you'll also reach it by taking the left-hand Souk Stailia at the fork by Rahba Kedima), centre of Marrakech's *babouches* industry. The ubiquitous leather slippers are the souks' iconic product and this is probably the best place to buy them, if you can face the task of choosing a colour and style from the enormous selection on offer. Parallel to Souk Smata to the north is Souk el Attarine, the spice and perfume souk. Heading west along Souk el Attarine brings you to one of the souks' great sights, the **Souk des Teinturiers**, or dyers' market, where wool recently dyed is draped over the walkways to dry.

Continuing past the skeins of wool brings you out of the souks at the Saadian **Fontaine Mouassine**, one of the medina's most beautiful fountains, and the 16th-century **Mosquée Mouassine**. This important mosque gives its name to this part of the medina.

North of the Souk el Attarine is the carpenters' **Souk Chouari**, one of many specialist areas in the tight northern souks that include ironworkers in Souk Haddadine, musical instruments in Souk Kimakhine and lanterns in Souk Jdid. This area of the souks, furthest from Jemaâ el Fna, is one of the best places to see craftsmen at work behind their stalls.

Before leaping into impulse purchases in the souks, it may be a good idea to get an idea of prices in shops in Guéliz, or in the Ensemble Artisanal on Mohamed V. Many people, however, get overly obsessed about getting a bargain; ultimately, the good price is the one you are happy to pay.

ON THE ROAD
Kids in Marrakech

There's plenty to entertain children in Marrakech, from the Jemaâ el Fna snake charmers to acrobats that will come somersaulting your way the moment you sit outside at a restaurant. But there's little that's specifically designed for kids. A day out at a pool outside the city is a good bet, and a trip to the mountains provides some needed space. A horse-drawn calèche tour of the city walls is a good way to see something without the scrum of street level, and places such as the Menara gardens sometimes have camels that can be ridden through the palm groves. For real wide-eyed excitement go for an early morning balloon ride over the nearby countryside (page 62).

FONDOUKS

Around the northern souks are many old *fondouks*. Originally these were inns, with bedrooms on the upper floors, and often stalls set up on the ground floor where passing tradesmen could sell their wares. Handsome old buildings, some have been restored and now house craft workshops. There are several around the junction of Rue Dar El Bacha and Rue Mouassine (including the Fondouk Kharbouch and Fondouk Almisane) and several more on Rue de Souk des Fassis, to the east of the medersa, where you'll also find Le Foundouk restaurant (see page 61). Visitors are usually free to look in.

MEDERSA BEN YOUSSEF

ⓘ *Daily 0900-1830, 40dh, 60dh with the museum and koubba.*

The city's most beautiful and most important Islamic monument, the 16th-century Medersa Ben Youssef is one of the few Islamic buildings open to the general public. Restored by the Fondation Ben Jelloun it is now Marrakech's architectural highlight. Cool, calm corridors, beautiful arches, *zellij* tiles and the light reflecting in the central pool make it a breathtaking place to visit.

Functioning as a boarding school for students of the religious sciences and law, and attached to the mosque of the same name, in its current incarnation it was founded in 1564-1565 by the Saadian Sultan Moulay Abdellah on the site of a previous 14th-century Merinid medersa. Though the name translates as 'school', it is likely that most lectures were carried out at the adjoining mosque.

Centred around a square courtyard containing a rectangular pool and with arcades on two sides, it is influenced by Moorish Andalucían architecture and shares similarities with the Alhambra in Granada. If you can avoid the tour groups, the sound of water running into the pool is about all you will hear: the contrast to the noise of the medina means that the peace is all the more marked.

Each student had a separate cell with a sleeping loft and a window looking onto the courtyard – these are decidedly more modest in style than the grand courtyard below. The intricate cedar wood decoration of the upper façades around the courtyard is worn but still beautiful. You will see fine *zellij* tiling on the arcade floor, walls and pillars. Inscriptions are in Kufic and cursive lettering, interwoven with floral patterns. Most impressive of all, however, is the stunning sense of space and calm that the interior's harmonious proportions achieve.

At the far end is the prayer hall covered with an eight-sided wooden dome. Beneath the dome plaster open-work windows illuminate the tilework. In the *qibla* wall is a five-sided *mihrab* indicating the direction of prayer. The stalactite ceiling of the *mihrab* and the carved stucco walls with pine cone motif are particularly impressive. The inscription here, dedicated to the Sultan, translates as: "I was constructed as a place of learning and prayer by the Prince of the Faithful, the descendant of the seal of the prophets, Abdellah, the most glorious of all Caliphs. Pray for him, all who enter here, so that his greatest hopes may be realized." The massive marble columns are carved out of Italian Carrara marble.

On the way out of the medersa, a visit to the toilets on the right of the vestibule reveals another elaborate stalactite design on the ceiling.

MUSEE DE MARRAKECH
ⓘ *Place Ben Youssef, T0524-441893, www.museedemarrakech.ma, daily 0900-1830, 40dh, 60dh with the medersa and koubba.*
In Dar M'nebhi, the early 20th-century palace of a former Moroccan minister of war, the setting of Marrakech's museum is more spectacular than its contents. After the entrance courtyard, a narrow corridor takes you into the exhibition areas proper. The simple whitewashed walls of the domestic wing shelter temporary exhibitions of contemporary art. Large pieces here are often striking, though quality varies. The main courtyard is protected by a plexi-glass roof that bathes the place in a strangely yellow light. Under this hangs a brass chandelier the size of a small spaceship, and there are plenty of nooks and comfortable seats in which to rest. A handful of photos of old Morocco have an air of abandonment, with cracked glass and skewed mounts cut from crumpled corrugated card. Rooms behind the main courtyard display Koran manuscripts, coins, ceramics and textiles. The Fès pottery is most impressive, dating from the 18th to the 20th century. Semi-abstracted fruit and flower motifs are mixed with geometric patterns in yellows and greens. The elaborate wooden façades in the rooms on the left show Portuguese influence. A small passageway to the left of the main reception room takes you through to the restored hammam. In front of the museum in the courtyard is a good café and a bookshop.

KOUBBA EL BAROUDIYINE
ⓘ *Place Ben Youssef, daily 0900-1830, 40dh, 60dh with the museum and medersa. There is a rather bureaucratic enforcement of the order in which you see the three Islamic monuments and the koubba should be the last of the three.*
Protected by wrought-iron railings, the 11th-century Almoravid *koubba* is the only complete Almoravid building surviving in Morocco. It dates from the reign of Ali bin Youssef (1107-1143), and perhaps formed part of the toilet and ablutions facilities of the mosque that at the time existed nearby. At first glance it is a simple building, with a dome surmounting a square stone and brick structure. However, the dome has a design of interlocking arches, plus a star and chevron motif on top. The arches leading into the *koubba* are different on each side. Climb down the stairs to view the ceiling of the dome, and you will begin to appreciate the architectural significance of the building, with its range of Almoravid motifs, including the pine cone and acanthus. Around the corniche is a dedicatory inscription in cursive script. Set into the floor is a small, almost square, basin. Finely proportioned, the building has many elements that became the standards of subsequent eras.

Standing with the *koubba* behind you, the minaret of the large 12th-century Ben Youssef Mosque, rebuilt in the 19th century, is clearly visible.

ON THE ROAD
Hammams

A ritual purification of the body is essential before Muslims can perform prayers and, in the days before bathrooms, the 'major ablutions' were generally done at the hammam (bath). Segregation of the sexes is, of course, the rule at the hammam. Some establishments are only open for women, others are only for men, most have a shift system (mornings and evenings for the men, all afternoon for women). In the old days, the hammam, along with the local *zaouïa* or saint's shrine, was an important place for women to gather and socialize, and even pick out a potential wife for a son.

Very often there are separate hammams for men and women next to each other on the ground floor of an apartment building. A passage leads into a large changing room/post-bath area, equipped with masonry benches for lounging on and (sometimes) small wooden lockers. Here you undress under a towel. Hammam gear today is usually shorts for men and knickers for women. If you're going to have a massage/scrub down, you take a token at the cash desk where shampoo can also be bought.

The next step is to proceed to the hot room: five to 10 minutes with your feet in a bucket of hot water will have you sweating nicely and you can then move back to the raised area where the masseurs are at work. After the expert removal of large quantities of dead skin, you go into one of the small cabins or *mathara* to finish washing. (Before doing this, find the person bringing in dry towels so that they can bring yours to you when you're in the *mathara*.) For women, in addition to a scrub and a wash there may be the pleasures of epilation with *sokar*, a mix of caramelized sugar and lemon. Men can undergo a *taksira*, which involves much pulling and stretching of the limbs. And remember, allow plenty of time to cool down, reclining in the changing area.

Hotel hammams include **Riad El Fenn**, see page 60, with a *gommage* treatment that ends with two halves of a fresh orange being squeezed over your body and a jar of wonderful-smelling rosewater being poured over your head and face. Richard Branson's **Kasbah Tamadot**, see page 76, in Asni, has a hammam a few steps away from a lovely dark blue swimming pool.

DAR BELLARJ
ⓘ *9 Toulalat Zaouiat Lahdar, T0524-444555, 0900-1800, free.*
Turning right out of the medersa, a brass sign indicates the entrance of Dar Bellarj, 'the House of Storks', on your left. The 1930s building, around a beautiful large, bright and open courtyard, was restored by Swiss artists. Previously there was a fondouk on the site, housing a hospital for birds. Today, the building, austerely but simply refurbished, houses a cultural foundation and is used as a gallery space for contemporary arts and displays. There are places to sit and contemplate and coffee and tea is also for sale.

MAISON DE LA PHOTOGRAPHIE
ⓘ *46 Rue Ahal Fès, T0524-385721, www.maisondelaphotographie.com, daily 0930-1900, 40dh, children free.*
Just yards from the Medersa Ben Youssef is a recently opened gallery of vintage Moroccan photographs. Thousands of sepia-tinted photos and glass negatives dating to the mid-1800s are displayed over the three floors in a restored riad, with a café on the roof terrace.

DAR CHERIFA

① 8 Derb Charfa Lakbir Mouassine, off Rue Mouassine, T0524-426463, www.marrakech-riads. net, daily 0900-1900.

A magically beautiful and peaceful place, Dar Cherifa is both a literary café (see page 62) and a fantastic contemporary art space. Wind down narrow alleyways off Rue Mouassine and knock on the door to be let in. Exhibitions of mostly local contemporary art are held downstairs and the café extends onto the roof terrace. The riad, one of the city's oldest, dates back to Saadian times, and has been wonderfully restored by Abdelatif Ben Abdellah, one of the key figures behind the rejuvenation of the medina. The soaring courtyard is one of the finest examples of Islamic architecture in Marrakech.

SIDI BEL ABBES

North of the Medersa Ben Youssef are quiet residential neighbourhoods where you will see few tourists. Built on an area of former orchards and market gardens, it is a more recent area of the medina, incorporated in the 18th century. Beyond the open square of **Bab Taghzaoute** is the **Zaouïa of Sidi Bel Abbes**. Usually considered the most important of the seven saints of Marrakech, and sometimes the patron saint of the city itself, Bel Abbes was born in Ceuta in 1130. He championed the cause of the blind in Marrakech and was patronized by Sultan Yaqoub al Mansour. You are free to wander through the religious complex, though non-Muslims are barred from the mausoleum. It's a striking place, with bright squares and shady alleyways. A series of arches is filled with potted plants and blind people chatting and waiting to receive food and alms. Nearby is the **Zaouïa of Sidi Ben Slimane el Jazouli**, a 14th-century sufi.

TANNERIES NEAR BAB DEBBAGH

The tanneries near Bab Debbagh ('Tanners' Gate') are one of the most interesting (if smelly) sites in Marrakech. Wandering towards the tanners' area, you will almost certainly be approached by someone who will offer to show you the tanneries – it's possible to see them without a guide, but easier with. Agree a price first and beware of excessive demands. You will be given a rather ineffective sprig of mint to hold to your nostrils to mask the stink and led through a small door into an area of foul-smelling pits, where men tread and rinse skins in nauseous liquids and dyes. In small lean-to buildings, you will find other artisans scraping and stretching the skins.

Located close to the seasonal water from the river, the Oued Issil, the odorous tanners were kept on the edge of the city with plenty of water and space to expand away from residential areas. Tanning in Marrakech is still a pre-industrial process, alive and functioning not far from the heart of the medina – even though the traditional dyes have largely been replaced with chemical products.

You may be told that there are two tanneries: one Arab, the other Berber. In fact there are several, and workforces are fairly ethnically mixed. There do remain specialities, however, with one set of tanners working mainly on the more difficult cow and camel skins, and the others on goat and sheep skins. You can get a view of the area from leather shop terraces next to Bab Debbagh – you will be charged for the privilege.

RAMPARTS AND GATES

The extensive ramparts of Marrakech, stretching for 16 km around the medina, were mostly built by the Almoravids in the 12th century, although they have been extensively restored since. The reconstruction is a continual process as the *pisé*-cement walls, made

The tanners are said to have been the first to settle in Marrakech at its foundation, and a gate is named after them, the only one to be named for a craft corporation. 'Bab Debbagh, bab deheb' – 'Tanners' Gate, gold gate' – the old adage goes, in reference to the tanners' prosperity. One legend runs that seven virgins are buried in the foundations of the gate (sisters of the seven protector saints of Marrakech) and that women who desire a child should offer them candles and henna. Another legend says that Bab Debbagh is inhabited by Malik Gharub, a genie who dared to lead a revolt against Sidna Suleyman, the Black King, only to be condemned to tan a cowhide and cut out *belgha* soles for eternity as punishment.

The tannery was considered both a dangerous place – as it was the entrance to the domain of the Other Ones – and a beneficial one, since skins were a symbol of preservation and fertility. Because the tanners spent their days in pits working the skins, they were said to be in contact with the unseen world of the dead and to be masters of fertility, being strong men, capable of giving a second life to dry, dead skin.

The process of tanning skins is strongly symbolic – the tanners say that the skin eats, drinks, sleeps and 'is born of the water'. When the skin is treated with lime, it is said to be thirsty; when it is treated with pigeon dung, it is said to receive *nafs*, a spirit. The *merkel* (treading) stage prepares the skin to live again, while the *takkut* of the tanning mixture is also used by women to dye their hair. At this point, the skin receives *ruh* (breath). Leather is thus born from the world of the dead and the *ighariyin*, the people of the grotto, and is fertilized in the swampy pool, the domain of the dead – who are also said to have the power to bring rain.

In the old days, the complex process of tanning would start with soaking the skins in a sort of swamp – or *iferd* – in the middle of the tannery, filled with a fermenting mixture of pigeon guano and tannery waste. Fermenting would last three days in summer, six in winter. Then the skins would be squeezed out and put to dry. Hair would be scraped off, then the skins would go into a pit of lime and argan-kernel ash. This would remove any remaining flesh or hair, and prepare the skin to receive the tanning products. The lime bath lasts 15-20 days in summer, up to 30 in winter. Then the skins are washed energetically, trodden to remove any lime, and any extra bits are cut off. Next the skins spend 24 hours in a *qasriya*, a round pit of more pigeon dung and fresh water. At this stage the skin becomes thinner and stretches. There follows soaking in wheat fibre and salt for 24 hours to remove any traces of lime and guano.

Then begins the actual tanning process. (The word *debbagh* actually means tannin.) Traditional tanneries used only plants – roots, barks and certain seeds and fruits. In Marrakech, acacia and oak bark are used, along with takkut, the ground-up fruit of the tamarisk. A water and tannin mix is prepared in a pit, and the skins get three soakings.

After this, the skins are prepared to receive the dye. They are scraped with pottery shards, beaten and coated with oil, alum and water. Then they are dyed by hand and left to dry in the sun (traditionally on the banks of the nearby Oued Issil). Finally, the skins are worked to make them smoother and more supple, stretched between two ropes and worked on smooth pottery surfaces.

of the red earth of the Haouz plains, gradually crumble. A ride in a horse-drawn *calèche* is a good way to see the ramparts; much of the route is now planted with rose gardens.

Grand gates punctuate the wall, including **Bab Rob**, near the buses and grands taxi on the southwest side of the medina. From the Almohad era, it is named after the grape juice which at one time was brought through this gate. **Bab Dabbagh** (the Tanners' gate, on the east side) is an intricate defensive gate with a twisted entrance route and wooden gates, which could shut off the various parts of the building for security. **Bab el Khemis**, on the northeast side, opens into the Souk el Khemis (Thursday market) and an important area of mechanics and craftsmen. Check out the junk market here on a Sunday morning. There is a small saint's tomb inside the gate building. **Bab Doukkala**, on the northwest side by the bus station, is a large gate with a horseshoe arch and two towers. The medina side has a horseshoe arch and a cusped, blind arch, with a variation on the *darj w ktaf* (step and shoulder) motif along the top. A newer road across the palm grove north of Bab Doukkala completes the circuit of the ramparts.

→ SOUTHERN MEDINA

South of Jemaâ el Fna the character of the medina changes somewhat: it is a more varied part of the city, with swanky palaces old and new interspersed with narrow, dirty streets and snippets of modernity. Rue de Bab Agnaou and Rue Ben Marine are busy, pedestrianized streets filled with banks, shops and glitz. To the east, Rue Riad Zitoun El Khedim and Rue Riad Zitoun El Jedid are long and unusually straight roads with more in common with the northern medina. Two museums devoted to Moroccan artistry, Dar Si Said and Maison Tiskiwin, both in attractive traditional settings, sit close together at the southern end of Riad Zitoun el Jedid. Beyond are the sparkling spaces of the Bahia palace and the crumbling openness of the El Badi palace. The nearby Saadian tombs are an intricately filigree example of aristocratic Moroccan design, whereas the attractively dishevelled Mellah area retains some of its poor Jewish roots, complete with synagogues and a large Jewish cemetery.

DAR SI SAID
ⓘ *T0524-442464, Wed-Mon 0900-1200, 1600-2100 summer, 1430-1800 winter, 30dh.*
Built by Si Said, Visir under Moulay El Hassan and half-brother of Ba Ahmed Ben Moussa (the former slave who built the nearby Palais de la Bahia, see below), Dar Si Said is a late 19th-century palace housing the Museum of Moroccan Arts and Crafts. The palace itself makes a visit worthwhile: an intimate and ornately decorated place, it has two storeys with rooms around arcaded courtyards.

The collection includes pottery, jewellery, leatherwork and Chichaoua carpets. It is particularly strong on Amazigh artefacts such as curved daggers, copperware and jewellery. On the first floor is a salon with Hispano-Moorish decoration and cedarwood furniture, while around the Andalucían-influenced garden courtyard you'll find old window and door frames. Look out for a primitive four-seater wooden ferris wheel of the type still found in *moussems* (country fairs) in Morocco.

Other highlights include a large 10th-century carved marble bath for ablutions, the carved cedar, octagonally domed ceiling in the reception room, and antique carpets from the Atlas.

MAISON TISKIWIN
ⓘ *8 Rue de la Bahia, T0524-389192, 15dh.*
Between the Dar Si Said and the Bahia Palace, a few streets further south is the fantastic Maison Tiskiwin (the House of the Horns), home to a fine collection of items related to

Northern African and Saharan culture and society. This small museum was lovingly put together by the Dutch art historian Bert Flint, who still lives here, though he has given the museum to Marrakech University. Flint still spends some of the year travelling and gathering objects to add to the collection and there is a strong sense of enthusiasm for the artefacts here, in strong contrast to some of the state-run museums. There are crafts from the Rif and the High Atlas, though the collection focuses primarily on the Sahara, and includes jewellery and costumes, musical instruments, carpets and furniture. The building itself, around a courtyard, is an authentic and well-maintained example of a traditional riad. There are excellent and copious notes in English. Groups tend to visit in the morning – if you go along in the afternoon you may get the museum all to yourself. Don't miss the beautiful Saharan leatherwork.

PALAIS DE LA BAHIA

ⓘ T0524-389221, Sat-Thu 0845-1145 and 1445-1745, Fri 0845-1130 and 1500-1745, 10dh.
Further to the south is the Bahia Palace (the name means 'brilliant'). It was built in the last years of the 19th century by the Vizir Ba Ahmed Ben Moussa, or Bou Ahmed, a former slave who rose to a position of power under sultans Moulay Hassan and Abd el-Aziz. Sunlight shines through wrought-iron bars creating beautiful patterns on the *zellij* tiles, and in the courtyard water ripples over green tiles around a beautiful fountain, surrounded by trees. There are tour groups, but there are also plenty of quiet corners in which lingering until they've passed is a pleasure. The palace is a maze of patios planted with fruit trees, passageways and empty chambers with painted ceilings. Guides will tell you that each wife and concubine had a room looking onto the patio. The story goes that Bou Ahmed was so hated that, on his death in 1900, his palace was looted and his possessions stolen by slaves, servants and members of his *harem*. Subsequently, the building was occupied by the French authorities. Bareness is still a feature of the palace, but it is one that accentuates the beauty of the architecture and space.

MELLAH

One of the city's most labyrinthine areas, the tight, enclosed streets of the Mellah are an atmospheric part of Marrakech, where riads and gentrification are only starting to make low-key inroads. South of the Bahia and east of the El Badi Palace, the *mellah*, or Jewish neighbourhood, was created in 1558. The second such area in Morocco, it was set up at around the same time as the ghetto in Rome. Despite the similarities of separation along religious lines, Moroccan Islamic attitudes seem to have been generally more tolerant towards Judaism than those in Christian Europe. Today the Jewish community has all but vanished, but there remain some signs to tell you of its former role in the life of Marrakech – many of the tall houses have distinctive enclosed balconies overlooking the narrow streets and you may be able to find some Hebrew lettering here and there. At one time there were many thousands of Jewish people living here, with several synagogues, and under the control of the rabbis, the area had considerable autonomy. Until the 1930s there were only two doors out into the rest of the medina. It's hard to get far down a Mellah street without someone offering to show you one of the synagogues. It's worth a visit, but agree a price first and expect double "donation to the synagogue"/"donation for the guide" requests. There are probably fewer than 150 practising Jewish people left in the Mellah and the remaining synagogues can be rather sad places, though the oldest, **Synagogue Lazama** (Sun-Fri), is still well looked after, with potted plants in its blue-painted and tiled courtyard.

MIAÂRA JEWISH CEMETERY

ⓘ *Rue Iman El Rhezoli, Sun-Fri approximately 0630-1900.*

To the east of the Mellah, two friendly brothers act as caretakers for the city's 17th-century Jewish cemetery. Visitors are welcome to wander among the old stones and the caretaker may also tell you about Jewish life in Marrakech. You'll probably find a dog or two lazing atop the weather-worn tombstones and shrines. It's a strangely affecting place: a bubble of complete calm around which the medina and the mountains crowd, it feels a little like a remnant of a lost civilisation. The smaller stones mark the resting places of children.

PLACE DES FERBLANTIERS AND AROUND

The traditional hub of the city's metalworkers, this square was once known as the Place du Mellah and was a part of the Jewish souk. These days, roses and lantern makers line its sides. Bar and restaurant Kosybar has an upstairs terrace that makes a good viewing platform from which to look down on the action below.

The **Grand Bijouterie**, the jewellery souk, is just to the northwest of the square, facing the entrance to the Palais de la Bahia. Its elaborate and glittering silver and gold are in marked contrast to the largely run-down Mellah. Other notable retail-based sights nearby include the dingy market stalls of **Souk Hay Essalam**, piled high with spices and cheap plastic tat (the entrance is directly opposite the jewellery souk) and, to the west, the **Marché Couverte**, the place to go should you want to purchase a live chicken.

PALAIS EL BADI

ⓘ *0830-1145 and 1430-1745 (Ramadan 0900-1600), 10dh plus another 10dh to see the Koutoubia minbar.*

The huge barren spaces of the ruined 16th-century El Badi Palace come as a bit of a shock after the cramped streets of the Marrakech medina. Orange trees grow in what were once enormous pools in the central courtyard, and storks nest noisily on the ruined walls. For five days in June, El Badi comes alive for the annual **Festival National des Arts Populaires**. Most of the year, however, it is a quiet sort of place, the high thick walls protecting the vast courtyard from the noise of the surrounding streets.

The palace was built by the Saadian Sultan Ahmed al Mansur ed-Dahbi (the Golden) between 1578 and 1593, following his accession after his victory over the Portuguese at the Battle of the Three Kings at Ksar el Kebir in northern Morocco. It marks the height of Saadian power, the centrepiece of an imperial capital. In its day it was a lavish display of the best craftsmanship of the period, using the most expensive materials, including gold, marble and onyx. The colonnades were of marble, apparently exchanged with Italian merchants for their equivalent weight in sugar.

The palace was largely destroyed in the 17th century by Moulay Ismaïl, who stripped it of its decorations and fittings and carried them off to Meknès. No austere royal fortress, the Badi was probably a palace for audiences – and it was at one of these great court ceremonies that the building's fate was predicted: "What do you think of this palace?" asked the sultan El-Mansour. "When it is demolished, it will make a big pile of earth", replied a visionary. El-Mansour is said to have felt a chill sense of foreboding.

The ruins on either side of the courtyard were probably summer houses, the one at the far end being called the **Koubba el Khamsiniya** (The Fifty Pavillion) after either the 50 cubits of its area, or the fact that it once had 50 columns.

The complex contains a small museum which includes the restored *minbar* (the sacred staired Islamic equivalent of a pulpit, from which the Imam delivers sermons) from the Koutoubia Mosque. Mark Minor, one of the conservators from the Metropolitan Museum of Art in New York who carried out the restoration, called it "one of the finest works of art in wood created by mankind". Constructed in Cordoba in Spain in 1139, it is covered in around 100 carvings. The minbar remained in use until 1962. The scattered ruins of the palace, with odd fragments of decoration amidst the debris, also include stables and dungeons.

PALAIS ROYAL DAR EL MAKHZEN
To the south of the El Badi Palace is the **Dar el Makhzen**, the modern-day Royal Palace, one of the late King Hassan II's favourite residences. It is closed to the public, however, and out of favour with the current king, who has had a new palace constructed, close to the Hotel Mamounia.

KASBAH
① *Follow Rue Bab Agnaou south from Jemaâ el Fna, or enter the medina at Bab Rob.*
Bab Agnaou, meaning the gate of the black people, marks the entrance to the Kasbah quarter from the west. The 12th-century gate is one of the city's most handsome, as well as one of its oldest structures. The Kasbah quarter dates from the reign of the Almohad Sultan Ya'qub al Mansour. The gateway was probably decorative rather than defensive, and would once have had a tower at each side, marking the entrance to the Almohad palace. It is surrounded by a series of arches within a rectangle of floral designs, with a shell or palmette in each corner and an outer band of Kufic inscription.

The road from the gate leads to Rue de la Kasbah, on which is the much restored **El Mansour**, or Kasbah Mosque, built at the end of the 12th century. It is one of the few remaining Almohad structures in the city, though rebuilding has given it a rather modern appearance. The minaret has original Almohad motifs on a background of green tiles, above which is a band of coloured tiles. The three balls on top are commonly known as the golden apples, though they are actually made of brass. The entrance to the Tombeaux Saadians (see opposite) is directly to the right of the mosque.

TOMBEAUX SAADIENS
① *0830-1145 and 1430-1745 (Ramadan 0900-1600), 10dh.*
The unrestrainedly opulent 16th-century Saadian Tombs were discovered thanks to aerial photography in 1917. The final resting place of the Saadian family, a dynasty from the Draâ valley that came to rule Morocco, the tombs were sealed off by Moulay Ismaïl in the 17th century in a vain attempt to condemn the Saadian rulers to oblivion. The claustrophobically narrow passage that leads to the tombs still emphasizes their hidden past.

Inside there are two mausoleums, containing a series of chambers set around a small garden and intricately decorated with an extraordinary profusion of Italian Carrara marble, carved cedar and plasterwork. A contrast to the much simpler Almohad style, the tombs contain some of Morocco's most striking Islamic architecture.

The *mihrab* (the niche indicating the direction of Mecca) in the first burial chamber is particularly impressive, supported by fine white marble columns. In this first room is the tomb of Prince Moulay Yazid. Known as the mad sultan, he was shot in the head by an uprising in 1792 and was the last to be buried here, after the tombs had been sealed off. The room was probably a prayer room before being used for burials.

The elaborate, domed second room is known as the Hall of 12 Columns and contains the central tomb of Ahmed al Mansour himself, the most famous of the Saadi rulers (1578-1603). Either side lie his descendants. It is a dramatic space, faintly lit from above, with beautiful *zellij* tiling.

The second, older and plainer mausoleum was built by Ahmed al Mansour for the tombs of his mother, Lalla Messaouda, and Mohamed esh Sheikh, founder of the Saadians. In the garden and courtyard are the tombs of more than 100 other princelings and members of court. Try to visit early in the day as the place can get overcrowded with tour groups.

JARDINS DE LA MAMOUNIA

ⓘ *Av Bab Jedid, T0524-388600, www.mamounia.com.*

Not just any old five-star hotel, La Mamounia is a byword for Moroccan opulence, its 1920s Art Deco style spruced up for the 21st century. The 13 ha of formal walled gardens, beloved of Winston Churchill, give their name to the hotel. Once royal playgrounds, they were given as an 18th-century wedding gift to Prince Moulay Mamoun by his father, King Sidi Mohamed Ben Abdellahand. The pavilion here is older, dating back as far as the Saadian empire in the 16th century. To the southwest of the Koutoubia, just inside the city walls, the gardens can be visited if you're smartly dressed and pop in for a pot of tea.

→ VILLE NOUVELLE AND THE GARDENS

Guéliz, the suburb laid out by the French in the 1920s, is a world apart from the medina. All glossy new apartment buildings and traffic, there are few sights but it is worth a wander for its cafés, upmarket boutiques and food market and it has many of the city's best restaurants. Moroccans dressed in smart Western clothes promenade up and down the main thoroughfare of Avenue Mohamed V in the evenings and lounge over long cups of coffee outside streetside cafés. There's a refreshing absence of hassle, but at times it's also easy to forget that you're in Morocco at all.

To the south, Hivernage offers a bigger, brasher version of the same, with wider streets and large hotels interspersed with occasional cafés, cocktail bars and casinos.

One of the most distinctive features of Marrakech is its gardens, and three in particular, around the peripheries of the city centre, are worth visiting.

GUELIZ

For a few remnants of French colonial architecture and a taste of a modern, buzzing Moroccan cityscape, Guéliz is the place to come for many of the city's designer boutiques and commercial contemporary galleries. Place du 16 Novembre is where the busiest roads (Avenue Mohamed V and Avenue Hassan II) converge; the most interesting parts of Guéliz are to the north of here, as is the Marché Municipale, a market with food stalls. The new, Charles Boccara-designed Théatre Royal, opposite the (even newer) train station, is worth a look – work on the place seems to have stalled but the guardian will probably be happy to show you around. The building is a good example of the incorporation of traditional Moroccan elements into contemporary architecture.

JARDIN MAJORELLE

ⓘ *Av Yakoub El Mansour, www.jardinmajorelle.com, Jun-Sep 0800-1800, Oct-May 0800-1700, 50dh, plus 25dh for the museum.*

A small tropical garden, this verdant splash of colour was first laid out by a French artist, Louis Majorelle, in 1924. A member of a family of cabinet-makers from Nancy who made their money with innovative art nouveau furniture, Majorelle portrayed the landscapes and people of the High Atlas in large, colourful paintings, some of which were used for tourism posters. The carefully restored garden belonged to Yves St Laurent, whose ashes were scattered here after his death in 2008. The cacti are large and sculptural and strong colours and forms dominate the garden, especially the walls, buildings and plant pots, which are a particularly vivid shade of cobalt blue. Bulbuls, monogamous songbirds often compared to nightingales, sing in the bamboo thickets and flit between the Washingtonia palms. A green-roofed garden pavilion houses the small **Musée d'Art Islamique** with a fine and easily digestible collection of North African art and objects from the personal collections of Pierre Bergé and Yves St Laurent, as well as works by Majorelle himself. The gardens are one of the city's most popular sights – try to visit early, late or at lunchtime to avoid the worst of the crowds.

JARDINS DE L'AGDAL
The large, tree-filled Agdal Gardens, stretching south of the medina, were established in the 12th century under Abd el-Moumen, and were expanded and reorganized by the Saadians. The vast expanse, over 400 ha, includes several pools, and extensive areas of olive, orange and pomegranate trees. They are usually closed when the king is in residence, but parts can be visited at other times. Of the pavilions, the **Dar al-Baida** was used by Sultan Moulay Hassan to house his harem. The largest pool, **Sahraj el Hana**, receives occasional coachloads of tourists, but at other times is a pleasant place to relax. As with the other gardens, swimming, however, is not allowed.

MENARA GARDENS
From the medina and the Agdal Gardens, Avenue de la Ménara leads to the Ménara Gardens, a large olive grove centring on a rectangular pool. The green-tiled pavilion beside the pool was originally built by the Saadian dynasty in the 16th century, and was renovated in 1869 by Sultan Abderrahmane. With palm trees and the Atlas Mountains as a backdrop, it is one of the city's prettiest sights and features on many Marrakech postcards. The large expanse of water generates a microclimate that is slightly cooler than the surrounding streets, and, being a short moped hop from central Marrakech, the gardens are popular with locals for picnics and romantic assignations. Together with the Agdal Gardens, the Ménara is listed as a UNESCO World Heritage Site.

MARRAKECH LISTINGS

WHERE TO STAY

€€€€ Maison MK, 14 Derb Sebaai, Quartier Ksar, T0524-376173, www.maison mk.com. Vibrant, bright and exceedingly hip, the 6 suites of the luxurious **Maison MK** combine traditional riad decoration standards – *tadelakt* and wrought iron – with contemporary Moroccan design elements and all mod cons. So funky is the place that even the mint teapots are brightly coloured and two-toned. The cinema room has a 2.5-m screen as well as an Xbox and you can put in advance requests for what you'd like in your minibar. Each room has iPod and mobile phone. For 22,000dh you can have the whole riad. Minimum stay of 3 nights, price includes airport transfers.

€€€€ Riad El Fenn, Derb Moullay Abdullah Ben Hezzian, Bab el Ksar, T0524-441210, www.riadelfenn.com. Possibly Marrakech's most spectacularly luxurious riad, **El Fenn** also does the simple things well. The design is striking – deep red walls coexist with more classic riad style, and a fine collection of contemporary art adorns the walls. There are 21 rooms, most of which have private fires, and one of which has a private, glass-bottomed rooftop pool, through which sunlight streams into the room below. Owned by Vanessa Branson, but run with laconic French style, **El Fenn** has some great ecological policies: it uses solar panels and has its own organic garden outside the city which provides the riad with fresh produce. There is a fine restaurant and bar, loads of cosy cushioned seating nooks and 3 pools with shaded terraces. The only danger is that once inside, you'll hardly want to venture out!

€€€ Riad Porte Royale, Derb el Matta 84, Diour Jdad, Zaouïa Sidi bel Abbes, T0524-376109, www.riadporteroyale.com. Owned by an English writer, **Porte Royale** brings a touch of British elegance to the northern edge of the medina. There's no over-the-top decoration or wild kaleidoscope of colours here, just pristine white walls, a few carefully chosen pieces of furniture and occasional rare fabrics. The stylish reserve of the decoration serves to emphasize the beauty of the building and contributes to an atmosphere of serenity. The location is a beautiful part of the medina that few tourists reach and service is superbly friendly and attentive. Excellent value.

€€€ Riad Tizwa, Derb Gueraba 26, Dar el Bacha, T0668-190872 (Morocco) or T07973-115471 (UK), www.riadtizwa.com. Stylish and good value, the Bee brothers' Marrakech riad is an elegant place near Dar el Bacha and claims to be "Marrakech's first environmentally recognized riad", sourcing produce from organic local suppliers. Well designed without being fussy, the 6 bedrooms, primarily white with splashes of colour, open into a central courtyard with a small fountain. Huge beds are exceptionally comfortable and the dressing areas are a great design feature – bring plenty of clothes in order to make full use of the inventive hanging space behind enormous tadelakt headboards. Bathrooms are luxurious, with innumerable thick towels and soft hooded dressing gowns you may never want to get out of. Wi-Fi, iPod docks and good food.

€€ Hotel Sherazade, 3 Derb Djama, T0524-429305, www.hotelsherazade.com. Beds are big, fabrics are bold and striped, there's lots of greenery and the vibe is friendly in this hotel southeast of Jemaâ el Fna. It's spotlessly clean and the 23 rooms are arranged around large courtyards. Breakfast is an extra 50dh for a buffet on the roof terrace. The owners also have 2 bungalows for rent 14 km north of the city. The street is the 3rd narrow one on your left as you head down Riad Zitoun el

Kedim from Jemaâ el Fna. Good value and very popular, so book well in advance.

€€ Hotel Ali, Rue Moulay Ismail, T0524-444979, www.hotel-ali.com. An old travellers' favourite, this large, rambling hotel is just off Jemaâ el Fna. It's a decent base for those intending to go climbing/trekking, as it is run by people from the Atlas and there are usually guides to be found hanging out here. Don't expect anything stylish; simple rooms have as many beds squeezed into them as possible, but all now have a/c and some have a balcony. Good-value restaurant and discounts for a week's stay. Fabulous views from roof terrace. No credit cards.

RESTAURANTS

€€€ Dar Zellij, Kaasour Sidi Benslimane, T0524-382627, www.darzellij.com. Converted from a 17th-century riad guesthouse to a restaurant, **Dar Zellij** now offers one of the most spectacular settings in the city in which to enjoy an evening meal. It's not easy to find but is well worth the effort. Waiters seem to float around the tree-filled courtyard in long white gowns, and the live music is subtle rather than intrusive. Tables come sprinkled with petals, there's an open fire, dark red walls, candles, enormous high ceilings, curtains and calligraphic art. The traditional Moroccan food is good too, though at times it can't quite match the extravagance of the surroundings or the service. Set menus 300-600dh.

€€ Le Foundouk, 55 Souk Hal Fassi, Kaât Ben Hadid, T0524-378190, www.foundouk.com. Tue-Sun 1200-2400. For those for whom insipid, overcooked tagines have become a chore, the succulent, well-spiced versions here will be something of a welcome surprise. Near the Medersa Ben Youssef, the licensed Foundouk, in a converted riad, is one of the most elegant restaurants in Marrakech. There are roses in glasses on the tables, contemporary art and mirrors on the walls, and modern jazz plays while a white, dark brown and burgundy colour scheme gives the place an air of contemporary sophistication. As well as the tagines (for around 130dh), there's European food, and vegetarians can find plenty of choice in the starters to make up an entire meal. Evening reservations recommended.

€€ Terrasse des Épices, 15 Souk Cherifa, Sidi Abdelaziz, T0524-375904, www.terrassedesepices.com. Daily 1200-2300. From the owners of the successful **Café des Épices**, the titular terrace is a surprisingly expansive and open space on the 1st floor of a building in the middle of the souks. Comfortable, shaded tables and private booths are spaced around the edge and, in the evening, it becomes especially atmospheric, as the sun sets and lanterns light the place. The food is excellent; as well as a traditional 100dh Moroccan menu (lunch only), there are inventive options, such as caramelized prunes with goat's cheese crème fraiche. No alcohol.

€ Jemaâ el Fna food stalls One of Marrakech's great experiences, eating in Jemaâ el Fna is not to be missed. Piles of salads and steaming tagines are set up under hissing gas lamps from early evening onwards. Each stall has a different variety of cooked food, from sheep heads to snails to fried fish to bowls of soup. It is best to go for the food cooked to order while waiting, and the most popular places obviously have a faster turnover of food. In general, however, eating here is no less safe than in most Moroccan restaurants, and there are rarely any problems. Walking along between the stalls is an experience in itself – you will be cajoled onto benches from all sides by young Moroccans who have somehow picked up a surreal line in mock cockney patter. Don't miss the stalls selling harira soup, served with dates and gateaux de miel for 9dh, or fresh fried fish at stall No 14. Make sure you know what you're getting – some unscrupulous stalls will keep enormous quantities of unordered dishes coming and then land you with a huge bill at the end.

Café des Épices, 75 Rahba Kedima, T0524-391770, www.cafedesepices.net. Daily 0800-2000. The open space of Rahba Kedima (the Spice Square), thronged with hat, basket and live reptile sellers, makes a great setting for the medina's best café. In a small and usually overflowing building, it offers good sandwiches and salads over 3 floors. The roof terrace is especially popular. Herbal teas are also served. Free Wi-Fi.

Dar Cherifa, 8 Derb Charfa Lakbir, Mouassine, off Rue Mouassine, T0524-426463. Daily 1200-1900. Hard to find and when you do you'll probably need to ring the bell to be let in, but that adds to the rarefied air of this gallery café in a tall, spacious riad. Downstairs is a contemporary art space, and the quiet café extends to the roof terrace upstairs and serves mint tea and saffron coffee. There are 2 lunch menus (90dh/120dh). Look out for occasional cultural evenings.

WHAT TO DO

Riads are often your best bet for arranging activities – almost anything is possible, and most places have a network of contacts and recommendations.

Ballooning
Ciel d'Afrique, 15 Rue Mauritanie, Guéliz, T0524-432843, T0661-137051 (mob), www.cieldafrique.info. Since 1990, huge balloons owned by **Ciel d'Afrique** have been drifting across the pale blue early-morning skies north of the Marrakech Palmeraie. For about an hour the balloon floats over Berber villages between the Oued Tensift and the Jbilet mountains, with views of Marrakech and the Atlas to the south. Passengers are picked up at their hotel at around 0600 and taken to the launch site, where the balloon is readied for take-off. After landing and, hopefully, being found by the 4WD support vehicles, mint tea is taken in a nearby village. For 2 people the cost of a flight is €205 each; for an extra €55 you can have champagne on board. **Ciel d'Afrique** also organize balloon trips further afield in the south of the country.

Cooking
Many riads offer cookery lessons – often these will be informal sessions with riad staff after a trip to the local market to buy produce and spices. The **Earth Café** offers lessons in traditional bread-making as a part of its visits.

Maison Arabe, 1 Derb Assehbé, Bab Doukkala, T0524-387010, www.la maisonarabe.com. The city's most professional cookery lesson set-up is in the **Maison Arabe** hotel. They also have a facility for lessons at the hotel's out-of-town swimming pool. Rates start at 50dh and depend on the number of people in a group.

Horse riding
Les Cavaliers de l'Atlas, T0672-845579, www.lescavaliersdelatlas.com. Just outside Marrakech is a professional stables that organizes rides through local countryside and villages. Half-day rides cost €50 pp, full-day rides with lunch €90 pp.

Rafting
Splash Rafting Morocco, 19 Bis Rue Fatima Zahra Rmila, T0659-346703, www.moroccoadventuretours.com. The best rafting conditions are in the winter and spring. Class III and IV whitewater rafting takes place in the Ourika Valley, Moulay Ibrahim Gorge and the Tizi-n-Test Gorge. Splash also run canyoning and river tubing at other times of the year.

HIGH ATLAS AND DRAÂ VALLEY

Three main roads lead south out of Marrakech into the western High Atlas. From west to east, they head over the Tizi-n-Test pass towards Taroudant; up the Ourika Valley to Setti Fatma, Oukaïmeden and the Toubkal National Park, and over the Tizi n'Tichka pass towards Ouarzazate.

On the R203 to the Tizi-n-Test, Asni is an important market town and Ouirgane is a strung-out holiday destination in the hills. Further south, the road curves and rises through the spectacular mountain valley to the awe-inspiring 12th-century mosque of Tin Mal, one of Morocco's most significant buildings, now partially restored. Back at Asni, a road branches south to Imlil and the Toubkal National Park, centring on North Africa's highest mountain. The landscapes are spectacular, and there are some great walking routes.

The route up the Ourika Valley from Marrakech is, initially at least, a gentler one, splitting to terminate at either the village of Setti Fatma, with its waterfalls and riverside restaurants, or the ski resort of Oukaïmeden.

Most switch-back of all, the N9 climbs to cross through the Tizi n'Tichka pass at 2260 m. Just east of here is the precipitous Kasbah of Telouet.

→ SOUTHWEST OF MARRAKECH

Take the main P2009 road south out of Marrakech (straight over at the junction near the **Hivernage**). The road forks a few kilometres after the **Club Royal Equestre**. You go right towards Amizmiz in the foothills of the Atlas. This road passes through a number of small settlements, including Tamesloht, and the Lalla Takerkoust Lake, where accommodation is available. Note that in a wet year, clay from the hillside may crumble onto the upper sections of the Amizmiz to Ouirgane road.

LALLA TAKERKOUST

Often referred to as 'the lake', Lalla Takerkoust, 40 km to the southwest of Marrakech, is actually a reservoir, formed by a hydroelectric dam (the Barrage Lalla Takerkoust) that provides Marrakech with a good portion of its electricity. It is a popular swimming and picnicking place for Marrakchis wanting to escape the oppressive heat of the city. Lapping at the red-earth foothills of the High Atlas, and with the high peaks as a backdrop, it's a strikingly beautiful place, and there are a couple of places to stay and eat (see page 77) too. If you have a car and decide not to head south to Ouirgane and Tin Mal, the route across the Kik plateau from here to Asni has extraordinary panoramic views across the high pastures to the Atlas peaks beyond.

OUIRGANE

Ouirgane is another pleasant place to pause on the R203, about one hour's drive (61 km) from Marrakech. The settlement's houses are scattered on the valley sides, some displaced by the building of a dam on the Oued Nfiss. Ouirgane can be reached by bus from Marrakech (the Taroudant service). Hotels in Ouirgane have good food (see page 77) and offer the opportunity to explore the valley on easy walks.

TIN MAL AND AROUND

A small settlement high in the Atlas mountains, Tin Mal was once the holy city of the Almohad Dynasty. It offers a rare opportunity for non-Muslims to see the interior of a major Moroccan mosque, with examples of 12th-century Almohad decor intact amidst the ruins. The Koutoubia at Marrakech (the Almohad capital from 1147) was modelled on Tin Mal. At the mosque the guardian will let you in and enthusiastically point out features such as the original doors piled up in a corner. He'll also ask for a donation when you leave.

Background In 1122, Ibn Toumert, after much roaming in search of wisdom, returned to Morocco. He created too much trouble in Marrakech, with his criticisms of the effete Almoravids, and shortly after, when the mountain tribes had sworn to support him and fight the Almoravids in the name of the doctrines he had taught them, he was proclaimed Mahdi, the rightly guided one. In 1125 he established his capital at Tin Mal, a fairly anonymous hamlet strategically situated in the heartland of his tribal supporters. The rough-and-ready village was replaced with a walled town, soon to become the spiritual centre of an empire. The first mosque was a simple affair. The building you see today, a low square structure, was the work of Ibn Toumert's successor, Abd el Mu'min – a student whom the future Mahdi had met in Bejaïa.

Tin Mal was the first *ribat*, as the austere Almohad fortresses were called, and was subject to a puritan discipline. The Mahdi himself was a sober, chaste person, an enemy of luxurious living. All his efforts went into persuading his followers of the truths of Islam, as he conceived them. Tin Mal was subject to a pitiless discipline. Prayers were led by the Mahdi himself and all had to attend. Public whippings and the threat of execution kept those lacking in religious fervour in line. As well as prayer leader, the Mahdi was judge, hearing and trying cases himself according to Muslim law, which had barely begun to penetrate the mountain regions.

After Ibn Toumert's death, his simple tomb became the focal point for a mausoleum for the Almohad sovereigns. Standing in the quiet mosque, today mostly open to the sky, looking down the carefully restored perspectives of the arcades, it is difficult to imagine what a hive of religious enthusiasm this place must have been.

Tin Mal mosque Completed in 1154, under Abd el Mu'min, the Tin Mal Mosque has a simple exterior. The mihrab (prayer niche) is built into the minaret. To the left, as one stands before the mihrab, is the imam's entrance to the right is a space for the minbar, the preacher's chair, which would have been pulled out for sermons. The decoration is simple: there are several cupolas with restored areas of stalactite plasterwork and there are examples of the *darj w ktaf* and palmette motifs, but little inscription. The technique used, plaster applied to brick, is a forerunner of later, larger Almohad decorative schemes.

When the new empire acquired Marrakech, a fine capital well located on the plain, Tin Mal remained its spiritual heart and a sort of reliable rear base. It was to Tin Mal that Abd el Mu'min sent the treasures of Ibn Tachfin the Almoravid. Even after the Merinid destruction of 1275-1276, the tombs of of Ibn Toumert and his successors inspired deep respect.

Eventually, the Almohads were to collapse in internecine struggles. The final act came in the 1270s, when the last Almohads took refuge in Tin Mal. However, the governor of Marrakech, El Mohallim pursued them into their mountain fastness, and besieged and took the seemingly impenetrable town. The Almohad caliph and his followers were taken prisoner and executed, and the great Almohad sovereigns, Abu Yaqoub and Abu Youssef, were pulled from their tombs and decapitated. The Almohads, one time conquerors of the whole of the Maghreb and much of Spain, were destroyed in their very capital, barely 150 years after they had swept away the Almoravids.

In the 1990s, around US$750,000 was put forward for restoration of the ruins. Work now seems to have ground to a halt, though the building is doubly impressive in its semi-ruined, semi-open-to-the-sky way.

Tizi-n-Test An hour or so's drive south of Tin Mal on the R203 will take you to the Tizi-n-Test pass, with its breathtaking views across the Souss valley to the Anti-Atlas mountains. Driving has been possible since the road, a traditional trading route, was formally opened in 1928, following the work of French engineers. Some of its sections are downright scary, but it is a recommended experience.

→ TOUBKAL NATIONAL PARK

Northern Africa's highest peak is one that many like to tick off their list, but the national park that surrounds it has plenty of other good walks, from afternoon strolls to serious treks. For details of walks in the park, see box, page 66.

ARRIVING IN TOUBKAL NATIONAL PARK

Best time to visit The best time for walking is after the main snows, at blossom time in the spring. Mules cannot negotiate passes until March/April. For some, summers are too hot and visibility in the heat haze is poor. November to February is too cold, and there is too much snow for walking, although frozen ground is often more comfortable than walking on the ever-moving scree. Deep snows and ice present few problems to those with ropes, ice axes, crampons and experience. Without these, stay away in winter.

Tourist information It's wise to purchase specialist hiking books (such as Alan Palmer's *Moroccan Atlas*) and maps. Mules and guides can be hired in Imlil, most easily in the Refuge. Having a local Tachelhit-speaking guide is essential on treks.

ASNI

The village of Asni is scattered in clusters in the valley and makes a good place for a quick break en route from Tin Mal if you can deal with the attentions of the trinket sellers. There are good walking routes along the Plateau du Kik to the west of Asni, north to Moulay Brahim and southwest to Ouirgane.

IMLIL

The most important village of the Aït Mizane Valley, Imlil is the start of the walks in the area, and also makes a good mountain hangout. In the centre of the village is the car park/taxi area with the stone-built Club Alpin Français hut. There are small cafés and shops, a good baker, a spice shop and a travel agent. Mules are 'parked' to the south of the village. When you arrive, you may be besieged by the men of the village, keen to help you in some way or other. The town's hammam has been built with money from Kasbah du Toubkal (see page 76).

Having a good local Tachelhit-speaking guide is essential on treks. The best time for walking is after the main snows, at blossom time in the spring: mules cannot negotiate the passes until March or April and summers can be too hot, with hazy visibility. From

Northern Africa's highest peak is one that many like to tick off their list, but the national park that surrounds it has plenty of other good walks, from afternoon strolls to serious treks. It's important to find a guide for longer walks here – conditions can be dangerous. The number of people who have to drop out of treks in the area due to stomach problems is high, so try to check on hygiene, when deciding who to use. If you're planning a trek in advance, Mountain Voyage, based in Marrakech (www.mountain-voyage.com), are recommended.

Walking options include the Aremd circuit, a refreshing hike through remote villages and past breathtaking views, and a hike to the Lac d'Ifni. Another is to walk to Setti Fatma, in the Ourika Valley.

Much more challenging is to climb Jbel Toubkal, the highest mountain in North Africa at 4167 m. It is necessary to break the walk at the Club Alpin Français Toubkal Refuge (ex-Refuge Neltner), a simple dormitory place with no meals at 3106 m. In winter this is a difficult trek and full equipment is essential. A specialist hiking book such as Alan Palmer's Moroccan Atlas – *The Trekking Guide* (Trailblazer, 2010) is recommended. Mules and guides can be hired in Imlil, most easily in the Refuge.

Imlil to Jbel Toubkal

Imlil is the end of the surfaced road but it is possible to reach Aremd (also spelt Aroumd) by car up the rough track. It takes about 45 minutes to walk. Café Soleil makes a good stop here. Sidi Chamharouchouch is reached in another 2½ hours, going steadily uphill. It is important to bear right after the marabout to find the initially very steep, but later steady slope up to the Toubkal refuges (3207 m). Allow 4½ hours from Imlil. There are two refuges here, at the base of the southern col. **Refuge du Toubkal** (www.refugedutoubkal.com) is older and simpler; **Les Mouflons** (www.refugetoubkal.com) is newer and smarter but also more expensive.

Jbel Toubkal by the South Cwm

This is the usual approach for walkers, a long day's walking and scrambling if you want to do up and back. The route is clearer on the map than it is on the ground. First observe the route from the rear of the Toubkal refuges and the large boulders on the skyline. These are a point to aim for. Leave the refuge and go down to the river. Cross over and up the other side is the main path to the foot of the first of the many screes. Take the scree path up to the boulders which can be reached in just over an hour. From there is a choice: the long scree slope to the north of the summit or the shorter, steeper slope to the south of the summit ridge. Either way, allow 3½ hours.

The summit is not in itself attractive but the stone shelters make fairly comfortable overnight camping for a good view of sunrise. Views are excellent – if there is no haze – to the Jbels Saghro and Siroua but as the summit here (4167 m) is a plateau, other views are limited. Be prepared for low temperatures at this altitude and for the bitter winds that blow three out of four days in the spring and autumn. The descent is quicker, allow 2-2½ hours.

November to February it is too cold and there is too much snow for walking. Without ropes, ice axes, crampons and experience, winter should be avoided.

SETTI FATMA AND THE OURIKA VALLEY

The Ourika Valley is a beautiful area of steep-sided gorges and green, terraced fields along the winding Oued Ourika, about 45 minutes' drive south of Marrakech. The accessibility of the valley makes it a very popular excursion for Marrakchis and tourists, and, in summer,

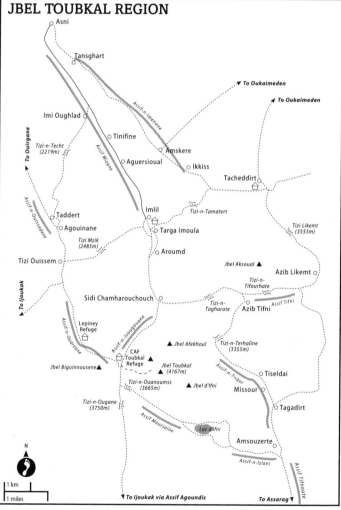

JBEL TOUBKAL REGION

sections of the valley get crowded with campers and day trippers happy to be away from the hot, dusty air of the plain. Just before Aghbalou, the P2017 splits, with a right-hand road taking you up to the ski resort of Oukaïmeden. The trail-head village of Setti Fatma is reached by going straight ahead. The valley has occasional problems with flash floods, the worst of which, in 1995, destroyed most of Setti Fatma and killed many people.

The road ends at **Setti Fatma**, famous for its seven waterfalls and 100-year-old walnut trees. There is a small weekly market, a **Bureau des Guides de Montagne** and a good choice of basic accommodation and riverside tagine outlets. Setti Fatma must once have been idyllic. There is breeze-block housing among the older stone homes now, but the stunning setting and the sound of the river make it picturesque nonetheless. The place is set up primarily for Moroccan rather than European visitors, but that gives it an unusual charm, and Setti Fatma would be a good starting point for a trek (see box, page 66).

The main part of Setti Fatma stretches beyond the end of the road. Precarious temporary rope bridges wobble visitors and locals carrying sheep across to a large number of café-restaurants along the bank. The seven cascades are a 30-minute scramble up from Setti Fatma, following the path up behind the first café, and there are plenty of young men and children who will help you find the way. There are more cafés en route and at times the path goes through the middle of souvenir shops. If you want to avoid the crowds, a walk up the main valley may be a better option.

OUKAÏMEDEN

Oukaïmeden, 'the meeting place of the four winds', is Morocco's premier ski resort, and Africa's highest. It's some 2600 m up in the Atlas and a 1½-hour drive from Marrakech. The highest lift goes up to 3250 m, and there are various runs down, not always very well marked. There are also four drag lifts and a tobogganing area. The resort is open for skiing from December to March; in summer it's less busy and many places are closed.

The quality of skiing is variable and good skiable snow cannot be counted on, though there's new investment and talk of snow cannons. The hot African sun means that the snow melts easily, only to freeze again at night, leaving slopes icy. Instructors work in the resort, and there are ski shops that rent equipment out and donkeys to carry you between lifts

In summer, visitors can walk, climb and even paraglide. Look out for the prehistoric carvings on the rocky outcrop below the dam wall. There are further carvings on the flat rocks among the new chalets.

→ TOWARDS OUARZATE VIA TIZI N'TICHKA

Completed in 1936 by the Foreign Legion, the N9 road from Marrakech to Ouarzazate gives stunning views. It runs through the full range of Atlas environments, from the Haouz plains, through the verdant foothills of the Oued Zat, to the barren peaks of the Atlas and the arid regions to the south. Drivers need maximum concentration on this route, especially in the twilight, when you will meet donkeys and flocks of sheep wandering across the road, guided by small children. Clapped-out local buses break down, and there are some especially narrow and vertiginous stretches leading up to the pass after Taddert. The eager fossil sellers who hang out at viewpoints and café stops are a further hazard. Note that in winter there can be heavy cloud, snow storms and icy rain, reducing visibility and making the road extremely slippery. In such conditions, the road is not much fun at night. If snow cuts the pass, the snow barriers will be down. The total distance from

Marrakech to Ouarzazate is nearly 200 km. Good places to stop include upper **Taddert** (very busy, 86 km from Marrakech), the **Tizi n'Tichka** itself (2260 m), which is almost exactly halfway, or **Ighrem-n-Ouagdal**, about 118 km from Marrakech, where there is an old *agadir* (granary) to visit.

A narrow road, in need of resurfacing and with nasty tyre-splitting edges, takes you from the Tizi n'Tichka road to Telouet (turn left 106 km from Marrakech). For those without their own vehicle, the trip is problematic, though there may be grands taxis up from Ighrem-n-Ouagdal, or you could hire a driver.

TELOUET

An eagle's nest of a place, high in the mountains, Telouet is something of a legend. It has one of the most spectacular kasbahs in the Atlas. Today, it is on the tourist circuit, as the hordes of 4WD vehicles testify. Within living memory, however, its name was synonymous with the repressive rule of the Glaoui brothers.

The history of Telouet and its kasbah is short but bloodthirsty. It is the story of how two brothers of the Glaoua tribe, sons of an Ethiopian slave woman, by force of arms and character, managed to achieve absolute dominance over much of southern Morocco in the early 20th century. Gavin Maxwell's *Lords of the Atlas* describes the turbulent times in Marrakech and the mountains, as first the Moroccan monarchy and then the French skirmished with the southern tribal leaders to achieve dominance. The denouement, which came shortly after Moroccan Independence in 1956, was fatal to Glaoui power.

Abandoned before completion, the Kasbah of Telouet as it survives today is mainly the result of 20th-century building schemes by the last great Glaoui lord, T'hami. Generally, as you arrive, someone will emerge to show you around. The great reception rooms, with their cedar ceilings and crumbling stucco, a transposition of 19th-century Moroccan urban taste to the mountains, are well worth a visit.

TELOUET TO OUARZAZATE VIA AÏT BENHADDOU

For those with 4WD, Telouet is the starting point for an 80-km route down to Ouarzazate. Ask for the road to Animiter, the first main village. Leaving Telouet, after a few kilometres, a turn-off to the left, near the foot of Jbel Amassine, takes you up to the source of the Glaoui family's wealth, a salt mine. **Animiter**, some 9 km east from Telouet, was famous in the early days of Moroccan tourism as its kasbah, painted by Jacques Majorelle, was featured on an early poster. Here the surfaced road runs out. It should be possible to camp near the Oued Mellah. The next village, **Timsal**, lies a few kilometres to the south. After Timsal, follow the track along the Adrar Taqqat, used when they put in electricity lines. You reach **Tioughassine**, and the track follows the Ounila Valley. At **Assaka**, look out for abandoned granaries under the cliffs. The track then follows up onto a sort of plateau above the canyon. Next, the main track drops steeply down to the valley bottom; **Tizgui-n-Barda** is the next main village, about 29 km from Telouet. Continue along the Assif Ounila to reach **Tamdacht**, meeting point of the *oueds* Marghene and Ounila and the start of the surfaced road.

This route was used in earlier times by caravans coming up from the south to pick up salt from the Telouet mine. Today, it is increasingly popular as an off-road excursion. In wet weather parts of the track turn to red-clay mud, difficult if you get stuck. As with other off-road adventures, it should be tackled by vehicles in pairs. If you get stuck, you will definitely need someone to help dig you out of trouble.

The next stop, **Aït Benhaddou**, is 50 km from Telouet and 30 km from Ouarzazate. The turn-off is clearly signed from the N10. The route follows the valley, with the river on the right, passing through the village of Tissergate. After a further 10 km the kasbah comes into view on the right, set up above the bright green of the irrigated fields.

On a dramatic hillside, the Kasbah of Aït Benhaddou is one of the largest complexes of traditional packed-earth buildings in Morocco, hence its place on the UNESCO World Heritage List. The place's fame has spread far and wide and in season coach after coach drives up, pauses for photographs to be taken and then leaves. Aït Benhaddou grew because of its strategic location on the south side of the Atlas, near the convergence of the Draâ and Dadès Valley routes.

The village is a must for tourists, both because of its unique architecture and its role in the film industry, with *Lawrence of Arabia*, *Jewel of the Nile* and *Gladiator* filmed here, as well as *Jesus of Nazareth*, for which part of the settlement was rebuilt. Despite all the visitors, the place is an awesome sight, and largely unspoilt.

Visitors are free to cross the river and wander through the kasbah, which is mostly an uninhabited shell these days. Despite money from the film industry and UNESCO to restore it, parts are much in need of repair. From the top, there are great views across the area and the old village also includes a large communal *agadir*, or store house. Back on the western side of the river, mud-walled hotels and restaurants make good use of the view.

In the village of Tifoultoute, the **Kasbah of Tifoultoute** ① *T0524-882813, 10 dh*, about 7 km north of Ouarzazate, is a splendid kasbah built for the Glaoui family in the early 20th century. It stands alongside the Oued Igissi. Still owned by the family, it has adequate food and magnificent views. Climb up to the roof terrace to see the surrounding countryside and a stork's nest on one of the turrets.

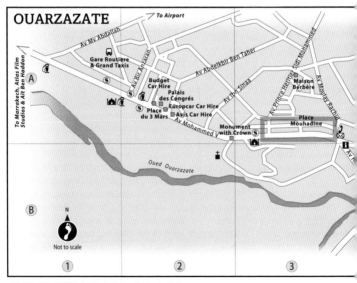

The very name Ouarzazate (pronounced 'waa-za-zat') evokes a desert fort, and there have been attempts in recent years to brand the town as the Moroccan Hollywood. The reality of Ouarzazate is a little more prosaic. The once-isolated French military outpost now has an international airport and a core of luxury hotels alongside its kasbah. Though the garrison remains, the needs of the regional administration and migrant workers have created a large and not especially attractive town. Ouarzazate is a solid, if sleepy, little town with a market on Sunday and Tuesday and a small handicrafts fair in May and the moussem of Sidi Daoud in September. It is best seen as a base for exploring valleys and oases south of the High Atlas, as a transit point for mountain and desert. The region is at its best in early spring when blossom is on the almond trees and snow still covers the summits of the Atlas.

ARRIVING IN OUARZAZATE

Getting there The CTM bus terminal is on Avenue Mohammed V, on the corner of Avenue Moulay Rachid, next to the post office. Private line buses and grands taxis arrive at the bus station at the western end of town, on Avenue Moulay Abdellah. It is a hefty walk from this bus station to the main hotels; best take a petit taxi. Ouarzazate has an international airport 1 km northeast of the centre of Ouarzazate.

Getting around Hotels in the town centre are mainly along Avenue Mohammed V and Avenue Moulay Rachid or over the causeway in Hayy Tabount. As you come down Avenue Mohammed V, heading east from the bus station, is the large **Place du 3 Mars**, a large square on your left. Here there are a few tour agencies, cafés and the Palais des Congrès. Further along the main street are banks, hotels, restaurants, cafés, shops, car rental

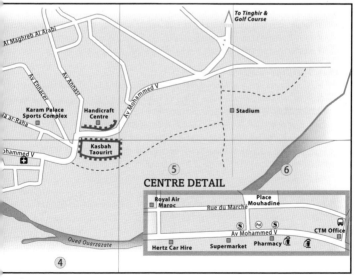

agencies, tour companies and petrol stations. The **old market** area is now closed to traffic and offers some interesting clothing, jewellery, spice and ceramics stalls before opening out onto to the **Place Al Mouahadine**, which in turn offers pavement snack-restaurants, an excellent patisserie and several desert tour agencies. The famous **Kasbah Taourirt** is located at the eastern edge of town and is an easy walk from the town centre.

Tourist information Délégation du Tourisme ① *Av Mohammed V, opposite CTM bus terminal, T0524-882485, Mon-Fri 0900-1200, 1430-1830.*

PLACES IN OUARZAZATE

Strategically placed at the confluence of three rivers, Ouarzazate has had a military presence since the Almohad period. In the late 19th century, the kasbah came under control of the Glaoui family, who used it as a power base to develop their control of the South. In 1926, the first airfield was built and, in 1928, a regular French military garrison was installed. Ouarzazate was henceforth the main administrative town for the region. A few buildings from this period straggle along the main street. Around and above them are the large hotels, built mainly in the 1980s.

The immediate vicinity of Ouarzazate is often used as a film location. Since *Lawrence of Arabia* was filmed at Aït Benhaddou, the region, close to mountains and desert, has been a popular director's choice. **Atlas Studios** ① *5 km along the road to Marrakech (look out for the mock Egyptian statues signalling the studios), T0524-882212, www.studiosatlas.com, 0900-1800, 50dh*, never seem to be out of work. *Hideous Kinky, Gladiator, Kundun, The Last Temptation of Christ, Babel* and *Alexander the Great* were all made here; you can see various bits of set and props on a 30-minute guided tour, as long as there's no filming in progress.

The historic highlight of Ouarzazate is the **Kasbah Taourirt** ① *east of the town centre along Av Mohammed V, daily 0800-1830, 20dh.* Constructed largely in the 19th century, the building had its heyday in the 1930s and would have housed the Glaoui chief's extended family, servants and followers, as well as a community of tradesmen, artisans and cultivators. Today it's one of Ouarzazate's poorest areas. The part adjacent to the road, probably quarters for the Glaoui family, has been maintained and can be visited.

AROUND OUARZAZATE

To the east of Ouarzazate, the **Mansour Eddhabi Dam** on the Oued Drâa has created a lake over 20 km long. Birdwatchers come here to see the wintering and migrating wildfowl. Winged visitors include spoonbills and flamingos, when there is sufficient water in the dam. In recent years, water levels have fallen spectacularly and the villas built as pricey lakeside retreats are now a fair way from the water. About 13 km from Ouarzazate, tracks from the N10 lead down towards the northern shore. The southern shore is more difficult to reach and access to the dam itself is prohibited. The best time to visit the lake is in spring or autumn.

For those with 4WDs or hardy cars, the **Oasis of Fint** is a possible destination, a few kilometres out in the desert west of Ouarzazate, across the Tabount causeway.

The road southeast from Ouarzazate to Zagora is spectacular, first winding its way across the Jbel Anaouar mountains, and then down along the Draâ Valley, a strip of intense cultivation, a band of vivid colour weaving through the desert, one of the most beautiful oasis valleys in Morocco. Here and there are red-earth coloured kasbahs and villages of flat-roofed houses, their rooftops edged with crenellations. Once, the Draâ was one of the longest rivers in Northwest Africa. Today, the cultivated areas give way to the desert near M'hamid, south of Zagora as the water seeps away into the parched ground. In this region, the classic sights are the village of Tamegroute, once famed as a centre of Islamic learning, and the dunes of Erg Lehoudi and Chigaga, popular for camel treks.

The Draâ Valley was not always so arid – there are ancient rock carvings of animals in the lower Draâ and the ancient writer Polybius mentions it as a river full of crocodiles. After Zagora, near M'hamid, the Draâ disappears into the sandy Debaïa Plain. The river only very rarely runs its full course to the Atlantic coast near Tan Tan, some 750 km away. In years of sufficient rainfall, there is good grazing for the nomads in the Debaïa, and even some cultivation.

ZAGORA

Zagora is the main town at the southern end of the Drâa Valley and the best place to overnight before heading off into the desert. In the 1990s, the town woke up to tourism. The arrival of 4WD vehicles and the improvement of the N9 road have allowed an influx of visitors and the desert settlement founded by an Arab tribe in the 13th century has been transformed out of all recognition. There's a **tourist information office** ① *Av Mohammed, T882485, Mon-Fri 0830-0430*, near the very grand provincial administration building and the famous '52 Days to Timbuktu' road sign. Given the poverty levels here, many locals compete fiercely for the tourist trade. To avoid potential hassle, try to make travel arrangements into the desert in advance, either through your hotel or through recommended agencies.

Although there are few architectural traces of the town's life before tourism, the paths through the date palm groves to the various *ksar* can help you imagine a time when the world was slower. Of these promenades, one of the more pleasant, despite the potential pestering, is around the **Amazrou** date palm oasis across the river. There is also some accommodation here and a kasbah once famed for its silverwork. Above Zagora and within walking distance are two hills, from which there are excellent views over the valley and towards the desert. Nearby are the ruins of an 11th-century **Almoravid fortress**.

During the *moulid* there is a major religious festival held in Zagora, the **Moussem of Moulay Abdelkader Jilala**. The town's **market** days are on Wednesday and Sunday. The souk is an important place for the exchange of produce and livestock for the surrounding region. **Musée des Arts et Traditions de la Vallée du Drâa** ① *8 km north of Zagora in the Ksar Tissergate, T0661-348388 (mob), 20dh*, is a very worthwhile museum of local antiquities housed in the ancient Kasbah. Displays are tagged in English.

TAMEGROUTE

Tamegroute, 20 km southeast from Zagora, lies on the left bank of the Oued Draâ and is visited mainly because of the zaouia, founded in the 17th century and headquarters of the influential Naciri Islamic.

ON THE ROAD
Draâ driving

Leaving Zagora, there are two main options if you want to avoid going northwards back over your tracks. The first route, the rough track running northeast from Zagora to Tazzarine, a settlement on the main metalled west to east route to Rissani in the Tafilalet, is for 4WD only and needs careful planning.

In a hire car, the R108 is a better route east which, although it means retracing steps 60 km up the Ouarzazate road as far as Tansikht, takes you across some wonderful arid scenery on metalled road all the way east to Rissani. There is a good stopover at **Nekob** (42 km from the junction), where the restored citadel has been given new life as the Kasbah Baha Baha, with a tiny ethnographic museum and lots of information on the region, including prehistoric rock art. After Nekob, **Mellal** is the next settlement before **Tazzarine** (75 km from the junction), a small place with petrol and basic shops, where the direct north-south track from Zagora joins the road. Tazzarine is a good base for searching out the *gravures rupestres* (prehistoric rock carvings) at Tiouririne or Aït Ouazik.

Tracks from the N12 to the Dadès road

With a solid 4WD, there are a couple of routes from the N12 across wild country to the N10 Rachidia to Ouarzazate road. Heading east out of Nekob, you will find a sign showing right for Tazzarine and left for **Iknioun**, a settlement lying some 65 km to the north in the Jbel Saghro. It is best to travel this route with a local as the tracks are confusing. Some of the better ones lead up to mines. After crossing the **Tizi-n-Tazazert-n-Mansour** (2200 m), you will have the option of going north on a rather better track to **Boumalne** (about 42 km), or right to Iknioun and then **Tineghir**, via the **Tizi-n-Tikkit**, a rougher but more beautiful route.

The easiest route up from the N12 to the N10 heads north from **Alnif**, however. Although it is best tackled in a 4WD, it can just about be done in a hire care with high clearance. After the **Tizi-n-Boujou**, the track takes you onto the N10 some 20 km east of Tineghir, 35 km west of Tinejdad.

West from Zagora to Foum Zguid

This route was off-limits for years due to the risk of Polisario rebel incursions from neighbouring Algeria. It is another difficult journey best attempted in a 4WD with accompanying vehicles. Much of the road (the 6953) is a very poor surface and 124 km in these conditions are not to be undertaken lightly. The thrill of the open spaces, the wide horizons and the faint prospect of sandstorms makes this a memorable journey. The road runs east-west following the line of the **Jbel Bani** to the south. From **Foum Zguid**, further rough tracks take you southwest and west towards **Tata** in the Anti-Atlas.

Always check you have a good spare tyre before setting out on rudimentary pistes into rough country, refuel whenever you can, and carry some spare in a can if possible.

M'HAMID

The village of M'Hamid marks the end of the tarmac road and is popular as a base for camel trips into the dunes. The most common destinations are the sands of the **Erg Lehoudi**, some 8 km north of M'hamid, and the magnificent unspoiled dunes of **Chigaga**, 55 km out towards the Algerian border, a two-hour drive by 4WD, or a three-day camel trek. There are plenty of outfits (and hustlers) here who will set you up with a trip of any length, from a short camel ride and a single night in a camp under the stars to a week-long camel trek west to Foum-Zguid. Shop around and make sure you know what you're getting. M'Hamid itself has basic facilities and a Monday souk. If visiting on this day, there may be some 'blue men of the desert' around, more for the benefit of tourists than tradition. The days of the great camel caravans led by indigo-swathed warriors are a mirage from the past, but you can get an idea of this cultural heritage at the annual **International Nomads Festival** in March (www.nomadsfestival.org).

HIGH ATLAS AND DRAÂ VALLEY LISTINGS

WHERE TO STAY

Asni

€€€€ Kasbah Tamadot, T0208-600 0430 (UK), T877-577 8777 (USA) or T0524-368200, www.kasbahtamadot.com. One of Morocco's best-known hotels, **Kasbah Tamadot** is run by Virgin and calls itself 'Sir Richard Branson's Moroccan Retreat', though chances are you won't bump into him here. Complete with all the creature comforts you can imagine, the cheapest of the 18 rooms is more than 3000dh a night and for your investment you get indoor and outdoor pools, gardens, spa and a hammam as well as some spectacular views. The restaurant uses ingredients from the hotel's own gardens and the library comes equipped with a telescope. Despite all its good points, however, ultimately the Kasbah has a little less character than its 2 main rivals, **Kasbah Toubkal** and **Kasbah Bab Ourika**.

Imlil and Aremd

€€€€ Kasbah du Toubkal, T0524-485611, www.kasbahdutoubkal.com. Imlil's restored Kasbah, perched spectacularly above the village, played the role of a Tibetan fortress in director Martin Scorsese's film *Kundun*. It is run by the UK-based travel agent **Discover Ltd**, in conjunction with locals, and is often cited as a good example of eco-tourism. There is a range of accommodation, from 3 dorms for groups, to 5 de luxe rooms. The best rooms come with CD players, slippers and even Berber clothes to borrow. The building, once HQ of the local *caïd*, is worth a visit – for a 20dh contribution to the local development fund, you can have mint tea and walnuts on the roof terrace. A day trip to the Kasbah can also be arranged from Marrakech for €85, including lunch, a mule ride and a visit to a Berber house.

Ourika Valley and Setti Fatma

€€€€ Kasbah Bab Ourika, 45 mins from Marrakech off the Setti Fatma road near Dar-Caid-Ouriki, T0524-389797 or T0661-252328 (mob), www.babourika. com. Unfusssily elegant, **Kasbah Bab Ourika** is in an extraordinary location, perched on its own personal hill overlooking the mouth of the Ourika valley, with craggy red mountain rock to one side and Marrakech in the distance behind. Built, set up and run by the owner of **Riad Edward**, the Kasbah is decorated with a similar insouciance – rooms are huge and have an antique, rustic style that makes guests feel immediately at home but are also luxurious, with thick rugs, generous bathrooms, open fires and wonderfully comfortable beds. The pool is spectacular, with views to the mountains, and the food is exquisite, with dishes such as chilled carrot soup and lemongrass beef brochette with stir-fried spinach and turmeric expertly mixing flavours. The environmental and social policies of the place are ground breaking and guests can take a guided walk through the extraordinarily fertile valley and Berber villages below. The track that needs to be navigated to reach the front door is an eroded adventure, but one that increases the dramatic sense of arrival, and of being in a very special place indeed.

€€€ Chez Momo II, coming from Marrakech, 800 m past La Roseraie, up a road on the left; T0524-485704, www. aubergemomo.com. After the original **Chez Momo** was engulfed in the water of Ouirgane's new reservoir in 2008, **Chez Momo II** was born, further up the hill, using local craftsmen and materials. Rooms are homely and elegant, with wrought-iron beds, bare wooden beams and lamps in alcoves. There's a beautiful horseshoe arch swimming pool out the front of the house, with trees, roses and sun loungers around, and 'trikking', on foot or on mule, is organized.

Setti Fatma

€€ **La Perle d'Ourika**, T0661 56 72 39, laperledourika@hotmail.com. A couple of mins downstream from Setti Fatma, the **Perle** has a degree of decoration rare in Setti Fatma, with furry sequined bed covers and painted floors. It's a little over the top, but it is at least an attempt at style. Good shared facilities, 24-hr hot water and a roof terrace with fantastic views up and down the valley. The restaurant is also recommended and has wine.

Lalla Takerkoust

€€ **Le Flouka**, BP45, Barrage Lalla Takerkoust, T0664-492660. Rooms are scattered around **Le Flouka**, right at the water's edge of Lalla Takerkoust. The 14 comfortable rooms are simply decorated with lamps and rugs and there are bare beams and open fires. There are also simpler tents and a de luxe 'tente de pacha', which comes with a built-in bathroom. Of

the 2 pools, 1 is reserved for hotel guests, though you can just as easily head straight out into the lake. Swimming straight towards the Atlas Mountains is hard to beat. There is a restaurant (€€) right beside the lake, serving dishes such as steak or mozzarella and tomato salad, as well as a bar, but it's generally a peaceful spot, big enough to absorb its visitors with laid-back ease.

Aït Benhaddou

€€ **Dar Mouna**, T05240-843054, www.darmouna.com. With a pool in an internal garden and views of the kasbah (for which you pay extra), this is a classy place with big beds and a restrained riad style.

Zagora

€€€ **Riad Lamane**, Amazrou (off the road to M'Hamid just after the bridge, turn right at the mini-roundabout), T0524-848388, www.riadlamane.com. Individually designed bungalows with coloured *tadelakt* walls and huge beds, all with African or Berber decorative touches. Also luxurious 'tent' rooms with bathrooms. Gorgeous gardens with pool and 2 restaurants. Desert excursions and camel trips offered.

RESTAURANTS

Asni

In the centre of the village are a number of stalls and cafés cooking harira soup and tagines. This is the last major place to stock up on basic supplies for a visit to the Toubkal region.

Ouirgane

The hotels in Ouirgane all have restaurants attached – **La Bergerie** is a good stopover for lunch.

Imlil and Aremd

Most places offer half board, so the stand-alone eating options are limited, but **Café Soleil** and **Atlas Tichka** offer good lunches.

Les Amis does good chicken brochettes and genuine coffee. **Café Grand Atlas** is more of a local place, where you can eat tagine on the roof terrace. **Café Imlil** was the first café in town, and hasn't changed much since. For something smarter, and for the best views, go to the **Kasbah de Toubkal**.

Setti Fatma

There's little to choose between the different waterside eateries – wander around and pick one that smells good, or go for a table with a view.

Oukaïmeden

Chez Juju is probably the best option.

DESERT TO COAST

To the west of Zagora, the parched, rocky landscape continues west until you reach the top of the fertile valley of the Souss at the walled market town of Taroudant, with its 16th-century walls and souks.

→ WEST ALONG THE N10: TAZENAKHT TO TALIOUINE

West of Zagora and Ouarzazate, Tazenakht is at an important junction, though much of the town stands to the northwest of the road. There's a market on Fridays and a number of carpet shops, displaying fine, geometrical wares produced by the local Ouzguita tribe. There are small shops and a mosque.

Between Tazenakht and Taliouine are two high passes, Tizi Ikhsane (1650 m) and Tizi-n-Taghatine (1886 m), with the small settlement of Tinfat and another imposing kasbah midway between. The highest pass, Tizi-n-Taghatine, incorporates some of the best scenery on this route: a mixture of landforms, terracing with small trees and views on all sides. Tizi-n-Taghatin marks the end of the Draâ and the beginning of the Souss basin. Between the passes there is patchy shifting cultivation and little else.

Taliouine is said to produce the best saffron in Morocco and has a magnificent kasbah to the south of the road. It's also a good starting point for walking in the Jbel Siroua (see box, page 80). There is a petrol station at the eastern end of town beyond the triumphal arches and another in the centre, almost opposite the Saffron Cooperative.

→ TAROUDANT

Taroudant is famous for its red-brown crenellated walls. Variously called 'the grandmother of Marrakech', or 'the elder brother of Marrakech', in reality it is not much more than a half-cousin. But it does have some of the character of its more famous neighbour across the Tizi-n-Test pass, albeit on a far smaller and sleepier scale. The medina is enclosed by impressive *pisé* (rammed earth) ramparts. Inside are two largish squares, higgledy-piggledy streets and some souks (although much of the older building has been replaced by concrete structures). Taroudant makes a good overnight stop on an exploration of Southern Morocco: Agadir and the coast are a short hop westwards; further afield are the pre-Saharan oases of Tata and Akka, with rock carvings close by; there is a spectacular mountain route to Tafraoute.

ARRIVING IN TAROUDANT
Getting there Buses and taxis arrive at Bab Zorgane outside the city walls.

Moving on To get to Essaouira (see page 82), go west to Inezgane before taking the coast road north. You'll need to change buses in Inezgane if you're travelling by public transport. The journey takes five hours (more if you have to wait for a connection). If you are on your way to Tafraoute (Dream Trip 2, see page 124) and have your own car, the route over the mountains via Aït Baha and Kasbah Tizourgane is impressive, if winding (3½ hours). By bus or shared taxi, you'll probably need to head west to the transport hub of Inezgane and change there. Buses from Inezgane to Tafraoute usually depart early in the morning.

Getting around The town centres on Place Assarag and Place Talmoklate. The sights, the ramparts and souk, can be done on foot. You might hire a bike from an outfit near Place Assarag to explore a bit more. From Taroudant, possible day trips include the old village of Freija, some 10 km from town, and the oasis of Tioute, which has an old kasbah. Pale-brown petits taxis do runs in the local area, and there are a few horse-drawn calèches, too.

BACKGROUND

Located at the heart of the fertile Souss valley, Taroudant was always an important regional centre and even managed to achieve national prominence on a few occasions. Taken by the Almoravids in 1056, it achieved a certain level of independence under the Almohads. Temporary fame came in the 16th century with the rise of the Saâdians. From 1510, the first Saâdian leader, Mohammed el Qa'im, was based in Taroudant as the Emir of the Souss. Even after the Saâdians had gained control of the rest of Morocco, Taroudant remained their capital for a while. Later, in the 17th century, Taroudant supported Moulay Ismaïl's nephew in his rebellion. When the great sultan took the town in 1687, he took his revenge by slaughtering the population and destroying much of the area. Decline set in, continuing into the 18th and 19th centuries. In the early years of the French protectorate, Taroudant harboured the rebel Sultan el Hiba and was consequently sacked by colonial forces. Today, the town is a regional market. A handful of riads have sprung up in recent years but many tourists are day trippers from Agadir or people overnighting on their way to other southern destinations. An inhabitant of Taroudant is called a Roudani.

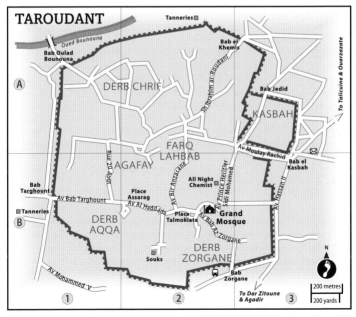

GOING FURTHER
Jbel Siroua

Rising to a twin peak of 3305 m, the Jbel Siroua is an arid, isolated region forming a sort of volcanic bridge between the High Atlas of Toubkal to the north and the Anti-Atlas to the south. There are comparatively few trekkers here, and communicating with locals can be a problem, unless you have fluent Tachelhit. Best trekked in autumn and spring, the best starting point for Jbel Siroua treks is Taliouine.

Possible treks
From Taliouine, there are numerous possibilities for trekking up into the Siroua. The **Auberge Souktana** ① *Taliouine, T0528-534075*, should be able to advise on short treks. Also try Naturally Morocco Guesthouse in Taroudant, as they have excellent contacts in the region. Another possibility would be to take a minibus from Taliouine up to Akhfamane, where many treks start. An irregular minibus service runs from the central garage in Taliouine up to Akhfamane, although it is possible to walk this in about five hours. At Akhfamane, there are a rooms available and mules for hire. A number of European-based travel companies run treks into the Jbel Siroua.

PLACES IN TAROUDANT
Walls The terracotta-coloured 16th- and early 17th-century Saâdian *pisé* walls, crenellated and set here and there with chunky square towers, are Taroudant's best sight. You could follow the walls round the town, possibly in a calèche (horse-drawn carriage), generally available from outside the **Hotel Salam** for around 40dh per hour. There were originally only five gates; running clockwise from the bus station they are Bab Zorgane, Bab Targhount, Bab Oulad Bounouna, Bab el Khemis and Bab el Kasbah. You can go up at least one of these for a look out over olive groves, orchards and building sites.

In the northeast corner of the medina is the kasbah, the most densely populated and poorest part of town. This was a fortress rebuilt by Moulay Ismaïl in the 17th century. Outside the walls, you can visit the tanneries by turning left from Bab el Khemis ('the Thursday gate'), where skins of a variety of animals are still cured using traditional methods.

Apart from its walls, Taroudant is not the most picturesque of places by day. Originally, part of the area within the walls was devoted to orchards and market gardening but much of this has now been built up, and the majority of the original low *pisé* buildings have long since been replaced by concrete housing. In the evening, however, Taroudant takes on a more interesting atmosphere, with men staying up late socializing in the cafés in the centre. It's also a relaxed place, where hassle is rare.

Souks The souks of Taroudant are an easy, calm place to look around for souvenirs. Thursday and Sunday are busy days, with people coming in from the surrounding villages. Specialities of the town include jewellery and carvings in local limestone. The main souks are in the block to the north of Avenue Mohammed V, between the two squares. Some hotels have a useful map of the souks, detailing areas of specialities.

DESERT TO COAST LISTINGS

WHERE TO STAY

Taroudant

€€€ **Dar Zitoune**, T0528-551141, www.darzitoune.com. A very smart, Swiss-owned place with 20 suites and bungalows among flowers and fruit trees, 2 km outside the city walls. Rooms are individually decorated but all share a warm colour palette and sleek design. The best have their own sitting rooms with open fires. The pool is beautiful, as is the bar – the only plain aspect of the place is the restaurant, though the food is good. Wi-Fi, satellite TV. Half and full board also available.

€€€ **Riad Maia**, 12 Tassoukt Ighezifen, T0641-037989, www.riad-maia-taroudant. com. A small, French/German-run riad with a cute salon and beautiful antique zellige tiles. The family room has a lovely turquoise sunken bathroom, and there's a multi-level roof terrace with sun loungers and views. Intimate and friendly.

€€€ **Riad Taroudant**, 243 Av Al Qods–Derb Jdid, T0528-852572, www.riad taroudant.com. Stylish and sophisticated, this riad is in an excellent position near the souk and has 16 rooms with *tadelakt* tiles, a courtyard pool and roof terrace with cacti and sun loungers. There's also a brick-vaulted hammam, which the French owner hopes to turn into a massage room.

€€ **Dar Infiane**, Douar Indfiane, T0661-610170, www.darinfiane.com. A French-owned converted kasbah with a small pool and attractive terraces with great views. Simple rooms manage to be both rustic and stylish. Look out for the low ceilings.

€€ **Naturally Morocco Guesthouse**, 422 Derb Afferdou, T0661-236627, www. naturallymorocco.co.uk. Originally run from the UK, the ecological and exceptionally friendly guesthouse is now managed by local staff who know the region well. Rooms, mostly en suite, are large and comfortable, decorated in simple Moroccan style, and there's a roof terrace with views of both the Atlas and the Anti-Atlas. Vegetarian food is a speciality and their cookery lessons are highly recommended. The kitchen can be used by guests, and rooms can easily be made into apartments for families or small groups. Staff organize unusually well-informed cultural tours of the region, and the hotel has won awards for its community projects. Guests have free use of the pool at Palais Salam. If you get lost, ask for 'La Maison Anglaise', which is how the locals know it.

€ **El Warda**, 8 Pl Tamoklate, T0528-852763. Absurdly cheap, especially for single rooms, and good value. Simple rooms have comfortable beds, some with balconies overlooking the stalls on Pl Tamoklate. Don't be fooled by the promise of en suite bathrooms though: you get a toilet and a sink but the baths aren't plumbed in.

RESTAURANTS

Taroudant

€€€ **La Gazelle d'Or**, Rte d'Amezgou, T0528-852039. In the hotel of the same name, this is high-class dining, with dishes made mostly from produce grown on the hotel's own organic farm. Dress up.

€ **L'Agence**, Av Sidi Mohammed, T0528-558270. Taroudant's most popular restaurant has sculpture, tablecloths and unusual Moroccan dishes, such as *safa*, chicken minced with almonds and cinnamon. A friendly and atmospheric little place.

ESSAOUIRA

Just three hours from the dusty heat of Marrakech, cool winds blow off the Atlantic onto the coast. The fishing town of Essaouira is the pretty, whitewashed and sand-blown highlight. A one-time military port, it was rebuilt as an international trading centre in the 18th century. International commerce has long since passed it by, but otherwise it hasn't changed much since. The walls are white, the windows and shutters cracked and faded blue, while stray cats and backpackers rest at the feet of sandy camel-brown arches and columns. Windsurfers and fanciful Jimi Hendrix myths hint at Essaouira's hippy heyday, the vestiges of which live on in a few cafés and a generally chilled pace to life. New flights to the airport have further reduced Essaouira's isolation, foreigners continue to buy up picturesque property and there are two successful music festivals.

→ ARRIVING IN ESSAOUIRA

GETTING THERE
Both **CTM** (www.ctm.ma) and private lines arrive at the bus station about 300 m northeast of the medina at Bab Doukkala – a five-minute walk with luggage or a 10dh petit taxi ride (15dh at night). Grands taxis also run to the bus station, although arrivals will be dropped off right next to the main entrance to the medina, Bab Doukkala. Drivers may want to use the car park (24-hour warden) close to the harbour next to Place Prince Moulay el Hassan.

MOVING ON
Around 190 km to the north of Essaouira, Oualidia (see page 90) can be reached by the slightly shorter and more scenic coast road, the R301, via Safi, or the faster, inland N1, branching left at El Agagcha onto the P3430. By both bus and grand taxi, it will probably be necessary to change in Safi; allow five hours including the change. With your own car it's quicker, around three hours.

GETTING AROUND
One of the most appealing aspects of Essaouira is that all the principal tourist sites can be comfortably reached on foot; cars can be left in the car park. There are some good walks along the windswept beach to Borj el Beroud. The walk to Cap Sim is an all-day excursion.

TOURIST INFORMATION
Délégation Provincial de Tourisme ⓘ *10 Av du Caire, T0524-783532, Mon-Fri 0900-1630.* Rather basic office with helpful staff, maps, leaflets and bus timetables.

→ BACKGROUND

Essaouira is a quiet sort of place with a long history. There was a small Phoenician settlement here, previously called Magdoura or Mogador, a corruption of the Berber word Amegdul, meaning 'well-protected'. The Romans were interested in the purple dye produced from the abundant shellfish on the rocky coast, which they used to colour the robes of the rich. Mogador was occupied in the 15th century by the Portuguese, who built the fortifications around the harbour. The town was one of their three most important bases, but was abandoned in 1541, from which time it went into decline. Mogador was also visited by Sir Francis Drake in Christmas 1577. In 1765, the Alaouite Sultan Sidi Mohammed Ibn Abdallah transformed Mogador into an open city, enticing overseas businessmen in with trade concessions, and it soon became a major commercial port, with a large foreign and Jewish population establishing the town as a major trading centre.

The sultan employed the French architect Théodore Cornut to design the city and its fortifications. In his design, Cornut chose a rectangular layout for the main streets, resulting

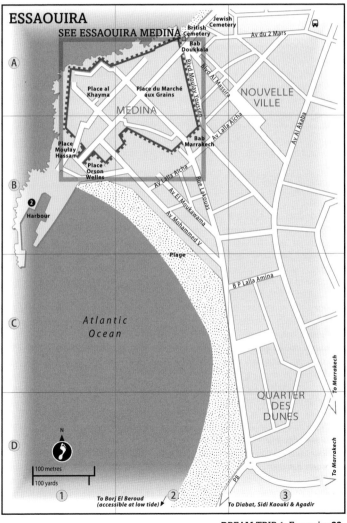

in a uniform style, and constructed ramparts in the Vauban style. The fortifications were not always that effective, however. From time to time, the tribesmen of the region would raid the town, carrying off booty and the merchants' wives – who it is said, were not always that happy to return. Perhaps life in rural Morocco was more pleasant than listening to the wind in the damp counting houses of Mogador.

Orson Welles stayed here for some time, filming part of *Othello* at the Skala du Port. At Independence the town's official name became Essaouira, the local Arabic name meaning 'little picture'. In the 1960s Essaouira had a brief reputation as a happening place, attracting hippies and rockstars, including Jimi Hendrix.

Now the town is emerging from several decades of decline, for on top of fishing, fish processing, a small market and handicraft industries, the town is attracting greater numbers of tourists, notably surfers. The burgeoning number of riads and their accompanying upmarket tourism has also brought some wealth to the inhabitants of this most relaxed town, without spoiling its gentle atmosphere, though an increase in the number of oversized hotels outside the city walls may have a more detrimental effect.

Essaouira has some useful friends in influential places, including André Azoulay, one of HM the King's special advisers, and there is an artistic lobby, too, including gallery owner Frédéric Damgaard and Edmond Amran-Mellah, the writer. Dar Souiri, on Avenue de Caire opposite the Délégation de Tourisme, is the hub of the town's cultural activities.

→ PLACES IN ESSAOUIRA

MEDINA
Essaouira does not have a lot in the way of formal sights, but has plenty of gently atmospheric streets to compensate. Enclosed by walls with five main gates, the medina is the major attraction. Entering from **Bab Doukkala** the main thoroughfare is Rue Mohammed Zerktouni, which leads into Avenue de l'Istiqlal, where there is the **Grand Mosque**, and just off, on Darb Laalouj, the **Ensemble Artisanal** and the **Museum of Sidi Mohammed Ibn Abdallah**, which houses the **Museum of Traditional Art and Heritage of Essaouira** ① *T0524-475300, Wed-Mon 0830-1200 and 1430-1800, 10dh*. This house, once the home of a pasha, has a collection of weapons and handicrafts, such as woodwork and carpets, and also has an interesting ethnographic collection, including examples of stringed instruments beautifully decorated with marquetry and documents on Berber music.

Avenue de l'Istiqlal leads into Avenue Okba Ibn Nafi, on which is located the small **Galerie d'Art Damgaard**. At the end of the street a gate on the right leads into **Place Moulay Hassan**, the heart of the town's social life. The town's souks are mainly around the junction between Rue Mohammed Zerktouni and Rue Mohammed el Gorry, although there is an area of woodworkers inside the Skala walls to the north of Place Moulay Hassan, where some fine pieces can be picked up with some good-natured bargaining. At the northeast end of Rue Zerktouni, close to Bab Doukkala, is the much-decayed **mellah**, the old Jewish quarter. Although the Jewish community no longer remains, it made a substantial contribution to the commercial and cultural development of the town.

Outside Bab Doukkala is the Consul's **cemetery** for the British officials who died here while converting Mogador into a trading post with strong UK links. Behind the high wall on the road to the bus station is the **Jewish cemetery**. If you find the man with the key, you may discover the resting place of Leslie Hore-Belisha, inventor of the first pedestrian crossing light.

THE HARBOUR AND SKALA DU PORT

Off Place Moulay Hassan is the small harbour, busy with its fishing fleet. The open-air restaurant stalls serving grilled fish have been smartened up in recent years but are still a great spot for lunch. The sea gate (**Porte de la Marine**), which serves to link the harbour with the medina, was built in 1769, it is said, by an Englishman who converted to Islam during the reign of Sidi Mohammed Ibn Abdallah. The gateway is built of stone in the classical style and the year of its construction (1184 of the Hegira) is inscribed on the pediment. It is connected to the ramparts on the **Skala**, an old Portuguese sea defence and battery, by a bridge which spans small primitive dry docks. Entry to the **Skala du Port** (10dh) is via a kiosk close to the Porte de la Marine, and from the top of the bastion there are extensive panoramic views of the harbour and the offshore islands, the Îles Purpuraires.

SKALA DE LA VILLE

Further to the north of Place Moulay Hassan, it is possible to get onto the ramparts of the Skala de la Ville from Rue de la Skala close to its junction with Rue Darb Laalouj. Entry here is free, and crenellated walls protect a 200-m-long raised artillery platform and an impressive array of decorated Spanish and other European cannon. This is a good spot from which to watch the sunset. From the tower of the **North Bastion** there are fine views of the old mellah, the medina, with its white buildings and blue shutters, and the coastline to the north. The **woodworkers' souks** are situated here in arched chambers underneath the ramparts.

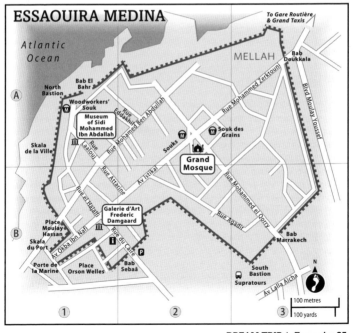

ESSAOUIRA MEDINA

BEACHES AND ISLANDS

Essaouira has fine beaches. The prevailing wind, known as the *alizée*, stirs up a lot of sand and makes it cold for swimming, but ideal for windsurfing, though not necessarily surfing. The northern **Plage de Safi** is fine in the summer, but can be dangerous during windy weather. South of the town, the wide beach is great for football, and there are usually games going on here. Past the Oued Ksob, you will see the waves breaking against the remains of Borj el Baroud, an old fortress. When walking far along the beach it should be noted that the incoming tide makes the Oued Ksob below the village of Diabat into an impassable river.

Diabat The one-time favourite hippy destination of Diabat, about 5 km from Essaouira, is easily reached by *petit* and grand taxi, say 40dh. The ruined palace/pavilion below Diabat is worth a visit. The building is said to have been swallowed by the sand after the people of the Souss put a curse on it because their trade was being ruined. The old fort was built by the Portuguese in the 18th century. A short walk up the road from Diabat will bring you to the **Auberge Tangaro**, one of Essaouira's better known hotels; 500 m further on, and you are at the crossroads with the N1 road from the south, which runs back into town.

Îles Purpuraires These islands to the southwest are a bird sanctuary, particularly for rare Eleonora's falcons. With a good telescope it's possible to see these falcons from the end of the jetty. Another area frequented by the birds is the mouth of **Oued Ksob**. The river mouth is also noted for a variety of migrating seabirds, including black, little, sandwich, whiskered and white-winged terns. The *oued* can be reached from a track off the N1 south of the town but access to the sea is not easy. Although now a nature reserve, it is possible to visit the main island, **Île de Mogador**, outside the breeding season (it's closed April to October). You can negotiate a private trip with a local fishing vessel to ferry you there and back, but first must obtain a permit (free) from the Port office.

→ SIDI KAOUKI

'Sans Stress', the hand-painted signs advertise, and they're not wrong. Sidi Kaouki is on the verge of comatose: apart from an occasional frisson of competition between the cluster of shack café bars around the centre of the village, and the to-ing and fro-ing of surfers across the gargantuan beach, there's very little going on here. And apart from the occasional young man with a camel politely enquiring if you're interested in a ride along the beach, there's a refreshing absence of hassle.

Sidi Kaouki is a huge surf beach, essentially, with a few scattered cafés and restaurants along the road. There are a couple of new hotels going up but there's a long way to go before it becomes anything like developed. If Essaouira's slower pace is still too frantic, and if the oyster bars of Oualidia aren't your thing, then the simple, seriously chilled pleasures of Sidi Kaouki might be the way forward.

LA PLAGE

The hub of Sidi Kaouki is a dusty patch behind the crumbling, whitewashed Mausoleum of Sidi Kaouki, resting place of a 19th-century local holy man with supposed powers to cure the infertile. From here the sandy beach stretches south for several kilometres, backed by dunes which shift shape and location through the seasons. The surf shack is a good place for renting boards or getting lessons and you don't have to hang around for long before you'll be offered a camel ride – some options are the half-hour trip north to Taguenza (50dh, see below), or the longer hour and a half or so south to waterfalls (300dh there and back). You could also just potter up and down the beach for 15 minutes. For those with transport, preferably 4WD, Iftan Plage, another isolated beach around 30 km south, would make a good destination for a day out.

TAGUENZA

About half an hour's walk north from the Mausoleum, Taguenza is another beach, backed with a huddle of stone fishermens' shacks and a café which is little more than some deck chairs on the sand and some strewn cushions inside. Peaceful and idyllic, it's a great spot for a picnic, a swim, wild camping or an alfresco fish meal straight out of the sea. The walk can mostly be done barefoot along sand and over rocks at the edge of the waves.

ESSAOUIRA LISTINGS

WHERE TO STAY

Essaouira

€€€ **Casa Lila**, 94 Rue Mohamed El Qouri, T0524-475545, www.casalila.ma. Exceptionally photogenic, even by riad standards, the antique **Casa Lila** goes big on dusty pastel shades, with lots of purples and lilacs. The towels are not as dazzlingly white as they once were – and rooms on the ground floor can be damp, but it mostly remains a charming spot, with smilingly good service and a great roof terrace with views across the medina.

€€€ **Madada Mogador**, 5 Rue Youssef el Fassi, T0524-475512, www.madada.com. Laid-back and French-run, **Madada Mogador** is a light and airy hotel with a spectacular roof terrace with wicker chairs and views of beach. Pale, warm colours and cool contemporary jazz fill the building. Rooms use traditional *tadelakt*, beds have huge headboards and there are spacious, stylish bathrooms. At the brilliantly equipped **Atelier Madada** downstairs, cookery lessons are offered.

€€€ **Riad Watier**, 16 Rue Ceuta, T0524-476204, www.ryad-watier-maroc.com. The French owner of this large and spacious riad has a boat, and may take you out fishing if you ask nicely. The building, an ex-school, is now home to a resident tortoise, a massage room, lots of plants, and state-of-the-art plumbing. White walls add to the sense of light and there are tiles, rugs, terracotta-coloured *tadelakt* and big showers in the 10 rooms. The views from the roof terrace north along the coast and of the sunset are spectacular. Master suites sleep 4 or 5 and would be good for families.

€€€ **Villa de l'Ô**, 3 Rue Mohamed Ben Messaoud, T0524-476375, www.villadelo.com. 12 rooms and suites are grouped around a huge courtyard in this grand, colonial-style hotel. Housed in a former almond store dating from the 18th century, it has kept many original features. Some rooms have sea views. Special offers are available with the golf course.

€€ **Riad Lalla Mira**, 12 Rue de l'Iraq, T0524-476744, www.lallamira.net. German-run, **Lalla Mira** emphasizes its eco-credentials, and has a hammam with various treatments which is also open to non-guests as well as a restaurant. Rooms have brick floors, draped beds and dark blue bathrooms.

Essaouira Hostel, 17 Rue Laghrissi, T0524-476481, T0661-709083 (mob), essaouira hostel@gmail.com. It's well hidden in the backstreets, but as long as you can find it, this excellent hostel offers a very warm welcome, with communal meals for 20dh, a bar, a frescoed roof terrace and well constructed dorms. Voted the best hostel in Morocco in the 2012 Hoscar awards. No credit cards.

Sidi Kaouki

€€ **Hotel Villa Soleil**, T070-233097 (mob), T0524-472092, www.hotel-villa-soleil.com. The 11 simple rooms and suites of **Hotel Villa Soleil** are just 1 min from the beach. Sandy tiles, whitewash and greys are punctuated with geraniums and splashes of colour. Massage, manicure and pedicure are all offered and there's a restaurant too. Breakfast is taken on the terrace which has views and basket chairs.

€€ **Windy Kaouki**, T0524-472279, www.windy-kaouki.com. This Italian-run place has 6 mini-apartments and a good pool in the courtyard. The restaurant serves fantastic grilled fish, octopus salad and aubergines.

€ **Auberge de la Plage**, T0524-476600, www.kaouki.com. A colourful and chilled place with Italian and German management. Of the 10 spacious rooms, 5 have private bathrooms. The colours all clash but solar energy and candles add to the atmosphere. The dining room has an open fire, the roof terrace has views over the sea, and horse riding and camel excursions can be arranged.

RESTAURANTS

Essaouira

€€€ After 5, 7 Rue Youssef El Fassi, T0524-473349. Open 1200-2300. Under huge stone arches and a pink ceiling, After 5 is a distinctly hip spot, with chilled lounge tunes and an imaginative Moroccan menu with Euro tinges. The place really comes alive in the evenings, however, when it doubles as a bar. Both chic and inviting, there is an open fire for winter, comfy cushions and free Wi-Fi. Striking design features include bold art and lightshades big enough to live in.

€€ Elizir, 1 Rue Agadir, T0524-472103. Open from 1930. Run by a Moroccan returned from living in the foodie hotspots of Italy, **Elizir** is about as good as a restaurant can get. The creative food uses top-notch ingredients and is exquisitely prepared – try the ravioli with ricotta, basil and pistachio, or the organic chicken, fresh fig and gorgonzola, but save some room for the mouth-wateringly delicious pear *pastilla* with chocolate, served with a cucumber sorbet. The wine's good too. Then there's the wonderfully eclectic decor. Sit out on the green and white roof terrace when it's warm.

€€ Le Patio, 28 Bis, Rue Moulay Rachid, T0524-474166. Evenings only, closed Mon. Styling themselves as a 'tapas ocean food' restaurant, funky **Le Patio** is a stylish, atmospheric little place with warm low lighting, brick arches, drapes and seductively flickering candles. The food is creative and tasty, with imaginative use of flavours such as vanilla and cinnamon.

€ Les Alizés, 26 Rue de la Skala, T0524-476819. One of the most popular places in town, and rightfully so. You can't reserve, but waiting at the small tables just inside the entrance with some olives and a bottle of wine is one of the pleasures of the place. Once you get a table you'll be plied with great Moroccan food – there's not an enormous choice but it's all good and the place is run with a rare combination of efficiency and good humour.

€ Port fish stalls, lunch only. The best cheap lunch options are the open-air restaurants between Pl Moulay Hassan and the port; usually served with a tomato salad, you can choose your fish before it's cooked. Hygiene is good and prices are fixed and written up on boards, but make sure you are clear on what you have and haven't ordered.

Sidi Kaouki

The café shacks at the centre of the village do sandwiches, snacks and tagines at lunchtime (1 or 2 open for breakfast too). **Café des Artistes**, attached to Hotel des Artistes, is another option, as is the lounge in the **Surfclub**. For a more satisfying meal, however, go to the excellent restaurant at **Windy Kaouki**.

WHAT TO DO

Camel riding

You'll get lots of offers at the southern end of the beach in Essaouira. If you want to get into camel riding in a big way, **La Maison du Chameaux** is the place for you.

The beach at Sidi Kaouki is a great spot to wobble about on the back of a camel.

Cookery courses

L'Atelier Madada, 7 Bis Rue Youssef El Fassi, T0524-475512. Mon-Sat 1030-1430, 450dh for the course and meal. Under the **Madada** hotel, this is a great place to learn the secrets of Moroccan cooking, or just to spend a fun couple of hours, after which you get to enjoy the fruits of your labour. Kids' lessons are also possible.

Surfing

Sidi Kaouki has a good surf club (www.sidi-kaouki.com) as does Essaouira (**Océan Vagabond**, www.oceanvagabond.com). Sidi Kaouki is generally better for surfing, Essaouira for windsurfing and kite surfing.

NORTH TO CASABLANCA

North of Essaouira, towards Casablanca, Morocco's economic powerhouse, the coast takes on a comparatively neglected air, with old towns built by European powers slowly crumbling away. In places, notably Oualidia, blessed with an extraordinary natural lagoon, holiday development is starting to take hold but, for the most part, tourists are a rare sight. Low hills slope down to the coast and tomato growers line each side of the road with trailers piled high with produce. El Jadida's old Portuguese centre is a spectacular filmset of a place and Azemmour also has its ancient ramparts.

→OUALIDIA AND AROUND

Almost midway between Essaouira and Casablanca, Oualidia (pronounced 'wa-lid-ee-a') has abundant natural beauty and is a restful sort of place, except in July and August when Moroccan tourists descend on it in their hordes. New holiday bungalows are beginning to cascade down the hillside but, for most of the year, it remains a chilled haven.

Named for the Saâdian Sultan el Oulalid, who built a kasbah there in the 1630s, the town is best known today for its oysters and its restaurants. There are caves, a lagoon, safe swimming – and ample amusement for birdwatchers, as the inlets and beaches are much appreciated by migrating birds in autumn and spring. It's also popular with surfers and, increasingly, kite-surfers, who ride the calmer waters in the lagoon. **Surfland** ① *between the road and the lagoon, T0523-366110,* offers surfing courses and other outfits set up in season on the beach.

ARRIVING IN OUALIDIA
Taxis and buses drop off in the higher part of the village on the Safi–El Jadida road. From here it's a petit taxi ride or a half-hour walk down to the hotels and restaurants by the sea.

MOVING ON
El Jadida (see page 91) is 80 km up the coast, accessible by both bus and shared taxis in about 1¼ hours.

PLACES IN OUALIDIA
The village of Oualidia forms a crescent around a peaceful lagoon, entered by the sea through two breaches in a natural breakwater. Above the beach, the skyline on the wooded hillside is dominated by the **kasbah**, built in 1634 by a Saâdian sultan to defend the pleasant and potentially useful harbour (a track right off the S121 opposite the turning to Tnine Gharbia leads up to the building). Below it is the now disused royal villa built by Mohammed V as a summer palace.

The town has a **market** (Saturday) for local agricultural produce. The lagoon and beach provide an ideal sheltered location for sailing, kite-surfing, windsurfing and fishing. From late June to September, Oualidia is very busy. The beach gets crowded and the water is none too clean. Off-season, you have the beautiful surroundings almost to yourself.

At the far end of the beach to the south of the town, about a 10-minute walk, rocky outcrops are threaded with **caves**, some of which have been artificially enlarged over the years, especially during times of war, when they made useful hideaways and lookouts. If you walk down this way, Mustapha, who is often to be found fishing on the rocks here, may well offer to give you a guided tour.

The Oualidia **oyster beds** came into production in the late 1950s, and annual production is around 200 tonnes, mainly for local consumption. Early fruit and vegetables, in particular tomatoes, are produced here under plastic for local and European markets.

For a change of scenery, you could head for **Lalla Fatna**, a wide sandy beach 50 km to the south. Sheltered by cliffs from the east wind, and with big northwest swells, it's a popular surfing spot. A café or two may spring up in summer, but there is little else in the way of facilities.

For those with a car, a possible side-excursion is to the **Kasbah Gharbia**, about 20 km to the southeast on the S1336. The kasbah is a huge enclosure, with a large white building in the centre.

→EL JADIDA (EX-MAZAGAN)

Popular in summer with Casablancans, El Jadida hibernates out of season. With its avenues and araucaria trees, it has a faint elegance reminiscent of some forgotten Mediterranean resort, making it the sort of place where you might film a Moroccan remake of *Death in Venice*. El Jadida is best known, however, for its massive-walled citadel, the Cité Portugaise, its bastions and lookouts harking back to a time of armies equipped with pikestaffs and blunderbusses.

ARRIVING IN EL JADIDA

Getting there The bus station is south of the centre, along Avenue Mohammed V. From here it is a five- or 10-minute walk to Place Mohammed V, the focus of the town. The train station lies 3 km south of El Jadida, off to the west of the N1 (the Marrakech road), and is not well signposted from the centre of town.

Moving on One hundred kilometres of motorway, the A5, links El Jadida with Casablanca. Buses and shared taxis do the journey in about 1¼ hours. Alternatively, there are eight trains daily from 0830 to 1930, which take one hour 20 minutes.

Getting around El Jadida is sufficiently small to do all the main sites on foot, and the reasonably priced hotels are all in the centre. The better beaches are a short taxi ride away; past the **Sidi Ouafi lighthouse** (Phare de Sidi Ouafi) is a beach popular with Moroccan families camping. The more distant **Sidi Bouzid beach** is also popular and has more facilities (take bus No 2 or a grand taxi). If you have your own transport, the coastal village of **Moulay Abdallah**, with its *zaouïa* complex, is 11 km southwards.

Tourist information Point Acceuil ① *Av Mohammed VI, T0523-352507*. Actually the office of an estate agent, this is the best place to come for information – they produce a small printed guide to the town as well as a map; both are free. **Syndicat d'Initiative** ① *Av Rafii opposite site of the Municipal Theatre, daily 0830-1200, 1430-1830.* Limited range of information available but helpful staff are happy to provide details of hotel accommodation, maps and tourist brochures of a general nature.

BACKGROUND

El Jadida is short for 'El Medina El Jadida', the 'New Town'. Over its long history, however, the town has had at least four other names – El Breija, 'Little Fort', Mazagão for the

Portuguese, El Mahdouma (The Destroyed) in the 18th century, and Mazagan under the French. The area was probably occupied by the Phoenicians and may well have been the trading post referred to as Rubisis by ancient authors. Apparently a safe mooring and a strong defensive position, the site was occupied by the Almohads, who built a *ribat*, or fortress, later abandoned. In the 16th century, the Iberian powers were building their

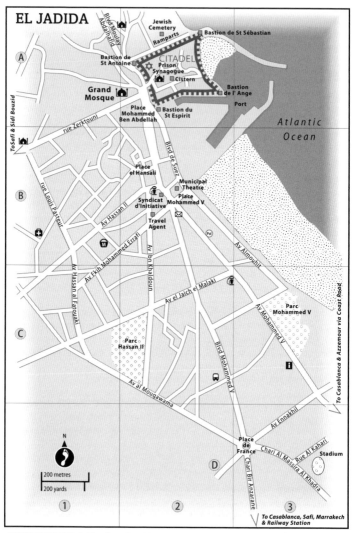

empires in the Indies and the Americas. With trade growing, Portugal was wealthy enough to establish strongpoints along the African coast, and the fortress town they founded and named Mazagão in 1515 was to become one of their most important bases, and one of the longest lived, holding out after the fall of their other enclaves in northwest Africa.

Sultan Mohammed Ben Abdallah retook the town in 1769. But the town had been mined by the defeated Portuguese who, according to legend, left someone behind to light the fuses; in the explosion, large numbers of celebrating Moroccan soldiers were killed. The old fortress town thus acquired a sinister reputation and the nickname El Mahdouma, 'The Demolished'. On the wild Atlantic coast, the massive defences left by the Portuguese were far too valuable to remain left abandoned for long. Reconstruction works were launched in 1815 by Sultan Sidi Abd al Rahman. In 1844, after the Moroccan forces had been defeated by the French at Isly – and the sultan's authority duly weakened – the Doukkala tribes looted the town. However, European merchants were to settle and the town began to expand beyond the walls of the original Portuguese city. There was also an influx of Jews from neighbouring Azemmour in the 19th century, and the town was further developed by the French as the chief town of the Doukkala region, also handling much of the trade with Marrakech. Under the French protectorate, the usual new avenues, gardens, along with administrative and residential neighbourhoods, were carefully laid out.

Today, El Jadida is a sleepy sort of small town, home to provincial administration, a university and a busy port with a sardine fishing industry. The summer influx of mainly Moroccan tourists is short (mid-July to mid-September), after which hibernation sets in. The Portuguese have put some money into the citadel, and the Moroccan authorities' emphasis on promoting beach resort tourism may have spin-offs for the town.

CITE PORTUGUESE

A magical sun-bleached place of dusty crumbling corners, playing children and peeling paint, the **Citadel** was built by the Portuguese from 1513. Its distinctive character was maintained after their departure in 1769 by European and Jewish merchants, who settled here from 1815. The quarter is small and easily explored and contains attractive Portuguese and Jewish houses with decorated, arched doorways and wrought-iron balconies.

You can wander around the **ramparts**, parts of which have been repaved, from ramps to either side of the main entrances and also from the Porte de le Mer. These are surmounted by the escutcheons of the Portuguese kings and were completed in 1541.

The **Bastion du St Esprit** is located at the southwest corner and, from here, the walk along the ramparts follows a canal on the south side, which is all that remains of the old moat that once surrounded the citadel.

From the **Bastion de l'Ange** at the southeast corner there is a superb panoramic view of the citadel, the fishing harbour and beach. Looking north, the walls are broken on the coastal side by the **Porte de la Mer**, the old sea gate from where the Portuguese finally left in 1769; many of the other interesting features of the old walled city – including a chapel, hospital, prison, Governor's palace and a lighthouse converted into the Grand Mosque – can be seen from this vantage point. The **minaret**, built on the foundations of an old watchtower, has five sides making it unique in the Islamic world. The old prison was converted into a **synagogue**; this building dominates the skyline to the north and the Star of David can be seen clearly high up on the façade. It is possible to gain entry to the building if you are able to find the guardian with the key but there is little of note to see

ON THE ROAD
Birds in paradise

Between Oualidia and El Jadida, but south of the industrial port of Jorf Lasfar, the coast starts to become of interest to birdwatchers. The range of habitats, including rocky coast, lagoons and salt flats, to dunes and scrub, makes for a variety of species. In addition, given its latitude, the area is important for over-wintering. All year there are flamingoes, cattle and little egrets, white storks and grey herons and even the tiny Sardinian warbler. Migrants include the collared pratincole and little tern, gulls and waders. The slender-billed curlew has also occasionally been spotted. Access is possible by bus, if you ask to be dropped off at a suitable place, but travel by car is far easier.

inside. Beyond the Porte de la Mer, the ramparts walk can be completed via the **Bastion de St Sébastian** and the **Bastion de St Antoine**. From this final section the old **Jewish cemetery** can be seen to the north outside the city walls.

Located between the entry gates and the Bastion du St Esprit is the **Church of Our Lady of the Assumption**, a Portuguese construction restored by the French in 1921, and later converted into a mosque.

In the centre of the citadel, the eerily beautiful and atmospheric underground **Cistern** ① *Rue Mohammed Ahehami Bahbai, 0900-1200, 1500-1800, 1500-1900 in summer, 10dh*, dates from the 16th century and was probably originally designed to store munitions. It served as a fencing school before being used, after completion of the town walls in 1541, as a tank to store water for times of shortage. When full, the Cistern reportedly held 4 million litres of water. The symmetrical construction has a vaulted roof supported by 25 circular and rectangular pillars, with just one central window in the ceiling, 3.5 m in diameter, producing a single shaft of light. Covering the flagstones is a shallow sheet of water, producing a shimmering reflection of the vaulted ceiling in the half-light. Orson Welles filmed scenes of his epic *Othello* in the Cistern. **Gallery Chaibia Tallal**, in the same block, has good exhibitions of contemporary art.

Outside the citadel, the other main focuses of interest are the **beach** and the area between **Place Mohammed V** and **Place Mohammed Ben Abdallah** and the immediately adjacent streets. The main shops, banks and restaurants are here, together with cinemas and the Municipal Theatre, and the pedestrianized **Place el Hansali** provides a pleasant alternative to the seafront for a relaxing drink on a café terrace.

AROUND EL JADIDA

The **beaches** south of El Jadida on the S121 are reached by bus No 2 and grands taxis. First is **Sidi Ouafi**, then the more developed (and polluted) **Sidi Bouzid**, with a bar, café-restaurants and a campsite. Here at Sidi Bouzid the gulls congregate in their hundreds between November and February each year.

Moulay Abdallah is a fishing village with an attached site of religious importance, lying 10 km from El Jadida. The minaret of Ismaïl Amghar dates from the Almoravid period and is almost intact. The shrine attracts up to 200,000 visitors to its annual *moussem* in August, one of the major festivals in the Moroccan calendar. Thousands of horsemen take part in the parades and displays, magnificent in their skill and their costumes.

Perhaps the least visited of the old Portuguese coastal bastions, Azemmour has a backwater air. It is a town with a dual identity. There are the obvious attractions – the walk along the old ramparts, the stroll through the narrow streets of the medina, the view of the Oum er Rbia River – and then there is the walk up to the Zaouïa of Moulay Bouchaïb. Here you can see the whole gammut of stalls and actitivites that are part of a pilgrimage centre. And for a summer swim, about 1 km from the town is Haouzia beach. Azemmour is an easy excursion from El Jadida, with plenty of grands taxis doing the 20-minute trip.

ARRIVING IN AZEMMOUR

The train station is a good 30-minute walk from the town. If you arrive by car, park near the ramparts, where there will be some sort of 'warden'. All the sights are in easy walking distance. A child may show you up to the ramparts, while the beach is about 30 minutes' walk away. The busy Rue Moulay Bouchaïb takes you up to the *zaouïa* of the same name.

BACKGROUND

There was a trading post here called Azama in the Carthaginian period, but earlier marble columns, dating back to Punic times, and Roman coins have also been found in the area. In the 15th century Azemmour was an important trading port on the routes between Portugal and West Africa, trading horses, carpets, jallabah and haiks with Guinea, and cereals with Portugal. The Portuguese occupied Azemmour in 1513 as a base from which to attack Marrakech, but under opposition from the Saâdians had to withdraw in 1541. The town assumed regional importance under the Saâdians, but soon lost ground to the growth of its near neighbour, El Jadida. The town is sometimes referred to as Moulay Bou Chaib, after its patron saint, who has a *zaouïa* above the town.

PLACES IN AZEMMOUR

Azemmour is still partly surrounded by imposing ochre **ramparts**, with several attractively carved bastions often decorated with cannon. From the hill above the bridge on the east side of the river there is a striking view of the medina with its white, square-fronted, flat-roofed houses stretching along the top of the steep bank opposite. The **beach** is also one of the best, but the town attracts few visitors. The walls of the old **medina** can be explored by the rampart walk, also with excellent views of the town; the steps are at the northeast end of the walls. Enter via **Bab es Souk**, with its clear Portuguese architectural influences and impressive wooden doors, generally round-arched with carved keystones. Also visit the *kissaria*, or covered market, and the **Sanctuary of Moulay Abdallah Ben Ahmed**. The doors of this house have a particular Portuguese style. A passageway to the left leads to the **kasbah**, which also had a role as a *mellah*, or Jewish quarter. In the kasbah, visit the **Dar el Baroud** building, the house of the powder, built within the ramparts between the medina and the kasbah. It is dominated by a tower from which there are views back over the rooftops towards the *oued*. The 16th-century **kasbah gate** is a strikingly simple semicircular arch; climb its tower for a view of the town.

To get to the **Gorges de Méhéoula**, also known as the Gorges des Orangers, take the road south out of Azemmour, turning right just before the Oued Oum er Rbia, and left at the first junction to keep alongside the *oued*. About 9 km from here, there is a signed turning left (north), giving the best view of this gorge.

NORTH TO CASABLANCA LISTINGS

WHERE TO STAY

Oualidia

Oualidia can get very crowded in high summer, when hotel reservations are essential. Prices drop in low season, Sep-Apr. Most restaurants also have places to stay.

€€€ Hotel Hippocampe, Route du Palais Oualidia, T0523-366108, www.hotel hippocampe.com. Bungalows around the edge of peaceful and amazingly floral gardens are set back from the lagoon. Among the profusion of geraniums and nasturtiums, rooms have wicker sofas and light contemporary furnishings. The licensed restaurant, serving lobster and the ubiquitous oysters, has patio doors opening onto a terrace with great views, and below this there's a pool.

€€ Issa Blanca, T0523-366148, www.hotel-issablanca-oualidia.com. Along the beach road, away from the lagoon, the 6 simple rooms here have clean, tiled, black and white bathrooms and metal frame beds; one has a private terrace. There's an open kitchen in the French-style restaurant – try the salad Issa Blanca, with oysters, of course, and something from a good list of Moroccan wines.

€€ L'Initiale, Oualidia Plage, T0523-366246. At the end of the road, this is a comfortable, modern place with a great licensed restaurant and, if you can, get room No 5 for a great sea view: sit up in bed and you'll see the waves crashing on the sand about 70 m away.

El Jadida

€€€ Riad Soleil d'Orient, 131 Derb El Hajjar, 0661-615074, www.riadsoleildorient.net. An elegant riad with 6 rooms and a verdant courtyard and a roof terrace.

€€ Dar del Mare, 18 rue Joseph Amiel, T0523-372807, www.dar-del-mare.com. In the Cité Portugaise, this little 4-room place has plenty of Antique Moroccan style and colour, with stained glass, cool black and white tiles and old wooden furniture.

Azemmour

€€€ L'Oum Erribia, 25 impasse Chtouka, T0523-347071, www.azemmour-hotel.com. This bright medina house has 5 spacious rooms, with big windows overlooking the river, and lots of contemporary art and modern style.

RESTAURANTS

Oualidia

As an alternative to the many excellent restaurants, take a bottle of wine to the beach in the evening, and oyster and urchin sellers will approach you with the freshest catch for sale. See also Where to stay, above: just about all the hotels here double up as good restaurants.

€€ Restaurant Les Roches, T0519-336793. A small and friendly place opposite L'Initiale, painted white and blue and offering a good 90dh 'menu touristique' with various seafood dishes.

El Jadida

€ Restaurant Portugaise, Rue Mohammed Ali Bahbai, Cité Portugaise. Despite the name, this unlicensed little family-run restaurant is predominantly French. There are red-and-white checked tablecloths and good-value omelettes and fish dishes as well as a *tagine du jour*. The waiter wears a bow tie, and everything is delightfully bijou.

€ Tchikito, Rue Mohammed Smiha. An El Jadida institution, Tchikito has sawdust on the floor, wipe-clean tablecloths and offers fresh fish dishes for 20-30dh.

CASABLANCA

In the 1930s, only two French achievements are said to have surprised the Americans: the First World War and Casablanca. A boom-town, nicknamed 'the African Marseilles', 'Casa' was a city where you could drive around at 130 kph and where the streets were filled with luxurious cars. The city grew from a small trading port at the end of the 19th century into one of Africa's biggest cities. With a centre planned by Henri Prost in the early 20th century, the city, with its wide avenues, elegant buildings and huge port, was held to be the finest achievement of French colonial urbanism. It has remained the economic capital of independent Morocco, the centre for trade and industry, finance and the stock exchange. Sprawling and dynamic and with a population of more than four million people, Casa is now a modern, noisy and chaotic metropolis with its fair share of urban problems, as well as some interesting neo-Moorish and art deco architecture, an enormous mosque and an enviable seafront location.

→ARRIVING IN CASABLANCA

GETTING THERE
Arriving by **train** at Casa-Voyageurs station (where connections arrive from other main cities), you will find that the taxi drivers do not want to take individual passengers. From Casa-Voyageurs to the city centre should not cost more than 15-20dh, depending on the traffic. Watch out for taxi drivers who will try various tricks to persuade you to go to hotels for which they are paid commission.

MOVING ON
To get to Mohammed V airport, either take a grand taxi (250dh, 300dh at night) from the city centre (where most of the hotels are) or a shuttle train (30dh) from either Casa-Port station (the terminus, close to the centre) or from Casa-Voyageurs (the main train station).

GETTING AROUND
Casablanca is a big place. The central area, with most of the interesting architecture, between the medina/Casa-Port station and the Parc de la Ligue Arabe, is just about small enough to do on foot. Other sites which you may want to visit – the seafront, or Corniche, with its restaurants and beach clubs at Aïn Diab, the Hassan II Mosque or the Quartier des Habous, a sort of garden city for Muslim notables – are short hops from the centre in one of Casablanca's red taxis (10-20dh for the trip, have change ready). There are numerous public and private bus lines, but it's better to maximize time by taking taxis.

Tourist information Office du Tourisme ① *55 Rue Omar Slaoui, T0522-271177*. Syndicat d'Initiative ① *98 Av Mohammed V, T0522-221524*. The latter is perhaps the more helpful of the two. There are also information booths in the city centre – they are friendly and eager to help but have almost no information to impart.

→BACKGROUND

Bold Phoenician pilots founded a trading post close to the present site of Casablanca during the seventh century BC, and the discovery of a Roman galley indicates use, if not settlement, of the area in the first century BC. (The silver coins found on this vessel are on show at the **Banque National du Maroc** in Rabat.) In the seventh century AD the Berber tribe, the Barghawata, held this area. It was conquered by the Almohads in 1188, and developed by Sultan Abd el Moumen as a port. In the 14th century the Portuguese established a settlement here on the site of the village of Anfa, but when it became a pirates' base in 1468, they destroyed it, repeating this act in 1515. The Portuguese re-established themselves in the late 16th century, and stayed until 1755, when an earthquake destroyed the settlement. The town was resurrected in the mid-18th century for strategic reasons, under Sultan Mohammed Ben Abdallah. There are various stories about how the town acquired its name ('the white house', Dar el Baydha in Arabic). One version says that it was named after the Caïd's house, a large white building visible from a distance.

FRENCH COLONIZATION

In the 19th century, European traders settled at Casablanca and, at the beginning of the 20th century the French obtained permission from Sultan Abd al Aziz to construct an artificial harbour. This was the beginning of Casablanca's rapid expansion. The French occupied the city in 1907 (and the rest of Morocco in 1912). Adventurers of all kinds were attracted to the place with its Wild West frontier feel. This first wave of French immigration greatly displeased the aristocratic resident-general, Lyautey, who wrote that "The citizens were Frenchmen who had built, beside the Moroccan city, a town to their own liking, but of the same disorderly, speculative and soulless nature as the American boom towns."

The town grew quickly: in 1907, the population was 20,000, including 5000 Jews and 1000 Europeans; by 1912, the population was 59,000, of which there were 20,000 Europeans and 9000 Jews. Morocco's first factory was founded in 1908 in Casablanca,

the first labour union was founded in 1910, and the first modern banks came with the protectorate. Land speculation was rampant, with both Muslims and Europeans involved.

Lyautey was highly suspicious of the European inhabitants of this boom town on the coast of 'traditional' Morocco. (When he decided that Rabat should be the capital in 1913, there were street protests in Casa.) However, it became imperative to do something for the city: in 1913, an observer described it as "an ocean of hovels, a sort of unstructured suburb to an as yet unbuilt metropolis."

PLANNING THE NEW CITY

In 1915 Lyautey and his chief architect, Henri Prost, began work on planning the new city centre, creating a grid of wide boulevards, lined with fine stucco office and apartment buildings. Key state buildings (as in Rabat) were styled with detailing derived from Moroccan traditional architecture, a style known as Arabiasance. And, one of the first acts of the new city administration was to create a 4 km ring boulevard, considered far too wide at the time. But the city was to grow far more rapidly than anyone predicted.

Prost certainly had no easy task, given the settler interests at stake. His plan covered an area of 1000 ha. With a proposed density of 150 people per hectare, the city was designed for 150,000 people – which led to accusations of megalomania. Industrial areas were situated north and east of the centre, on rocky ground, while residential areas, on more fertile soil, were to the west and southwest. Between the two, Prost laid out a centre focusing on two large public squares, the Place de France, centre for commercial activity, and the Place Lyautey, site of the main administrative buildings. The walls of the medina were in part demolished. The Avenue du 4ème Zouaves, today's Avenue Houphouêt

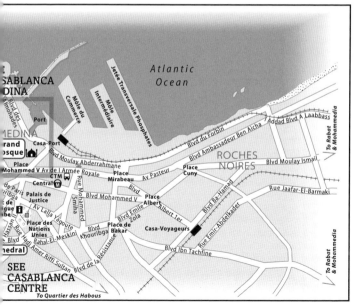

Boigny, led down to the railway station and the port. A fan-shaped system of roads and ring boulevards structured the new city – and it is a tribute to Prost's planning that the traffic runs as smoothly as it does today.

In terms of physical planning, colonial Casablanca was a relatively successful city – even though Prost's zoning was not always respected, and the suburbs subsequently sprawled far beyond the core, with vast planned projects and unplanned *bidonvilles* (the original *bidonville* or tin can city was in Casablanca). Between 1921 and 1951 the number of inhabitants grew by 85% due to an exodus from the Moroccan countryside and arrivals fleeing the wars of Europe. At the end of the Second World War Casablanca had a population of 700,000. With rising unrest in the expanding slums, it was essential to improve housing conditions. Planner Ecochard and the Atbat-Afrique team developed the concept of culturally adapted housing for the masses, that is to say inward-looking, multi-storey patio houses for the poor Muslim communities. However, as André Adam, chronicler of Casablanca's development, put it, "in her hanging patio, today's woman is like a bird in a cage".

AFTER THE WAR
In 1950, Casablanca was an exciting place to be, drawing in capitalists fleeing the socialist government in France, and where the focus of debates was Moroccan independence. A new building boom produced some modest skyscrapers and Casablanca-based trade unions were important in the nationalist struggle, notably in the riots of 1952 and insurrection from 1953 to 1955.

The city has continued to expand and has constructed a number of new architectural landmarks: the gigantic Hassan II Mosque, right on the Atlantic, and, on the Boulevard Zerktouni, the Twin Center, designed by Catalan architect Richard Bofill, dwarfing the Maârif neighbourhood.

Despite the increased building speculation at the expense of older property, it seems that Casablanca's architectural heritage is gaining recognition and there is increased official awareness that the city's architecture is potentially a draw for tourists. But Casablanca also has problems. The mix of ocean-humid air and diesel pollution makes an unpleasant cocktail. There are huge economic disparities between the wealthy villa quarters of Anfa Supérieur and Aïn Diab and extensive areas of sub-standard housing. There are still numerous *bidonville* areas. Some, like Beni Msick, have seen major rehousing projects, others huddle on odd strips of land next to railway lines and derelict factories.

UPSTART CITY
Casablanca, grimy and frayed at the edges though it may be, also has a glitzy side. Alongside the imperial cities, it is an upstart. Its streets bear the names of rebel heroes, of French and Moroccan cities, and of trees and artists. If Rabat is a home-loving civil servant and Fès an austere imam, then Casablanca is a golden boy, often stressed-out but always on the move. Casablanca has a go-getting air, which builds glamorous careers for some – and leaves many in the gutter. The old Lusitanian port, destination for camel and mule trains coming up from plains and mountains far inland, is a very long way away. Casablanca is a place where an anonymity impossible in the traditional city can be found, where identities can sometimes break free of the old constraints. Although not the most attractive or hospitable of places to visitors, it is definitely the place where Morocco's

ON THE ROAD

Laboratory of urban planning

For Resident-General Lyautey, Casablanca was to be the commercial nerve centre of the French protectorate. The decision was taken to build a vast new port at a site which many critics saw as totally impracticable. But the technical difficulties were overcome and, in 1921, the new port complex, with its kilometre-long **Delure Jetty**, was inaugurated, confirming Casablanca's world port status.

As for the rest of the city, the architecture of the early period of the protectorate was characterized by a variant of the neo-Moorish style, already used in Algeria and Tunisia. Lyautey wanted Morocco's official buildings to be simple and sobre in style, and some of the results can be seen in **Place Mohammed V**.

Later, in the interwar period, a local variant of art deco took root, using geometric motifs in low relief and wrought ironwork, and occasionally incorporating plaques of Moroccan *zellige* mosaic decoration. Set-back terraces on the top storeys and horizontal detailing gave the larger buildings a sculptural quality. The art deco aesthetic, strengthened by the success of the 1925 Paris Exhibition of Decorative Arts and Modern Industries, can be traced in buildings as diverse as the **Hôtel de Ville** (by Marius Boyer, undoubtedly the leading architect of the city) and Paul Tournon's towering white **Cathédrale du Sacré Coeur**, occasionally used as a performance space.

One of the first cities to be planned using aerial photography and formal zoning regulations, Casablanca was also one of the first places to see the use of revolutionary construction techniques like concrete formwork. In the early 1930s, streamlining and speed stripes were all the fashion – hence the horizontal window bands of many buildings – and the first mini-skyscrapers appeared, marking a break with the six-storey apartment buildings. Plot size and land prices (and the enterprising spirit of 'French California') allowed the construction of buildings difficult to envisage in the crowded cities of France. And, of course, there were numerous adaptations to local conditions: terraces and belvederes, granito floorings for the daily washing of floors, and separate servants' quarters. The year 1951 saw the completion of Morandi's **Immeuble Liberté** – 17 storeys high and in the finest ocean-liner style. (If you have time, take a look at the **Villa Souissi**, near the Espace Anfa, a private 1950s home transformed into a bakery and pâtisserie.)

With the arrival of the Allies in 1942 and the new US base at Nouasseur, American influence grew. American cinema and its capital Hollywood (with a similar climate to Casablanca), inspired the city's wealthy families. The new villas of the *zones de plaisance*, such as Anfa and Le Polo, were luxurious and functional according to the tenets of the modern movement. In a few decades, the city had acquired the most up-to-date facilities for work and leisure, and cinemas had a key place: the Rialto (1930) and the Vox (by Boyer, 1930, now demolished).

Casablanca was always more than just another colonial city and somehow it epitomized Jazz Age modernity. Today, the city has a great architectural heritage of which its inhabitants are increasingly aware. The demolition of the Boyer-designed **Villa el Mokri** in 1995 aroused widespread criticism and media interest, and the association **Casa Mémoire** (www.casamemoire.org) is now working for the preservation of the city's unique heritage of buildings.

future is made. Casablanca, stylish child of French colonial capitalism, has grown up. The vast city, made a household name by a Hollywood film, watches the world on satellite TV. Morocco-watchers observe its potentially turbulent suburbs and listen to the gossip in its villas and cafés to follow how things in the wider country are going.

The Casablanca suicide bombings of 2003, in which 45 people died, and the bomb of 2007, which killed a further five people, were carried out by young men from the shanty towns and poorest suburbs of the city. Since 2003, efforts have been made to help the poor of the city, with education and literacy programs and attempts to improve housing. Many Moroccans blame Algerian influences for the fundamentalist streaks in Casablancan society, but most of the contributory factors are probably nearer to home. These contributory factors of high unemployment and rising poverty were brought to the forefront in 2011 when Casablanca, like all of Morocco's big cities, experienced mass protest rallies as part of the Arab Spring. Whether these problems can be tackled sufficiently to appease critics, remains to be seen.

→PLACES IN CASABLANCA

When visiting Casablanca, you may notice changes in street names. The older French names in the central area are still in use, but on new plaques, the French 'rue' is written in Latin letters as 'zanka', while 'avenue' is 'chari'.

HASSAN II MOSQUE
① *Blvd Sidi Mohammed Ben Abdallah, T0522-482886. Open to non-Muslims by 45-min guided tour only from the western side of the mosque 0900, 1000 and 1100, also at 1400 Sep-Jun, and 1400 and 1500 Jul-Aug. During Ramadan, tours are at 0900, 1000 and 1100, and on Fri at 0900 and 1400. 120dh.*

In many ways impeccably modern, with its traditional decorative detailing, including ceramic mosaic, carved plasterwork and painted wood, the Hassan II mosque is often also heralded as a symbol of the renaissance of Moroccan craftskills. Inaugurated in 1993, it is the world's fifth biggest mosque and took five years of intensive labour by over 30,000 workers and craftsmen to complete. Works were undertaken by French contractors Bouygues, also responsible for the huge Basilica of Yamasoukrou on the Côte d'Ivoire. The minaret, some 200 m high, was inspired by the minaret of the Koutoubia Mosque in Marrakech, and is Casablanca's chief landmark. Sometimes a laser beam, visible over 35 km away, indicating the direction of Mecca, probes the night sky. The mosque is huge: in terms of covered area, it is the largest in the world and has space for 80,000 worshippers. There are upper prayer areas on a mezzanine floor that has space for 5000 female worshippers.

The mosque is built on a rocky site, right next to the ocean, with the water practically lapping the bay windows of the prayer hall (which has a mobile roof allowing it to be opened to the sky and a partially glass floor so that certain VIP worshippers can kneel over the Atlantic as they pray). Visitors pass through the main prayer hall, the ablutions room (ritual ablutions are compulsory before prayer) and the two public baths, beautifully decorated but still closed. As one approaches the wide esplanade leading to the mosque, the buildings on either side were planned to house a *medersa*, a library and a museum of Islamic art but the necessary funding has yet to be found. The costly operation was all paid for by public subscription and, unusually for a mosque in the city, it is managed by the **Agence urbaine de Casablanca.**

ON THE ROAD
24 hours in Casablanca

Start the day with a coffee and pastry and a stroll around the central neighbourhood near the market on the **Avenue Mohammed V** and the **Rue du Prince Moulay Abdallah**. Take a petit taxi over to the **Grande Mosquée Hassan II**, right on the Atlantic shore, the westernmost mosque of the Islamic lands, for one of the morning guided tours. There will probably be time for a quick stroll along the seafront before lunch at the **Restaurant du Port de peche**, inside the port compound. Next, take a petit taxi over to the **Quartier des Habous**, a perfectly planned 1920s neighbourhood built for the notables of Fès to get them to settle in Casablanca. There are some good souvenir places here, and have a look at the **Tribunal du Pacha**. Then take another petit taxi out to Maârif to visit the **Villa des Arts** and the nearby **Cathedral du Sacré Coeur**. Finally, in the early evening, those who like the crowds might want to explore the medina or the area round the **Parc de la Ligue arabe**. Evening activities could include a trip to a hammam, perhaps the **Bain Zaiani**, or one of the hammams near Boulevard Zerktouni and the Mosquée el Badr. Casablanca has plenty of good restaurants: try **Taverne du Dauphin** in the town centre or the expensive **A Ma Bretagne** out beyond Ain Diab. Casa nightlife centres on the **Corniche**, the beachfront, where there are bars and clubs to suit most tastes.

THE MEDINA

The medina, site of the old city, is a ramshackle quarter, dating primarily from the 19th century (the fortifications are 18th century). Still densely populated, it can easily be explored in a couple of hours, entering from Place Mohammed V. There were three main sections: a bourgeois area with consuls, merchants, government officials and Europeans; a *mellah* or Jewish neighbourhood – which dominated the medina for much of the 20th century, and the *tnaker*, housing rural migrants (the term refers to a compound with a cactus hedge.) The **Grand Mosque** was built by Sultan Sidi Mohammed Ibn Abdallah at the end of the 18th century to celebrate the recapture of Anfa from the Portuguese.

The **Koubba of Sidi Bou Smara** stands in the southwest corner of the medina near an old banyan tree. It is said that, in the 10th century, Sidi Bou Smara ('man of the nails') was passing through the town and asked for water to perform his ritual washing before praying. Insults and stones were thrown at him instead. Undaunted, he struck the ground with his staff and there issued from that place a spring which continued to flow. It seems that the inhabitants' earlier inclination to send him away changed to a reluctance to let him go, so he settled in the corner of the medina and planted a banyan tree which grew quickly and to an immense size. The tree is now studded with nails driven in by supplicants for the saint's assistance.

The **Koubba of Sidi Beliout** (off-limits to non-Muslims) is the small complex of whitewashed buildings to your left on the Avenue Houphouêt Boigny (ex-Avenue du 4ème Zouaves) as you walk towards the city from Casa-Port station. It used to be in the medina, until the demolitions created the boulevard linking station and city. Sidi Beliout is said to have blinded himself and gone to live with wild animals, finding them preferable to the human race. The animals cared for him, and a lion carried him to this resting place after his death. He is appealed to by those needing consolation. Near his shrine is a fountain. Those who drink the water will reputedly return to Casablanca. Sidi Beliout is now the name of the central district close to the shrine.

The remains of Sidi Allal el Kairouani and his daughter Lalla Beida are in a **mosque** on Rue Tnaker to the north of the medina. He was the patron of fishermen, and she was known as the White Princess due to the pale colour of her skin. One story goes that Dar el Baydha (House of the White Princess) was the name given to the town in 1770 when it was rebuilt, and that it only later took the Spanish translation Casa Blanca. The story recounts how Sidi Kairouani, travelling from Tunisia to Senegal, was shipwrecked off the coast here, but rescued by the locals. He sent for his motherless daughter who was not so fortunate. Her ship sank too but she drowned. Her body was carried to her grieving father who buried her facing the sea and left a place beside her for himself.

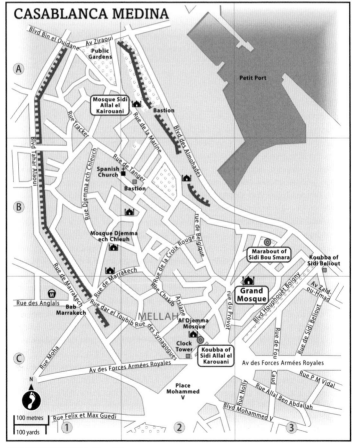

ON THE ROAD
Modern medina

Resident-General Lyautey's respect for things Moroccan reached an apogee at the Quartier des Habous. Only too aware of the housing problems facing the Muslim population, Lyautey's planner Henri Prost proposed a new traditional town. The aim was to provide medium-cost housing for Muslims. Top families from Fès, wary of settling in 'impure' areas inhabited by Europeans, were to be attracted to a stylish mini-medina, close to the Sultan's new palace but a fair distance from the new city centre. The land was put forward by the Habous, a sort of religious property institution. (In Islam, land or other property can be held in mortmain to benefit descendants.) A Jewish merchant added a plot, but as the Habous could not accept gifts from Jews, he gave the land to Sultan Moulay Youssef, who turned it over for development.

The task of designing the area was given to architect Albert Laprade, a great observer of traditional architectures in Europe. Too busy designing the residency in Rabat, however, he handed the project to Cadet and Brion, who produced a whole neo-traditional area with all the necessary modern infrastructure. There were all the facilities familiar to former residents of an old city: a market, public ovens, hammams, Koran schools, and mosques. Wealthy Fassis moved to the area, keen to be close to the heart of things while living in a traditional environment.

OUTSIDE THE MEDINA

Though rather abandoned, the **Cathédrale du Sacré Coeur** is a tall elegant white structure built in 1930 with nods to Moroccan as well as European architecture. Inside, the white space is pin-pricked by coloured glass and elevated by slender white columns. For 20dh the guardian will let you up the tower for good views over the city. Be warned, though, that you may have to fight your way past the pigeons, and it wouldn't pass any health and safety examinations. Look out for occasional events staged here.

Villa des Arts ① *30 Blvd Brahim Roudani, T0522-295087, Tue-Sun 0930-1900, 10dh*, is a contemporary art gallery in a restored and whitewashed 1934 art deco building. Outside, fountains are embedded in the paving, while inside, polished wood floors and big white walls are a good setting for rotating displays of Moroccan and international art.

Notre Dame de Lourdes ① *junction of Av du 2 Mars and the Rond-Point de l'Europe,* was built in the 1950s and is famous for its stained-glass windows by Gabriel Loire.

Quartier des Habous is 4 km southeast of the centre close to Mers Sultan train station, but it's better to take a petit taxi and ask for 'Derb el Habous'. An attempt to create a modern medina (see box, above), the Habous is a strangely artificial residential suburb – a surreally neat and tidy version of Morocco. The **Pasha's Courtrooms** (Mahkamat el Pacha), completed in the 1950s and rather Lutyens in style, make a focal point, but generally it's a place to wander and gawp. There are a number of shops selling *belgha* (leather slippers), Moroccan clothing and copperwork. Close to the Pasha's Courtrooms are a number of good bookshops, stocking mainly Arabic titles.

BEACHFRONT

① *The ocean promenade, Blvd de la Corniche, west of the medina is easily reached by petit taxi or by local bus (No 9) from the junction of Blvd de Paris and Av des Forces Armées Royales.*

ON THE ROAD
Sidi Abderrahman, the flautist

The story of Sidi Abderrahman – like that of so many saints – has been smudged over like an old manuscript. Sidi Abderrahman was a pious man or *wali salih*, who took refuge on an islet off the Atlantic coast to better contemplate the Almighty. But he was unable to pray. To serve the Lord, he played sweet music on a reed flute. Another *wali*, Sidi Bouchaïb Arradad, hearing of the piety of Sidi Abderrahman, came to see him and said that he should lay down his flute and that he would explain to him the intricacies of prayer. The two remained together for seven days and, on the eighth day, Sidi Bouchaïb spread his carpet on the sea and went away. Deep in prayer, Sidi Abderrahman didn't see him leave. When he realized that his guide had left, he called him back, then threw himself into the sea to try to catch up. The waves drew back and an island appeared. Sidi Bouchaïb, seeing this miracle, cried out, "Oh Sidi Abderrahman, forget what I taught you and play your flute. Your *baraka* is greater than mine." And so Sidi Abderrahman stayed on his island to worship God until he passed away.

Of course there are many other legends explaining the past of Sidi Abderrahman. His tiny island retains a mystic fascination; it is a place where women may go to seek the saint's blessing, a cure for sterility, bad health and other maledictions. They come from all over Morocco, travel across to the island on makeshift 'boats', consult soothsayers in tiny damp rooms, visit the shrine, maybe organize a *lila* – a night-time ritual of dance and trance – and return home relieved of their cares.

The beachfront, or Corniche, is most definitely a place to stroll and be seen. Along the ocean front, beach clubs with open-air pools have been built on the rocks. Beyond the beach clubs and hotels, the beach becomes public, and games of football take place on the big expanses of sand. Out on the coast road, you will come to the **shrine of Sidi Abderrahman**, built on a rocky islet (see box, opposite).

→MOHAMMEDIA

Mohammedia, known as 'Fedala' until 1960, when it was renamed after the present king's father, Mohammed V, is a curious, sleepy sort of town. It is home to the Samir Refinery, and is the second biggest port in the country. There is a small walled medina, a neighbourhood of fine, wide avenues lined with palm trees, and a park with a modern church – all somehow on a scale unsuited to such a quiet place. It is as though grandiose plans for city development in the 1920s never actually quite got off the ground. Beachside Mohammedia, with its promenade and cafés, comes alive in summer. A likeable little town, it could be the place to spend a last night at the end of a trip, perhaps if you have a late flight out of Casablanca the following day.

Arriving in Mohammedia Mohammedia is easily reached by the shuttle train running between Casablanca (10 minutes) and Rabat (25 minutes). Another option is to take a grand taxi from Boulevard Moulay Abderrahman in Casablanca (turn first left just before the Centre 2000 as you leave Casa-Port station). The town is easily explored on foot, although there are plenty of lime-green petits taxis if you need to get back to the station quickly. **Tourist information** ① *14 Rue al Jahid, T0523-324299.*

Background Just to the north of modern Casablanca, Mohammedia was a thriving port in the 14th and 15th centuries. Its trade with Europe expanded in the 17th and 18th centuries, notably with the export of horses, and the kasbah was built in 1773 to support this activity. A decline in trade left Mohammedia subordinate to adjacent Rabat. However, specializing in the handling of petroleum gave it a new lease of life, and the oil refinery, opened in 1961, raised its status to one of Morocco's major ports. Industrial activities are centred around a rock salt factory. Its 3 km of sandy beaches make it a popular recreational area for the people of Casablanca, both for weekend breaks and as a summer holiday haunt.

Places in Mohammedia The distinctive mosque, **Jamaâ Radouane**, was opened in 1991. There are three doors in arched apertures, approached by shallow steps across a gleaming white marble courtyard. More impressive is the wide open park but most come to Mohammedia solely for its beach.

CASABLANCA LISTINGS

WHERE TO STAY

€€€ **Novotel Casablanca City Centre**, Angle Bld Zaîd Ouhmad Sidi Belyout, T0522-466500, www.novotel.com. It may not have an inspiring name, but the **Novotel City Centre** is a surprisingly stylish hotel, with 281 rooms and a chic bar with colourful low lighting and billowing white drapes. Sleek modern rooms have prints on the walls, widescreen TVs, orange cushions and minibars.

€€€ **Transatlantique**, 79 Rue Chaouia, T0522-294551, www.transatcasa.com. Open since 1922, the **Transatlantique** claims to be the oldest hotel in Casablanca. Public areas have lots of carved wood and art deco details, though the rooms themselves are plainer. Each has comfortable wooden furniture and a/c, and the best rooms have balconies over the street. There's a piano bar and nightclub downstairs; go for rooms higher up if you're worried about the noise.

€€ **Hotel Guynemer**, 2 Rue Mohammed Belloul, T0522-275764. Exceptionally friendly and helpful, the well-run **Guynemer** is no longer a secret and the 29 rooms here fill up fast. Clean, quiet and central, there is free internet in the lobby, as well as Wi-Fi. They can arrange airport transfer, run daily city tours and can sort out just about anything else you might want. Rooms are comfy, peach coloured and modern. Quieter rooms overlook an ugly internal courtyard. Those at the front are lighter but noisier. Nice old pictures of Casablanca decorate the stairs.

€€ **Hotel Maamoura**, 59 Rue Ibn Batouta, T0522-452967, www.hotelmaamoura.com. A rare central hotel which has a modicum of traditional Moroccan style in its carved plaster ceilings and hanging lamps. Private parking, room service and Wi-Fi.

€€ **Volubilis**, 20-22 Rue Abdelkrim Diouri, T0522-272771. www.volubiliscasa.com. Decorated with a bit of originality, this is run by the same management as the **Transatlantique** (see above), onto which it backs. There's even a connecting door between them, and guests here can use the facilities of the **Transatlantique**. There's a pizzeria and bar, and the 45 rooms have floral bedspreads your granny would be proud of, plus good tiled bathrooms.

€ **Hotel de Paris**, Rue Prince Moulay Abdallah, T022-273871. In the pedestrianized part of the centre of Casablanca, this is a friendly hotel whose staff really go the extra mile to help. The rooms are very decent for the price, with TV, a/c, nice balcony and extremely small bathroom. It can be noisy so pack your earplugs.

€ **Hotel de Seville**, 19 Rue Nationale, T0522-271311. The rooms at the front of this central hotel have good balconies overlooking the street. They are simple but clean and comfortable, with tiled floors and aged bedspreads. Good value.

RESTAURANTS

€€€ **A Ma Bretagne**, Sidi Abderrahman, Blvd de la Corniche beyond Aïn Diab, T0522-397979. Mon-Sat. Excellent French restaurant with a good wine cellar. Classy without being stuffy and wonderful sea views as well as superior food. One of the best in Casablanca. It's pricey (mains 180-320dh) but recommended.

€€€ **La Fibule**, Blvd de la Corniche, T0522-360641. Smart and atmospheric Moroccan restaurant near the El Hank lighthouse, with an emphasis on seafood. The carved ceilings are impressive and there's an open fire for the winter. Sip one of the 11 Moroccan wines as you look down on the waves below.

€€€ **Ostréa**, just inside port compound on the right, T0522-441390. Daily 1100-2300, even in Ramadan. A smartly contemporary restaurant, where the oysters are the star attraction (an oyster farmer started the place) and the seafood is some of the best in town. Try to get a table by the window upstairs so you can look down on the bustle of the port below.

€€€ **Rick's Cafe**, 248 Rue Sour Jdid, T0522-274207/08. Taking its name from the eponymous café in the film, this is something of an institution among visitors to the city. There's atmosphere by the bucketload, a piano player and, for film buffs, Casablanca is played every night. The food is good, if a bit pricey, but the ambience can't be beaten.

€€ **Al Mounia**, 95 Rue du Prince Moulay Abdallah, T0522-222669. One of the best places for traditional Moroccan food in Casablanca. There are tables outside under an enormous tree or you can eat inside in tiled and carved surrounds. All the usual Moroccan dishes – *pastilla*, tagines – are well executed and service is very good.

€€ **La Bodega**, 129 Rue Allal Ben Abdallah, T0522-541842. Open until 0100. A lively tapas bar, with Spanish cocktails upstairs and a DJ and dancefloor downstairs. Fills up with Casablanca's beautiful people.

€€ **La Corrida**, 59 Rue Guy Lussac, T0522-278155. Closed Sun and Sep. Good Spanish food, faded decor tells of the days when Casablanca had a bullring. Grilled fish and tapas are specialities, as is the sangria. Outdoor seating.

€€ **Matsuri**, 21 Rue Zaïd Bnou Rifaâ, T0522-252563. A stylish conveyor-belt sushi restaurant, **Matsuri** has some nice touches, such as fresh lilies in alcoves on the walls and good use of bamboo. Norwegian salmon is brought in specially.

€€ **Restaurant du Port de Pêche**, close to the medina in the fishing port compound, T0522-318561. Excellent fish dishes in smart but simple atmosphere. It's a good lunchtime spot but service is on the slow side. Try to reserve. To get there, leave Casa-Port station on your right, go straight ahead and then turn left for port area.

BARS AND CLUBS

Most of the nightclubs are situated on the beachfront, liveliest in summer, and open around 2400-0400. Punters are an interesting mix of media people, expatriate kids, prostitutes, fashionistas, Saudis, hustlers and a handful of gay men.

Allow around 200dh for entry, which will generally include your first drink. In order to procure a table, you'll usually be expected to buy a bottle of whisky for around 1300dh. Jeans are normally OK, but trainers are frowned upon.

WHAT TO DO

Swimming
Take out a day-ticket at one of the private beach clubs at Aïn Diab and mix with Casablanca's young and trendy set. Both

Tahiti and **Miami** offer day entrance for around 70dh, rising to 120dh at the weekend. Beyond the beach clubs the beach is free.

DREAM TRIP 2
Agadir→Anti-Atlas→Coast→Marrakech 21 days

Agadir 2 nights, page 113

Taghazoute 3 nights, page 119
Bus or shared taxi from Agadir (1 hr)

Immouzer des Ida Outanane 1 night, page 119
Car from Taghazoute (2 hrs)

Taroudant 2 nights, page 78
Car from Immouzer (3 hrs)

Tafraoute 3 nights, page 124
Car from Taroudant (4 hrs) or bus/shared taxi changing at Inezgane (6 hrs)

Tiznit 1 night, page 129
Bus (2½ hrs) or shared taxi (2 hrs) from Tafraoute

Mirleft 3 nights, page 131
Shared taxi from Tiznit (45 mins)

Sidi Ifni 2 nights, page 131
Bus or shared taxi from Mirleft (30 mins)

Agadir 1 night, page 113
Bus from Sidi Ifni (3 hrs)

Marrakech 3 nights, page 35
Bus, from Agadir (3½ hrs)

GOING FURTHER

Tata and Akka page 126
Shared taxi (changing in Igherm) from Tafraoute (4 hrs)

DREAM TRIP 2
Agadir→Anti-Atlas→Coast→Marrakech

South of the High Atlas, the scenery of the Anti-Atlas is like a geology dissection, with the mountains' inner workings turned out and laid bare, the land risen and folded over on itself.

Catch some rays, sip beer and eat pizza in Agadir before heading north up the coast to Morocco's surfing hotspots.

Then wind up into the mountains, passing beehives (stop for a jar of honey) and palm groves on your way to the market and waterfall of Immouzer des Ida Outanane.

To the south is Taroudant, its souks and streets protected behind handsomely crenellated red-earth *pisé* walls and surrounded by the beginnings of the Anti-Atlas. The vertiginous, winding route from here to Tafraoute, passes the Kasbah Tizourgane, rising majestically out of the landscape around it.

Tafraoute and the Ameln Valley are dominated by their rocky surrounds, and there are plenty of exhilarating routes to detain climbers, walkers and cyclists.

Tiznit has shoe shops and jewellery souks among its attractive warren of streets and just enough of a buzz that you'll appreciate the extreme laid-back nature of Mirleft and Sidi Ifni and their great beaches.

Marrakech, by contrast, hums with activity, especially in Jemaâ el Fna, where half the city seems to descend nightly to stroll and talk and perform.

AGADIR

Atlantic Agadir, at the mouth of the Souss Valley, is named after a Berber fortified granary. But simple rural life is long forgotten in today's city of around 200,000 people, which has grown up along the sweeping 9-km beach. A further half a million live in the surrounding area. A microclimate of year-round sun and swimming ensures that Agadir receives the largest number of tourists in all Morocco. And, while most of its visitors don't stray far from its large package holiday hotels, the city has the advantage of being near interesting villages and natural sights – as well as having good onward connections.

→ ARRIVING IN AGADIR

GETTING THERE
The vast majority of tourists arrive in Agadir by air. **Aéroport d'Agadir-Massira** ① *on the Taroudant road, T0528-839122, www.agadir-airport.com*, is 26 km inland from the city. Package holiday companies have buses to shuttle clients to their hotels, and car hire companies have offices at the airport. Otherwise, there are six-passenger grands taxis outside the airport (170dh to the town centre, 220dh at night; you could arrange to share). If Agadir is not your main holiday base, then you could take a grand taxi to Inezgane, a transport hub south of the city with good connections to various destinations. There is also a bus, No 22, for Inezgane, but no bus that goes direct to Agadir.

Intercity buses arrive at the *gare routière*, outside the town. Some buses from southern destinations only go as far as Inezgane, so you will need to take a grand taxi (around 5dh a place) or a local bus (Nos 5 and 6) to get into the city. Local buses and grands taxis arrive at the southern edge of the city centre on the Rue de Fès, close to the Avenue el Mouqawama.

Arriving by road, from the north you will come in on the N8, leading into Avenue Mohammed V; from Marrakech and the N8, turn left along Boulevard Mohammed Cheikh Saadi into the town centre. From the airport and Inezgane, and beyond along the N10 to Taroudant or the N12 to Tiznit and the South, the route goes along either Avenue Hassan II or Avenue Mohammed V.

GETTING AROUND
Agadir is not a huge place, and most things can be done on foot. There are plenty of petits taxis, useful for getting to some of the more distant hotels.

MOVING ON
Take a shared taxi north to Taghazoute (see page 119) from the bus station or take bus No 12.

TOURIST INFORMATION
Office du Tourisme ① *Av Mohammed V, T0528-846377, Mon-Fri 0830-1630.* Near the north end of town, the tourist office is almost entirely useless.

Agadir has little that is distinctively Moroccan. The old town was almost totally destroyed in the earthquake of 1960, and has been rebuilt as an international beach resort.

AGADIR'S RISE AND FALL

Agadir first features in written history in the early 16th century, when a Portuguese noble built a fortress named Santa Cruz de Cap de Gué, somewhere close to the present city. The fort was sold on to the King of Portugal in 1513 and, for a while, it became a link in a chain of trading posts the Portuguese established along the Atlantic coast of Africa. The Imazighen of the Souss valley launched a jihad against this isolated fort, and the Saâdian Emir of the Souss, Mohammed Echeikh el Mehdi, captured it in 1541, heralding the Portuguese departure from most of their other Atlantic strongholds. His son, Moulay Abdallah el Ahalib, built the kasbah on the hill overlooking the city, the ruins of which still stand.

As the Saâdians developed farming in the Souss valley, Agadir grew in importance, eventually becoming a big trading centre in the 17th and 18th centuries. Exports were sugar cane, olive oil, gold and spices, both from the Souss valley and the Sahara. However, Agadir declined during the reign of Sidi Mohammed Ben Abdallah, who preferred to develop Essaouira, to the north, and closed down Agadir's port. By the beginning of the 19th century, Agadir had all but disappeared.

In the early 20th century, Agadir briefly hit the international headlines. The European powers were running out of places to colonize, and Germany, under Kaiser Wilhelm II, was annoyed at the growing influence of France and Spain in Morocco. In 1911 an incident occurred in the Bay of Agadir when a German gunboat appeared 'to protect German interests'. The crisis was settled by negotiations between the French and Germans which recognized France's rights in Morocco in exchange for territorial concessions in the Congo. The French occupied Agadir in 1913. They constructed the port in 1914 and enlarged it in 1930 and 1953.

On 29 February 1960, disaster struck: old Agadir was completely destroyed by a terrible earthquake, killing an estimated 15,000 people. Newly independent Morocco faced the challenge of rebuilding the town. An entire new settlement was laid out south of the old centre and planned for development as a major tourist resort, with distinct functional zones separated by green swathes, the large hotels carefully distanced from the local residential areas. The ruined kasbah was encased in concrete. Set in the wall are Mohammed V's words, commemorating the dead: "If destiny desired the destruction of Agadir, its reconstruction depends on our faith and our determination." More clearly visible on an arid hillside, in giant Arabic letters, is the national motto: "Allah, Al Watan, Al Malik" ("God, the Nation, the King"). With reconstruction, the city gained some functional buildings, all brutalist concrete, by the likes of star 1960s Moroccan architect Jean-François Zevaco. The port, which escaped total destruction, was developed as the base for a large fishing fleet and as the centre of an industrial zone.

AGADIR TODAY

In the 1990s, tourism in Agadir suffered from the impact of the Gulf War and the huge growth in the popularity of Marrakech. Agadir had no nightlife to compete with the Balearics or the Canaries and, instead, the town became a destination for a wealthy Gulf Arab clientele. From the town's nightclubs, prostitution developed. Poor housing areas on the margins expanded, with rural people fleeing the drought-stricken countryside in the late 1990s. Thanks to this exodus, Agadir is now the largest Tachelhit-speaking city in Morocco, and its people, the Gadiris, are proud of their Amazigh origins. There is a dynamic local bourgeoisie with business interests across Morocco. Since the turn of the millennium, tourism in the city has attempted a move upmarket, with the Agadir Marina development at the northern end of the bay.

→ PLACES IN AGADIR

THE BEACH AND PROMENADE

The beach is Agadir's main asset, groomed daily and well provided with cafés, camel rides and watersports. A long swathe of sand, it stretches around the bay as far as Agadir itself. It's usually fairly well sheltered from wind and waves, and hassle is kept to a minimum. Due to the preponderance of superhotels at the edge of the sand, the beach can feel removed from the centre of the town, especially at its southern end. The beach in front of the hotels is patrolled by wardens who keep trinket-sellers at bay. On the more public stretches of sand you may get more attention from salesmen. There can be a strong undertow in the sea and small children should not be left to paddle unattended.

At the edge of the sand, Agadir's promenade has been much improved over the years and makes for a fascinating wander, especially in the early evening, when you might see

jugglers, visiting Casablancans in high heels and gold clothes, toy sellers and European families with ice creams. Brick-tiled and palm-fringed, there are plenty of cafés and restaurants alongside.

Sunbed hire, around 30dh per day, often includes toilet and shower facilities, usually attached to snack bars and restaurants.

THE MARINA
Beyond the beach's northern end, the new yacht-filled marina has Western shops and some smart cafés and restaurants. A couple of boats here, including the **Jolly Roger** ① *T0654 310 159*, offer tours and fishing trips.

KASBAH
The kasbah was a densely populated area of the old town and many died here in the 1960 earthquake. It's reached by a winding road to the north of the centre, off Avenue Mohammed V, a petit taxi ride for all but the most energetic. The kasbah was built in 1540 to launch an attack on the Portuguese city and was retained after the victory as a fortification against local insurrection. The ramparts and entrance have been maintained in a reasonable condition, as Agadir's one historic site and a memorial to those who died. Despite its view over Agadir, it was not resettled after 1960.

CITY CENTRE
Architecturally the city is memorable for the buildings from the 1960s reconstruction period. The main post office, by Zevaco, is typical of the minimalist reinforced concrete austerity. The modern **Grand Mosque** is on Avenue des Forces Armées Royales.

The **Vallée des Oiseaux** (Valley of the birds), between Avenue Mohammed V and Boulevard du 20 Août, is a pleasant place to wander and listen to bird song, although the llamas and mountain goats look rather as if they're missing life in the countryside.

Musée Amazighe ① *Passage Aït Souss, between Blvd Hassan II and Blvd Mohammed V, T0552-821632, open 0930-1730, 20dh*, has a small but interesting display of jewellery, carpets, pottery and wooden craftwork from southern Morocco, as well as occasional temporary displays. The collection was assembled over the years by Dutch local art specialist Bert Flint, one of the founders of the Casablanca École des Beaux Arts, who now runs the Maison Tiskiwine in Marrakech.

Jardim de Olhão ① *corner of Rue Kennedy and Av des FAR, Tue-Sun 1430-1830*, is a small park that was created to mark the twinning of Agadir and the Portuguese town of Olhão. It's a cool and peaceful oasis of green with a playground. A small exhibition shows photos of Agadir before the 1960 earthquake.

BEYOND THE CENTRE
Souk al Had ① *Av Abderrahim Bouabid, Tue-Sat, a 20-min walk or a short taxi ride from the centre*, is Agadir's Moroccan market. It doesn't give quite the same shopping experience as Marrakech or Fès, but it does offer a taste of local life, with stalls selling carefully piled spices, boxes, shoes, crafts and tagines.

Médina d'Agadir ① *T0528-280253, www.medinapolizzi.com, open 0900-1800, 40dh*, is a small, village-sized and spotlessly clean version of the old medina of the city between Agadir and Inezgane, designed and built by an Italian architect. Traditional methods and materials have been used, and the project includes workspaces for artisans and a restaurant.

AGADIR LISTINGS

WHERE TO STAY

A couple of boutique options have opened in recent years on the outskirts of town, and there is a handful of good mid-range places in the city centre. Otherwise, despite the huge numbers of hotels, there are few choices between the huge 5-star beachside enclaves and the rather seedy budget options in the Talborjt area, away from the beach. Street-facing rooms on the 2 main avenues can suffer from traffic noise.

€€€ Riad Atlas Kasbah Ecolodge, Tighanimine El Baz, 15 km inland from the centre of Agadir, T0661-488504, www.atlaskasbah.com. Sound ecological principles, a beautifully designed traditional building and a great location in the hills east of Agadir make this a romantic place to stay. The 8 rooms and 3 suites are kitted out in riad style, with ochre tones and traditional fabrics. Activities such as cookery classes and an astronomy night are available on request. Home-cooked food but no alcohol licence; it's fine to bring your own drinks.

€€€ Riad Villa Blanche, Baie des Palmiers, T0528-211313, www. riadvillablanche.com. Sleek, contemporary Moroccan style and a manageable size (there are 28 rooms) set this place apart from the super-hotel competition. There are 2 good pools, a large spa, a library, a restaurant and a bar at the southern end of Agadir's bay. It's a fair walk to the centre but you may not want to leave that much.

€€ Atlantic, Av Hassan II, T0528-843661, www.atlantichotelagadir.com. Competing with the nearby Kamal to be Agadir's best-value accommodation, the Atlantic is set back from the road with immaculate, comfortable rooms, a good (if rather cold in winter) pool and some Moroccan touches that give the place an element of style, lifting it above the average concrete Agadir block. Service is friendly and it's bang in the centre of town, albeit a 10-min walk from the beach. Price includes a reasonable buffet breakfast. Check their website for occasional discounts.

€€ Kamal, Av Hassan II, T0528-842817, www.hotel-kamal.com. An excellent mid-priced hotel in the centre of the city. It's large, with 128 rooms, but the welcome is friendly and there's a sparkling pool at the rear. The pastel decor has a slight 1980s feel but everything is spotlessly clean and there's a bar and restaurant.

€ Petite Suede, Av Hassan II, T0528-840779, www.petitesuede.com. A friendly place with plain but well-priced and comfortable rooms not far from the beach. The hotel is in a quiet part of the centre but some rooms still suffer from street noise; choose a room at the back if you can.

RESTAURANTS

The new marina area has some good upmarket restaurants; the city centre has some surprisingly authentic pizza joints. Stalls by the port have excellent fresh fish and good prices maintained through hectic competition. (Take a petit taxi there for 10dh, or bus No 1.) The Nouveau Talborjt area has a few options on the tree-shaded Pl Lahcen Tamri.

€€ La Madrague, La Marina d'Agadir, T0528-842424. A sophisticated marina restaurant, La Madrague's white tablecloths, red leather seats, up-lit glass floor and grey *tadelakt* walls give it a striking appearance. Outside heaters mean you can sit and watch the boats all year round, and there's a menu of fish, seafood and meaty options.

€€ Le Quai, La Marina d'Agadir, T0661-605822. Contemporary and stylish, this restaurant has white chairs and low lighting and offers modern European food, with an emphasis on fish and seafood. There are tables inside and out, with patio heaters for cooler winter nights.

€€ Les Blancs, La Marina d'Agadir, T0528-828393, dir@gmail.com. A terrace restaurant and bar in a fantastic position at the north end of the beach near the new marina development, this lounge beach bar and restaurant shows little trace of Morocco. Comfy shaded sofas, laid-back tunes, strutting staff in faded jeans and black t-shirts. The menu has a Spanish flavour, with good tapas and cocktails. There's even an area of private beach reserved for customers.

€ Daffy, Rue des Orangers, T0528-820068. A friendly little place serving traditional Moroccan food: couscous and tagines for around 50dh. There are a few wooden tables and chairs outside on the quiet street set back from Hassan II.

€ Little Italy, Av Hassan II, T0528-820039. Next door to Agadir's other decent pizza restaurant, Little Italy makes a reasonable stab at pizzeria authenticity. There are wooden beams and various bits of Italiana hung between black and white photos of film stars. Usually busy, the atmosphere and the pizzas are the highlights. Grab one of the outside tables if the prospect of other diners smoking bothers you.

€ Mille et Une Nuits, Pl Lahcen. A popular, good-value place on the square in Nouveau Talborjt with good Moroccan fish dishes and tagines for around 30dh. There are tables outside, and they serve food all afternoon, though the waiters can be a little pushy.

€ Via Veneto, Av Hassan II, opposite the Vallée des Oiseaux, T0528-841467. A high-quality pizzeria with a real wood oven and alcohol licence. They also do other Italian and some Moroccan food. Fish tanks and candles decorate the place and Western pop plays on the stereo. Book ahead in high season.

Cafés

€€ Yacout, Av Février 29, T0528-846588. A pâtisserie, bakery and café with a green and shady seating area: a good spot for coffee or breakfast, and makes excellent cakes and biscuits. There's also a branch inside the Marché Centrale.

€ Venezia Ice, La Marina d'Agadir. No cones but good-quality ice cream for a cool accompaniment to a stroll around the marina. Alternatively, they have wicker chairs outside under parasols.

NORTH OF AGADIR

The coast to the north of Agadir has great surfing beaches, especially around Taghazout. Although developers are moving in, the area remains largely tranquil, with Paradise Beach and others stretching 30 km northwards from Agadir. Inland, Paradise Valley is a beautiful gorge and river basin, dotted with palm trees and waterfalls, leading up into the mountains and the village of Immouzer des Ida Outanane.

→ TAGHAZOUT

Morocco's surfing centre, Taghazout (19 km north of Agadir) was once a sleepy, hippy village. Today, it is waking up to making money out of its fame, but for now it remains a laid-back, pretty little town, centred on a small bay where fishermen hang out, smoking around their upturned boats. Surfers from all over the world gather and discuss the waves, and a handful of cafés and restaurants sell banoffee pie and smoothies alongside the tagines. The nearby beaches are superb, and you don't have to go far to get more great surfing away from the crowds. The accommodation is excellent, and there are good surf schools too, offering equipment hire, beginner's lessons and tips and transport for experts. The best surfing, and therefore Taghazout's high season, is from autumn to spring when the Atlantic winds work their magic. Summer is quieter and hotter, but there are usually still some waves to be had. All year round there are possibilities for horse riding and quad biking, too. To get there, catch bus No 12 or 14 from Place Salam in Agadir. Bear in mind that the nearest ATM is in Aourir, a couple of kilometres down the coast.

Rocky reefs, sandy beaches and the Atlantic swell combine here for some fantastic surfing conditions. There's plenty of space for hanging out on the wide sands too. The beach in Taghazout itself is picturesque but has sewage problems. **Panorama's** is immediately south of the town, a short stroll to a big expanse of beach with decent waves for all abilities, especially when there's a big swell. Further south, just before Aourir, **Crocs** is good for beginners. Famous surfing spots, **Anchor Point**, **Killers** and **Mysteries**, are all within walking distance to the north, though they can be crowded. It's worth taking a bus from the square to **Aourir** to the south or to **Boilers** and **Tamri Plage** to the north. Tickets are cheap and the buses run every 30 minutes. Having a car opens up other seldom-surfed possibilities along the N1; there are plenty of hire options. See box, page 120, for more details on the best breaks. For beginners, Taghazout is a good place to learn.

→ IMMOUZER DES IDA OUTANANE

Named after the local confederation of Berber tribes, Immouzer des Ida Outanane is small mountain town at the end of a spectacular winding drive up from the coast through the palm-filled **Paradise Valley** (where there are some good walking opportunities and possibilities for wild swimming) into the hills. Around 50 km northwest of Aourir, at an altitude of 1160 m, Immouzer is a cool, relaxing place for a day trip or a short stay, with pine, olive and eucalyptus trees, terraced fields and little or no hassling of visitors. It is a markedly Moroccan and rural experience in contrast to the international cafés and surf schools on the coast. The local claim to fame is honey: there's a festival in May and plenty of roadside honey stalls on the road from the coast. If you stop and ask, someone will

Anchor Point

Anchor Point at Taghazout is a wave of world renown. The relaxed Vee-Dub camper vibe of the 1970s may have gone – and expect the line-up to be packed every time the wave breaks – but the wave is the same. It still offers that big, green wall, those long, leg-aching rides and, at eight foot plus when the wave really comes into its own, a world-class challenge. Stretching north from the edge of Taghazout, this rocky ledge of a point leads out to the old anchor factory that gives the place its name. Don't expect many barrels, as this wave is all about big walls.

Boilers

This right-hander north of Taghazout, off the N1, is probably the most consistent point in the region and, while not exactly the longest, it certainly is a rewarding wave. Named after the huge ship's boiler that sits next to the peak, this spot is a great indicator reef and is clearly visible from the coast road. The main downside is the crowds and, at times, the line-up is packed and can get hassley.

Immessouane

The days of catching Immessouane to yourself are long gone, the line-ups are now crowded whenever the swell kicks in (and even when it doesn't) but this headland, about 30 km north of Taghazout, boasts at least three waves that will tempt you. The first has walls wrapping off the end of the rocky headland through to the inside of the bay. A few hundred metres to the south, a stark defensive wall guards the harbour. Firing across in front, this second right is a hollow and powerful wave with a steep take-off that offers adrenaline-fuelled barrels. Inside the bay lies the most popular and longest of the three right-handers. It starts to break at the southern end of the harbour mouth and peels through to the beach at low tide. Suitable for all surfers, this excellent, long-walling wave breaks over sand and rocks.

Killer Point

The points around the Taghazout region all have a similar geological make-up. The flat rock reefs have a deposit of sand that builds up over them during the quiet of the summer and is then groomed by the season's early swells into long sandbars. Some years these can be epic, while in others a wave may not break at all. Killer Point is one such place: catch it good and you'll be rewarded with the best wave in the whole of the region, outclassing Anchor Point and all other contenders. At other times it will be sectiony, rippy and frustrating.

Panorama's

A real Jekyll and Hyde wave, this point break can be a speeding hollow gem, a slow frustrating wall or a closeout, depending on the combination of swell, tide and sand banks. Catch it good and it can deliver some of the most exciting waves in the area. If Anchor Point is firing, Panorama's should be too, which helps keep crowds down. It's a low-tide break, where barrel after barrel spins off the point, but it's not for the faint-hearted. A rip pushes away from the take-off point by the apartments and a difficult, steep take-off leads into a fast, driving section.

probably be happy to show you their hives. Thursday's market is a bustling local affair, with the village filled with sellers of meat, homemade metal buckets and plastic furniture. Immouzer's most famous sight, however, is its seasonal waterfall, impressive in spring after a wet winter and worth a visit at other times for its extraordinary limestone rock formations. This is an arid region and, generally, the water is used, more prosaically, for irrigation. To reach the foot of the waterfalls, located below the village, turn left in the main square (signposted) and descend for 4 km. There's a car park from where you can walk the five minutes through olive groves to the foot of the falls. The falls are popular for both sightseeing and swimming; there are pools where the water has gouged out deep holes into which daredevil divers plunge from rocks high above. Immouzer is also a good place for birdwatching and walking.

MOVING ON
To Taroudant

From Immouzer, it's a three-hour drive to Taroudant, see page 78.

WHERE TO STAY

Taghazout

Surf Maroc, Moroccan Surf Adventures, Surf Berbere and Dfrost are among the Taghazout outfits offering organized surfing with accommodation included. All encourage package stays of a week or more together with lessons but they also accept bookings for shorter stays, and there's no obligation to surf. It's a competitive market and you get much more for your money than in Agadir, plus a friendly, international and communal vibe. All the above companies also have, or can organize, good apartments for rent. Some surfers rent rooms from local families; you can get good prices, but don't expect too much in the way of facilities and check on security.

€€€ Villa Amouar, www.surfmaroc.com. Still being built at the time of writing, this promises to take the successful, British-run Surf Maroc model and elevate it, with more space and a boutique feel. Recycled vintage furniture mixed with contemporary touches and abstract art should create a posh surf vibe. All rooms will have big en suite bathrooms and most will come with sea views and private terraces. There's a great pool looking out onto the sea with a sunken bar next door. Touches, such as outdoor showers attached to the trees, will up the cool quotient and it promises to become a seriously chic place to stay.

€€ Dfrost Surf House Villa, T0528-200522, www.dfrostsurfmorocco.nl. A friendly, Dutch-run, surf-centred operation near Hash Point, at Taghazout's northern end. The villa's great terrace has a hot tub and good views of the surf. The 7 rooms range from shared dorms to 'premium double'. There's a good breakfast and optional home-cooked evening meals too, plus a big cinema screen and daily roof-terrace yoga classes. A barbecue is served every Sun night. The company also has various apartments

for rent nearby. The website has some of the best information on the surfing conditions in the Taghazout area. Minimum 3-night stay; weekly deals available.

€€ Surf Camp, Tamraght, T0528-314874, www.morocsurf.com. Moroccan Surf Adventures' purpose-built accommodation is in Tamraght, 2 km down the coast from Taghazout. There's a new terrace, complete with hammock, a restaurant and simple, clean, comfortable rooms.

€€ Taghazout Surf Camp, T0528-200290, www.surfberbere.com. The Surf Berbere team emphasize local culture and organize trips for flat days. Their surf camp is on 4 levels at Hash Point, right next to the sea with a big roof terrace and sunset yoga.

€€ Taghazout Villa, www.surfmaroc.co.uk. The 2 communal terraces both have great views straight out to sea and along the coast to Anchors. There's a very friendly communal vibe, and a slightly more upmarket feel than at the Auberge (see below). Rooms are simple but comfortable and attractively decorated, with a combination of dorms and doubles. Evening meals are taken all together on wooden tables after home-made dips are served. There's Wi-Fi, a constant supply of fruit, and an honesty fridge for drinks and chocolate. For the surfing, Surf Maroc offer plenty of serious expertise and kit.

€€ Villa Mandala, www.surfmaroc.co.uk. Yoga and surf make good bedfellows in this spacious villa in a quiet (if a little isolated) spot near the sea in Aouir, run by Surf Maroc. There's plenty of communal space, a small pool, a hammam and everyone eats together in a beautifully decorated and sunny room. There's a more homely, feminine vibe than in the Taghazout Villa, with bougainvillea and rooms beautifully decorated with splashes of colour and plenty of Moroccan touches: fabrics, cushions, rugs and mirrors. Free Wi-Fi and a spectacular yoga space on the roof with views of Banana Beach.

€ Auberge, www.surfmaroc.co.uk. Right in the heart of Taghazout, on the town's beach, this friendly and great-value place is the nearest thing around to a conventional hotel. Above the ground-floor restaurant and café are 11 compact but nicely decorated rooms in colourful seaside tones with photos on the walls and blue slatted shutters. There's a great traveller atmosphere and terraces that overlook the fishing boats and the sea below. On Thu guests from all **Surf Maroc**'s accommodation gather for a barbecue.

Immouzer des Ida Outanane

€€ Hotel des Cascades, T0528-826016. A slightly dated hotel in an extraordinary location, with 27 en suite rooms, with terraces or balconies. There's good French-Moroccan food in the restaurant, a bar, a tennis court, a pool lined with pomegranate and pear trees, and a beautiful tiered garden of fruit and olive trees located above the seasonal waterfalls. Lunch on the shaded terrace with wonderful views of the mountains is a popular option.

Camping is possible near the **Café de Miel** near the foot of the cascades.

RESTAURANTS

Taghazout

As well as the restaurants and cafés below, there are fried fish stalls in the market next to the buses at the southern end of town.

€ Aftas, Taghazout beach. Opposite the **Auberge**, down on the beach, this place has drinks and sandwiches and good Moroccan food. Stools outside on the street are good viewpoints from which to watch Taghazout go by.

€ Auberge, Taghazout beach. The buzzing restaurant of Taghazout's hotel is the heart of international traveller life in town, offering good post-surfing food and excellent banoffee pie. Managing to be both funky and romantic, it has a greenery-covered terrace and candles, with views of the beach, though outside it can also be distinctly smelly. Inside there's a colourful bar with a big screen. The food is an international mix of pizzas, curries, fried fish, burgers and tagines.

€ Banana Beach, Km 14 near Tamraght. This chilled beach café has a volleyball court and sun-loungers and serves beer; an excellent place to relax for an afternoon.

€ Le New Port, T0613-411845. The best option along Taghazout's main street, this French-owned (and English-speaking) place offers a mix of European and Moroccan food. The fried fish is good, served with generous portions of beans and rice, and there are tagines too. The terrace gives good views of the street and the mosque. Service can be slow.

€ Le Spot. Good pizzas and fast food on the main street.

€ Tamazirt, just up the hill from the **Auberge**, this little café sells good smoothies and granola.

Immouzer des Ida Outanane

The **Hotel des Cascades** (see Where to stay, above) has the town's best restaurant.

€ La Belle Vallée, Km 33.5, Rte de Miel, T070-379642. On a bend in the road to Immouzer next to a tree-fringed stream, this little café-restaurant knocks up great food on request: delicious omelettes and one of the best Moroccan salads you'll find anywhere, served with warm bread. If you fancy staying around here, the Auberge Bab Immouzer, 3 km down the road, has a pool and good views.

TAFRAOUTE AND AROUND

Located 1200 m up in a natural Anti-Atlas amphitheatre near the Ameln Valley, Tafraoute is a rewarding town for climbers, walkers, mountain bikers and those who just want to chill in a spectacular mountain setting. Winter and early spring are good times to visit, when the almond trees are in blossom (usually late January and early February) and the pink and ochre boulders contrast with the sharp green of the early barley and palms in the small oases. To match the colour scheme, even the village houses are painted pink. There are rewarding and easily organized excursions to see canyons and prehistoric art, but it's the rocks that dominate – strangely beautiful and often awesomely large, they were shaped in the distant past to look like enormous Henry Moore sculptures.

→ TAFRAOUTE

With a population of about 4000, the village is the administrative centre for a large surrounding area. There is an almond festival here, the **Fête des Amandiers**, in January and February, with music and dance, and a market on Wednesday, which brings in large numbers of people from the surrounding villages. There are stalls making and selling a variety of crafts, in particular *babouches* (traditional shoes), which are a local speciality – you'll find varieties here that are rare in Marrakech.

ARRIVING IN TAFRAOUTE
Southwest out of Taroudant, cross over the N10 on the P1714 before branching left on the long straight road to Imi Mqourn. After this, the land rises and the road climbs towards towards Aït Baha. Driving here requires concentration, as stretches of the narrow winding road need repair after damage by heavy rain. Aït Baha, 95 km from Tafraoute, has a basic hotel and a souk on Wednesday. There are one or two small villages, such as Hadz Aït Mezzal, and abandoned houses high up the slopes. As the road swings over the cols, there are good views. The landscape grows increasingly other-wordly, with the strata of the hills and mountains waving across the landscape. Fifty kilometres from Tafraoute the R105 passes the extraordinary Kasbah Tizourgane, which is well worth a visit (see page 125). After the Tizi-n-Taraktine pass (1500 m) you sweep down into the Ameln Valley (see below).

MOVING ON
There are three buses a day (2½ hours) to Tiznit (see page 129), especially in the morning. Shared taxis (two hours) are also frequent.

→ VALLEE DES AMELN

The Valley of Almonds' is scattered with villages in between areas of irrigated agriculture, producing argan oil and almonds. The north side of the valley is walled off by an enormous expanse of rock, much loved by climbers. The majority of the villages are precariously positioned on the south-facing slopes of Jbel el Kest. Older stone and *pisé* buildings, generally higher up above the agricultural land where springs emerge from the mountainside, are crumbling. Newer buildings are made using reinforced concrete, with dark red rendering picked out in white. The Vallée des Ameln is best explored on foot or mountain bike. PTT has mountain bikes for rent.

From Tafraoute, the valley makes an excellent day's walk. You can take a guide for this but, as long as you have a map, it shouldn't be necessary. Head northwest out of town between the cemetery and the campsite and you will find that paths converge over a col between two rocky outcrops. From here the path descends steeply into the valley below.

Once in the valley itself, paths to the north of the road connect the various villages. The best way back is southeast from **Azrou Ouadou**, over some dramatic high plateaus and along rocky paths. The paths coming back tend to peter out but, as long as you keep heading southeast, Tafraout will eventually come into view. Allow five or six hours for the walk.

Adaï, 3 km southwest on the Tiznit road, is particularly picturesque. The rock formations caused by weathering and reminiscent of onion rings are most unusual. Other villages, either on the road like **Taguenza** or high up to the left like **Annameur**, are also worth a visit. It is more interesting to walk the upper track (a distance of around 7 km) that connects these villages. **Oumesnate** is another popular stop, as there is a traditional house here open to visitors. The French-speaking blind owner does a guided tour.

→ AROUND TAFRAOUTE

NAPOLEON'S HAT AND THE PAINTED ROCKS

To the south of Tafraoute, just 3 km on the new road to Tiznit, is **Agard Oudad**, an interesting village built below a rock referred to as *le chapeau de Napoléon*. From here you can walk or cycle west to see the local artistic landscape, *les pierres bleues*. These are rocks and mountainsides, painted in various colours by the Belgian landscape artist Jean Vérame, known for his massive-scale art projects. Now faded and a little shabby, it's questionable whether the rocks are an enhancement to the landscape, or an act of environmental vandalism.

GORGE AIT MANSOUR

About 15 km south of Tafraoute, the gorges of Aït Mansour have birdsong and palms, with glimpses of towering pink rocks through the branches. This is a great spot for a peaceful walk alongside the water, passing people collecting dates.

In **Tizght**, **Chez Massaoud** café (T0528-801245) makes a good resting point, and there is a fruit stall opposite. You can even stay overnight here if you wish.

PREHISTORIC CARVINGS

Another 15 km or so south of the gorges, the landscape opens up into wide, dry, stony, flat-bottomed valleys, almost entirely empty but for the occasional nomadic encampment. There are some excellent prehistoric rock engravings at **Ukas**. You'll probably need a guide to find them, and a willingness to clamber up some rocks, but the beautiful animal and human figures are well worth the effort.

KASBAH TIZOURGANE

Around 50 km north from Tafroute on the Agadir road, the extraordinary **Kasbah Tizourgane** ① *T0661-941350, www.tizourgane-kasbah.com, 20dh*, rises high out of the surrounding landscape like an intricately decorated cake. The kasbah has been lovingly restored and is open to visitors, with paved paths winding among the dusty pink buildings and opening out to give amazing views of the romantically bleak, undulating surroundings. A part of the kasbah operates as a simple hotel (see below). Be patient for someone to come and open the entrance gate for you.

GOING FURTHER
Tata, Akka and prehistoric rock art

The main town of the Jbel Beni region, built alongside an oasis, the rose-pink houses of Tata focus on an arcaded main street and dusty market square. The place has the feel of a desert garrison outpost. There are banks, an ATM, a post office and basic café-restaurants. Fill your tank in Tata as service stations in this region can often run out of fuel.

A good half-day side trip from Tata is to the impressively large *ksar* of **Tazaght**. Just before Addis, and after a big village on your left, turn left (east) off the 7084 to Akka. Tazaght is just visible across several kilometres of gravelly plain traversed by tracks. Follow the piste and park up near the new pink mosque and walk around the ridge to the right. The oldest part of the village, largely stone-built, sits atop a rocky crest, while other sections closer to the cultivated area crumble back into the earth. Look out for the original mosque which has a massive whitewashed simplicity recalling the Almoravid *kouba* in Marrakech. You can clamber round the semi-ruined houses and walk down to the oasis. There seems to be no trace of the once large Jewish community of the *ksar*.

The region southwest of Tata is rich in prehistoric rock art. You will see overlapping images of elegant gazelles, other beasts, spirals and human feet, carved on large flat stones in the unlikeliest of locations – witness to the civilization resident here in a time before the desert. A good selection of sites can be covered in a long day's exploring, if you have your own vehicle. For those dependent on public transport, the excellent site of **Adrar Metgourine** can be reached from Akka (70 km southwest of Tata) on foot. If you want to stay overnight here, there is one inexpensive hotel, **Tamdoult**, on the main road, but it's pretty grotty. Akka also has cafés and shops, with souks on Thursday and Sunday.

The best guide to rock art in the area is **Mouloud Taâret**, T0662-291864 (mob). He lives in **Douar Touzounine**, a roadside settlement a few kilometres south of Akka, handy for the rock-art site of **Tamdoult**. He also has a base in **Oum el Aleg**, a village south of the main road a few kilometres east of Akka. A guide is essential if you want to find the best of the carvings. They tend to be on flat boulders on low ridges which run parallel to the 7084 road. You may also see open-air sites where neolithic people worked flints. These tend to be more visible after winter rain. Watch out for snakes and wear good shoes.

Between Oum el Alek and Tata, there are two minor rock-art sites close to the 7084, **Oued Meskaou** (on your left, coming from Tata) and **Aman Ighriben** (on your right). The better of the two is Oued Meskaou. From the Tata direction, look out for the Akka 24-km post which is just a few metres after the turn-off for the site. As you come from Akka, look out for the Taroudant 234-km post, also a sign for Oued Meskaou and the Commune Rurale de Tata. Turn off right between the concrete bollards. Park under the thorn trees near the gap between two ridges. The engravings are on the ridge tops, an interesting mix of smoothed and *piqueté* technique carvings, including some spirals. The chess-board designs, the so-called *bijoux berbères*, are probably recent nomad scratchings. Out in the distance, near a higher ridge line, is the oasis of **Ghans**, which has a *guelta* (pool) in rainy years.

Aman Ighriben is 12 km further on, 12.5 km from Akka. Turn off near the marker 259 km to Tiznit, 246 km to Taroudant. Coming from Tata, turn off right a couple of kilometres after the Guelmim 255-km marker, just before the white markers. You should park near the palm trees some 200 m from the road. The carvings are on a low (10 m high) stoney rise close to palms and thorn bushes. The site, probably because it is so accessible, is much deteriorated, although there are still some nice gazelles.

TAFRAOUTE AND AROUND LISTINGS

WHERE TO STAY

€€ Les Amandiers, T0528-800088, www.hotel-lesamandiers.com. Once a very smart establishment, located on a rock above the town, the **Amandiers** has good views and a pool but is looking a little tired around the edges these days. There are 60 plain rooms with a/c and satellite TV and a large restaurant and bar. Tour groups occasionally invade, otherwise it's a calm spot, popular with climbers.

€€ Saint' Antoine, T0528-801497, www.hotelsaintantoine-tafraout.com. This fairly contemporary hotel, with a 1980s feel, has a pool, a lift, room service, internet access, restaurant and a/c.

€ Salama, T0528-800026, www.hotelsalama.com. Plum in the town centre, the large pink **Salama** has comfortable modern rooms with a/c, en suite bathrooms, excellent showers and internet connections in rooms. They even do 24-hr room service, if occasionally reluctantly. The only possible downsides are the lack of heating for cold winter nights and the decidedly average café on the ground floor.

€ Tafraoute, Pl Moulay Rachid, T0528-800060. In the town centre near the petrol station. Hot water, simple rooms and friendly staff. Light and airy but on a noisy junction.

€ Tanger, T0528-800190. Close to the bridge, this place has 9 small rooms and a plain roof terrace with a washing line. It's a basic place with shared showers, but has friendly staff and good food.

Camping

Camping Les Trois Palmiers, 15 mins' walk out of town, along the Tiznit road, T0666-098403. A small site reasonably equipped and with a café. Popular with motor caravaners. Also has a few rooms for rent.

Around Tafraoute

€€ Kasbah Tizourgane, T0661-941350, www.tizourgane-kasbah.com. Part of the restored kasbah operates as a simple hotel. Half or full board, it makes a stunning, if isolated place to stay.

€€ Kerdous, about 35 km out of town on the Tafraout–Tiznit road (54 km from Tiznit), T0528-862063, www.hotel-kerdous.com. This is in a spectacular spot with great views of the surrounding mountains. 39 rooms, pool, a/c, telephone, TV, restaurant, 2 bars, panoramic terrace, shop and secure parking.

RESTAURANTS

€€ Chez Sabir, Rue d'Amelne, T0528-800636. The chef who runs this atmospheric place is married to an English author and it closes in summer when they decamp to Cornwall. Worth seeking out for its superior Moroccan cuisine, using the best local ingredients.

€€ Hotel Les Amandiers (see Where to stay, above). This has a large restaurant and the only bar in town. The contrast of the white-jacketed waiters and the echoing school dinner hall atmosphere is striking but you'll get good traditional Moroccan food and there's wine too, should you wish. Functional rather than atmospheric.

€€ La Kasbah, Rte Agard Oudad, T0528-800536, T072-303909. About 5-mins' walk out of the centre, **La Kasbah** gets little passing traffic but deserves to be busier, with excellent quality Moroccan food. The tasty *kalia*, a spicy meat, tomato and onion dish with beaten egg on top, is a speciality. Wine available on request.

€ Marrakech, this popular local spot just up from the bus stop has few frills but does good traditional Moroccan food and makes a good lunch stop.

Cafés and bakeries
Café Étoile d'Agadir, with tables outside on one of the main squares, where it catches the morning sun, this is the town's best spot for breakfast. It also does a fine line in smoothies and juices. Lunch and dinner menus for 40dh and 75dh respectively.

Boulangerie Artisanal, between the mock-Berber towers just over the bridge and past the market stalls, it would be easy to miss this subterranean baker who has built a traditional oven where the bread cooks on hot pebbles. If you ask he'll let you go in and have a look. The crusty white loaves, with a subtle aniseed flavor, are a good cut or two above the usual Moroccan fare.

SHOPPING

Stalls in the small souk around the market square specialize in local *babouches* (Moroccan shoes), some of which are in styles not usually found in Marrakech.

Maison du Troc, 155 Rte Amiane, T0528-820536. Locally made carpets and rugs, this is also a good place to get information or guides for walks and climbing.

WHAT TO DO

Climbing
If you're interested in climbing, Claude Davies' Cicerone book, *Climbing in the Moroccan Anti-Atlas*, is highly recommended. The climbing scene in Tafraoute is still relatively young and you may be able to find some good undocumented routes. **Hotel les Amandiers** (see Where to stay, above) has Davies' new routes log book.

Cycling
Said Oussid, opposite **Maison Touareg**, on the **Hotel les Amandiers** road, T070-409384. Has a good selection of mountain bikes for hire. 50dh a day for basic models up to 100dh a day for specialized bikes.

Swimming
You can use the pool at the **Hotel les Amandiers** for a small fee.

Tour operators and guides
Tafraout Aventure, T0528-801368, www.tafraout-aventure.com. Can arrange 4WD trips and trekking guides. They can also give you a map of the area should you want to strike out alone. A good day trip (300dh pp) goes to the Aït Mansour gorge for a walk and includes lunch before continuing to the prehistoric rock carvings in Ukas and returning via the Timguelchte gorges. Longer trips can also be arranged all the way to the coast or southeast into the desert.

Good local guides can be found at **Maison du Troc** (see Shopping, above), or ask for the well-connected, all-purpose fixer Houssine Laroussi (T0661-627921), who has a tiny shop, **Coin Nomade**, on the corner of the market square and can provide maps, advice and guidebooks from his piles on the floor.
Brahim Bahou, T06618-22677, brahim-izanzaran@hotmail.com. Brahim is an official Guide de Montagne. He speaks English and has a small office with maps and porters. Prices start at 300dh for a 4-hr trek.

SOUTH OF AGADIR

Along the coast south of Agadir, Morocco's landscapes become increasingly barren, the hills and mountains of the interior subsiding into the desert. Tiznit, 90 km south of Agadir and a transport junction for routes south, has a seldom-visited walled centre and a jewellery souk. Out on the coast, Mirleft and Sidi Ifni have the added advantages of spectacular coastline. Sidi Ifni was an outpost of Spain until well into the 20th century; now its white colonial architecture is crumbling. Mirleft, by contrast, seems like a place of the future; championed by a handful of enthusiastic young French and British hotel and restaurant owners, it is a bastion of hip. And between and around the two towns are plenty of excellent beaches.

→TIZNIT AND AROUND

Tiznit, seemingly ancient, and famed for its great red-ochre *pisé* walls, is, in fact, barely 100 years old. Although the town does not have much to offer in the way of sights, it's well worth a wander around after an overnight stop. The once-famed Source Bleue, the Blue Spring, close to the Great Mosque, is stagnant green today but the shopping is excellent: the quality of silverwork in the Souk des Bijoutiers is high and Rue Imzlin has some great shoe workshops. Tiznit is a laid-back and unexpectedly attractive town with very few tourists.

ARRIVING IN TIZNIT

Getting there Coming in by bus you get off near Place du Mechouar, the central square. Most grands taxis stop on nearby Boulevard Mohammed V, opposite the post office. Most of the cheap hotels are situated close by.

Moving on Mirleft (see page 131) is an easy half-hour in a shared taxi.

Getting around Tiznit is a small place, easily explored on foot. You may, however, wish to go to the beach near Sidi Moussa d'Aglou, 17 km out of town, where there are some cave dwellings. Grands taxis from Avenue Hassan II run out to Aglou village, and the coast is a couple of kilometres further on. **Syndicat d'Initiative** ① *T0528-869199.*

BACKGROUND

One theory is that Tiznit derives its name from Lalla Zninia, a woman of dubious morals, whose repentance here was supposedly rewarded by God creating the blue spring, or the Source Bleu de Lalla Tiznit. The main town was established in 1882 by the great reforming sultan Moulay Hassan (1873-1894), part of a general policy of strengthening the Alaouite Dynasty's authority in the south. He had a number of separate *ksar* enclosed within the 5 km of walls. There are 36 towers and, although there are eight gates in all, the three most important are Bab Ait Jarrar, Bab Jadid and Bab Laaouina – a later addition by the French.

It was at Tiznit that El Hiba had himself proclaimed sultan in 1912, challenging the French who were extending their power. In 1912, the French already controlled northeastern Morocco, the Chaouia and Casablanca. El Hiba, acting on the same basis of uniting the Muslims of Morocco to resist the infidel, organized southern resistance, declaring himself defender of the faith. A powerful confederacy seemed to be emerging, and El Hiba entered

Marrakech in August 1912 unchallenged. The adventure ended in September, however, when French troops under Colonel Mangin stormed the city, outgunning El Hiba's forces.

PLACES IN TIZNIT

The open-air **souk** is on Bab Ait Jarrar, main days Thursday and Friday. Along Rue de l'Hôpital from the square is the **Grand Mosque**. The minaret has distinctive protruding wooden perches; the story is that these are to assist the dead as they climb to paradise; they probably also had a more prosaic function in the construction of the tower. Adjacent to the mosque is the **Source Bleue de Lalla Tiznit**, named after the town's saint, a reformed prostitute: where she died a spring appeared. Steps lead down to a large square pool but these days the water is a lurid shade of stagnant green. The town's walls are its other main attraction, and you can walk around the inside of most of the 3-km perimeter, along quiet dusty streets where children play football, men stand and chat and women scurry home with shopping. There are two religious **festivals** in Tiznit in August: the Moussem of Sidi Abderrahman, and the acrobat's Moussem of Sidi Ahmed ou Moussa, a village some 50 km away in the Tafraoute direction. On the Sidi Moussa/Sidi Ifni junction, the new **mosque**, buff with green tiles and a green cupola, is a distinctive landmark.

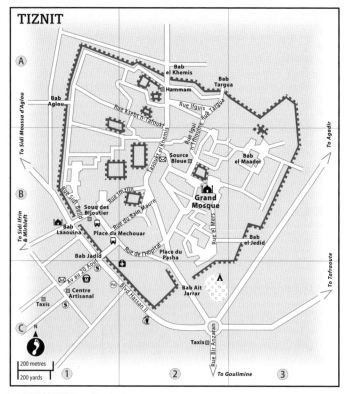

AROUND TIZNIT

The nearest beaches (be careful bathing and aware of the Atlantic's strong undertow) are at **Sidi Moussa d'Aglou**, 17 km northwest of Tiznit. In winter, the beach is deserted apart from a few surfers and well organized people in camper vans. In summer, however, the place gets crowded, mainly with locals camping out. New homes are being built and there are some seasonal restaurants. From Aglou, you can take a track some 4 km along the beach to reach a fishing village, after which there is a small troglodyte community. The campsite opens only in summer. Exceptionally cheap, it is none too secure. As well as good food, the **Café-Restaurant Ouazize** has rooms.

The **Oued Massa nature reserve** (see page 133) is also easily accessible. Off the Sidi Ifni road, the **Domaine de Khenfouf** (T0661-657566, www.khenfouf.com) is an artisan, organic cooperative that opens to the public every Saturday and sells argan products and embroidery. If you're interested in exploring the local area, **Bab el Maader** is a great source of information and maps.

MIRLEFT AND AROUND

Until very recently Mirleft barely qualified as a one-horse village. Now, however, a stroll down its dusty street reveals a hive of activity as hip young Europeans create an enclave of laid-back bars and restaurants and cheap-yet-groovy hotels. Buoyed by the presence of surfers and paragliders, who come for the great beaches and the updrafts, and many others who come to hang out in the great year-round climate, Mirleft is very clearly a place on the up.

This was once the border between Morocco and Spanish Sidi Ifni. You can climb to old **fortifications** on the hill above the village, and longer walks are possible into the hills behind. There's also a Monday **market** and a handful of interesting shops but, otherwise, the attractions are the beaches and the waves.

The centre of Mirleft is set back 1 km or so from the coast, on the eastern side of the road but it just about joins up with **Les Amicales**, clustered on the clifftop overlooking **Imin Tourga beach**, the best local spot for swimming. Due west of the centre of Mirleft (cross over the main road by the bus stop and head straight down the hill through the houses) is the small but beautiful **Aftas Plage**, with a cluster of new cafés and restaurants. Further south, but still just about within walking distance, are the larger bays of **Plage Sidi Mohamed Ben Abdallah** (also known as Marabou) and **Plage Sauvage**, and **Sidi Ouafi**, the latter being the best surfing spot. At 10 km before Sidi Ifni is the beach of **Legzira**, famous for its spectacular natural rock bridge that curves over the sand. Popular with surfers, it has a couple of beachside hotels and restaurants.

→SIDI IFNI AND AROUND

One of the most unlikely towns in Morocco, Sidi Ifni was, until 1969, Spanish territory and known principally to stamp collectors. Today, for much of the year, it is a quiet port town with a distinctive Iberian feel and some unusual buildings in the art deco/neo-kasbah vein, many of them beginning to crumble. Surfers have a number of spots nearby, while camper vans line the town beach in winter, escaping the cold weather further north. In July and August, Sidi Ifni fills up with returning migrant workers and occasional sea mist. Though it can feel like more of a ghost town than its upwardly mobile neighbour Mirleft, there are early signs of European money also arriving in Sidi Ifni, and there is an increasing choice of good places to stay and eat.

BACKGROUND

Sidi Ifni was occupied by the Spanish from 1476 to 1524 and, again from 1860, as a consequence of the Treaty of Tetouan. The town was always an enclave, surrounded by Morocco from 1860 to 1912 and from 1956 to 1969, and between 1912 and 1956 by the French protectorate. The town had a port and an airstrip, and a role as a duty free zone. The economic survival of the town was based on the fact that the border was open to trade. In the 1960s Morocco grew tired of the continuing Spanish presence and forced Spain into negotiations from 1966. The enclave was returned in 1969.

PLACES IN SIDI IFNI

Sidi Ifni is much bigger on atmosphere than sights. **Place Hassan II**, still commonly referred to as Plaza de España, is the centre of the town. Around it are buildings with a

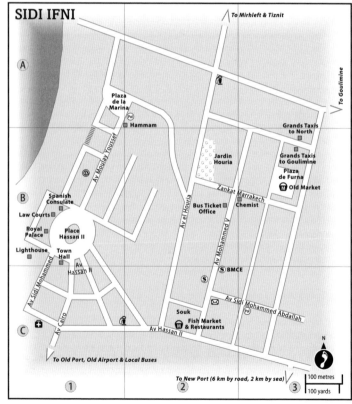

SIDI IFNI

To Mirhleft & Tiznit

To Goulimine

A

Plaza de la Marina

Pol

Hammam

Jardin Houria

Grands Taxis to North

Grands Taxis to Goulimine

Plaza de Furna

Old Market

Av Moulay Youssef

Zankat Marrakech

B

Spanish Consulate

Law Courts

Royal Palace

Place Hassan II

Lighthouse

Town Hall

Av Hassan II

Av el Houria

Bus Ticket Office

Chemist

Av Mohammed V

BMCE

Av Sidi Mohammed

Av Cairo

Souk

Fish Market & Restaurants

Av Sidi Mohammed Abdallah

Pol

C

Av Hassan II

To Old Port, Old Airport & Local Buses

To New Port (6 km by road, 2 km by sea)

N

100 metres
100 yards

1   2   3

1930s feel: running clockwise as you face the **Hotel Belle Vue** are the former church, now home to the law courts, the very faded Spanish consulate (open one day a month), the town hall, and the discreet Royal Palace. Past the palace and behind the police villa is an attractive lighthouse with neo-Moorish detailing. Past the hospital and campsite is a new housing development, with the aerodrome on your left. From here you can drop down to the beach and the port. Offshore, the massive concrete structure was once linked to the mainland by cable. Ships would moor here and everything would be hoisted ashore.

There's a **fish market** at the top of town, which quickly turns from soporific to lively once the catch comes in, usually around 1600-2000. The weekly **market** is held on Sunday on the old airfield. Sidi Ifni hosts a large **moussem** in June. At low tide it's possible to walk north along the shore to the local saint's **tomb** or *koubba*.

→ SIDI IFNI TO AGADIR

OUED MASSA NATURE RESERVE

ⓘ *Ignore any faux guides at the entrance to the park telling you that you have to pay a fee. At Issoh you may find fishermen in the caves who will cook you up some of their catch.*

From Sidi Ifni it's a three-hour drive back up the coast to Agadir. Off the Agadir road from Tiznit, take the left turn marked to Sidi Rbat. The road surface stops very suddenly, turning into sandy track over open farmland. Depending on your vehicle, you may have to cover the last few kilometres to the reserve on foot.

Held back by large sandbanks, the waters of the Oued Massa have formed a lagoon. The vast reed beds, the massive fringing dunes to the southwest, sandbanks at the mouth of the river, the water course itself and the mud banks to the north provide a home to both birds and mammals. Visit between February and April, or between September and November when there are over-wintering birds. The estuary can be home to crane, avocet, spoonbill, great flamingo, osprey, and night, squacco and purple heron. One of the few surviving groups of the endangered bald ibis live here; the other main site is north of Agadir at Tidzi. Several kinds of raptor are attracted by the populations of other birds, including small groups of ospreys.

About 5 km west of the transport hub of Inezgane, just south of Agadir is the mouth of the **Oued Souss**, an important place for birdwatchers. The best visiting times are February to April and September to November, when many varieties of gulls and terns are in residence. The surrounding area has more colourful birds, including the black-headed bush shrike, the great grey shrike, brown-throated sand martin and De Moussier's redstart.

MOVING ON
To Marrakech

From Agadir it's 250 km (about three hours) to Marrakech via the A7 superhighway for the final three days of this trip. See pages 35-62.

WHERE TO STAY

Tiznit

Budget travellers have a range of options near the Pl du Mechouar; a handful of smarter places have sprung up in the medina in recent years.

€€ **Bab El Maader**, 132 Rue El Haj Ali, T0673-907314, www.bab-el-maader.com. A homely guesthouse run by a French couple, Michèle and Yann, in a quiet part of town. All on the ground level, stylish rooms have plenty of carefully selected Moroccan details, and there's a courtyard with red ochre *tadelakt* seats. The owners are real enthusiasts for the area and a mine of good information and maps.

€€ **Maison du Soleil**, 470 Rue Tafoukt, T0676-360387, www.maison-du-soleil.com. Traditional Moroccan touches – fabrics, tiles, *tadelakt* – elevate this little guesthouse beyond the ordinary. Rooms at the top of the house are lighter, and there's a great roof terrace, where breakfast is served. The owners don't live here, however, and it doesn't feel as homely as the other riads in town.

€€ **Riad Janoub**, 193 Rue de la Grande Mosquée, T0679-005510, www.riadjanoub.com. Immaculately decorated, this is a new building constructed in traditional Moroccan style, albeit on a bigger scale than most. Large rooms on 2 floors around a pool are individually decorated, with pale walls and contrasting fabrics. They have their own water supply and solar heating. An extensive top terrace has cushions and sunbeds, and there's a small Berber tent and a barrel-vaulted hammam and massage room.

€ **Hotel des Touristes**, 80 Pl El Mechouar, T0528-862018. Clean and bright, with 12 small rooms and 24-hr hot showers. Probably the best budget bet in town.

€ **Riad Le Lieu**, 273 impasse Issaoui, T0528-600019, www.riad-le-lieu.com. Very good value, this riad, on a side-street off Rue Imzilin in the centre of Tiznit, also has a fantastic restaurant and a *salon du thé*. Elegant rooms are decorated in pale, romantic tones: white and silver predominate. There's free Wi-Fi and French newspapers. On the roof, the terrace has a Moroccan tent that can be used for dining or sleeping. 2 rooms have private terraces.

Mirleft and around

€€€ **Kasbah Tabelkoukt**, T0528-719395, T0661-582749 (mob), www.kasbah-tabelkoukt.com. 7 themed, spacious and elegant bedrooms, beautiful tiled bathrooms, sea views and an infinity pool are the highlights of this smart place 4 km south of Mirleft. Rooms are individually themed. Separate from the main building, stone houses give more independence and are a good mix of tradition and modernity.

€€€ **Dar Najmat**, Plage Sidi Mohammed Ben Abdallah, T0528-719056, www.darnajmat.com. 2 km south of Mirleft at Marabout Beach, this is a mellow spot where you'll hear little other than the crashing of the Atlantic waves. It has beautiful rooms and a pool that looks right onto the beach. Decorated in white, greys and sandy shades with dark wood, there are antique touches too, such as the spectacular front door. Restaurant, and half board comes as standard.

€€€ **Les 3 Chameaux**, T0528-719187, T0666-548579, www.3chameaux.com. Bringing the style of a French country house to the hill high above Mirleft, the **Three Camels** has 12 suites and 10 rooms of old-school colonial elegance. There's an international library, a swimming pool, with great views north over the hills, and ancient tiled floors. Airport transfer from Agadir 250dh.

€€ **Aftas Beach Guest House**, Aftas Beach, T0528-719540. A chilled little

English-run place right on the beach at Aftas Plage, this has a great colourful salon, with a traveller/ surf vibe, good beach café food and some fabulous quirky details. There's Wi-Fi too, and a hotel laptop. Rooms are comfortable but small and rather plain for the price.

€€ Riad de l'Oasis, T0528-719347, T0661-231677 (mob), www.mirleft-tourismir.com. Near the beach in Les Amicales, this riad has a turquoise pool surrounded by dusty pink walls and tiled rooms with draped beds. The roof terrace has an open grill as well as comfy seats. The owners have other properties, including 2 villas for rent.

€€ Sally's B&B, Les Amicales, T0528-719402, T0661-469888 (mob), www.sally mirleft.com. This high-quality English B&B is on the edge of the cliff in Les Amicales, Mirleft's coastal satellite. Sally herself is a friendly, talkative host, who will happily cook full English breakfasts. Beds are big and comfortable, and there are stunning, vertiginous views over the waves and the beach below. From the roof terrace the views are even better, and there's a stylish self-contained studio with its own terrace and a barbecue.

€€ Un Thé Au Bout Du Monde, T0661-975742, www.untheauboutdumonde.com. 5 mins' drive up the coast north of Mirleft, this new place is beautifully put together, if a little isolated. Rooms and apartments are in 5 separate low-rise buildings in immaculate gardens. There's a good pool and a well-regarded café-restaurant that uses home-grown produce in its French and Moroccan dishes. Sea views, though the place itself is set back from the coast.

€ Abertih, T0528-719304, www.abertih. com. Upstairs, there are 11 simple but very clean rooms. Only 5 have en suite bathrooms, but the shared facilities are excellent. Downstairs, there's a very laid-back bar and restaurant (evenings only), decorated in warm reds and yellows and with free Wi-Fi. There are rugs and black

and white photographs, a good roof terrace with plants and candlesticks and occasional yoga sessions. The owner is a paragliding guide, and paragliding groups sometimes take the whole place over, usually in Nov and Mar.

€ Atlas-Mirleft, T0528-719309, www. atlas-mirleft.com. Pink walls, comfy chairs and atmospheric low lighting set the tone for this café-restaurant and hotel on Mirleft's main street. Ownership has changed twice in recent years but the model remains the same: 9 rooms are straightforward and carefully decorated with fabrics and complementary colours. There's a great roof terrace with a grill and a tent in summer. The restaurant serves good French food. Good-value rates include breakfast with unlimited drinks.

Sidi Ifni and around
See www.ifniriad.com for villas that can be rented in and around Sidi Ifni.

€€ Xanadu, 5 Rue el Jadida, T0528-876718, www.maisonxanadu.com. Warm pink tones, cosy rooms and a roof terrace with views.

€ Belle Vue, 9 Pl Hassan II, T0528-875072. In an old building on the main square, the Belle Vue has sea views and a good terrace restaurant and bar. Wi-Fi in some areas and an alcohol licence.

€ Residence Sidi Ifni, 4 Av My Abdellah, T0528-876776. Above café-restaurant **La Barandilla** are spacious, cosy, en suite apartments, some with a sea view. The restaurant has a 70dh menu and there's a bar.

€ Suerte Loca, bottom of road leading from Pl Hassan II, T0528-875350. Multilingual, popular, friendly and overlooks the sea, though its rooms could do with some TLC. The café-restaurant has a pool table and excellent food in the evenings and at breakfast, when there are pancakes, juices and shakes on offer. Ask about small flats for rent.

The fishing village of Sidi Ouarsik, 17 km south of Sidi Ifni, is about 1 hr's drive from the town. There's cheap accommodation to rent – ask at **Hotel Suerte Loca**. You can get there by Landrover taxi from the grand taxi station in Sidi Ifni.

RESTAURANTS

Tiznit

€€ Riad Le Lieu, 273 impasse Issaoui, T0528 600019, www.riad-le-lieu.com. Daily lunch and dinner. Superbly good Moroccan-French food is served on lamp-lit tables in the courtyard of this central, 16th-century riad (see Where to stay, above). Flavour-filled dishes might include sardine tagine and a tomato and cheese millefeuille. Lots of fresh herbs are used, and you might even get some live piano-playing from the owner. The only downside might be the lack of an alcohol licence. Good enough to justify a visit to Tiznit just to eat here.

€ Hotel de Paris, Av Mohammed V, T0528-862865. Tagines, couscous and alcohol are all served on the ground floor of this hotel outside the city walls.

Mirleft and around

See Where to stay, above; most good places to eat in the centre of Mirleft (notably **Atlas** and **Abertih**) are also hotels.

€ Atrim, T0528-719352. A friendly, sophisticated family-run Italian restaurant in the middle of Mirleft, with candles, abstract art, black and white photos and a balcony overlooking the comings and going on the street below. The pasta is fresh and perfectly cooked; try the excellent ravioli with sage and butter. There's wine, too, and a very convivial, laid-back atmosphere.

€ Café Aftas, Aftas Beach, T0656-183762, www.cafeaftas.com. A popular German-run café-restaurant and surf school right on Aftas beach, with no electricity but plenty of candles. They'll cook up a tagine or couscous on demand and they can arrange accommodation too. Surf school **Chasseurs de Vagues** is also based here.

€ Café des Pecheurs, Aftas Beach. The only really Moroccan place at Aftas, and by far the longest standing ("since the hippies!"), offering good, simple dishes of fried fish.

€ Said Surf Café, Aftas Beach. As well as renting out boards and organizing trips to visit Said's mother's village in the hills, this little beach shack café does a good line in tagines, couscous and grilled fish. In the morning there are breakfasts too, with Moroccan crêpes and pancakes.

Sidi Ifni and around

In the market there are a cluster of cheap tagine stalls – depending on the catch, these may also offer grilled fish. **Suerte Loca** (see Where to stay, above) does excellent food and drinks all through the day.

€ Adou Art, opposite the Hotel de Ville, just off the main square. A chilled little café with comfy seats, cinema posters and photos.

€ Café Restaurant El Hourria, Av Hourria, T0528-876343. Moroccan and European food and drink in a modern setting at the bottom of town. The garden, with trees and flowers, is a good place for a sandwich.

€ Café Restaurant Mar Péqueña, 20 Av Elmowahidine. Excellent modern Moroccan food in a cosy little place near the seafront, with petal-scattered tables. Portions are huge; try the spicy octopus and vegetables.

€ Ocean Miramar, 3 Av Prince Moulay Abdellan, T0528-876637. Pizzas and good seafood served on a terrace overlooking the sea.

DREAM TRIP 3
Fès➔Desert➔Gorges➔Marrakech 21 days

Fès 4 nights, page 139

Meknès 2 nights, page 164
Train from Fès (1 hr)

Moulay Idriss and Volubilis en route,
pages 172 and 173
Day trip from Meknès

Azrou and Ifrane 1 night, pages 177
and 179
Car from Meknès (1¼ hrs)

Midelt 1 night, page 179
Car from Azrou (2 hrs)

Er Rachidia 1 night, page 184
Car from Midelt (2 hrs)

Merzouga 3 nights, page 188
Car from Er Rachidia (2 hrs)

Tineghir and Todra Gorge 2 nights,
pages 191 and 192
Car from Merzouga (2½ hrs)

Boumalne du Dadès and Dadès Gorge
2 nights, page 193
Car from Tineghir (1 hr)

Aït Benhaddou 1 night, page 70
Car from Boumalne du Dadès (2½ hrs)

Marrakech 4 nights, page 35
Car from Aït Benhaddou (4 hrs)
for flight home

GOING FURTHER

Taza page 158
Train from Fès (2 hrs)

DREAM TRIP 3
Fès➔Desert➔Gorges➔Marrakech

Fès is Morocco at its most mysterious. Coming straight from Europe, some suffer from culture shock when first exposed to its smells, its steep medieval streets and its apparent chaos. But get under its skin and it's a spectacular, magical place, especially once you're through its grand gates into the warren of its traffic-free medina. Nearby Meknès is more accessible, and has some impressive monuments from its past as the country's capital.

The Middle Atlas are a range of mountains also tinged with otherworldly flavours, their hazy blue contours and cedar forests hiding Barbary apes and pseudo-Alpine ski resorts.

Flecks and strips of fertility punctuate the south-facing slopes of the Atlas as they tilt down towards the barren Sahara, where the sand dunes of Erg Chebbi are a beautifully sculpted landscape of shifting shadows.

Skirting the furthest edge of the Atlas on the journey west, the route passes two slices cut into the rock, the Todra and Dadès gorges, where mountain springs and meltwater feed a narrowing strip of green at the base of rust-red cliffs. At the head of the gorges, their roads snake increasingly as they wind up through spectacularly tight defiles and out into the mountains.

Aït Benhaddou, especially if you can stay once the day trippers have gone, is a magical sandcastle of a kasbah and a restful spot in which to gather your energy for the hair-raising drive over the mountain pass of Tizi n'Tichka and down into Marrakech.

If the Atlas are the spine of the country, Marrakech is its heart. Behind its walls are exquisitely ornate riads, palaces, tombs and gardens, while the amazing energy and spectacle of its rambling square is a distillation and exaggeration of Morocco.

FES AND AROUND

Fès (also spelt Fez in English) is a fascinating city – perhaps as near to the Middle Ages as you can get in a couple of hours by air from Europe. It is not an easy city to get to know, but repays the time and effort spent on it. With three main sections, the city has numerous historic buildings, around the Qaraouiyine Mosque and some memorable souks. Fès is also a base from which to explore nearby regions: Bhalil and Sefrou to the south, the spa towns of Sidi Harazem and Moulay Yacoub, as well as sites further afield, such as the Middle Atlas resorts of Azrou and Ifrane. Also nearby is the other central Moroccan imperial city of Meknès, with Volubilis and Moulay Idriss close by.

→ ARRIVING IN FES

GETTING THERE

To get to town from the **Aéroport de Fès-Saïss**, 15 km south of the centre, take a grand taxi (150dh) or catch bus No 16. There are two bus stations: the main one is outside the city walls near Bab Mahrouk, while the **CTM** station is on Av Mohammed V in the town centre (Ville Nouvelle). If you come in from Taza and all points east, you will probably arrive at yet another bus terminus, at Bab Ftouh. The railway station is at the end of Boulevard Chenguit in the Ville Nouvelle, T0535-622501. To get to the Ville Nouvelle, head down this road and slightly to the left into Avenue de la Liberté; this joins Avenue Hassan II at Place de Florence.

MOVING ON

The train to Meknès (see page 164) takes one hour and is the most civillized way of moving on. There's often a morning train and then a long gap until a cluster of trains in the evening. Buses or shared taxis offer an alternative.

To get to Chefchaouen (see page 246) on Dream Trip 4, you can take a bus to Ouezzane (see page 245) and then take a grand taxi on to Chefchaouen (four hours).

ORIENTATION

Fès is spectacular, but not as immediately attractive as Marrakech. Unlike the capital of the South, a crossroads for caravans and peoples, Fès is more secretive, its old ways hidden behind the cliff-like walls of its alleyways. Its sights are not easily discovered and several days are really necessary to take in the city's atmosphere. Essentially, there are three main areas to visit: **Fès el Bali**, the oldest part of the city, a medina divided by the river into Adwa al Andalusiyin (the Andalucían quarter on the east bank) and Adwa al Qaraouiyine (the Qaraouiyine quarter on the west bank); **Fès el Jedid**, containing the royal palace and the mellah and founded under the Merinids (you need half a day); and the **Ville Nouvelle**, the city built by the French, which has taken over many of the political, administrative and commercial functions of old Fès. You'd be well advised to save some energy to get up to the Borj Nord/Merinid tombs for views across Fès el Bali at sundown. While Fès el Jedid is fairly flat, Fès el Bali has long sloping streets. In the winter it can rain heavily, turning Talaâ Sghira and Talaâ Kebira into minor torrents. That said, restoration in the old town continues apace (see box, page 141), with areas like the riverfront in r'Cif starting to look quite smart, and its appeal grows with every visit.

GETTING AROUND

Fès is a spread out sort of place, and distances are greater than they may at first seem, so look forward to some considerable hikes from one place to another or petit taxi rides. If you are based in a Ville Nouvelle hotel, you can get a taxi from the Place Mohammed V, or the main PTT on the Avenue Hassan II, or simply by flagging one down. Getting around the historic neighbourhoods of Fès, which divide into **Fès el Bali** (the Old) and **Fès el Jedid** (the New), is another matter. You will be dealing with a complex network of lanes and alleys and, in the case of Fès el Bali, much of it is pedestrianized anyway. If time is limited, it may be better to engage an official guide – rather than get lost and have (possibly unpleasant) dealings with an unofficial guide. From the tourist information office on Place de la Résistance in the Ville Nouvelle to Bab Boujeloud, effectively the beginning of Fès el Bali, is a 3-km trot. The train station is a similar distance from Fès el Bali; the CTM terminus roughly 4 km.

TOURIST INFORMATION

Office du Tourisme ① *Pl de la Résistance, T0535-623460.* Syndicat d'Initiative ① *Av Mohammed V, T0535-625301.*

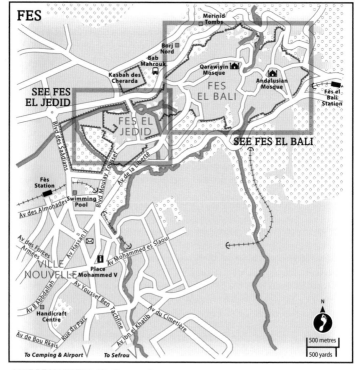

ON THE ROAD
Saving Fès

During the 20th century Fès was largely overshadowed by the growth of Rabat and Casablanca, even though many Fassi notables did well out of the protectorate – witness the palaces and splendid houses of the Ziat, Douh and Batha areas of the medina. The city declined in the post-independence period as the élite moved to the cities of the Atlantic coast, leaving their fine courtyard homes to the poorer members of the family or to rural immigrants. The money for the upkeep of large, ageing buildings has gone elsewhere and, today, much of the medina faces critical problems, not the least of which is the pollution of the Oued Fès and the Oued Sebou, along with the disintegration of the historic, but much decayed, drinking water network.

Today the crumbling houses of Old Fès are home to a poor population. Official figures give 35% of the old city's population as being under the poverty line, the figure rising to more than 40% in some areas. The ADER (Agence pour la dédensification et la réhabilitation de Fès) was set up to improve living conditions – to date with only limited success. With the houses regularly disintegrating after the winter rains, the ADER's main aim is to ensure that people are moved out of the most dangerous housing – so reducing the potential for street protests. In 1981, the city was added to the UNESCO World Heritage List. In the 1990s, the ADER began restoration works on a small number of gates and monuments and a special traditional building crafts training centre was established.

The scale of the problems of Fès is enormous, however. In 1985, UNESCO estimated that US$585 million was needed to save the old city. In 1995, the World Bank came up with US$14 million for infrastructure improvement and works finally got underway. More than 20 years after being listed, the medina continues to decay, with demolitions leading to gaps in the once dense urban fabric. There has been much controversy over the building of two roads into the centre, one leading to Talaâ Kebira and the other over the existing course of Oued Fès. Although some restoration projects seem to go on forever, private and foreign finance has been used to restore a number of buildings at the heart of Fès el Bali, including the Foundouq Najjarine (Fondation Lamrani) and Dar Adil (Italian foreign ministry). To really save Fès, official bodies like the Municipality, the ADER, the Urban Planning Agency and the Ministry of Culture will have to work more closely together. In particular, some sort of housing improvement loan policy will have to be created to persuade the often absent owners to invest in their historic property.

On a much more positive note, however, Fès now has a fast-increasing number of upmarket riads and some European-owned cafés and restaurants. This outside investment and the economic benefits that a flood of new visitors can bring, should help the old city survive.

→ BACKGROUND

SPIRITUAL CAPITAL

Fès has a highly strategic location. The city is situated in the Oued Sebou basin, astride the traditional trade route from the Sahara to the Mediterranean, as well as on the path from Algeria and the Islamic heartland beyond into Morocco. For centuries, the dominant axis within Morocco was between Fès and Marrakech, two cities linked by their immense power as well as by their rivalry. Even today, while the coastal belt centred on Rabat and

Casablanca dominates the country in demographic, political and economic terms, Fès continues to fascinate, for it has another characteristic, perhaps its dominant feature: Fès is a religious place and is felt to be the spiritual capital of Morocco. The word Fès in Arabic means axe – a possible reference to tools used in its construction.

The influence of a saintly person, the *baraka* or blessing of a protector, was felt to be essential for a Moroccan city in times gone by. Fès, founded by Idriss II, El Azhar, 'the Splendid', had its patron too, and the life of the city once gravitated around the cathedral-mosque where Moulay Idriss and his descendants are buried. In recent memory, the end of each summer saw great celebrations for the *moussem* of Moulay Idriss. The craftsmen's corporations would take part in great processions to the shrine of the city's founder; a sacrificial bull, horns and head decorated with henna the heart of every procession.

The people of Fès were deeply religious. Some early European writers saw the city as a great Mont-St-Michel, a prayer-saturated place with its mosques, *zaouïas* (sanctuaries) and oratories. Dr Edmond Secret, writing in the 1930s, said that "the majority do their five daily prayers. Draped in modesty in the enveloping folds of their cloaks, the bourgeois, prayer carpets under their arms, recall monks in their dignity." This air of religiosity still clings to the city, especially during Ramadan. And, on every night of the year, in the hours which precede the dawn, a time hard for those who are sick and in pain, a company of muezzins maintains a vigil in the minaret of the Andalucían Mosque, praying for those asleep and those awake.

INTELLECTUAL HERITAGE

The city's religious life was closely tied to education. "If learning was born in Medina, maintained in Mecca and milled in Egypt, then it was sieved in Fès," went the adage. In the early Middle Ages, it was a centre of cultural exchange. One Gerbert d'Aurillac, later to become Pope Sylvester II from 999 to 1003, studied in Fès in his youth and brought Arabic numerals back to Europe. Famous names to have studied or taught in Fès include Maimonides, the Jewish philosopher and doctor, Ibn' Arabi (died 1240) the mystic, Ibn Khaldoun (died 1282), and the mathematician, Ibn el Banna (died 1321).

Thus, Fès supplied the intellectual élite of the country, along with many of its leading merchants and craftsmen, and you will find Fassis (the people of Fès) in most towns and cities. They are rightly proud of their city; their self-confidence, verging at times on self-satisfaction, is a distinctive trait, making them rather different from most other Moroccans. Fès does not have the immediate friendliness of the villages, the mountains or the desert, but it is a city well worth spending time in – like it or not, it will not leave you indifferent. Driss Chraïbi, for one, in his 1954 breakthrough novel *Le Passé Simple*, certainly did not mince his words: "I do not like this city. It is my past and I don't like my past. I have grown up, I have pruned myself back. Fès has quite simply shrivelled up. However, I know that as I go deeper into the city it seizes me and makes me entity, quantum, brick among bricks, lizard, dust – without me needing to be aware of it. Is it not the city of the Lords?"

SETTLERS FROM ANDALUCIA AND KAIROUAN

The first settlement here was the village Medinat Fès founded in 789/90 by Moulay Idriss. However the town proper was founded by his son Idriss II as Al Aliya in 808/9. Muslim families, refugees from Córdoba and surrounding areas of Andalucía soon took up residence in the Adwa al Andalusiyin quarter. Later 300 families from Kairouan (in contemporary Tunisia), then one of the largest Muslim towns in North Africa, settled on the opposite bank, forming Adwa al Qaraouiyine. The Qaraouiyine Mosque, perhaps the

ON THE ROAD
A child's survival guide to Fès

When your parents say to you "son, we're going to Fès," your first reaction might be: "Where's Fès?" The next is: "Will they have pizza?"

In reality Fès is one of the most brilliant cities I've ever been to. Wandering around the medina, you see groups of street children, vibrant coloured washing hanging over into the streets, and best of all, the amazing market. In the markets nothing is fixed-price and there's always some clever deal or haggling going on.

Me and my brother and sister decided to test our haggling skills to the limit by playing a Moroccan version of *The Apprentice* and seeing who could buy the same standard items – a coloured glass, a slipper keyring and a pencil case – for the least money. Sadly, I lost by quite a bit!

At least I was helped in my bargaining by having done the **Café Clock** download course. This is a short session (about 1½ hours, 150dh) that Café Clock runs to teach you some simple Arabic phrases and a bit about the culture and what hand signals mean. My favourite was 'smehily' meaning "sorry", which you pronounce "smelly", and I used a lot bumping into people.

Café Clock is a great place to be, in the heart of the medina, and it does great milkshakes and burgers – and when I say burger I don't mean beef, pork or even lamb – but camelburger! (Which is actually delicious.)

And about the pizza – no, you won't find much in the medina, but they do have Malawi bread, like a thin wide sugary crêpe which is good for breakfast with soft cheese.

Dos
- Have a chocolate and banana milkshake at **Café Clock**.
- Go for a swim in one of the hotels.
- Learn a few phrases of Arabic.

Don'ts
- Go into a carpet shop if you haven't got at least half an hour and don't mind being patted on the head by the owner.
- Run away screaming if your parents even mention it.
- Visit the Roman ruins at Volubilis. Because 1) they are ruins 2) they are Roman 3) you have to drive three hours to get there and back. And no, they're not educational.

by Leo Thomson (age 11)

---

foremost religious centre of Morocco, is the centre of a university founded in 859, one of the most prestigious in the Arab World. The influence of the university grew a few centuries later under the Merinids, with the construction of colleges or *medersas*. On the right bank of the Oued Boukhrareb, the Jamaâ Madlous or Andalucían Mosque was also founded in the ninth century and remains the main mosque of Adoua el Andalus.

ALMORAVIDS AND ALMOHADS
The two parts of Fès el Bali were united by the Almoravids in the 11th century, and Fès became one of the major cities of Islam. In the 12th century the Qaraouiyine mosque was enlarged to its present form; one of the largest in North Africa, it can take up to 22,000

worshippers. The Almohads strengthened the fortifications of the great city. Under both dynasties Fès was in competition with the southern capital of Marrakech.

GROWTH OF FES UNDER THE MERINIDS

Fès reached its peak in the Merinid period, when the dynasty built the new capital of Fès el Jedid containing the green-roofed Dar al Makhzen still occupied by the monarch, the Grand Mosque with its distinctive polychrome minaret dating from 1279, and the mellah, to which the Jews of Fès el Bali were moved in 1438. The Merinid sultans Abu Said Uthman and Abu Inan left a particularly notable legacy of public buildings, including the Medersa Bou Inania, several mosques and the Merinid Tombs. The Zaouïa of Moulay Idriss, housing the tomb of Idriss II, was rebuilt in 1437. In the 15th century Fès consolidated its position as a major centre for craft industries and trade.

FROM SAADIAN FES TO THE PRESENT

Under the Saâdians (15th to 16th centuries) Fès declined, with a degree of antagonism between the authorities and the people. The Saâdians did, however, refortify the city, adding the Borj Sud and Borj Nord fortresses on the hills to the south and north of the city.

Under the Alaouites, Fès lost ground to the expanding coastal towns, which were far better located to benefit from trade with Europe. The occupation of Algeria also meant Fès was out of phase with the huge changes taking place to the east. In 1889 the French writer Pierre Loti described it as a dead city. However, the dynasty had added a number of new *medersas* and mosques, and reconstructed other important buildings.

The French entered Fès in 1911, but proved unable to gain full control of the city and its hinterland. Plans to make it the protectorate's capital were thus abandoned. In any case, Rabat on the coast was better located with respect to fertile farmlands and ports. Although the Ville Nouvelle, also often referred to as Dar Dbibagh, was founded in 1916, it dates principally from the late 1920s. French policy was to leave the historic quarters intact, preserved in their traditional form. Since the early 1990s, the city has exploded beyond its former limits, with huge new areas of low-rise housing on the hills behind the Borj Sud at Sahrij Gnaoua and to the north at Dhar Khemis and Bab Siffer.

→FES EL BALI: ADOUA EL QUARAOUIYINE

On the left bank of the Oued Boukhrareb, the **Adoua el Quaraouiyine** is a rewarding area to visit, as long as you don't expect too many well-structured heritage sites. If time is very short, then the minimum half-day circuit will allow you to get down the main street, **Talaâ Kebira**, to the central **souks** and main religious monuments, the **Moulay Idriss Zaouïa** and the **Qaraouiyine Mosque** (closed to non-Muslim visitors). At the start or the end of the tour, take a look in at the Dar Batha, a 19th-century Hispano-Moorish palace and now home to a **Museum of Moroccan Arts and Handicrafts**. With more time, you could also take in beautifully restored **Fondouk Nejjarine**, now a museum of wood and carpentry, and head up to the right bank, **Adoua el Andalus**. A couple of days in Fès will give you time to get to know the souks thoroughly and explore the higher, upscale neighbourhoods of **Douh**, **Zerbtana** and **Ziat**, where some of the largest of the city's palaces are located (see box, page 154).

Fès el Bali can only be explored on foot. The layout is complex and it may save time to engage the services of an official guide, as long as the balance between sites of interest and expensive shops is agreed in advance. Avoid unofficial guides and 'students' offering their

FESTIVALS

Fès Festival of Sacred Music

For 10 days in June Fès vibrates to the rhythmic drumming and soaring voices of the **Festival de Fès des musiques sacrées du monde** (Fès Festival of Sacred Music). From sufi to gospel, the range is wide, and there is a scattering of dance too. Free open-air concerts take place in the square outside Bab Boujeloud, with other ticketed events at locations such as the Batha Museum and Bab Makina. Prices for individual concerts range from around 150dh to 600dh, or you can buy a pass for all the concerts for 2900dh. Tickets are available online at www.fesfestival.com.

services. So saying, sometimes you do get lost and need someone to guide you out (10dh is a reasonable tip). The points from which you can get taxis are Errecif, down at the bottom, between the two halves of Fès el Bali, and Batha (pronounced 'bat-Ha'), up at the top.

TOWARDS FES EL BALI

Approaching Fès el Bali from the **Boujeloud Gardens** (Jnène Sbil or Jardins de la Marche Verte) ① *Tue-Sun 0900-1800*, you could follow Rue de l'UNESCO right round past the **Dar el Beida**, a late 19th-century palace, on your left. The road continues past a line of early 20th-century buildings (Pension Campini, police station), then the Préfecture on your right, before you reach the rather undistinguished entrance to the **Musée Dar Batha** ① *T0535-634116, Wed-Mon 0830-1630*, on your left almost opposite the Préfecture. The most important displays are the carpets and the distinctive Fès pottery. A 10th-century technique, enabled by the use of cobalt, produced the famous 'Fès blue'. (On Talaâ Kebira there are a couple of shops stocking this traditional pottery.) In the museum also look out for the *minbar* or preacher's chair from the Medersa Bou Inania.

BAB BOUJELOUD AND AROUND

If you're staying in a cheap hotel, it's likely that you'll be somewhere near Bab Boujeloud. The neighbourhood takes its name from the striking gate, which marks the main western entrance to Fès el Bali. With blue *zellige* tiles on the outside and green on the inside, Bab Boujeloud makes a fittingly stylish access point to the city, and was revamped under the French in 1913. Just to the right of the gate, as you arrive from the Place Boujeloud, there is a small gate in the wall, generally kept closed, which leads into the restored **brick water collector**. Though this may not sound very exciting, it is a good piece of late mediaeval hydraulic engineering, channeling the waters of the Oued Fès into underground pipes, which supplied the distributors of each neighbourhood. The whole system was still in operation in the late 19th century. The two minarets visible from the gate are those of the 14th-century **Medersa Bou Inania** and the simpler ninth-century **Sidi Lazzaz Mosque**.

On your left as you arrive at Bab Boujeloud, the impressive gate flanked by twin octagonal towers is **Bab Chorfa**, leading into Kasbah En Nouar, or Kasbah Filala, so named because it was once occupied by people from the Tafilalet who arrived with the early Alaouite rulers.

There are two main thoroughfares in Fès el Bali. **Talaâ Seghira** leads to the right. **Talaâ Kebira** leads to the left, directly past the Sidi Lazzaz Mosque, and the next major building, the Bou Inania Medersa, one of the most important sites in Fès, and straight on down through the medina to the Qaraouiyine Mosque.

BOU INANIA MEDERSA

ⓘ 0830-1730, 10dh, open to non-Muslims.

Fès's most spectacular sight, and one of Morocco's most beautiful buildings, the 14th-century Medersa Bou Inania is located handily close to Bab Boujeloud, the entrance near the top of Talaâ Kebira. Built by the Merinid Sultan Abu Inan between 1350 and 1355, it was

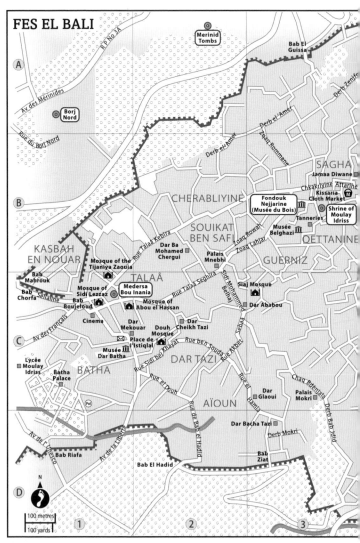

FES EL BALI

used to accommodate students until the 1960s and is now open to the public after a lengthy restoration. You enter through a highly decorated vestibule roofed by a stalactite dome. The building centres on a large, stone-flagged courtyard, at the far end of which is a sort of dry moat, where water taken from the Oued Fès once flowed, which separates the prayer hall from the square courtyard. The mosque area has a highly decorated minaret, indicating

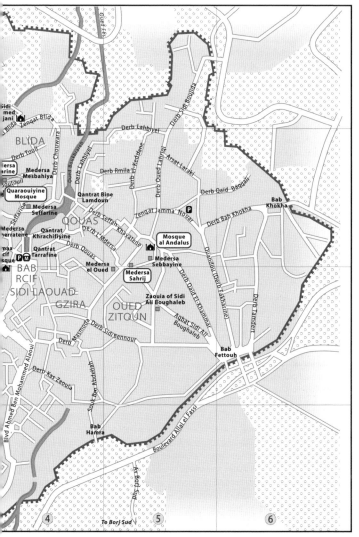

that it was far more important than most *medersas*, which normally do not have minarets or even pulpits for the Friday prayer. Indeed, the *medersa* has the status of a Friday mosque and, for a time, rivalled the Qaraouiyine Mosque. For the best view of the minaret, go for a coffee and a cake on the roof terrace of **Café Clock**, opposite (see page 163). The courtyard is decorated with ceramic mosaic, Koranic inscriptions and some fine carved woodwork. On the ground and first floors are the students' cell-like rooms, some with decorated ceilings.

There used to be a complex 14th-century *clepsydra* (**water clock**) built in the wall opposite the *medersa*. Using brass bowls and the dripping of water, and complete with chimes, it is said to have been used to allow the Medersa Bou Inania, visible from both the Qaraouiyine Mosque and the Mosque of Fès el Jedid, to signal the correct time for prayer. The wooden structure has been restored and, at some point, the clock may actually be made to work again.

TALAÂ KEBIRA TO THE QARAOUIYINE, SOUKS AND MEDERSAS

The narrow Talaâ Kebira, the principal street in Adoua el Qaraouiyine, descends steeply towards the spiritual and commercial heart of the city, a tangle of streets and alleys around the shrine (*zaouïa*) of Moulay Idriss and the Qaraouiyine Mosque. The 20-minute walk from Bab Boujeloud is many people's most memorable experience of Fès, an extraordinary wander through noises, smells, sights and a mass of humanity, from camels' heads on display at the butchers to aged mint sellers to heavily laden mules carrying goods across the city, guided by muleteers crying out 'Balak!' to warn pedestrians. Once you get to the bottom of Talaâ Kebira, the main religious monuments are off limits to non-Muslims, though the doors to the Qaraouiyine Mosque are often open, allowing a quick glimpse of the interior. It may be possible, depending on restoration works, to get into one of the *medersas* that ring the Qaraouiyine Mosque. Try to see the Medersa el Attarine, and don't miss the restored Foundouk Nejjarine, the Carpenters' Fondouk, which is the main accessible historic building in the central part of Fès el Bali. The other don't-miss sight is the main tannery, Dar Debbagh, located quite close to the well-signed Musée Belghazi.

As Talaâ Kebira descends, it goes through frequent identity changes, taking on the name of the different crafts which are (or were) practised along different sections of the street. First it becomes **Rue Cherabliyine** (slippermakers), where each afternoon except Friday people hawk second-hand shoes and slippers. The **Cherabliyine Mosque** dates from 1342, the reign of Sultan Abul Hassan, and has a small and attractive minaret tiled in green and white including the *darj w ktaf* motif. Further on, Rue Cherabliyin is called **Aïn Allou**, where leather articles are auctioned every day except Friday. After Aïn Allou, the street is named for the basket weavers (Msamriyine) and bag makers (Chakakyrine), before becoming the **Souk el Attarine**, the former perfumers' souk, the most prestigious in the medina. Between Attarine and the Zaouïa of Moulay Idriss is the lively main **kissaria**, the place to buy traditional clothing.

Before getting tangled up in Souk el Attarine, take a right and then a left down some steps off Cherabliyine to get to the square in front of the 18th-century **Fondouk Nejjarine**, an impressive building now home to the **Musée du Bois** ① *38 Rue Abdelazuz Boutaleb, T0535-621706, 1000-1700, 20dh*, an interesting museum of wooden crafts and tools. The beautiful space is filled with some interesting pieces that showcase Fassi carpentry to great effect, such as carved doors and windows, handsome coffers and musical instruments. There's also an impressive doorknocker carved from one piece of wood. The fondouk is also worth a visit for its roof terrace, where there's a good, if rather pricey, café –

ON THE ROAD
Saintly Sultan Abou Inane

A number of ancient colleges in the medinas of Morocco – among them *medersas* in Meknès, Salé and Fès – bear the name Bou Inania, after their royal founder. Sultan Abou Inane's most important building works were in Fès: he constructed the Jamaâ Zhar, a fine mosque close to his palace, and the Koubba of the Karaouiyine Library. Today's non-Muslim visitor can see the Medersa Bou Inania, considered to be one of the finest in existence. Tradition has it that when the sultan was presented with the final accounts, he tore up the paperwork, declaring that "Beauty is not expensive, whatever the sum may be. A thing which pleases man cannot be paid too dear."

Born in Fès in 1329, Abou Inane Faris de-throned his father at the tender age of 20, and had himself proclaimed sultan at Tlemcen in June 1348. By all accounts he was an imposing figure. Wrote Ibn el Ahmar, chronicler of the Merinids: "He was taller than everybody else. His body was slim, his nose long and well-made. He had hairy arms. His voice was deep, but he spoke quickly in a staccato manner, so that it was sometimes difficult to understand him. He had beautiful, finely shaped eyes, full eyebrows, and an agreeable face of great beauty … My eyes have never seen in his army a soldier with a fuller beard, a finer and more pleasing figure." Abou Inane was also, by all accounts, a skilled horseman, and had a good knowledge of law, arithmetic and Arabic. Ibn el Ahmar also mentions that he left behind 325 children.

On being proclaimed sultan, Abou Inane took the throne name of El Moutawakkil, 'he who places trust in God'. Although a strong ruler, he was also a pious man (he knew the Koran by heart), and this was reflected in a number of ways. He instituted a tradition of having a blue flag hoisted to the top of the minarets on Friday to indicate prayer time, and had oil-lamps placed on the minarets to show prayer times at night.

Like many a medieval ruler, however, Abou Inane had an unfortunate end. In 1358, returning to Fès from Tunis, he fell sick. Arriving in his capital on the eve of Aïd el Kebir, he had sufficient strength to lead the great prayers on the *musalla* outside the city. He was too ill, however, to receive homage from the notables of the realm. The vizier, Hassan el Foudoudi, who had been plotting in the wings had the sick sultan smothered in his bedclothes.

The burial place of Abou Inane, however, remains something of a mystery. Perhaps it was too risky to allow such a good ruler to have a mausoleum, which might then become a focus for public gatherings and discontent.

a good spot to take a break from the frenetic activity of the souks. Back on the square, the **Nejjarine Fountain**, also carefully restored, is reputed for the fever-curing properties of its waters. On the far side of the square from the fondouk is **Hammam Laraïs**, the wedding baths, once much used by grooms and brides before a pre-marriage trip to the Zaouïa of Moulay Idriss. The tanneries of **Dar Debbagh** are close by. To get there, go right at the far end of the Nejjarine square and follow the street round.

Surrounded by narrow streets, the 18th-century **Zaouïa of Moulay Idriss**, last resting place of the ninth-century ruler Idriss II, is off-limits to non-Muslim visitors, although parts of the interior can be seen by tactful glances through the large, unscreened doorways. Shops around the *zaouïa* sell candles and other artefacts for pilgrims, the distinctive nougat sweets which are taken home as souvenirs of a pilgrimage, and silverware. Each entrance to the precinct is crossed by a wooden bar, ensuring no pack animals go wandering into the sacred area. On your way round, note a circular porthole through which offerings can be discreetly passed.

The Qaraouiyine Mosque (see below) is also surrounded by narrow streets on all sides. In the immediate vicinity of the mosque are four *medersas*: going clockwise, **Medersa Attarine** (the most important and visitable, see below), **Medersa Mesbahiya** (partly ruined), **Medersa Seffarine** (the Coppersmiths' Medersa, recently restored), and **Medersa Cherratène** (more modern, three storeys). All were in use well within living memory.

Dating from 1323, the **Medersa Attarine** (currently undergoing restoration) was built by Merinid Sultan Abu Said. It used to accommodate students studying at the nearby Qaraouiyine University. The courtyard is one of the most elaborately decorated in Morocco, with the usual carved stucco and cedar wood, and *zellige* tiling. The courtyard has a solid, white marble fountain bowl. In the dark prayer hall, a chandelier bears the name of the *medersa*'s founder and the date. As with most *medersas*, the second floor has a succession of students' cells. From the roof (if accessible) there is a good view of the minaret and courtyard of the Qaraouiyine Mosque.

QARAOUIYINE MOSQUE
ⓘ *Inaccessible to non-Muslims. From the narrow streets, you may be able to take diplomatic glances through unscreened entrances.*

At the end of Souk el Attarine, the Quaraouiyine Mosque, the focal point of Fès el Bali, is probably the most important religious building in Morocco and was once a major centre of medieval learning, with professors in law, theology, algebra, mathematics, philosophy, and astronomy. With space for some 20,000 worshippers, it is one of the biggest mosques in North Africa. Original funding to build this mosque was provided in 857 by a wealthy immigrant family from Kairouan (in present day Tunisia), hence the name. The building was enlarged in 956 and again – most importantly – under the Almoravids between 1135 and 1144. The Almohads added a large ablution hall, the Merinids rebuilt the courtyard and minaret. The twin pavilions in the courtyard are 17th-century Saâdian additions. While the minaret goes back to 956, the 'Trumpeters' Tower' or Borj an-Naffara is later and is used during Ramadan to signal the time to begin fasting again. Built under Sultan Abou Inan in the second half of the 14th century, the tower originally functioned as an observatory. There are said to be plans to convert the tower into a museum dedicated to astrolabes and astrology – an important science in the Muslim world given the religion's use of a lunar calendar and the need to calculate the precise direction of Mecca for prayer. The Qaraouiyine has 14 doors, 275 pillars and three areas for ablutions. Features include elaborate Almohad carving and a venerable wooden pulpit. Some of the chandeliers were made from church bells. Women have a separate worship area, on a mezzanine floor, behind the men.

A minor sight on the Derb Bou Touil, the street running along the eastern side of the mosque, is the 14th-century three-storey **Fondouk Titouani**, originally built to accommodate merchants from Tetouan and, today, used by artisans and a carpet shop. Both this and the nearby **Palais de Fès** restaurant have good views of the Qaraouiyine's courtyard.

PLACE SEFFARINE
On the southeast side of the Qaraouiyine, the triangular Place Seffarine (Brassworkers' Square) is marked by a tree visible from the north or south Borj. On the right is the **Qaraouiyine Library**, founded in 1349 and still operational. You can usually enter the courtyard and entrance hall; non-Muslims are not allowed in the library itself. Of passing

ON THE ROAD
Bathtime blues

Early in the 19th century, Fès was visited by the Spaniard Domingo Badia y Leblich, travelling under the pseudonym Ali Bey el Abbassi. He noted the importance of the public baths or hammams of Fès: "The baths are open to the public all day. The men go in the morning, the women in the afternoon. I generally used to go in the evening, taking the whole bathhouse for myself so that there would be no outsiders … The first time I went there, I noted that there were buckets of water placed symmetrically in the corner of each room and each cubicle. I asked what they were for. 'Do not touch them, sir,' the personnel of the hammam replied in haste. 'Why?' 'These are buckets for the people down below.' 'Who are they?' 'The demons who come to wash during the night'."

A few centuries earlier, Leo Africanus described the traditions of the hammams of Fès: "The companions and the owners of the steam-baths hold festivities once a year, celebrating in the following way. First of all they invite all their friends, and go through the city to fife, tambourine and trumpets, then they take a hyacinth bulb, placing it in a fine copper container which they cover with a white cloth. Then they go back through the city, accompanied by music, to the door of the hammam. There they put the bulb in a basket which they hang over the door, saying, 'This will bring seed to the hammam, because of it there will be many visitors'."

Traditions related to the hammam seem to have died away today. But, even in the 1920s and 1930s, superstitions were very much alive. Dr Edmond Secret, a French doctor working in Fès, noted how those who went to the hammam very early, washing alone, were considered courageous, and genies were held to live in damp corners and the water pipes.

interest, behind the tree on Hyadriyine are two of the oldest **hammams** in Fès, which are currently being renovated, though an opening date remains elusive.

The **Medersa Seffarine**, built in 1271, was the first in the city and is much simpler in style than the later *medersas*. It continues to be used by students and, for a 10dh tip to the man on the door, you can have a quick guided tour – it's interesting to see a working *medersa* but it's a little like looking around a youth hostel, albeit a very ancient one.

If you head left of the tree on Seffarine, you can follow through to one of the bridges over the Oued Boukhrareb, either Qantrat Kharchifiyine or, after Sebbaghine, Qantrat Tarrafine. Here you come out onto **Rcif**, home to the best fresh produce market in the medina and a useful point for getting a petit taxi.

CHOUARA TANNERIES

The most colourful sight in Fès, the Chouara tanneries have not really changed since medieval times. At the bottom of the valley, they use the water of the Oued Boukhrareb, as well as a smelly mix of urine and guano to turn animal hides into dyed, usable leather. To get there from the Medersa Seffarine, follow Derb Mechattine (the narrow right-hand street of the two at the top of the square) around to the left onto Zanka Chouara. The best views of the tanneries are from leather shops that have terraces from where you can view the work going on below. Afterwards, you'll be expected to have a look at the handiwork for sale; there's no obligation to buy anything, although the quality is high, and you could do much worse for a souvenir of the city. See box, page 53, for a full account of the traditional tanning process.

ADOUA EL ANDALUS

Probably the poorest area of the medina, the Andalus quarter, the right bank of Fès el Bali, has fewer obvious sights than the left bank. However, the Medersa Sahrij, next to the Mosque al Andalus, is worth a visit. You can approach the neighbourhood from the southeast, taking a petit taxi to Bab Fettouh, or by climbing up out of Bab Rcif, losing yourself in the maze of streets of the Qouas neighbourhood.

With its green and white minaret, the **Mosque al Andalus** is a distinctive building dating from the same period as the great Qaraouiyine Mosque. The minaret dates from the 10th century, and the mosque was enlarged in the 13th century, with an architect from Toledo designing the grand main doorway, particularly impressive if you approach the mosque coming up the steps from below. If interested in a relic of the city's commercial life, take a look in at the **Fondouk el Madlous**, a few steps down from the mosque entrance on the left. Restored under Moulay Hassan I in the 19th century, this fondouk is still used for accommodation and storage.

As you face the main door of the mosque, go right along Derb Yasmina to reach the entrance of the nearby **Medersa Sahrij** ('School of the Reflecting Pool'), built 1321-1323 to house students studying at the mosque. There has been no major restoration campaign here yet and cats snooze on the weathered wood screens topped with scallop designs. The white marble basin, after which the *medersa* was named, has been removed from the courtyard. The large prayer hall contained the library against the *qibla* wall at either side of the mihrab. Try to get up onto the roof for the view. In between the mosque and the *medersa* is the **Medersa Sebbayine**, now closed. After visiting the Medersa Sahrij, you could carry along the same street, past the unmarked Medersa el Oued on your right. A few metres further on, a sharp right will take you onto Derb Gzira. Just after the turn is a house which bears the strange name of **Dar Gdam Nbi**, the 'house of the Prophet's foot', so called because a sandal which supposedly once belonged to the Prophet Mohammed was conserved there. Once a year, just before the Prophet's birthday or Mouloud, the Tahiri family would open their home to allow the faithful to approach the semi-sacred item of footwear. Unfortunately, the owners have sold up and the property has been divided. Continue therefore on Derb Gzira, which winds back down to Rcif, where you could find a bus (No 18) to take you back up to Place de la Résistance in the Ville Nouvelle. There are plenty of red petits taxis here as well.

FES VANTAGE POINTS

The **Borj nord**, built by the Saâdian Sultan Ahmad al Mansour in 1582, is a small but interesting example of 16th-century fortress architecture. There are good views of parts of Fès el Bali from the roof. Inside, the **Arms Museum** ⓘ *T0535-645241, closed Tue,* has displays of weapons and military paraphernalia from all periods, including European cannon. The collections have been built up mainly as a result of royal donations and include a number of rare pieces. Many of these killing tools have a certain splendour as crafted items. Look out for the largest weapon of all, a 5-m-long cannon weighing 12 tonnes used during the Battle of the Three Kings. From the Borj nord, you can head along the hillside to the 14th-century **Merinid Tombs**. The tombs are ruins, and much of the ornamentation described by earlier visitors has not survived. (Note that this is not a safe place to go alone at night.) In the late afternoon, the garden promenade behind the Borj nord and tombs is busy with locals out for a stroll. The views over Fès el Bali are splendid.

Nearby is the **Hotel des Merinides**, also with an excellent view and a pool, which non-guests can use for a small fee in the summer.

From the 13th-century **Borj sud**, south of the centre, occupied by the military, you can look north over Fès. The nearby *son et lumière* auditorium bathes Fès el Bali in white light. Unfortunately there are no lasers to pick out the parts of the city being described in the commentary. Until the late 1990s, this southern military outpost of the city stood in isolation but nowadays the low-rise flats of the sprawling Sahrij Gnaoua neighbourhood have marched up the hills, threatening to engulf it.

→ FES EL JEDID

The one-time Merinid capital, containing the Royal Palace and the old Jewish quarter (the *mellah*) is now a pleasant haven between the hustle and bustle of Fès el Bali and the Ville Nouvelle. Allow half a day here, perhaps in the late afternoon, before heading for the Borj Nord at sunset.

MELLAH

The best place to start is probably at the **Place des Alaouites**, close to the Royal Palace, and instantly recognisable by its spectacular doors giving onto a vast esplanade, used essentially on ceremonial occasions – or, in the early 1990s, during urban riots. Over on the right, at the edge of a small garden terrace, is the elegant **Bab Lamar**. Between this and the Rue Bou Ksissat, opt for the small gate which takes you into Rue des Mérinides in

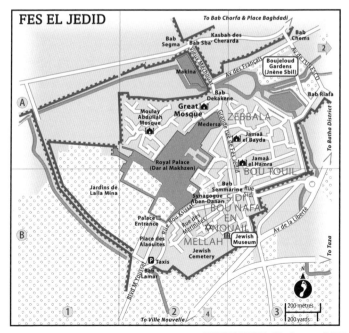

ON THE ROAD
The palaces of Fès

Hidden in the narrow streets of the Douh, Zerbatana and Ziat neighbourhoods, just east of the Batha, are some truly huge 19th- and early 20th-century palaces. The heirs have long since migrated to more promising elsewheres, and the high-ceilinged rooms are semi-squatted by poor relatives or rural migrants. If your time is limited, try to see Dar el Glaoui and Dar el Mokri. You will need to find a local to guide you in and a tip to the owner of around 20dh per visitor is probably reasonable for the disturbance. **Riad Fès** guesthouse, T0535-741012, may be able to put you in touch with a suitable guide. Try also the multilingual Abdellatif Riffi Mbarki, T0668-220112 (mob).

Most often visited, as it is right on Talaâ Seghira, is the **Palais Mnebhi**, which now functions rather efficiently as a restaurant. Its former owner was a minister of war under Sultan Moulay Abd el Aziz, and Maréchal Lyautey, first résident-général, resided here. Try to get a peek at the garden patio of **Dar Ba Mohamed Chergui**, on Derb Horra, linking Talaâ Kebira to Talaâ Seghira. The overgrown raised flowerbeds are laid out according to the *mtemmen*, figure-of-eight motif traditional in *zellige* (ceramic-mosaic). On Rue Sidi Mohammed el Haj, a right off Talaâ Seghira as you descend, is **Dar Ababou** which has a garden courtyard overlooked by balconies.

Dar el Glaoui is the most easily visited of the big palaces. Three tennis courts, if not four, would have easily fitted into the main courtyard. From the roof terraces there are views across the city. When the Glaoui family fell from favour after independence, the palace was abandoned. No less splendid is **Dar el Mokri**, named for the grand vizir El Mokri who held office for the whole of the French period. There are some 1930s additions and a sadly run-down garden. Off the big courtyard, the rooms are partly converted to workshops, partly squatted. There is an off-chance that if you are passing down Derb Chaq Bedenjala on your way to Bab Jedid a lad will spot you and ask if you want to take a look at the palace.

Close to the Batha (*batha* is Arabic for open area) are a number of easily located patrician residences. Right on the square, **Dar Mekouar**, once a cradle of the nationalist movement, is a few metres to the left of the **Maison Bleue** guesthouse (see plaque on wall). Next to the café to the right of the Maison Bleue, a narrow street, Derb Salaj, runs directly into Fès el Bali. Follow along and you will find, down a blind alley, the house used by the local **Institut Français** for occasional concerts. Further along, the very chic **Riad Fès** guesthouse is signposted, and you will find **Dar Cheikh Tazi**, now headquarters of the Association Fès-Saïss, an organization working to promote the region.

the **mellah**. The term, used throughout Morocco, probably derives from the Oued Melah, literally 'salty river', which once ran close to this part of Fès, but which, like so many of the watercourses in the region, has disappeared. Off Rue des Mérinides, the streets once had names that reflected the area's Jewish past. Take the fourth street on the right, Rue de Temara, which will take you to the **Synagogue Aben-Danan**. (There used to be two other synagogues, the Em Habbanim and the Mansour.) In fact, until the 13th century, the Jews lived in Fès el Bali in the Bab Guissa area, still referred to as Fondouq el Yahoudi. In the main hall of the synagogue, there is a collection of objects giving some idea of the material context of Fassi Jewish life. After the synagogue, past a small square, head across to the **Nouaïl** area. Next to the Jewish cemetery, the **Jewish Museum** is an intriguing collection of photos, newspaper clippings and artefacts of the community that lived here. (If you go right here, the street leads down to a door which will take you down to the American animal hospital or **Fondouk el Amerikan**.) From the Nouaïl area try to cut through to the continuation of Rue des Mérinides, Rue Sekkakine and the imposing **Bab Semmarine**, which leads you to Fès el Jedid proper. (If you double back on Rue des Mérinides, you'll find **Bab Magana**, the 'clock gate', whose scruffy timepiece stopped a while ago.) All along the street are the elegant façades of the houses built by prosperous Jewish families in the early 20th century.

BAB SEMMARINE TO BAB SBA'

Bab Semmarine, a chunky structure characterized by a double horseshoe arch and lozenge motifs, takes you through into the wide main street of **Fès el Jedid**, often referred to as Avenue Moulay Slimane. This divides the *madina al bayda*, the white city founded by the Merinids in 1276, in two and takes you through to **Bab Dekakene**. On the right, **Jamaâ el Hamra** 'the red mosque' is the first of the two mosques, so called because it was founded by a red woman from the Tafilalelt. The second mosque on your right is the **Jamaâ el Bayda**. Continue straight ahead and, at the end of the avenue, you can cut through an arched gate in the walls to your right taking you past the dry course of the Oued Chrachar to a decrepit waterwheel and a small café-restaurant. Double back, cut through left, and you are at **Bab Dekakene**. Here you want to go through to the right to the walled square referred to as the **Vieux Mechouar**. On the left are the Italianate entrance gates to the **Makina**, originally built in the 19th century to house an arms factory; it now has various functions, including a rug factory and youth club. Going straight ahead, you come to **Bab Sba'**, which takes you through onto the main road running along the north side of the city, linking the Ville Nouvelle to Fès el Bali. You might take a look at the unusual twin octagonal towers of **Bab Segma**, flanking the ring road. The fortified structure to the north is the **Kasbah des Cherarda**, built 1670 by Sultan Moulay Rachid and today housing a branch of the university and a hospital.

For those with plenty of time, the trail through Fès el Jedid should include a dawdle through the **Moulay Abdullah** neighbourhood, north of the palace. There are a couple of mosques for non-Muslims to look at from the exterior here. Those with plenty of energy should head through the Boujeloud gardens and along Avenue des Français to **Bab Boujeloud** at the western end of Fès el Bali (see page 145).

➜ AROUND FES

MOULAY YACOUB

Every bit a country spa town, Moulay Yacoub, 20 km northwest of Fès, is a short 45-minute journey through rolling countryside and some interesting capital-intensive irrigated farming. Taxis from Bab Boujeloud stop near the car park above the village. Steep flights of steps lead down into the village. There are plenty of hammams, small shops, cafés and a number of cheap lodging houses, some with rudimentary self-catering facilities.

Moulay Yacoub is a destination for local tourists, and a visit to one of the **hammams** can be quite an experience. There are baths for both men and women. The buildings date from the 1930s and could do with some maintenance but, at the price, you can't complain. The men's hammam has a pool of extremely hot sulphurous water – a bucket of Moulay Yacoub water poured on your head is guaranteed to boil your brains. There are few foreigners; beware the masseur, who may well delight in making an exhibition of you with a poolside pummel and stretching designed for Olympic athletes. Merely bathing in the hot spring water will leave you exhausted – and hopefully rejuvenated. There is also a luxury spa down in the valley.

SIDI HARAZEM

In restaurants all over Morocco, Sidi Ali and Sidi Harazem are the most widely available mineral waters, along with sparkling Oulmès. The saintly Sidi Harazem is said to have died in Fès in 1164. He taught at the Qaraouiyin Mosque and, it is said, his classes and lectures were so interesting that even the *djinn*, the mischievous spirits of Moroccan folklore, attended. The village of Sidi Harazem, with its spring and spa centre, is only 4 km along the N6 from Fès, with buses leaving from the CTM bus station and Bab Boujeloud, and other buses and grands taxis from Bab Ftouh. The area around the thermal baths is still very popular for swimming and picnics. There is a 17th-century *koubba*, dating from the time of the village's establishment as a resort under Sultan Moulay Rachid.

If you want to stay, there is the pricey (for what it is) **Hotel Sidi Harazem** (T0535-690135, www.sogatour.ma), with 62 air-conditioned rooms, health facilities, restaurant and bar (**€€**).

BHALIL

En route to Sefrou, 5 km before the town off the N8, is Bhalil. This small hill village may have had a Christian population before the coming of Islam. Behind the picturesque village are several **troglodyte dwellings**, with people still inhabiting the caves. The road takes you round the town, giving excellent views on all sides, and there are two good, clean cafés on the outskirts when approaching from the east.

SEFROU

Sefrou is 32 km south of Fès along the N8. It is not the sort of place you would visit if travelling south, as the N8/N13, via Ifrane and Azrou, is a better route from Fès to Er Rachidia and the South. However, Sefrou is certainly worth visiting as a side trip from Fès or even for an overnight stay, as it is one of the most appealing towns in Morocco, a poor but relatively unspoilt historic walled town lying in a beautiful wooded valley, with a calm and genuinely friendly atmosphere.

Arriving in Sefrou Both buses and taxis arrive and leave from Place Moulay Hassan, by Bab Taksebt and Bab M'kam, where the road from Fès meets the old town. Buses from Fès leave from Bab Boujeloud and many go on to Er Rachidia. Grands taxis from Fès leave from Bab Ftouh. **Syndicat d'Initiative** ① *past the Jardin publique, T0535-660380.*

Background Although now bypassed by new roads, Sefrou once lay astride the major caravan routes from Fès and the north, to the south and the Sahara beyond. It does, however, remain an important market place for the surrounding agricultural region. Like Debdou and Demnate, Sefrou was one of those small inland Moroccan towns that had a distinctive character because of its large Jewish population, which predated the Islamic conquest. Although many Berbers and Jews were converted to Islam by Moulay Idriss, Sefrou's Jewish element was reinforced with the migration of Jews from Tafilalet and Algeria in the 13th century. After the Second World War, large numbers of Jews emigrated to Morocco's large cities, Europe and Israel. The 1967 Arab-Israeli War was the final blow.

Sefrou has fascinated American academics, with the likes of anthropologists Geertz, Rosen and Rabinow carrying out research here. Recently Sefrou was created capital of a new province, receiving new and badly needed investment. A town declining into shabby anonymity, it may yet rescue something of its heritage and find a place on the tourist map.

Places in Sefrou The market place below and east of Avenue Mohammed V is a relaxed area to wander, best during the Thursday **market**. The town, which is known for olive and cherry production, has a large **Fête des Cerises** in June, and other smaller *fêtes* during the year. There is a *moussem*, or religious gathering, for Sidi Lahcen Lyoussi.

Entering from the north, the road curves down to the Oued Aggaï, past the **Centre Artisanal** ① *Mon-Sat 0800-1200 and 1400-1900,* into the busy Place Moulay Hassan. From here, **Bab M'kam** is the main entrance to the medina, which lies north of the river, and **Bab Taksebt** is the main entrance, over the bridge, into the *mellah*. Both are small, maze-like quarters, but it is difficult to get seriously lost. The **mellah** can also be entered from the covered marketplace through **Bab M'Rabja**. Beside a mosque built into the wall, turn right and down the main street, beside small restaurants, butchers', shops and craftsmen, and then left to reach one of several small bridges over the Oued Aggaï. Alternatively, take one of the small side turnings to discover the cramped design of the *mellah*, now mainly occupied by poor rural migrants, with houses often built over the narrow streets.

In the medina, the **Grand Mosque**, restored in the 19th century, lies beside the river and the souks just upstream. Past the souks is the **Zaouïa of Sidi Lahcen ben Ahmed**. In the medina there is a clearly discernible difference in the design of the quarter, reflecting the strict regulations and conditions under which Jews in the *mellah* lived. Sefrou is quite remarkable, however, in that the mellah is as large as the medina.

Avenue Moulay Hassan crosses the Oued Aggaï, where there is a **Syndicat d'Initiative** which has a **swimming pool** and continues as Avenue Mohammed V, the main street of the unexciting new town, with the post office and a few shops and simple café-restaurants. Turn into Rue Ziad by the post office, past **Hotel Sidi Lahcen Lyoussi**, and continue uphill on the black-top road. Camping is signed to the left but continue up to the **Koubba of Sidi Bou Ali**, with its white walls and distinctive green-tiled roof. There is a café, a few stalls and a magnificent view. Another small excursion beginning south of the river leads west to a small **waterfall** (*les cascades*).

GOING FURTHER
Taza

There was a time when Taza was quite a happening place, given its strategic location controlling the easiest route from the Moroccan heartland of Fès and Meknès to the eastern plains. The town, rather quiet today, is divided into three quite separate parts: the area around the railway and bus station; the **Ville Nouvelle** around Place de l'Indépendence, and the quiet medina on the hill with its narrow streets. After the hurly-burly of Fès, low-key Taza makes a good base from which to explore up into the hills of the Jbel Tazzeka National Park.

ARRIVING IN TAZA

Arriving by train, bus or grand taxi, you will come into the north of the Ville Nouvelle. The medina is a fair 3-km trek away and, as there is only one hotel there, you will probably stay in the Ville Nouvelle. (Go straight down Avenue de la Gare; there are three hotels on Place de l'Indépendence at the end.) There is a regular bus service from Place de l'Indépendence to Place Moulay Hassan in the medina. A light blue petit taxi will cost you around 3dh from station to Place de l'Indépendence, and 6dh from the station to the medina.

BACKGROUND

The site was first settled in Neolithic times. Later it was developed by Meknassa Amazigh groups, eventually becoming an important, but ultimately unsuccessful fortification against the advance of the Fatimids from the east. The Almohads under Sultan Abd el Moumen captured the city in 1141-1142, making it their second capital, and using it to attack the Almoravids. The Almohads built a mosque and expanded the fortifications.

Taza was the first city taken by the Merinids, who extended the Almohad city considerably. Its important defensive role continued under the Merinids and the Saâdians, and was again pivotal in the rise to power of the Alaouites, who further extended and fortified the city, later using it as a strong point in their defence against the threat from French-occupied Algeria to the east.

The eccentric pretender, Bou Hamra, 'the man on the she-donkey', proclaimed himself sultan here in 1902 and controlled much of eastern Morocco until 1912, when he was caught and killed. He was known as a wandering miracle-maker, travelling Morocco on his faithful beast. Taza was occupied by the French in 1914, and became an important military centre, located on the route linking Algeria with the Atlantic plains of *le Maroc utile*, between the remote mountains and plateaux of eastern Morocco and the great cities to the west. Today, with the decline in cross-border trade with Algeria, Taza, like its distant neighbour Oujda, sees far less passing traffic than it did and has a distinctly sleepy feel to it. A couple of the hotels have been upgraded, however, and you could well stay here for a couple of nights if exploring or birdwatching up in the Jbel Tazzeka National Park.

PLACES IN TAZA

The **Ville Nouvelle** – for hotels, restaurants, banks and other services – is a quiet place centred around early and mid-20th-century buildings on Place de l'Indépendence. The older buildings are in the small, attractive **medina** perched on the hill 3 km away from the railway station and 2 km from the centre of the new town. From the bottom of the hill there is an interesting short cut to the **kasbah** via a flight of steps which provide remarkable views. Beyond this point, further along the main road on the right, are the **Kifane el Ghomari caves**, inhabited in Neolithic times. Note that the main historic buildings in the medina are closed to non-Muslims.

MEDINA

The transport hub of the old town is **Place Moulay Hassan**, just outside the main entrance to the **souk**. The focus of the old quarter is the main street, commonly called the Mechouar from end to end, which runs behind Place Moulay Hassan along the entire length of the medina, from the Andalucían Mosque to the Grand Mosque at the opposite end of town by the Bab er Rih gate. Between the two mosques are the various souks. Hassle is practically non-existent, as there are few articles thought to interest the tourist. The fact that there is no motor traffic in the medina makes it all the more pleasant. The best thing to do is just wander – the old neighbourhoods are quite small and sooner or later you will come out on the outside road ringing the town.

Turning left just past the main gate to the souk, by the **Cinema Friouato**, is the jewellery section of the souk. From here you can turn left along a very straight and narrow section of road towards the Andalucían Mosque, or right towards the Grand Mosque. Following the latter route, the food and spice souk is off to the left, behind the broader section of the Mechouar. Further along, you may get a glimpse of the **Zaouïa of Sidi Azouz** (note its beautiful wall-basin by the door). It is difficult to gain a good view of the **Grand Mosque**, built by the Almohads in the second half of the 12th century, with further elaboration by the Merinids in the late 13th century, and the Alaouites in the 17th. In its classic proportions of 1:5, the minaret resembles that of the Koutoubia Mosque in Marrakech. Only Muslims can view the beautiful chandelier bearing 514 oil lamps, which lights the mosque.

To the right of the Grand Mosque, down a steep flight of steps, you reach a section of the **ramparts**, with good views over the surrounding countryside, lower Taza, and the mountains beyond. Going left after the steps to start a rampart tour, the first section, with some steep drops, is referred to as **Bab er Rih**, 'the Gate of the Wind'. From here you have perhaps the best view of the Almohad minaret. Eventually, keeping to the outside of the town, you could look out for the circular **Sarasine Tower**, also dating back to the Almohad times – and showing clear European influence.

At the far end of the mechouar from Bab er Rih is the **Andalucían Mosque**, with its 12th-century minaret. Just before, on the right, stands the 14th-century **Medersa of Abu el Hassan**, named after a Merinid sultan. This is closed, but the exterior shows a carved lintel in cedar wood and a porch roof overhanging the road. In a lane to the right of the mosque, Zankat Dar el Makhzen, there is the former house of Bou Hamra the pretender. The weekly **market** takes place outside the walls at this end of town, outside **Bab Titi**.

FES LISTINGS

WHERE TO STAY

There are hotels and riads in Fès to suit all budgets, including some very luxurious ones in and around the tangled lanes of the medina – certainly the best place to stay if you want to get a real feel of old Fès. If you want to stay in a riad, a reservation is essential and someone will be sent to meet you.

New riads are opening all the time, and they tend to be owned by a slightly younger crowd than in Marrakech. Fès also has a disproportionate number of British riad owners compared to other Moroccan cities. **Fez Riads**, T0672-513357, www.fez-riads.com, is an excellent agency offering luxury accommodation in the medina.

€€€€ Dar Bensouda, 14 Zkak El Bghel, Quettanine, T0535-638949, www.riaddarbensouda.com. This chic hotel is in one of the more obscure parts of the medina and is well worth the effort of finding. Owned by Moroccan hotelier Abdellatif Aït Ben Abdellah, who made his mark with several respected riads and restaurants in Marrakech, he's brought his own sense of style to Fès. A large courtyard is minimally furnished with butterfly chairs, linen drapes and saffron-coloured rugs. Rooms are individually decorated with pared-down elegance, and 1 luxury suite has a private courtyard at an accessible price. Another courtyard is home to an inviting plunge pool, the restaurant (warmed by a log fire in the winter) serves a wide range of Moroccan cuisine, while the roof terrace provides a full 360° view of the medina and surrounds.

€€€€ Riad 9, 9 Derb Lamsside, Souiket Ben Safi, Zkak el Ma, T0535-634045, www.riad9.com. Sophisticated and elegant, **Riad 9** has everything necessary to make a stay in Fès unusually stylish, from books, jazz, Chinese lanterns and panoramic views to a hyperactive cat. Run by a French designer, it has the rugs and architectural features but goes a step further, with great touches like tree trunk underwear drawers, dentists' chairs in bathrooms, canary yellow python skin pouffes and turtle doves on the roof. Old antiques mix with inventive contemporary design to create something very special. Rooms are rented individually or you can rent the whole place.

€€€€ Riad Fès, 5 Derb Ben Sliman Zerbtana, T0535-741206, www.riadfes.com. This vast house, originally built in 1900, was one of the first in Fès to be transformed into upscale accommodation, and it remains one of the city's most luxurious places to stay. Particularly at night, its poolside bar is spectacular and seriously hip. The 26 rooms are split into 3 different design themes depending on your tastes – Baraco Andalous, traditional Moroccan or Oriental – and although they don't quite live up to the wow-factor of the rest of the place, they still feel special. The roof terrace provides a more upmarket spot in the medina for lunch and has fantastic views.

€€€€ Riad Laaroussa, 3 Derb Bechara, T0674-187639, www.riad-laaroussa.com. One of the first wave of contemporary riads in Fès, this 17th-century riad opens out around a grass and pebble courtyard with fountains and orange trees. As well as 4-poster beds, fireplaces in some of the rooms (a huge bonus during the rather damp and cold winters) and a striking tadelakt roof terrace, there are plenty of quirky touches such as kettles for taps, adding an air of the unexpected. The dining room has black and white photos and jazz playing, while the 7 bedrooms are all themed around a colour. There's an elegant hammam and spa and copious amounts of intricately carved plaster.

€€€ Dar Attajali, 2 Derb Qettana, Zqaq Rommane, T0535-637728, T0677-081192 (mob), www.attajalli.com. Attajali is one of the most exquisite renovations in the medina, highly traditional with a feminine feel. Think lots of pinks, purples and silky fabrics, soothing Arabic music and an air of quiet serenity. 5 individually decorated rooms have wooden ceilings, pretty zellige tiles, antiques, comfortable mattresses, imported German duvets and traditional Moroccan beauty products in the bathrooms. The 'purple suite' has a spectacular draped 4-poster bed, if you're after a romantic weekend away. This is the only vegetarian guesthouse in Fès, and the food is excellent, making good use of locally sourced fruit and vegetables. Breakfast and dinner are served in a rooftop dining room, with wonderful views across the medina.

€€€ Dar Roumana, 30 Derb el Amer, Zkak Roumane, T035-741637, www.darroumana. com. One of the first foreign-owned guesthouses to open in the medina (and still one of the best). The American owner Jennifer Smith has created one of the friendliest places you could hope to stay in. Big on traditional Moroccan decor, such as zellige, intricate plasterwork and painted ceilings, it has a wonderful feeling of space and light, with a large central courtyard, library, TV room and sprawling roof terrace with excellent views of the Merinid tombs. All 5 suites are large, well proportioned and feature the works of local craftsmen, as well as unique characteristics, such as the claw-footed bath in the Roumana suite, or the private balcony off the Yasmina suite. Jennifer has always been known for her excellent cuisine and, as well as offering cooking lessons, she's upped the ante again recently by bringing in a French chef, Vincent Bonnin, to head the restaurant (now also open to the public), which offers a daily changing menu Tue-Sat. Booking recommended.

€€€ Dar Seffarine, 14 Sbaa Louyate, T035-635205, www.darseffarine.com. The 750-year-old **Dar Seffarine** is an architectural gem built around a spectacular tiled courtyard with high arches. The creation of Kate (a Norwegian graphic designer and photographer) and

Alla (an Iraqi architect), their attention to detail from the restoration of the house's intricate features to the choosing of antique carpets, furniture and linens is impeccable. Decor is minimal to allow the house to speak for itself, but a museum it's not. The couple are gregarious hosts and every evening guests are invited for drinks in their small, homely courtyard just off the kitchen, or can dine together in the rooftop dining room (the food is excellent). Located just around the corner from the Qaraouiyine Mosque, it's also well positioned for some of the medina's key sights, and with easy access to the parking and taxis at Rcif.

€€€ Riad Tizwa, Derb Guebbas 15, Douh Batha, T07973-238444 (UK mob) or T068-190872 (Morocco mob), www.riadtizwa. com. Sibling to the more established **Tizwa** in Marrakech, **Tizwa Fès** has 9 chic double bedrooms and a sprawling, lushly planted roof terrace, where excellent breakfasts are served. All rooms are generously appointed with some useful modern details, such as iPod docking stations, which is indicative of the Bee brothers' laid-back approach to hospitality that makes the place so pleasurable. Bathrooms are all done out in *tadelakt*, with organic rose petal soap and luxuriously thick bathrobes, and tea and coffee is secretly delivered to your door in the mornings, a nice touch. Communal spaces are warm and welcoming, with an open fireplace in the living room and a richly furnished courtyard for chilling out over mint tea in the afternoons. A truly comfortable home-away-from-home.

€€-€ Pension Dar Bouanania, 21 Derb Ben Salem, Talaâ Kebira, T035-637282. A rarity in the medina, **Dar Bouanania** is a good-value hotel with some style. Packed with painted wood, plaster and traditional tiles, it's a great way to get a taste of the architecture on a budget. Rooms – some en suite – sleep up to 4 and have big rugs and ornate furniture. Great value if you're travelling as a family or a group.

€ **Hotel Cascade**, 26 Rue Serrajine, T035-638442. A backpackers' institution, the busy Cascade is in the very heart of the action, just inside the main gate of Bab Boujeloud. Rooms are very basic but OK for the price and, on the upside, it's a great place to watch over the comings and goings down below. If money is really tight, you can also sleep cheaply on the roof terrace.

€ **Youth hostel**, 18 Rue Abdesslam Serghini, in the Ville Nouvelle, T035-624085, www.fesyouth-hostel.com. In the Ville Nouvelle, this is a spotless and very professional outfit, worth considering even if you don't usually stay in youth hostels. There's a very pleasant courtyard and garden, with lilies, trees and birds, and they have single-sex dorms and smaller rooms for 2-7 guests. You can do laundry on the roof and they offer good information. Reception open 0800-2200 but rooms closed 1000-1200 and 1500-1800. No HI card necessary.

RESTAURANTS

The medina is changing fast and although the majority of places to eat are still traditional Moroccan restaurants or street food, there are also increasing numbers of hip, foreign-owned places. The British-run **Café Clock** (see Cafés, below) has become the essential meeting point of anyone travelling to Fès. But for fine dining, visit the new boutique hotels like **Dar Bensouda** (see page 160) and **Dar Roumana**.

€€€ **Al Fassia**, in the Hotel Palais Jamaï, Bab el Guissa, T035-634331. Open lunch and dinner. Cooling views of the pool and verdant gardens make a lovely setting for a high-quality buffet lunch. Choose from a wide variety of salads, Moroccan and international dishes and fresh fish and meat grilled on the spot. They also have a good wine list, including some very drinkable Moroccan bottles.

€€€ **Le Jardin des Biehn**, 13 Akbat Sbaa, Douh, T0664 647 679, www.jardines biehn. com. Open breakfast, lunch and dinner. The **Jardin des Biehn** combines several riad-style suites around a private organic garden with the colourful **Café Fès** at one end. Once a Pasha's summer palace, it is a wonderfully atmospheric place for a lazy lunch (yes, they do serve wine), or dinner beneath the stars. Michel Biehn, a well-known collector of antique textiles, lends his touch throughout, and you can see the art gallery and or stroll in the gardens. The traditional Moroccan, or lighter French and Italian dishes, feature many home-grown products, and there are also pizzas baked in a wood-fired oven.

€€€ **Maison Blanche**, 12 rue Ahmed Chaouki, T0535-622727, www.maison-blanche.ma. Open lunch and dinner. In the Ville Nouvelle, arguably Fès's best restaurant, it is also its trendiest, combining a large, slate-clad dining room with an elegant 1st-floor bar and lounge. It is hugely popular among the city's groovers and shakers and is a satisfying choice if you're looking for somewhere special to splash your cash. Food is Franco-Moroccan with lots of creative touches, such as grilled John Dory with a preserved lemon marmalade or fillet of beef with pistachio butter. The wine list and cocktails are excellent, and there's even a cigar bar for lovers of a nice, fat Cubano, but it can get pricey. The 2-course menu for 200dh is a more affordable option.

€€€ **Palais Tijani**, 51-53 Derb Ben Chekroune Lablida, T035-741128. Open lunch and dinner. A classic palace restaurant, with lots of intricate ornamentation, low tables, scattered rose petals and a focus on providing a true taste of Morocco. Service is charming, and dishes include celebratory pigeon *b'stilla* (pie), hearty tagines and couscous. No alcohol licence.

€€ **Café Medina**, open 1000-2300. Located just outside Bab Boujeloud, this is a peaceful spot to hang out on a roof terrace. It is a little bit more upmarket than its neighbours and offers good-quality Moroccan options.

€ **Fez et Gestes**, 39 Arsat El Hamoumi, Ziat, T0535-638532, T0668-601791, www.fes-et-gestes.ma. Open lunch and dinner. Housed in an Italian-style villa, with a pretty, walled garden, this is one of the loveliest spots in the medina and is the creation of charming French expat, Cecile. In the shade of a jacaranda tree, refuel on perfectly executed Moroccan salads, tagines and pastries. In winter, 2 plump leather armchairs in the library provide a cosy nook for hot mint tea and a good book.

There is no shortage of cheap eats in Fès el Bali, particularly just inside Bab Boujeloud, where there is a busy row of cafés with outdoor tables, all of which are good for an evening meal. Of these, local celebrity **Thami's**, tucked into a corner under the tree, is the most often recommended and the tastiest. His *kefta* and egg tagine is excellent, as are his steaming great cauldrons of *lobia* (white bean stew) and *maakouda* (potato pancakes with hot chilli sauce). It's also arguably the best place in town for a spot of people watching. Open noon-midnight.

Cafés

Café Clock, 7 Derb el Magana, Talaâ Kebira, T035-637855, www.cafeclock.com. Daily 0900-2300. In a beautiful old building just off Talaâ Kebira, in the heart of the medina, **Café Clock** is so much more than just a café. It has become the epicentre of traveller and expat Fès since opening in 2006, and understandably so. Hip, young, and energetic, there always seems to be something going on, whether it's a photo exhibition by a local artist, Arabic conversation classes or a calligraphy lesson in one of the upstairs lounges. It's also a great place to eat, with a contemporary riff on Moroccan classics. People come from far and wide to get a taste of their eponymous camel burger, or for afternoon tea and home-baked cakes on the roof with its stunning view of the minaret of the Medersa Bou Inania across the other side of Talaâ Kebira. There's even free Wi-Fi and, if you want to find anything out about the city, you'll probably find someone here who will be happy to tell you.

Cremerie de Place, on the northern point of Pl Seffarine. A well-loved little spot for sitting out on the square and watching the copper beaters at work. There's something almost musical about the chink, chink, chink of so many little hammers, and it's a good place to get to know locals who stop for a chat minus the endless haggle. Coffee, *panache* (mixed fruit juice) and cakes are all good here, and it's ideal for catching your breath after a couple of hours losing yourself in the souks.

Óuali's Café, Pl Bouros, Talaâ Kebira. An unmarked and unprepossessing café with a few rickety outdoor tables on the right as you head down Talaâ Kebira, the much-photographed and rather ancient Óuali will serve you an exquisitely spiced coffee with commendable *panache*. You even get a home-made leather holder to stop your hands from burning.

WHAT TO DO

Fez Food, www.fez-food.com. Designed for foodie travellers who want to experience the gourmet delights of the medina or learn about spices, taste wine in the vineyards of Meknès, or try rolling couscous in the Atlas. They also have more traditional cooking lessons.

Tours Around Fez, www.toursaround fez. com. Hikes and sunset picnics on Mt Zalagh to 4WD trips through the Middle Atlas, with a focus on responsible tourism.

MEKNES AND AROUND

Meknès never set out to be an 'imperial city'. But, as chance would have it, the inhabitants of Fès and Marrakech showed little enthusiasm for 17th-century ruler and builder Moulay Ismaïl, and so he turned his attentions towards Meknès. Strategically situated at the heart of Morocco, Meknès became his capital, and he embarked on a massive building programme. Meknès is known as a city of minarets – gentle green or grey in colour, the tall, angular, linear towers dominate the old town, which, with its cream colour-washed houses and terraces sits above the narrow valley of the Oued Boufekrane. There are pleasant souks, a medersa – but, above all, an easy pace that is almost relaxing after the tension and press of Fès. The most famous monument is the great Bab Mansour el Aleuj and, although today little is left except for vast pisé walls, once upon a time this great gate to a palace complex was worthy of the Thousand and One Nights. Meknès also offers some rewarding side trips – to the Roman site of Volubilis, and to the pilgrimage centre of Moulay Idriss.

→ ARRIVING IN MEKNES

GETTING THERE

The new bus station (private long-distance buses) is at Bab el Khemis, on the far side of the medina from the Ville Nouvelle. The old CTM bus station is at 47 Avenue Mohammed V in the Ville Nouvelle, and some grands taxis leave from nearby on Avenue des FAR. Private local buses arrive at the terminal below Bab Mansour. The main train station is some way from the centre and 1 km from the medina. If you are going to stay in Ville Nouvelle, get off at the Meknès Amir Abdelkader station, the first of the two stations in Meknès as you come from Casa/Rabat. This station is just below Avenue Mohammed V and closer to the centre of the Ville Nouvelle than the other main station.

MOVING ON

Azrou (see page 177) is 1¼ hours away by car. Getting across the Atlas by public transport is possible, but from here on the advantages of a car are huge, not least the ability to stop and look at some of the great views. Grands taxis to Azrou leave from the car park below Place el Hedim, opposite the private line buses. Ask the drivers hanging around for the destination. For Moulay Idriss and then a short walk to Volubilis (see pages 172 and 173) taxis leave from near the Shell station on your right as Avenue Hassan II descends.

GETTING AROUND

Meknès is a fairly spread-out place. The medina, along with the ruined palace complexes of the 17th century, is situated across the valley of the Oued Boufekrane. When visiting Meknès in summer, it can get hot, and the distances between the different parts of the 17th-century palace city are considerable. You will probably need a full day, with most of a morning dedicated to the palace complex. In half a day, you could do the medina easily.

TOURIST INFORMATION

Office du Tourisme (ONMT) ⓘ *27 Pl Batha-l'Istiqlal, T0535-521286.* Helpful, although not overly endowed with information.

Coming up to Meknès by road from Rabat, you get a good idea of why Moulay Ismaïl chose the town as his capital. The N6 passes through the Mamora Forest and a belt of fertile, relatively prosperous countryside. Meknès was originally a kasbah from the eighth century, used by the Kharajite Berbers against the Arabs. The town itself was founded by the Zenata Amazigh tribe called Meknassa in the 10th century and then destroyed by the Almoravids in 1069. A later kasbah was destroyed by the Almohad Sultan Abd el Moumen in order to build a new grid-patterned medina, some features of which still remain. This city was ruined during the conflict between the Almohads and the Merinids, but was partially rebuilt and repopulated in 1276 under Sultan Moulay Youssef. A fine *medersa* was built under the Merinids, as they sought to expand Sunni orthodoxy to reduce the influence of Soufi leaders.

THE REIGN OF MOULAY ISMAIL

The reign of the Alaouite sultan, Moulay Ismaïl (1672-1727), saw Meknès raised to the status of imperial capital. Even before his succession to the imperial throne, Moulay Ismaïl developed the city. Meknès was chosen as his capital rather than the rebellious and self-important rivals of Fès and Marrakech. Moulay Ismaïl is renowned for his ruthless violence, but many of the stories recounted by the guides may be apocryphal. What is certain is that he made an impression on European visitors to the court. Meknès was described as a Moroccan Versailles. Indeed, some suggest that the sultan was trying to rival Louis XIV, then involved in building his palace complex outside Paris. Having conquered Morocco, Moulay Ismaïl left his mark all over the country. Kasbahs were built by his troops as they pacified the tribes, cities acquired mosques and public buildings.

Moulay Ismaïl's vision of Meknès was vast and, although much of the *pisé* and rubble walls are in ruins, those still standing are testimony to its original scale. The city was built by a massive army of slaves, both Muslim and Christian, and the sultan was notorious for his barbaric treatment of these people, supposedly having them buried in the walls among other horrors. He built several palaces to accommodate his wives, concubines, children and court, as well as quarters for his army, the Abid Bukhari, an élite praetorian guard of black slaves, the chief instrument of his power. The city contained within it all that was necessary for such a large military machine, with store houses, stables, armouries, gardens and reservoirs.

AFTER MOULAY ISMAIL

After Moulay Ismaïl's death, Meknès gradually declined. His huge court and army could not be held together without his immense ego, and his successors, Moulay Abdallah and Sidi Mohammed, returned the emphasis to Fès and Marrakech. Furthermore, the earthquake of 1755 destroyed many of Moulay Ismaïl's creations. The French revitalized Meknès, appreciating its strategic position in the corridor linking eastern Morocco and Algeria with the coastal belt around Rabat and Casablanca. They built their Ville Nouvelle apart from the medina and the imperial city, on the east bank of the Oued Boufekrane, as part of their policy of separate development of Moroccan and European quarters. During the protectorate, Meknès became the most important garrison town in Morocco and continued as an important military town after independence.

MEKNES TODAY

Although Meknès is perhaps overshadowed by its near-neighbour Fès, it is today the fifth largest city in Morocco, with both tourism and industrial activities, and is the centre of a highly productive agricultural region. After a period of relative stagnation, Meknès is re-emerging as an important town. National planners made the city capital of the Meknès-Tafilalelt region, which extends southeast to Er Rachidia, Erfoud and Rissani down one of the country's most strategic lines of communication. The late 1990s saw a spate of new building, not all of it in keeping with the city's character. Along with assorted concrete

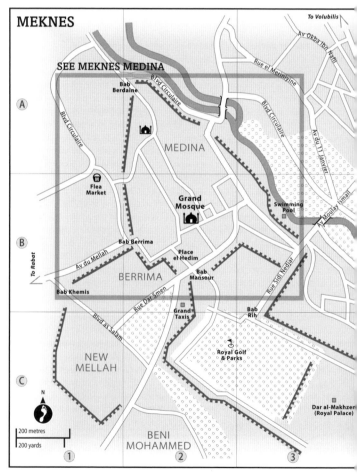

blocks, a McDonald's has gone up on the corridor of parkland designed as a green lung for the heart of the city. And, horror of horrors, some philistine has put up a low-rise housing block in the heart of the medina, higher than some of the minarets.

Lovers of Moroccan red wines will find place names in the region south of Meknès familiar. The country's best vineyards are located here, near settlements like Aït Souala, Aït Yazm and Agouraï. Quality is improving, with foreign investors putting money into improved vinification methods and makers from Bordeaux and other renowned wine regions bringing their knowledge to the industry.

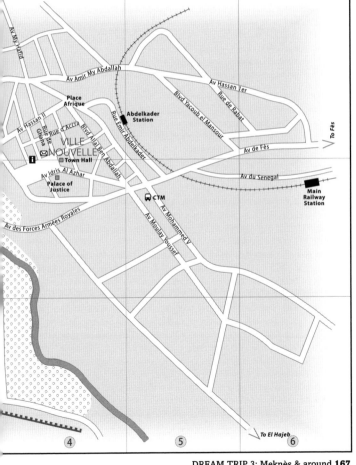

Meknès is a striking town, a fact accentuated by the distant backdrop views of the **Jbel Zerhoun**, which rises to over 1000 m to the north. The wooded foothills and orchards of olives, apples and pears below provide a green setting to the city for much of the year. One of the great imperial cities of Morocco, it is now more memorable for the impressive sense of scale and feeling of space than for any existing historic architecture. Another distinct part of Meknès is the **medina**, which includes the intricately decorated Medersa Bou Inania, vibrant souks, the Dar Jamaï palace museum and numerous mosques. The cream-washed walls and daily life of the residential areas just behind Rue Dar Smen still carry an antiquated 'Morocco that was' feel about them. To the east of the medina, on the opposite bank of the Oued Boufekrane, there stands the early 20th-century Ville Nouvelle. Carefully laid out by planner Henri Prost, the new town commands impressive (and as yet unspoiled) views over both medina and the imperial city. It has a relaxed atmosphere and is a calm place to drink a coffee or tea and watch the evening promenade. Meknès is one of the easiest imperial cities to explore independently, but there is no shortage of faux guides offering their services in Place el Hedim and nearby. If you need assistance, obtain an official guide from the tourist office or one of the larger hotels. About 150dh is a realistic fee.

MEDINA

Place el Hedim (the Square of Destruction), opposite Bab Mansour, is the centre of Meknès' old city and the best starting point for exploration. The biggest open square in the city, it was once as busy as the Jemaâ el Fna in Marrakech (see page 43), filled with acrobats, storytellers and snake charmers plying their trade. Despite its name, the square is now a quiet place with some cheap cafés at the far end, opposite Bab Mansour. Renovation works are underway and, hopefully, the square will remain the central place to stroll on a Meknès evening rather than becoming a car park. To the left of the square is a crowded, covered **food market**, with bright displays of fresh vegetables and pickles; definitely worth a look. On the right-hand corner of the square down a few steps is **Dar Jamaï**, a 19th-century palace, owned by officials at the court of Sultan Moulay Hassan, and now the **Museum of Moroccan Arts** ① *T0535-530863, Wed-Mon 0900-1700, 10dh.* Built in 1882, it was the residence of the Jamaï family, two members of which were ministers to Moulay Hassan. It was used as a military hospital after 1912 and in 1920 became a museum. Exploring the house gives an insight into the lifestyle of the 19th-century Muslim élite. On display are wrought iron, carved wood, weaving, leather and metal work, and various antique household items. Look out for richly painted wooden chests and panels. Upstairs is a furnished reception room. The garden planted with cypress and fruit trees is a pleasant halt in the heat of the day.

The medina of Meknès has seven traditional **souks**, which, while not quite of the order of those in Marrakech or Fès, are nevertheless well worth exploring. Immediately to the left of the Dar Jamaï a small entrance leads to the souks. The alley bends around to the right behind Dar Jamaï past some undistinguished clothes shops. Just before a carpet shop turn left. The passage, now covered, widens slightly, and continues past a range of shops selling modern goods, a bank, and various minor side turnings. At the junction, on the left, is **Souk Nejjarine**, which includes textile-sellers and carpenters, another entrance to the carpet souk and a fondouk hardly changed since it was built. This route passes the Almoravid **Nejjarine Mosque**. At the end, one can turn left towards the mellah or Place el Hedim or right into the dusty and noisy **Souk Sraira**, just inside the city walls, used by carpenters and metalworkers. At the very end, on the left, is the 12th-century Almohad **Bab Jedid** gate, around which are some interesting stalls selling musical instruments. **Souk Cherchira**, initially occupied by tent-makers, runs parallel to Souk Sraira but outside the city walls. **Souk Sebbat** is the right-hand turning opposite Souk Nejjarine and includes sellers of *babouches*, modern clothes and caftans, several tourist and handicraft shops, a *fondouk* on the right and another on the left, before the Bou Inania Medersa. A turning on the right opposite the *medersa* leads directly onto Rue Dar Smen, a good alternative route to remember.

Best approached from Souk Sebbat is the **Medersa Bou Inania** ① *0900-1200, 1500-1800. Climb up onto the roof for a view of the medina, including the roofs of the Great Mosque, the minaret of the Nejjarine and other mosques.* Founded circa 1345 by Merinid Sultan Abou el Hassan, this former college dispensing religious and legal instruction is a must-visit. The door to the *medersa*, part of a cedar screen, is just under a dome (notable for its ribbed design) at an intersection in the souk. Altogether, the college had 40 cells for its students, on both floors, around an oblong courtyard including a pool, with arcades surrounded by a screened passageway. As with many of the *medersas*, there is eye-catching *zellige* tiling and carved wood lintels. Take a look at the green-and-yellow tiled prayer hall. The doorway is ornamented with *zellige* tiling, as well as the customary and, perhaps, a little over-the-top stalactite-style plasterwork.

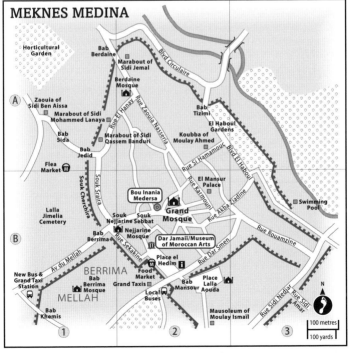

MEKNES MEDINA

Horticultural Garden
Bab Berdaine
Marabout of Sidi Jemal
Blvd Circulaire
Berdaine Mosque
(A)
Zaouia of Sidi Ben Aissa
Marabout of Sidi Mohammed Lanaya
Rue El Hanaf
Rue Zaouia Nasseria
Bab Tizimi
Bab Sida
Marabout of Sidi Qassem Banduri
El Haboul Gardens
Koubba of Moulay Ahmed
Bab Jedid
Rue Si Hamamou
Blvd El Haboul
Flea Market
Souk Sraira
Souk Cherchira
El Mansur Palace
Rue Karmoun
Swimming Pool
Bou Inania Medersa
Lalla Jimelia Cemetery
Souk Nejjarine Sebbat
Grand Mosque
Rue Akba Hadine
(B)
Nejjarine Mosque
Dar Jamaii/Museum of Moroccan Arts
Rue Rouamzine
Bab Berrima
Rue Sekakine
Rue Dar Smen
Av du Mellah
BERRIMA
Place el Hedim
New Bus & Grand Taxi Station
Bab Berrima Mosque
Food Market
Grand Taxis
Bab Mansour
Place Lalla Aouda
Rue Sidi Nediar
Rue Sidi Amar
MELLAH
Local Buses
Bab Khemis
Mausoleum of Moulay Ismaïl
N
100 metres
100 yards
(1)   (2)   (3)

Nearby, the **Grand Mosque**, situated in the heart of the medina, is a 12th-century Almoravid foundation with 14th-century alterations. It is one of the oldest in Meknès and also the largest. Although non-Muslims are not permitted to enter the mosque, it is possible to view its lovely green-tiled roof and the minaret from the neighbouring Medersa Bou Inania (see above).

MELLAH

To the west of Place el Hedim, through a street popular with hawkers of household goods, turn left into Avenue de Mellah. On the left is the mellah, a quarter built by Moulay Ismaïl in 1682 for his large Jewish community, which was walled off from the Muslim medina. The **Bab Berrima Mosque** dates from the 18th century, a time when the mellah was becoming increasingly Muslim. Few members of Meknès's once important Jewish community remain today, however.

BAB EL KHEMIS

Heading southwest towards Rabat, the city wall is broken by Bab el Khemis, built by Moulay Ismaïl, with a range of different arches, decoration and calligraphy. This is the only remaining piece of the garden quarter attributed to Moulay Ismaïl. The rest has gone. It was destroyed by Moulay Abdallah, son of the great Moulay Ismaïl, who was not pleased by the reception he received from the inhabitants when he returned from an unsuccessful campaign. After this, the Boulevard Circulaire leads past a cemetery containing the 18th-century tomb of Sidi Mohammed Ben Aissa, founder of the important religious brotherhood of the Aissoua. It's closed to non-Muslims but worth a look from a respectable distance. The Ben Aissa religious ceremonies are still held on the Mouloud (Prophet Mohammed's birthday). The Boulevard Circulaire continues round to Bab Berdaine, the entrance to the north medina.

NORTHERN MEDINA

Less frequented by tourists, the northern medina is reached by either weaving through the streets from the *medersa* or the souks or, more easily, coming round on the Boulevard Circulaire. **Bab Berdaine** dates from the 17th century, a building decorated by Jamaâ el Rouah and flanked by two immense towers. Inside, on Place el Berdaine, is the **Berdaine Mosque**. Travelling south, the streets continue through an area of the traditional medina, only occasionally spoilt by insensitive new building. Here you are in traditional neighbourhoods where private and public space are clearly differentiated, each quarter having its own mosque, hammam and public oven.

Back on the Boulevard Circulaire, the next major gate around towards Oued Boufekrane is **Bab Tizmi**, near to **Restaurant Zitouna**. Opposite Bab Tizmi is the quiet **Parc el Haboul**, part of an area of gardens and recreational facilities in the valley, dividing the medina and the Ville Nouvelle.

BAB MANSOUR

Claimed by some to be the finest gateway in North Africa, Meknès is dominated by this monumental gate at the top of the hill in the medina, opposite Place el Hedim. It dates from the reign of Sultan Moulay Ismaïl and was completed by his son Moulay Mohammed Ben Abdallah in 1732, and marks the entrance to the huge grounds of his imperial city. The gate is named after one of the sultan's Christian slaves, Mansour the Infidel. The huge size is more of a testimony to its sultan than a reflection of defensive strength. The gate is clearly more about imperial splendour than anything else. The decorated flanking towers do not even have firing posts. The outrepassé arch is surrounded by a blind arch, including the usual lozenge network motif and *zellige* tiling. Between the arch and framing band is a black-tiled area with floral patterns. The overall effect of the main gate is exuberant and powerful. The gate has come to be a symbol of Meknès, even of Morocco as a whole.

IMPERIAL CITY

The imperial city of Moulay Ismaïl is a massive area of crumbling walls and ruins, well worth taking a day to explore at leisure. Immediately through Bab Mansour from Place el Hedim is **Place Lalla Aouda**, once the public meeting point during the period of Moulay Ismaïl and now a relaxing and pleasant area to rest. In the far corner is the **Lalla Aouda Mosque**, the story being that it was built by Princess Aouda as penance for eating a peach during the Ramadan fast.

Directly opposite Bab Mansour, in the right-hand corner of the square, a space in the walls leads through to a second square, the **Mechouar**. To the right note the domed **Koubat al Khayyatine** ① *on the left of the entrance to the building, tickets 10dh*, a plain building with pleasing simple decor situated in a small park behind a fence. In the 18th century this was used to receive ambassadors and, later, to make uniforms. Koubat el Khayyatine translates as 'the tailors' dome'. Inside is a display of photos of old Meknès. Outside, right of the entrance, a flight of stairs leads down to dank and vaulted underground chambers, said by guides to be the prison of the Christian slaves, although why one should want to keep a workforce down here is anyone's guess.

In the wall opposite the small park the right-hand gate leads to a golf course. This was originally to have been a lake, but was converted to its present use by the king. Behind the golf course is a later palace of Moulay Ismaïl, the **Royal Palace** or **Dar al Makhzen** ① *closed to visitors*, still in use and now heavily restored.

South of Place Lalla Aouda, the **Mausoleum of Moulay Ismaïl** ① *access via the monumental entrance in the cream wall opposite an arcade of craft shops (stock-up on film here), entrance fee (sometimes)*, contains the tombs of Moulay Ismaïl, his wife and Moulay Ahmed. Unusually for religious buildings in Morocco, the mausoleum is open to non-Muslims. These visitors can enter as far as an annex to the mosque section and admire from there the plaster stucco, *zellige* tiling and distinctive and exuberant colouring. The guardian normally allows visitors to take photos of the interior of the mosque from the annex.

Just past the mausoleum is an entrance to **Dar el Kebira** ('the big house'), Moulay Ismaïl's late 17th-century palace. The palace is in ruins, but the nature of the original structure of the building can be discerned. Since the 18th century, houses have been built into the walls of the palace. Back out on the road, pass under the passage of the **Bab ar Rih** ('Gate of the Winds'), a long, arched structure. Follow the walled road, running between the Dar el Kebira and the Dar al Makhzen and turn right at the end. Carry straight ahead through another arch and, after around 200 m, you reach another chunky *pisé* wall, the Heri es Souani building.

HERI ES-SOUANI

① *0830-1200, 1430-1830*.
Close to the city campsite and a hefty 35-minute walk from the medina, Heri es Souani, also called Dar el Ma ('the Water Palace'), is a large, impressive structure, also dating from

the reign of Moulay Ismaïl and used variously as granary, warehouse and water point to provide for the court, army and followers in either the normal run of events or in case of emergencies, such as conflict or drought. It is a good indication of the scale of Moulay Ismaïl's imperial ambitions. From the roof there would be a good view, if one were allowed up. The nearby Agdal basin is now used for storing water for irrigation purposes. Once it was presumably a vital reserve in case of siege. Popular with strollers at weekends and on summer evenings, the location is a little stark on a hot summer afternoon, so have a post-visit drink at the café in the nearby campsite.

→MOULAY IDRISS AND VOLUBILIS

The shrine town of Moulay Idriss and the Roman ruins at Volubilis are an easy day trip from Meknès, although there is a hotel at Volubilis and more at Moulay Idriss for those who want to stay over and get a really early start, a good idea in summer when the heat can be oppressive. Volubilis, set in open fields, is a delight in spring, with wild flowers abounding. The ruins, covering over 40 ha, have poetic names – the House of Orpheus and the House of the Nymphs, the House of the Athlete and the House of the Ephèbe, and there is a noble forum, a triumphal arch to Caracalla as well as ancient oil presses. The vanished splendour of Volubilis is echoed by legendary evocations of early Islam at Moulay Idriss nearby. This most venerable pilgrimage centre, set between steep hillsides, was founded in the eighth century by one Idriss Ibn Abdallah, great-grandson of Ali and Fatima, the Prophet Mohammed's daughter. Today he is referred to as Idriss el Akbar, 'the Great'. His son, Idriss II, is buried and venerated in Fès.

ARRIVING IN MOULAY IDRISS AND VOLUBILIS

Getting there Moulay Idriss is 30 km north of Meknès; Volubilis a little further north. For Moulay Idriss, take a grand taxi from Rue de Yougoslavie, or from the square below Place el Hedim (a 10dh ride). There are also regular buses from below Bab Mansour. The last bus back is at 1900. Volubilis is a clearly signposted 5-km drive from Moulay Idriss, a pleasant walk on a nice day, or a short taxi ride. Alternatively, for Volubilis bargain in Meknès for a grand taxi (split cost with others, say 50dh the trip), or take a bus for Ouezzane and get dropped off near the site. If travelling by car, leave Meknès by Rue de Yougoslavie in the Ville Nouvelle, and follow the R410 as far as Aïn el Kerma, and from there the N13 to Moulay Idriss.

MOULAY IDRISS

Coming round the last bend from Meknès, Moulay Idriss is a dramatic sight; houses and mosques piled up around two rocky outcrops, with the *zaouïa*, or sanctuary, in between. The centre of the Jbel Zerhoun region, Moulay Idriss is a pilgrimage centre, including as it does the tomb of its namesake, Idriss Ben Abdallah Ben Hassan Ben Ali, the great-great-grandson of the prophet Mohammed. The town is an alternative to Mecca in Morocco for those unable to do the ultimate pilgrimage. Moulay Idriss came to Morocco from Arabia, after defeat at the Battle of Fakh in 786. In 788 he was accepted as imam by the Amazigh Aurora tribe at Volubilis and continued the rest of his life in Morocco, before he was poisoned in 791, to win over the loyalty of the tribes to the Idrissid Dynasty he established, and to spread the faith of Islam. This town and Fès were two of his major legacies.

However, the town of Moulay Idriss was mainly developed in the 18th century by Sultan Moulay Ismaïl, in part using materials lifted from nearby Volubilis, which the sultan plundered without restraint. Moulay Idriss was closed to non-Muslims until 1912 and, even today, is primarily a Muslim sanctuary, best visited during the day as an excursion and, although not unfriendly, certainly a place to be treated with cautious respect. A religious festival, or *moussem*, is held here in August, when the town is transformed by an influx of pilgrims and a sea of tents.

Buses and taxis stop in the main square, where there are some basic restaurants and cafés. Above it is the **Zaouïa of Moulay Idriss**, as well as shops for various souvenir items associated with pilgrimage: rosaries, scarves, candles and a delicious array of nougats, candies and nuts. The sanctuary itself, with its green-tiled roofs, a succession of prayer halls, ablution areas and tombs, is closed to non-Muslims.

Looking up from the square, the medina clings to the two hills, on the left is Khiba, while Tasga is on the right. Steep paths climb through the residential areas. After the climb, there is a rewarding view over the sanctuary, showing the courtyards and roofs, and the adjacent royal guesthouse. The road through the town, keeping right, leads to a Roman bath just above the stream. Further on, beyond the road, there is a ruined 18th-century palace with a good view of the town.

VOLUBILIS

ⓘ *Below the Jbel Zerhoun and 5 km from Moulay Idriss along the N13, the site is signed from the road, has parking (10dh usually), a café and ticket office but little else. It can be viewed in a day trip. In summer, start early to avoid the heat. On the way in, note the collection of mosaics and sculptures, an 'open-air museum'. Open 0800 to sunset. 20dh.*

Volubilis is by far the most impressive Roman site in Morocco and sits in a spectacular spot, with the hills and Moulay Idriss behind, vast views over the plain below. While much has been removed to adorn other cities over the centuries, or taken to museums such as the one in Rabat, the structure of the town is largely intact, the design of the buildings clearly discernible from the ruins. Many floor mosaics remain, remarkably unaffected by the passing centuries.

Background Archaeological evidence points to the possibility of a Neolithic settlement at Volubilis, while tablets found show there was a third-century BC Phoenician settlement. In AD 24 it was the western capital of the Roman kingdom of Mauretania, and from AD 45 to 285 the capital of the Roman province of Mauretania Tingitana. Under the Romans the immediate region prospered from producing olive oil. However, as Volubilis was at the southeastern extremity of the province, connected to Rome through the Atlantic ports, its weak position necessitated extensive city walls.

Under the Emperor Diocletian, Rome withdrew to the coastal areas, leaving Volubilis at the mercy of neighbouring tribes. The city survived but its Christian and Jewish population diminished in importance, becoming the Christian enclave of Oualila during the eighth century. Though proclaimed sultan in Volubilis, Moulay Idriss preferred Fès. By the 11th century, Volubilis was totally deserted. It suffered again when Moulay Ismaïl ransacked the ruins to build Meknès and, further, in the earthquake of 1755. French excavations and reconstruction began in 1915. The metal tracks on the site date from this period.

The site From the ticket office the entrance to the city is by the southeastern gate. A path, with sculptures and tombstones alongside it, leads down to a bridge across the

Oued Fetassa. Up on the other side the first important remains in an area of small houses and industrial units are of an **olive press complex**. The mill stones, for crushing the olives, and the tanks for collecting and separating the oil, can be seen. Olive presses can be found through much of the city, as olive oil production was as essential an element in its economy as it is in the area today. Many of the same techniques are still used.

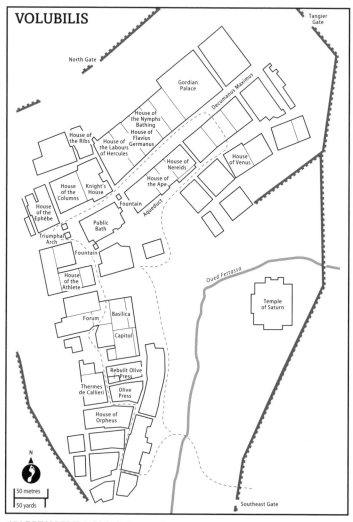

VOLUBILIS

Tangier Gate

North Gate

Gordian Palace

Decumanus Maximus

House of the Nymphs Bathing

House of the Ribs

House of Flavius Germanus

House of the Labours of Hercules

House of Nereids

House of Venus

House of the Columns

Knight's House

House of the Ape

House of the Éphèbe

Fountain

Aqueduct

Triumphal Arch

Public Bath

Fountain

House of the Athlete

Oued Fertassa

Temple of Saturn

Forum

Basilica

Capitol

Rebuilt Olive Press

Thermes de Callieri

Olive Press

House of Orpheus

N

50 metres
50 yards

Southeast Gate

Right of the olive press is the **House of Orpheus**, a large mansion. In this building, as in most, some areas will be clearly roped off, and it is advisable to respect this, to avoid the whistle and wrath of the otherwise very friendly guardian. The first entrance gives access to a room with an intricate dolphin mosaic, to a kitchen with a niche for religious figures, and to a paved bathroom and boiler room. Note the complex heating system. The second entrance leads to an open court with a mosaic of the goddess Amphitrite, with living rooms around it, including a dining room with an Orpheus mosaic, showing the hero playing his harp.

Roman imperial settlements, even the most provincial, had impressive arrays of public buildings to cement a general feeling of Romanity. This was architecture as identity, and Volubilis was no exception. Heading further down into the site, and then to the right, lie the **Baths of Gallienus**, public baths which are the distant ancestor of the Moroccan hammam. Beyond this, the large public square in front of the Basilica is the **Forum**. In this area are a number of monuments to leading Roman figures. The **Basilica** is one of the most impressive ruins, with a number of columns still intact. This third-century building was the court house for the city.

Beside the Basilica is the **Capitol**, also with columns. In the court in front there is an altar and steps leading up to the **temple** dedicated to Juno, Minerva and Jupiter Optimus Maximus. This building had great state importance, being the place where the council would assemble on great occasions.

Adjacent to the Forum is the **House of the Athlete**, named after the mosaic of an athlete winning a cup. The Triumphal Arch dominates the skyline, as well as the Decumanus Maximus, the roadway leading to the Tangier Gate. This was built in AD 217 to honour Emperor Caracalla and his mother Julia Domna. Originally finished with fountains and medallions, the arch was heavily reconstructed by French archaeologists. Although not of the same finesse as the honorary arches surviving in the Roman cities of Tunisia and Libya, it is nevertheless impressive. The Decumanus Maximus, the main street, had a colonnade with small shops, in front of a series of large houses, some containing interesting mosaics.

Starting on the left, from just beside the Triumphal Arch, the **House of the Ephèbe** was built around a courtyard with a pool. The house is named after the bronze statue of a beautiful boy or *ephebos* found in the ruins. Adjacent is the **House of Columns** and then the **Knight's House**, which has an interesting mosaic of Bacchus, good-time god of wine. In a more serious taste, the **House of the Labours of Hercules** has a mosaic with individual pictures of Hercules's life, and another of Jupiter. Further up, the **House of the Nymphs Bathing** has a mosaic showing nymphs undressing. The largest house on this side, the **Gordian Palace**, is fronted by columns, but the remains are quite plain. This may have been the governor's residence from the time of Gordian III, with both domestic quarters and offices.

On the right-hand side of Decumanus Maximus from the Triumphal Arch there is a large **public bath and fountains**, fed by an aqueduct. Three houses up is the **House of Nereids** with a pool mosaic. Behind this and one up is the House of Venus, which has one of the best arrays of mosaics. The central courtyard pool has a mosaic of chariots. There are also mosaics of Bacchus, on the left, and Hylos and two nymphs, on the right. Nearby is a mosaic of Diana and the horned Actaeon. From the House of Venus cross back over the Oued Fetassa to the remains of the **Temple of Saturn**, a Phoenician temple before the Romans took it over. From here, follow the path back to the entrance, perhaps for refreshments in the café.

MEKNES AND AROUND LISTINGS

WHERE TO STAY

€€€ Riad Safir, 1 Derb Lalla Alamia, Bab Aissi, T035-534785, riadsafir@menara.ma. This riad expanded recently and now combines 2 quite different, though equally stylish, spaces. The 1st house is cosy and bohemian, filled with warm red and orange textiles and lots of carved wood detailing. The 2nd offers a more contemporary interpretation of Moroccan architecture, with cooling greys and greens. All 7 rooms have bags of character and plenty of space.

€€ Riyad Bahia, 13 Tiberbarine, T035-554541, www.ryad-bahia.com. This is a pretty little guesthouse with a comfortable, laid-back vibe. Rooms are decorated with antique wooden doors, low tables and cushions, and all have big beds with soft linens; suites have fireplaces. Bouchra's cooking is among the best in Morocco.

€€-€ Riad El Ma, 4 derb Sidi Besri, T0661-514824, www.riad-el-ma.com. An atmospheric riad, big on original details, such as ornate plasterwork, painted doors and zellige tiles, complemented by home-away-from-home service. The 6 rooms have colour themes, private bathrooms and big, comfortable beds. The large central courtyard creates a great sense of space. There's also a library, a dining room for breakfasts and evening meals (book in advance) and a small, corner rooftop pool.

€ Hotel Majestic, 19 Av Mohammed V, T035-522033. A quirky, but in some ways quite fabulous old 1930s-style place, this is a great pad for lovers of kitsch. There are 47 clean rooms, each panelled in dark wood beneath layers of varnish and purple bedspreads. Rooms on the street are on the noisy side, so it's worth opting for a quieter inner room.

€ Youth hostel, Av Okba Ibn Nafii, near the municipal stadium and **Hotel Transatlantique**, T035-524698, www.hihostels.com. Open 1000-1200 and 1600-1700. This is the HI's headquarters in Morocco and is one of the best and friendliest hostels in the country, with dorms arranged around a garden. Clean, comfortable and well maintained.

Moulay Idriss

Accommodation is slowly improving, though much of it is still fairly basic.

€€ Dar Zerhoune, T0642-247793, www.buttonsinn.com. Far and away the best place in town. A boutique-style guesthouse with just 4 rooms, all simply but very comfortably decorated, with large bathrooms, quality bed linens and some great details, such as the sea serpent table legs and flea market finds.

RESTAURANTS

Meknès

Two sides of Pl el Hedim fill up with street foodstalls selling mostly brochettes.

€€ Café Restaurant Gambrinus, Av Omar Ibn el Ass, opposite the market, off Av Hassan II, T035-520258. This friendly little place serves French, Spanish and Moroccan cuisine, and it's a reliable lunch stop for refuelling. Interesting wall murals give it the edge over similar places.

€€ Restaurant Riad, 79 Ksar Chaacha, T035-530542. This rather grand medina restaurant offers a range of traditional Moroccan dishes such as beef and prune tagine, pigeon *pastilla* and couscous on Fri. It has no alcohol licence and can fill up with tour groups, but you can eat outside in a garden filled with flowers and cacti and a small, slightly unkempt pool.

€ Oumnia, 8 Ain Fouki Rouamzine, T035-533938. A cosy little family-run place with a good-value fixed menu of Moroccan staples. Follow the signs off Rue Rouamzine.

MIDDLE ATLAS

From Fès or Meknès there are a number of interesting towns to visit in the Middle Atlas, possibly as stopovers to break a journey south to Marrakech, or as places to escape the summer heat and do some walking in the hills and cedar forests. In a week you could comfortably combine Fès and Meknès (plus Volubilis and Moulay Idriss) with a circuit southwards, which might include overnights in Azrou, Ifrane, Sefrou or Immouzer du Kandar. A loop southwest of Azrou would take you down to Khénifra and back up via the Aguelmane Azigza and Oum er Rbia, Morocco's largest river, which flows into the Atlantic at Azzemour. Strategically located on the road between the imperial cities and Tafilalet, and next to magnificent mountains, Midelt at an altitude of 1525 m, looks as though it will have a good future as a base for hikers.

→AZROU AND AROUND

Azrou, 70 km south of Meknès, is a small Amazigh market town and hill resort at the heart of the Middle Atlas. The name means rock in Tamazight and refers to the rock in the middle of the town next to the large new mosque. The town has a relaxed air and good hiking in the wooded vicinity. The ruined kasbah was built by Moulay Ismaïl. If you have a car, there are some very scenic routes south of Azrou where the landscapes are truly spectacular. One loop would take you up to **Aïn Leuh**, past Lac Ouiouane and across the **Plateau des Cèdres** to the source of the **Oum er Rbia** (Morocco's major river) and onto the **Aguelmane Azigza** and **Khénifra** (a possible overnight stop), or back up from Khénifra on the main N8 to Azrou via Mrirt (large Thursday souk).

ARRIVING IN AZROU
All buses, except those of CTM, arrive at the bus station opposite the Grand Mosque, near Place Mohammed V. The grand taxi station is close by, near the roundabout. Azrou is a one-horse sort of place, so there are no difficulties getting around.

MOVING ON
Midelt (see page 179) is a couple of hours away by car, bus or shared taxi. Two CTM buses come through at night but there's also one in the afternoon.

BACKGROUND
One of Azrou's claims to fame is that under the French protectorate, it was chosen to be home to the Collège berbère, a training school for Moroccan Berbers, which was founded on the premise that Arabs and Imazighen were fundamentally different – and should be educated and ruled as such. The divide-and-rule policy backfired – it was in the interests of neither Arabs nor Imazighen for a colonial regime to continue to control Morocco; in any case, loyalty to Islam and the Alaouite throne proved to be stronger than ethnic ties, a fact which somehow escaped French colonial ethnographers. After Independence, the Collège berbère became the Lycée Tarik Ibn Zayid, symbolically named for the Arab conqueror of Andalucía. In the late 1990s, Amazigh cultural movements began demanding more official recognition of their cultural identity; it will be interesting to see how Morocco handles its large Amazigh minorities in coming years.

PLACES IN AZROU

Azrou's traditional character, once created by the green-tiled roofs of the arcades round the market square, has taken a beating. Although there are a few good hotels and it is ideally located as a base for exploring the cedar forests, it has yet to find its place in the tourist market. It seems to function as a sort of suburb to its more upmarket neighbour, Ifrane. The heart of Azrou, **Place Mohammed V**, is to the right on leaving the bus stop. There is a covered **market** near Place Mohammed V, while the **Ensemble Artisanal** ① *0830-1200, 1430-1800*, is situated off Avenue Mohammed V, with a fixed-price shop and a number of craftsmen working on the premises – look out for the Middle Atlas carpets. A large **Amazigh souk** is held just above the town on Tuesday, with vegetables, textiles and some interesting Middle Atlas carpets, as well as traditional entertainment from musicians and others. The town also has a small pool for summer use.

AROUND AZROU

If you have time, seek out the region's largest and most famous cedar, the **Cèdre de Gouraud**, named after some half-forgotten French military commander. This is signposted to the right off the Azrou to Ifrane road, down a narrow, winding road. Barbary apes will be eagerly waiting among the trees to share the contents of your picnic.

Of more specialized interest is the abandoned **Benedictine monastery** at **Tioumliline** ① *turn right a few hundred metres up the hill after the Ifriquia petrol station above Azrou on the Midelt road.* The monastery, founded in 1920, was finally relinquished in 1963, becoming a vocational training centre, abandoned along with the dispensary in the 1980s. Low stone buildings, a cloister planted with cypress, lilac, and a Judas tree survive on this beautiful site, as does the church building and the graves of five fathers. The monastery was important as a meeting place for Moroccan intellectuals in the heady days after independence, providing a refuge to abstract painter Gharbaoui, amongst others. The location is lovely, and birdwatchers may find things of interest in the mixed deciduous/cedar woodlands here.

At 19 km south of Azrou, a turning off the N8 leads to **Aïn Leuh**, an Amazigh village with a Wednesday souk important to the semi-nomadic Beni M'Guild tribe, a ruined kasbah from the reign of Moulay Ismaïl, and nearby waterfalls. You then follow a narrow road through cedar forest and across a plateau, past **Lac Ouiouane** and its 1930s chalets to the source of the River Oum er Rbia, 20 km away. In places, the cedar forest has been cut back to form a thick green crown on the tops of the hills. The villages here are desperately poor, there is little traffic and children will come racing out at the first sign of a passing vehicle. Many of the houses are little more than stone shelters with crude plank roofs, now partly rendered more watertight with plastic. Drive slowly as the road is narrow. Eventually, you drop down to the source of **Oum er Rbia**, clearly visible with its water works from above. There is a car park (lots of men wanting to warden your car) and steps leading to a series of concrete platforms built on the rocks where the river waters come boiling out from between the boulders. (Some of the springs are said to be sweet, others salty.) After the platforms, you can clamber up to see where the water comes crashing into a small, but not actually very deep pool (no diving). After the source, you can head west on a narrow and in places much deteriorated metalled road through beautiful landscape to join the main N8 south of Mrirt. The other option is to continue on south to **Aguelmane Azigza**, a crater lake surrounded by forest and ideal for swimming. The tree-lined spot has its devoted followers among Moroccan campers and is a fine location for some birdwatching. There also may be accommodation on offer in a local café. The road continues to rejoin the N8 at Khénifra.

→IFRANE AND THE LAKES

Ifrane, 17 km north of Azrou and 63 km south of Fès, is a mountain resort founded by the French in 1929 which today has numerous large villas and chalets, as well as a royal palace and hunting lodge. It still manages to have something of a colonial hill-station feel to it, despite the arrival of a large new campus university housed in chalet-type buildings and vast new social housing developments on the Azrou side of town. When the palace is occupied by the king, the town becomes busy with staff and politicians. From the town there are good walks in the cedar forests, and a drivable excursion round the *dayats* (crater lakes). There is some skiing to be had at the nearby resort of **Mischliffen** and there is a small airport maintained for private and royal flights.

THE DAYAT LAKES
North of Ifrane, leave the N8 to the east for a tour of the dayats, seasonal limestone lakes which are a haven for wildlife, especially birds. There are four lying between the N8 and the R503: Aaoua and Ifrah are the largest but you can also visit Afourgah and Iffer. **Dayat Aaoua**, 12 km from Ifrane, is a scenic place to picnic if the lake is full, which is not the case in drought years and can make the area disappointing for birdwatchers. In good circumstances, however, the dayats are home to coots, herons and egrets; look out for the black-winged stilt and numerous reed warblers. The surrounding woodland, made up mainly of holm-oak and cedar, is alive with birds: tits, chaffinches, short-toed treecreeper, jays, greater spotted woodpeckers and raptors including black and red kite, Egyptian vulture and booted eagle. In the woodland Barbary apes can be seen and, where the woodland gives way to more open plateau, look out for the jackals.

IMMOUZER DU KANDAR
A small hill resort, 80 km south of Fès and beautiful in spring with the apple blossom, Immouzer is a popular excursion from Fès, easily accessed with regular buses and grands taxis. It is also a lively place during the **Fête des Pommes** in July. Market day takes place on Mondays in the ruined kasbah. Just north of Immouzer du Kandar are the popular picnic/ camping springs, **Aïn Seban** and **Aïn Chifa**, clearly signposted to the west of the road. In drought conditions they are less attractive.

→MIDELT

For many, the rough-and-ready mining town of Midelt is a handy overnight stop about halfway between the imperial cities and the Tafilalet. Despite high unemployment, the town has a calm, friendly atmosphere and a souk on Sunday. Those in need of a little retail therapy should think carpets in Midelt. These can be bought from the weaving school (*atelier de tissage*) of the **Kasbah Meriem**, the local name for the monastery/convent of **Notre Dame de l'Atlas** ① *T0535-580858,* which is run by Franciscan sisters in premises off the road to Tattiouine. There is also a tiny community of Trappist monks here who relocated from Algeria. The sisters may also be a good source of information about the region. To get there, head north out of Midelt town centre, take a left turn onto the track after the bridge, follow the track towards the kasbah village, where you then take a sharp right and go almost immediately left up the hill. After about 1 km, the Kasbah Meriem is signed on the left, down a dip and up again, its presence indicated by trees. The atelier is left of the large metal gate. Inside, there is a simple church with a small icon of the seven sleepers of Ephesus, symbol of a myth present both in Christianity and Islam. The Franciscan sisters do lots of good work in the region, travelling off into the countryside with mules and a dispensary tent. While the covert funding by USA churches of Protestant missionary activity has attracted criticism in the Moroccan press, the Franciscans' efforts are much appreciated by locals.

For more on **hiking** opportunities and other possible excursions in the area, head for **Aït Ayach**, halfway between Midelt and Zeïda on the N13, where the **Auberge-Restaurant Timnay** can help with vehicle hire and guides (see page 182).

→ AROUND MIDELT

Midelt works well as base for excursions, to the abandoned mines of Ahouli in a defile of the Oued Moulouya, or an off-road trip to the Cirque de Jaffar, a natural amphitheatre in the side of Jbel Ayyachi, paramount peak of the region. In the heart of the eastern High Atlas, Imilchil is now feasible as a long day trip on the metalled road via Rich. Note that, as elsewhere in this plateau region, the winters are very cold and the summers very hot, so the best time to visit is the spring. Here the spring is later, and May or even early June are recommended for walking.

MINES OF AHOULI
For those with a hire car, this excursion north from Midelt goes along the S317 to **Mibladene** (10 km) and over the head of the Oued Moulouya to the abandoned mining settlement of Ahouli. The road is signed right a few metres north from the central bus station junction in Midelt. The first long straight section to Mibladene is badly potholed but it then improves slightly after Mibladene, a former mining community, to the right of the road. You then wind into spectacular gorges. The road deteriorates again after an Indiana Jones-style bridge, parts of it washed away by floods.

Ahouli must once have been a hive of activity. Copper and lead were the main products. The gorge is beautiful, with poplar, oleander and even the odd weeping willow. Mine infrastructure and housing clings to the cliffs. The community even had its own rather splendid cinema (now sanded up) and swimming pool. The lower floors of the houses had heavy metal doors, to keep out eventual floodwater. There is a caretaker here, and he or his son may show you round.

After Ahouli, you can drive up out of the gorges on a well-made track, turning left to more abandoned dwellings on the plateau. Turning left, a couple of kilometres brings you to the small village and semi-abandoned *ksar of* **Ouled Taïr** next to the *oued*, reached by a wobbly footbridge.

Note When driving out to Mibladene, men will try to flag the car down. Most will be selling fossils or stones of some kind. With all three mines in the region (Mibladene, Ahouli and Zaïda) now closed, there is a lot of poverty; selling stones is about the only thing left to do for many.

JBEL AYYACHI

Midelt is also the jumping-off place for treks up to Jbel Ayyachi, which at 3747 m is eastern Morocco at its highest, an impressive 45 km stretch of solid mountain, unbroken by any peaks. First conquered in July 1901 by the Marquis de Segonzac, the heights can remain snow-covered well into late June. In the right conditions, on a long summer's day, the climb can be done in a day, but it's probably better to take two days and bivouac out on the mountain. To tackle the Jbel Ayyachi, head first for **Tattiouine**, 12 km from Midelt (grand taxi transport available). Here it should be possible to find mules and a guide. For a fit party, the climb and back should take around 12 hours. Make sure you have plenty of water. Even in summer, it can be very cold at the summit.

Impressive and seemingly impenetrable with its snow-capped heights, the Jbel Ayyachi functions as a water tower for southeastern Morocco, its meltwater feeding both the Moulouya to the north and the Oued Ziz to the south. Jbel Ayyachi derives its name from the local Aït Ayyach tribe. Within living memory, caves in the cliffs were occupied by freedom fighters resisting the Makhzen and the incoming French. The last of such mountain strongholds were only finally taken by the central authorities in 1932.

CIRQUE DU JAFFAR

One of Morocco's best known 4WD excursions takes intrepid off-roaders up to the Cirque de Jaffar (map NI-30-II-3), one of the natural arenas hollowed out on the north side of the Jbel Ayyachi. In fact, in a good off-road vehicle, it is just about possible to travel over from Midelt, via the Oued Jaffar, to **Imilchil**, a distance of 160 km. The initial part through the Oued Jaffar gorges is the most scenic. The route is not to be attempted in winter, however, and certainly not risked in spring if there are April snows. Consult the **Gendarmerie royale** in Midelt or the people at **Auberge-Restaurant Timnay** on the Zeïda road (see page 182).

GORGES DU ZIZ

The N13 north to the Gorges of the Ziz is a superb route. For the first 20 km the road follows the Oued Ziz. Caves can be seen cut into the cliff, no doubt used to store crops. On your right is the western shore of the **Barrage de Hassan Addakhil**, completed in 1971. The dam supplies water to Er Rachidia and the region's oases. It also limits the potentially destructive flash flooding of the Oued Ziz. Migrating birds stop over on the lake, too. If you travel along this route in the evening, the sun accentuates the landforms, highlighting bands of hard rock with screes between. Then you come to the **Gorges of the Ziz**, a spectacular ride in a narrow defile 2 km in length. At around 29 km from Er Rachidia, where a bridge crosses the river, there is the small settlement of **Ifri** where picnicking and camping are possible.

If you have lots of time, then continue on the N13, through the Legionaire's Tunnel, to the hot springs of **Moulay Ali Cherif**, 42 km north of Er Rachidia. Follow through to the gardens of **Tirhiourine**. The surfaced road links with the N10 a few kilometres east of Er Rachidia, near the airport.

MIDDLE ATLAS LISTINGS

WHERE TO STAY

Azrou and around

€€ Hotel Panorama, T035-562010, panorama@extra.net.ma. This is the best hotel in Azrou and, as the name suggests, the one with the best views. All of the 38 rooms have a balcony or terrace from which to admire them and, slightly less attractively, they also have large TVs should your penchant be for late-night Arabic TV. Elsewhere the hotel is pleasant enough, with some good-quality contemporary photographs decorating the walls and a restaurant and bar for a sundowner. It's good value for money too.

€ Hotel Azrou, Rte de Khénifra opposite the Crédit agricole, about 600 m down from central mosque, T035-562116. This is simple, no-frills accommodation at its best, with freshly painted walls and clean en suite rooms with single beds (but not 24-hr hot water). There's a bar and restaurant that seems to open depending on business. Private parking.

€ Hotel Salam (Chez Jamal), Pl Saouika off Pl Mohammed V, T035-562562. This is quite a sweet little place overlooking the main square (the entrance is at the rear), if you don't mind getting back to basics. The decor is of the colourful birthday cake variety so beloved by Moroccans, but the management is friendly and willing and they'll do their best to ensure a happy stay. Some rooms are en suite (hot water costs 8dh) and it has a pleasant roof terrace.

Ifrane

€€€€ Michlifen Ifrane Suites and Spa, Av Hassan II 18, T0535-864000, www.michlifenifrane.com. Under the same ownership as **La Moumounia** in Marrakech, this brings a touch of glamour to the alpine-esque town of Ifrane. Expect 5-star service with bells on. There's a luxury spa and hamman, beautiful bedrooms, several excellent restaurants and stunning views of snow-capped mountains. Design-wise, think American lodge luxury and sleek, Nordic minimalism, with plenty of wow-factor. There's even a log-fire by the indoor pool.

€€ Hotel Le Chamonix, T0535 566028. A good, mid-range option, with 64 bright clean rooms, with fairly chintzy communal areas and simple, comfortable decor in the rooms. It could do with a bit of TLC these days, but friendly service and a willing attitude make up for it. The restaurant serves alcohol, and you can hire skis from the bar.

€€ Hotel Perce Neige, Rue des Asphodelles, T0535-566210, www.hotel-leperceneige.com. This is a friendly little place of just 22 rooms and 5 suites, which is good value if a little jaded. In the centre of town, it's a suitable base for exploring and has a good-value restaurant and bar.

€ Gite Dayet Aoua, Rte d'Immouzer a Ifrane, Km7, T0535-604880, T0661-351257, www.gite-dayetaoua.com. About 7 km outside Ifrane, this basic gîte is set in stunning countryside. Peacocks and chickens roam the gardens, decor is a cut above most gîtes of this level, each room individually and carefully decorated with local textiles and crafts. Don't expect modern luxuries but if you want to get away from the mob, sample home-cooked Moroccan food served in a Berber tent, or go on long walks from your back door, it's a winner. They can also arrange bivouacs for camping in the hills, canoe trips and guides.

Midelt

There is only the most basic of accommodation in Midelt itself, and it's worth getting off the beaten path a little to find the best of it. Reservations are recommended in the spring.

€ Auberge-Restaurant Timnay, Aït Ayach, halfway between Midelt and Zeïda on the N13, 20 km from Midelt, T0535-583434, timnay@iam.net.ma.

This is an efficient set-up, with a range of accommodation, including simple rooms, camping, nomad tents and sites for campervans. There is a restaurant, shop and pool, also 4WD rental, with guide for exploring the region. For a 4WD, you may feel that 4 people are necessary to cover costs. Possible circuits on offer include Zaouïa Sidi Hamza and the upper Taâraârt Valley (2 days, 415dh pp). There are also good day trips to Canyon de Tatrout.

€ **Hotel Atlas**, Rue Mohammed Amraoui, T035-582938. This small family-run hotel is very clean, with pale blue rooms, colourful bedspreads and a roof terrace with mountain views. Shower 10dh, besara soup 5dh. Great value for money.

€ **Hotel Bougafer**, 7 Av Mohammed V, T0535-583099. Up the hill round behind the bus station, this place has good, clean en suite rooms and simple 3- and 4-bed rooms on the top floor. There's internet access from 2 computers and the restaurant has a cinema-sized TV screen, which pulls in locals as well as tourists.

RESTAURANTS

Azrou and around

€€ **Hotel Panorama**, T0535-562010 (see also Where to stay, above). With its crackling wood fire and 100dh menu, including mountain delicacies such as Middle Atlas trout and *lapin à la moutarde*, this is a great choice, especially after a hard day's hiking.

€€ **Hotel Restaurant des Cèdres**, Pl Mohammed V, T0535-562326. Behind the net curtains, there are 2 fixed menus, one 'gastronomique', one 'touristique', though you may find it's cheaper to order the same things à la carte. Service is attentive and the fish is good.

Boulangerie Pâtisserie L'Escalade, 5 Pl Hassan II, T0535-563419. Excellent little baker with very good cakes and biscuits.

Ifrane

€ **Café-Restaurant de la Rose**, 7 Rue des Erables, next to the Mobil station, T0535-566215. This is a fairly basic place that nevertheless offers a hearty menu (70dh) that hits the spot. The special is the *truite en papillottes*. No alcohol. You can also ask

for obliging local mountain guide Izem here, who knows some good routes in the local outback.

Le Croustillant Boulangerie Pâtisserie, does reasonable coffee and has a good selection of pastries in a setting reminiscent of a European cafeteria.

Midelt

€ **Hotel Roi de la Bière**, Av des FAR, T035- 582625. This Moroccan salon offers free internet and lots of Barbie-pink decor, along with a good-value 80dh fixed menu.

€ **Restaurant de Fès**, 2 Av Mohammed, T062-057754. Couscous is the order of the day here, along with some excellent options for vegetarians. Choose from 7 different *salades Marocaine* and an excellent 10-vegetable tagine. Small, welcoming and enthusiastic, it gets filled up with groups, so it's worth trying to bag your table early. 3-course menu for 80dh.

There are some cheap roadside places just up from the station offering mainly tagines – try **Restaurant Lespoir** or **Restaurant du Centre**.

WHAT TO DO

Skiing

The season is Jan-Mar, and the resort at Mischliffen near Ifrane has good, but short, slopes, sometimes with patchy snow cover. Hire equipment from the **Chamonix** restaurant in Ifrane and take a taxi to the resort. This is a small area with cafés and ski lifts but little else. During summer the area is popular with walkers.

ER RACHIDIA TO ERG CHEBBI

The variety and scale of the landscapes is the attraction of east-central Morocco. South of the Gorges of the Ziz and relaxed Er Rachidia are the palm-filled canyons of the Tafilalet on the Ziz river, one of the biggest oases in the world and famous (as well as historically important) for its dates. Further south, there is a crumbling ksar (fortified kasbah) *at Rissani and the high dunes of Merzouga, site of many a Saharan fantasy – both cinematic and personal – as travellers flock to ride camels out into a photogenic ideal of the desert.*

→ER RACHIDIA AND AROUND

Er Rachidia was previously known as Ksar es Souk or 'the village of markets', due to its importance as a trading crossroads for the trans-Saharan caravans. It was renamed after independence for the first Alaouite leader, 17th-century sultan Moulay Rachid. The present town was established by the French, initially by the Foreign Legion, as a military and administrative centre, a role it retains today. The town, with its mix of new concrete and older mud-walled buildings, has little in the way of sights beyond a 19th-century *ksar* near the Erfoud exit, but it is a convenient stopping point at the meeting of routes to Ouarzazate, Erfoud (south), Midelt and Meknès (north), and distant Figuig (east), and so has reasonable facilities and a relaxed atmosphere. It is generally used by visitors as an overnight stop on a 'round the High Atlas' circuit and makes a good place to pause before heading down to Rissani (more crumbling kasbahs) and the dunes of Merzouga. If you can't get accommodation at Merzouga or Erfoud, the dunes are visitable from Er Rachidia on a long day out. Evenings in the town are pleasant, with lots of people out strolling in the streets after the heat of the day, and the main market days are Sunday, Tuesday and Thursday.

ARRIVING IN ER RACHIDIA
Getting there There are several buses a day from Midelt (three hours), Fès (nine hours) and Meknès (eight hours).

Moving on Buses run to Erfoud and Rissani (two hours, see pages 186 and 187). You could get to the dunes of Erg Chebbi by staying in Erfoud or Rissani, but it's preferable to be in one of the Merzouga hotels along the dunes' edge, to the north of Merzouga village (see page 189). A hire car or a grand taxi and an arrangement for someone to meet you at the road's edge for the last leg across the desert is the best bet.

Getting around The grid-iron street pattern, so typical of French garrison towns in the Sahara, makes orientation simple. The main road, Avenue Moulay Ali Cherif, leads down to the new bridge over the Oued Ziz, after which it becomes Avenue el Massira. The *gare routière* is on the right in the town centre on Rue M'Daghra as you head east. The CTM bus company is located here too (T0535-572024). Grands taxis are 200 m further north along the main road.

Tourist information Tourist office ① *44 Rue My Abdellah (near bus station), T0535-570944, Mon-Fri 0830-1630.*

PLACES IN ER RACHIDIA

Er Rachidia is not blessed with myriad sights. You may want to take a look at the historic **Ksar Targa**, about 5 km from the centre. Also of passing interest are the social housing developments on either side of the Midelt road. Here the architects put new homes within neo-*ksar* type walls, which are painted a strong, Marrakech terracotta colour. As the largest town in the southeast, close to the Algerian frontier, the modern Moroccan state clearly needed to mark its presence by such projects. You will also notice quite a number of soldiers – there is a large garrison – and lots of shoeshiners, who will readily apply black polish to dusty walking boots.

→TAFILALET

Heading south from Er Rachidia towards Merzouga, the southern stretches of the Ziz valley, known as the Tafilalet, are particularly fertile. Historically, the region was of considerable importance, due in part to its location on the trans-Saharan trade routes. In the eighth and ninth centuries the region was a separate kingdom and became known as a centre of religious unorthodoxy – of the Kharijite Berber heresy and later of Shi'ism. The ruling Alaouite Dynasty originated in Rissani. From 1916 to 1931 French control of the region was challenged and effectively thwarted by local forces. Many of the settlements of the valley were destroyed in a flood in 1965. Today the region produces figs, olives and dates, but is noted especially for its tamarisk trees. (Dried tamarisk fruit is used in the leather industry for its tannin, essential to the curing process.)

MESKI

Heading for the Tafilalet from Er Rachidia, it's a 94 km journey to Rissani. Meski, lying to the west of the Erfoud road about 18 km east of Er Rachidia, is the first halt, famed for its **Source Bleu**. Developed by the Foreign Legion, Meski has a springwater pool surrounded by palms, and a popular camp site, the **Camping de la Source Bleu**. The **Ksar of Meski** is around 500 years old and the ruins make an attractive silhouette. To get to Meski from Er Rachidia, take a grand taxi, paying the same price as for Erfoud – the Source and campsite are a few hundred metres from the road. Moving on from Meski, you might be able to get a bus, or (easier) hitch a lift with other tourists.

Continuing south on the N13 towards Erfoud, you could easily miss one of the most spectacular views in Morocco. Keeping an eye out, you will eventually glimpse the huge oasis-canyon of the Oued Ziz to the right (west). There is a track, marked by a small cairn, which runs to the edge of the gorge. The view is magnificent – and there will be others there admiring the scenery too.

ALONG THE ZIZ CANYON

After the viewpoints, the road soon drops down into the valley, some 20 km long, where a succession of *ksar* house the farming people who make their living from the area.

If you have time, take a 4WD and a guide along the small roads by the river through the small settlements rather than speeding along the N13. Here you will see a great contrast between the green fertile ribbon of palms and oasis gardens and the surrounding scorched landscape. In each loop of the river stands a *ksar* (fortressed village) made of mud brick guarding the valley and providing protection for the village as well as supervision for the trade in slaves and precious metals that once used this route.

At 28 km from Er Rachidia, the route drops to the valley floor along a road descending down the cliff face. **Zouala** is the first settlement. You could take time to explore the oasis here. Above are soaring crags, below are palms and water: a fine dual environment for birds, the green contrasting with the rock faces. Further on, the large settlement strung out along the road is **Aoufouss**, about 45 km from Rachidia. There is an **Afriquia** petrol station and a CTM stop. Red-washed concrete houses line the road; the old *pisé* dwellings are clearly visible further back. For a break, try the café attached to the petrol station where food is usually good and the bathrooms clean. The road then rises out of the canyon floor onto an arid plain for the final approach to Erfoud.

At **Borj Yerdi**, 14 km north of Erfoud, the first small dunes come into view and, if driving, watch out for sand on the road, despite the tiny fences of palm fronds put up to control the shifting dunes.

North of Erfoud, on the eastern side of the road, is the *ksar* of **Ma'adid**. Here it is said the streets are so narrow and the arrangement so complicated that only locals can find their way in and, more importantly, out. Take a guide if you visit. There will be crowds of excitable children, eager, as usual, for *bonbons* and *stylos*.

→ERFOUD

Erfoud is a southern Moroccan garrison town, founded by the French in the 1930s to administer their desert territories. The modern centre of the Tafilalet region, it makes an excellent base for exploring the valley and nearby desert areas. The small town of Rissani and its *ksar* and the dunes of Erg Chebbi are close by, though to see the latter at their best, you're probably best continuing to Merzouga. Lovers of dates may try to time their visit to coincide with the annual date festival held in October, though it is a movable feast and hard to pin down.

Getting around Erfoud is a small place, easily explored on foot. You will probably want to visit the *ksar* at Rissani, however, which is easily accessible by grand taxi. A number of other *ksar* are a few kilometres outside the main settlement. The Erg Chebbi dunes can be reached by 4WD excursion, with most hotels in Erfoud offering the trip, as well as local desert tour agencies. There are grands taxis and minivans in the early morning between Merzouga and Rissani, leaving from next to the bus station.

PLACES IN ERFOUD

On the other side of the river from the town of Erfoud is the **Borj Est**, a military fort (no admittance, but get a taxi up to the top for the view) overlooking the village and palms, the Tafilalet oasis and the desert. There is a **market** on Sunday in the centre.

At the **Marmar Marble Factory** they polish a black rock estimated to be about 650 million years old, embedded with fossilized shells known as goniatites (ammonites). The slabs, rather reminiscent of tombstones, appear in all the hotels and bars in town. The main quarries are out of town on the road to Merzouga.

Rissani, 22 km south of Erfoud and birthplace of the Alaouite Dynasty, is a sprawling modern village close to the site of the ruined town of Sijilmassa. It has a 17th-century *ksar* which houses most of the population, and the main street has a bank and a few cafés. If you are feeling energetic and have your own transport, you may want to explore other local *ksar* on a heritage trail, the *circuit touristique*.

PLACES IN RISSANI

Sijilmassa was once the Berber capital of the Tafilalet region, and a major trading centre. It was founded in 757 by the Arab leader Moussa ben Nasser and its location on the major Sahel to Europe trade route, from Niger to Tangier, gave it considerable importance and prosperity, trading in gold. Its fame grew, as did its size. The ruins, little of which remain, are between the town and the river. A major new kasbah was put up by Moulay Ismaïl, but the Aït Atta tribe destroyed the town in 1818. The current Alaouite Dynasty settled in the surrounding region in the 13th century before gaining the Moroccan Sultanate in the 17th century. The ruins are really of historical interest only and the guides are often not very well informed – although they can be entertaining. Tales of earthquake destruction are on the fanciful side.

To find out more about Rissani's past, you might call in at the **Centre d'Études et Recherches Alaouites (CERA)** ① *T0535-770305, Mon-Fri 0830-1630*, located in the large austere *ksar* on the main square, just along from the **Hotel Sijilmassa**. There is a library and a small museum, which is just a few small cases of pots from recent excavations and large panels with information in French about the region's history. There is a detailed 1:100,000 scale map of the region, and some of the staff may helpfully speak English.

THE KSAR CIRCUIT AROUND RISSANI

The feel of the Rissani oasis is rather Mesopotamian, with mud monuments crumbling away to fine dust. The region was once prosperous, the palace buildings dotted around designed by architects, unlike the *ksar* villages.

To the southeast of Rissani is the **Zaouïa of Moulay Ali Cherif**, the founder of the Alaouite Dynasty. This is a new building as the previous one was destroyed by flash flood. Non-Muslims may not enter and are prevented therefore from viewing the beautiful glazed tilework, the central courtyard with fountain and surrounded by palms. Moulay Ali Cherif was buried here in 1640. Near here is the **Ksar Akbar**, a ruined Alaouite palace from the 19th century, which once held vast treasures and the rejects of important families. It is also said to be the palace of Moulay Abd el Rahmane, brother of reforming 19th-century sultan Hassan I.

About 2 km to the south is the **Ksar Ouled Abd el Helim**, nicknamed the 'Alhambra of the Tafilalet'. It was built in 1900 by Moulay Rachid, elder brother of Moulay Hassan, as a governor's residence. Its decorated towers, monumental gateway and cloistered courtyards provide a little grandeur in the oasis.

Tinrheras is the most southerly *ksar* at 770 m above sea level. There is a splendid view from the walls of the hammada to the south and the panorama of the oasis to the north. Off the road to Erfoud, in the vicinity of the **Hotel Kasbah Asmaa**, are some more minor sights, including **Ksar Jebril**, a large, still-populated village to the west, and **Al Mansouria**, another village to the east, about 300 m into the palm groves. Here there are yet more crumbling remains of vanished palaces, including a rather spectacular gate.

Some 61 km southwest of Erfoud, Merzouga has one attraction: the 150-m-high dunes of Erg Chebbi, a vast pile of sand stretching into the Sahara. The dunes are an offshoot of a much bigger area of dunes across the border in Algeria but, because of the relative accessibility of Erg Chebbi, they have often been used as a film set by Hollywood directors. And it's not hard to see why. As the sun shifts across the sky during the day, the dunes change colour, from the palest cream to deep oranges and reds, and their beautiful shapes and patterns are constantly sculpted by the wind. Despite the popularity of the dunes, it's easy to escape any sign of human habitation, especially if you get up early for a walk. Bear in mind, however, that what might at first appear no more than a lifeless expanse of sand is, in fact, a fragile ecosystem and one that quad bike tours are in danger of destroying.

All of the hotels along the edge of Erg Chebbi organize **camel treks** into the dunes – usually out to semi-permanent tent encampments where you stay a night before coming back to the hotel. The cheaper trips tend to go a short distance to a communal camp where you may find that the romance of a night under the bright Saharan stars is spoiled by the crowds. Pay a bit more and you should get a small camp, with varying degrees of comfort. Camps to the northern or southern slopes of the dunes tend to be quieter. There is little else, beside the other tourists and a small village with a Saturday souk, but the calm and the wilderness are a big part of the appeal. There is occasionally good birdwatching in the adjacent **Dayat Merzouga**, when it has water. Another (summer) option is to have a sand bath, said to be good for rheumatism.

The *piste* continues south to **Taouz**, and with a 4WD you can travel along the once 'forbidden track' (shown as the *piste interdite* on the maps) west to Remlia and the confluence of the dry river valleys of the Gheris and Ziz.

WHERE TO STAY

Er Rachidia

€€€ Hotel Kenzi-Rissani, Av Moulay Ali Cherif, in the direction of Erfoud, T0535-572584, www.kenzi-hotels.com. Pleasant location on the town's outskirts, 62 rooms, restaurant, bar, tennis and pool, open to non-residents for 50dh daily. Can get very booked up by tour groups at peak times. Better deals available online.

€€€ Hotel Le Riad, Zone touristique d'Errachidia, Rte de Goulmima, T0535-791006, www.hotelleriad.com. A smart place outside the city, with 24 a/c rooms around a good-sized pool.

€ Hotel Errachidia, 31 Rue Ibnou Batouta, T0535-570453. This is a reliable, clean, modern place just behind the bus station. Rooms have TVs, desk and comfy beds. It's far from beautiful, but it does the job.

€ Hotel M'Daghra, Rue Allal Ben Abdallah (if coming from west, turn left at **Café Lipton** on main drag, hotel is 100 m down on right), T0535-574047. Another modern option in the centre, with 26 rooms with decent showers, good beds and some with balconies.

Tafilalet

Camping Tissirt, 30 km south of Er Rachidia, heading to Erfoud, T0662-141378, www.campingtissirtziz.free.fr. On the edge of the Ziz Canyon, the site has great views, shaded garden, a big Berber tent and a couple of pisé bungalows.

Merzouga and Erg Chebbi

Spread out along the edge of the dunes, most of Merzouga's hotels are north of the village itself. In fact those further away tend to be preferable – they generally have more space and easy access to the less visited areas of the dunes. Most have obligatory half board and do their own excursions out onto the dunes. Many close in the summer,

when it becomes too hot to go out on the dunes. Flash floods in 2006 destroyed several hotels, some of which have since been rebuilt.

Signs off to the east of the new sealed road from Rissani lead across the sand on bumpy pistes, to ubiquitous pisé, kasbah-style accommodation, with high walls around a large central courtyard. Most hotels will offer to meet you out on the main road, which is highly advisable. Note that there are numerous faux guides in the area who will do their best to convince you that certain auberges are closed and lead you elsewhere. If you have GPS, contact the auberge for their precise location, or get someone to come and meet you.

€€€ Auberge Kasbah Derkaoua, T0535-577140, www.aubergederkaoua. com. At the northern end of the dunes, **Derkaoua** is best reached heading southeast out of Erfoud, rather than from the Rissani–Merzouga road. Popular, and a cut above most of the other options, there's a licensed restaurant, a pool, hammam and a tennis court. Rooms are decorated with Moroccan fabrics and the food is magnificent. Book in advance. Bivouac from 550dh pp.

€€€ Hotel Kasbah Tombuctou, Hassi Labied, Merzouga, T0535-577091, www. xaluca.com. Rising from the foot of the dunes like a Sahara theme park, this Xaluca-owned hotel is a bit garish, but full of luxury. Rooms are cool, finished in coloured *tadelakt*, some with enormous bathrooms. Huge pool, restaurant and its own bivouac for getting deeper into the sand. All mod cons. Live the dream in the Royal Suite (**€€€€**).

€€ Auberge du Sud, T0661-216166 (mob), www.aubergedusud.com. 20 differently themed rooms and a big dining area. Camel trips (600dh pp) involve

2 or 3 hrs' trekking to a camp with showers and toilets. Each room has its own terrace overlooking the dunes. Solar panels provide electricity and hot water. Free collection from Rissani.

€€ Auberge Ksar Sania, by the Grand Dune and the seasonal lake, T0535-577414, www.ksarsaniahotelmerzouga.com. Run by Gérard and Françoise Tommaso, **Ksar Saniya** was among the places destroyed by flooding in 2006, but has been rebuilt as an unusual hexagonal eco-lodge, with attractive rooms shaped from traditional materials, palms and *tadelakt*. Also offers cheaper self-cooling mud-built 'huts' in the garden. Pool.

€€ Chez Julia, right in the village of Merzouga itself, T0535-573182. This place offers a very different experience to all the kasbah-style hotels. Small and personal, it's run by the eponymous Austrian owner. The 9 rooms, decorated in pastel tones, have comfortable big beds; the room at the top has good views over Merzouga to the dunes. Facilities are shared but everything is spotlessly clean. Breakfast (40dh) is taken on the roof terrace and there are lots of Moroccan choices for dinner – especially good for vegetarians – and Austrian desserts too.

€ Auberge Camping Sahara, Hassi Labied, T0535-577039, www.auberge sahara.com. Simple family-run *auberge* with shaded camping sites (25dh pp), showers and respectable washing facilities. Also has 20 homely guest rooms, a pool and a restaurant.

RESTAURANTS

Er Rachidia
€ Hotel-Café La Renaissance, 19 Rue Moulay Youssef, T0535-572633. Reliable, with excellent couscous.

€ Hotel Oasis, 4 Rue Sidi Abou Abdallah, T0535-572519. Serves Moroccan food and alcohol.

There are other cheap places along Av Mohammed V.

Erfoud
You can eat in (relative) luxury at any of the hotels in Erfoud. The **Kasbah Xaluca** lunch-buffet is delicious for 210dh. For those on a budget, there are places on Av Moulay Ismail and Av Mohammed V.

€€ Dadani, 103 Av Mohammed V, T0535-577958. An excellent little café-restaurant with traditional (and comfortable) Moroccan seating upstairs and a Western-style café downstairs. Very good *kalia*, though don't expect it to come in a hurry.

There's even an apartment for rent, should you like it so much you want to stay.

Rissani
There are not that many eating options in Rissani but the restaurant at **Kasbah Ennasra** is open to the public and serves good Moroccan set menus. Also the **Restaurant Café Merzouga** on Av Moulay Ali Cherif, near the main market, is recommended.

Merzouga
Most people eat where they're staying, so there's not much in the way of standalone eating options. However, the **Café Nora**, T0667-612191, in Khamlia, just 7 km south of Merzouga on the Taouz road is well worth a visit for a tasty organic lunch or mint tea prepared by Hassan and Souad. Combine it with a visit to the **Dar Gnawa** next door.

TODRA AND DADES GORGES

The 'Road of the Thousand Kasbahs', as it is marketed, runs between Er Rachidia and Ouarzazate, through arid plains and oases with a backdrop of harsh mountain landscapes, where semi-nomadic Berbers pasture their flocks. The modern world has arrived, however: tourist buses and 4WDs bring their flocks to the growing villages at the start of the spectacular gorges, and the new buildings replacing the crumbling kasbahs these days use concrete breeze blocks rather than pisé. Nevertheless, there is plenty to see, as well as walking opportunities along this route. Skoura is an oasis town with old kasbahs and El Kalaâ is the centre of Morocco's rose-growing industry. Those with 4WDs can try the bumpy mountain tracks leading into the Massif du Mgoun, or the rugged gorge-to-gorge route from Tineghir to Boumalne.

→ WEST TO TINEGHIR

TINEJDAD

At the junction of the Er Rachidia, Tineghir and Erfoud roads, Tinejdad is an Amazigh and Haratine town in a large oasis, with some significant kasbahs, notably the Ksar Asrir. There are a lot of bicycles in Tinejdad, so be particularly careful if driving through. The central square has a post office, the town gardens, town hall, telephones, taxis and petrol station.

TINEGHIR

Once a tiny oasis settlement, Tineghir is now a modern administrative centre, its population swelled by technicians and staff working for the local mining company. Tourism is taking on importance, and the town is an ideal stay on the road east to the Tafilalet. It also makes a good first night stop on a walking holiday.

Tineghir is an unexpectedly large place. There is the modern hub, now ribboning east and west along the N10, as well as the older kasbah settlements a few kilometres north from the town, overlooking the irrigated plain as one climbs out of the town towards the Gorge du Todra. The contrast of magnificent barren mountains and verdant oases is stark. For the rushed, there are views from the gorge road, otherwise you might explore on foot; hire a guide for 40dh. You will find olive and fruit trees inter-cropped with cereals and vegetables, herds of sheep and goats out to pasture in the foothills. As elsewhere in the region, there is much new building along the roads, the old *ksar* partly abandoned to the side. The main population belong to the Aït Atta tribe. Try to visit the **Kasbah el Glaoui** on the hill above the town. Although officially closed, it is normally possible to get in.

SOUTH FROM TINEGHIR

The village of **Aït Mohammed** is southeast of Tineghir and clearly visible from the main road. It stands on the minor road that goes along the *oued* to **El Hart-n'Igouramène**. A track due south leads into the **Jbel Saghro**, aiming for the village of **Iknioun**, which nestles under the central heights. It eventually connects with the desert road from Erfoud to Zagora.

The Todra Gorge, particularly spectacular in the evening, when the rocks are coloured in bands of bright sunlight and dark shadow, is narrower and more winding than the Dadès Gorge. There are campsites and places to stay near the narrowest part of the gorge, a highly recommended break from the activity of the major towns.

The 14-km route up the gorge is very narrow, and you will have to slow down for kids playing near the road. Also watch out for the tyre-splitting road edge when you move over for a bus thundering towards you. (Tourist buses and 4WDs head up to the gorge for lunch.)

Just north of Tineghir, as the road climbs up, is the village of **Aït Ouaritane**. There are many good views and some stopping places on the road. The safest place to stop is generally picketed with camels; the most spectacular has fossil and scarf sellers. Neat strips of crops in the oasis gardens and crumbling kasbah villages spread out below.

Some 9 km from Tineghir are campsites in an idyllic location in a palm grove. About 6 km further on is the most visited section of the gorge, where the high cliffs leave just enough space for the road and river. As you might imagine, rocks, palm groves and river make this a good environment for birds. There are some hotels (eg **La Vallée**) before the ford (which should present no problems for ordinary cars) and you can then carry on up to the next two hotels, **Les Roches** and **Yasmina**, which squat in bogus kasbah style under a spectacular overhanging bit of gorge.

TAMTATOUCHTE AND BEYOND
The more adventurous will want to continue beyond the narrow confines of the Gorge du Todra. The village of Tamtatouchte is a steady climb of about four hours. The **Auberge Baddou**, the **Auberge Bougafer** and various other rudimentary establishments provide food and accommodation. A few lorries returning from the souk use this route and may provide you with a lift, if necessary. With 4WD, many of the smaller villages to the north can be reached. With a good driver, connections can be made westwards to the Dadès Gorge or northwards to Imilchil.

GORGE TO GORGE
Though rough, the 42 km west to **Msemrir** and the Dadès Gorge from Tamtatouchte, rising to 2800 m, isa popular 4WD route. It can be done in five hours. This journey is best undertaken in a good 4WD vehicle with reliable local driver. Ensure that tyre pressure is higher than normal, as tracks are very stony, and that you have a full petrol tank. Find out about the condition of the piste before departure. This route is best undertaken between May and September. At other times of year, potential flash floods make it dangerous. It is probably best to do this route starting at the Todra Gorge so you do the most difficult pass, the one after Tamtatouche, 2800 m, first. At Msemrir, a popular base village for treks, there are a couple of simple places to stay, including the **Auberge el Ouarda** and the **Auberge Agdal**.

BOUMALNE DU DADES

Boumalne is a small town, with a reasonable selection of hotels, though most people prefer to head on up the Dadès valley and stay there. The town grew from a very basic settlement to its current size mainly in the second half of the 20th century. In the Muslim cemetery there is the domed shrine of one Sidi Daoud. He is commemorated in an annual festival, when bread is baked from flour left at the grave and fed to husbands to ensure their fertility. Wednesday is market day. Approaching from the west, there is usually a Gendarmerie royale checkpoint at the intersection before the bridge, so slow down.

From a high point above the town, a barracks and some hotels look out over the harsh and rocky landscape. If you are a birdwatcher, you may well want to head off south to the **Vallée des Oiseaux** (on the road from Boumalne to Iknioun). The track southeast which leaves the N10 road just east of Boumalne gives easy access into the desert. It rises steadily to Tagdilt and provides possibilities for spotting desert birds and, less likely, desert fauna.

THROUGH THE GORGE

The R704 leaves the N10 at Boumalne and follows the Oued Dadès through limestone cliffs, which form the striking Dadès Gorge. The principal destination is the section of the gorge following Aït Oudinar, but the track continues up into the High Atlas, with public transport as far as Msemrir. There are very basic pistes into the mountains and around into the Todra Gorge (see page 192).

Just beyond Boumalne is **Aït Arbi**, where there are a series of striking *ksar* above the road. The road continues past areas of unusual rock formations, through Tamnalt and **Aït Oudinar**, where there is basic accommodation. The valley narrows after Aït Oudinar, creating the most striking area of the gorge, where the cliffs are vivid shades of red. The road continues alongside the *oued* as far as **Msemrir**, just beyond which it branches. The right-hand branch turns into a difficult track, running east across the pass (2800 m) and continuing to link with the R703 through the Todra Gorge, or up into the High Atlas. The gorges and crags offer a good environment for golden and Bonelli's eagles and lammergeiers, and the scree slopes for blue rock thrushes.

EL KALAA DES MGOUNA AND THE VALLEE DES ROSES

A ribbon-development place, El Kalaâ des Mgouna, 1¼ hours' drive from Ouarzazate, is the capital of the Moroccan rose-essence industry and centre of the Mgouna tribe. (The name means 'Citadel of the Mgouna' and is also spelt Qalat Mgouna.) The former French administrative centre has become a sprawling town, with banks, police, small shops for provisions, petrol and a Wednesday market. The blooms in the Vallée des Roses flower in late spring. The rose festival is held in early May, with dances and processions under a shower of rose petals to celebrate the harvest. The children at the roadside will try to sell bunches of roses and garlands of rose petals, and there are plenty of shops selling rose water, *crème à la rose*, rose-scented soap and dried roses.

A picturesque local legend runs that pilgrims travelling back from Mecca brought with them 'the Mother of All Flowers', the Damascus rose, initiating the rose industry. It may be, however, that sometime in the 20th century, French perfumers realized that conditions in this out-of-the-way part of southern Morocco would be ideal for the large-scale cultivation of the bushy *Rosa centifolia*. Today, there are hundreds of kilometres of rose bush hedges, co-existing with other crops, and two factories, distilling rose essence. The one in a kasbah-like building can be visited. To produce a litre of good quality rose oil requires around five tonnes of petals, you will be told. The locals feel, however, that the price paid by the factories is too low and prefer to sell dried rose petals on local markets. Pounded up, the petals can be used mixed with henna or other preparations.

While based in El Kalaâ, if you are feeling energetic you may want to head northwards 15 km up the Mgoun Valley to the **Ksar de Bou Thrarar**, at the entrance of the **Mgoun Gorges**. Less adventurously, there is a dagger-making workshop and showroom, **Co-operative Artisan du Poignards Azlag**, on the eastern outskirts of the town.

SKOURA OASIS
The large oasis fed by the Oued Idelssan has irrigated land growing palms, olives and cereals. The Oued Hajag crosses the road on the western side of Skoura. The small settlement here has a white square mosque with white cupola. You can now bypass the town on the main road. Nevertheless, the palm groves are worth stopping to explore on foot, bicycle or even on horseback.

Before the actual village, to the left of the road (if coming from Ouarzazate), is **Kasbah Amerhidl**, the largest of Skoura's kasbahs. The village also includes two kasbahs formerly occupied by the El Glaoui family, **Dar Toundout** and **Dar Lahsoune**.

MOVING ON

To Ouarzazate
From Skoura Oasis it's 40 km to Ouarzazate. See Dream Trip 1, page 71.

To Aït Benhaddou
From Ouarzazate it's 34 km (40 minutes) to Aït Benhaddou. See Dream Trip 1, page 70.

To Marrakech
From Aït Benhaddou it's 190 km (four hours) to Marrakech via the N9 for the final three days of this trip. See pages 35-62.

TODRA AND DADES GORGES LISTINGS

WHERE TO STAY

Goulmima

€€€ Chez Pauline, Tadighoust, 15 km from Goulmima, T0535-885425, www.gite chezpauline.com. French-run guesthouse surrounded by peach, fig and olive trees, with the odd chicken scuttling across the farm. 4 rustic whitewashed en suite rooms in the main house sleep 2-5 people and are tastefully decorated with African artefacts. Each has a/c. 2 annexes offer dorm-style accommodation at 120dh per person. Camping also available. Excellent food.

Tinejdad

€€€ Ksar el Khorbat, T0535-880355, www.elkhorbat.com. Built within an 18th-century ksar, there are 10 huge, characterful rooms with bathrooms and plenty of Moroccan rugs. Pool, restaurant and library. Winner of the 2010 Responsible Tourism Award. Obligatory half board.

Tineghir

€€ Hotel Tomboctou, 126 Av Bir Anzane (take 1st major left coming into Tineghir from west), T0524-835291, www.hotel tomboctou.com. Good cool rooms in a restored kasbah, eco-savvy, with small pool, secure car parking available. Mountain bikes for rent, plus sketch maps of region. The best option in town.

Todra Gorge

In winter it gets pretty chilly at night and, in late summer, the river can swell suddenly after thunderstorms in the mountains, so choose your camping place with care.
€€ Dar Ayour, 13 km up the gorge, just before the narrowest point, T0524-895271, www.darayour.com. Stylish guesthouse with plum-coloured *tadelakt* walls, Berber rugs and a warm welcome. Built right on the edge of the river, overlooking the gardens. Rooms are colourful, with tiny en suite bathrooms.

Boumalne du Dadès

€€€ La Perle du Dadès, 5 km from town centre on a very rough track on the Er-Rachidia side of the river, T0524-850548, www.perledudades.com. Beautifully restored Kasbah with 14 spacious rooms, split-level suites and novel 'troglodyte' cave-rooms. Full of homely furnishings, basketware, books, an old piano and cosy nooks. There's a pool, views from the terrace are great and there are lots activities. On the downside, the food can be disappointing and not much English is spoken.

Dadès Gorge

€€ Les 5 Lunes, Ait Oudinar, T0524-830723, www.les5lunes.com. Belgian/Moroccan-run, this traditionally built little place has a different vibe to most of the accommodation in the valley. Flamenco music plays, there are old Berber wooden locks on the doors and the freshly made pancakes for breakfast are excellent. There are only 5 rooms, a salon with a fire, and a roof terrace with good views over the greenest part of the valley. Thoroughly laid-back.
€€ Timzillite, T0677-264347. Up above the much-photographed hairpins at the top of the canyon, **Timzillite** has views that are hard to beat, as long as you don't suffer from vertigo. 6 rooms are small but cosy, and there's solar power for electricity and water. The roadside café is a popular stopping place.
€ Atlas Berbere. T0524-831742.
All rooms here have heating and a view, and some have 2: over the stream and down the valley. The food is good and there are veggie options, such as ratatouille. The friendly owner will proudly tell you that he is the creator of the fake *pisé* wall effect ubiquitous in the Dadès valley. There's music every evening and a wood fire. It's worth trying to bargain on the price. You can sleep on the roof terrace for 25dh.

El Kalaâ
€€ Kasbah Itran, 3 km from El Kelaâ des Mgouna heading to Bou Tharar, T0524-837103, www.kasbahitran.com. A tiny **auberge** run by a Spanish-Moroccan partnership, perched up on a cliff on the road up to Bou Tharar and into the Massif du Mgoun. 6 attractive, homely rooms, 3 with en suite bathrooms. Great views of Kasbah Mirna to the south and Kasbah du Glaoui to the north.

Skoura oasis
€€€ Jardins de Skoura, www.lesjardins deskoura.com. Hammocks by the pool, breakfast in the gardens and open fires for cold winter evenings. Beautiful *pisé* rooms and *tadelakt* bathrooms. A popular stopping-off point deep in the *palmeraie* and from where you might not want to move on.
€€€€ Kasbah Aït Ben Moro, 3 km west of Skoura proper, T0524-852116, www. aitbenmoro.com. A beautifully refurbished building a few metres off the main bypass. Rooms are dark, as kasbah rooms tend to be, decor is austere and elegant. From the roof terrace and garden there are views over the palm groves to the Kasbah d'Amerdihil. 13 rooms, 4 suites and 3 tower rooms (660dh) with shared bath.

RESTAURANTS

Apart from roadside cafés, there are few separate eating options in this area.

Tinejdad
Café el Fath, **Café Assagm** and **Café Ferkla** are possibilities for refreshment.

Tineghir
There are no exciting gastronomic choices here. **La Gazelle d'Or**, in the town centre, is good. **La Kasbah**, Av Mohammed V, is a friendly place.

Boumalne du Dadès
A few decent options frequented by tourists are along the main road, just across the river and at the bottom of the Av Mohammed V. **Café Atlas**, in the centre, is good for food or just a tea or coffee. **Hotel-Restaurant Salam**, in the centre, serves food, tea or coffee. **Restaurant Chems**, just outside Boumalne, on the Er Rachidia road, is perhaps the best option with its pleasant terrace.

El Kalaâ
Café-Restaurant Rendez-Vous des Amis, Av Mohammed V, T0661-871443. Popular and reliable for tasty tagines and snacks.

WHAT TO DO

Boumalne du Dadès
Trekking
Bureau des Guides, bottom of Av Mohammed V, main street, T0667-593292.

El Kalaâ
Trekking
El Kelaâ is a good base town for trekking; call the **Bureau des Guides de Montagne**, 1 km before the town centre, on south side of road, T0524-836577, T0661-796101 (mob). The **Kasbah Assafar** also has plenty of contacts with guides. Ambitious walkers in late spring and summer may want to try to climb Irhil Mgoun, at 4068 m it is one of the highest peaks in the central High Atlas.

Skoura oasis
Horse riding
Skoura Equestrian Centre, 2 km from Skoura on Toundout road, T0661-432163 (mob). Lessons and treks through the Skoura oasis. For beginners and experienced riders.

DREAM TRIP 4
Tangier→Rabat→Chefchaouen→Ceuta 21 days

Tangier 3 nights, page 199

Asilah 2 nights, page 211
Bus or grand taxi from Tangier (45 mins)
or train (35 mins)

Larache and Lixus 2 nights, page 214
Bus (1 hr) or shared taxi from Asilah
(45 mins)

Rabat 3 nights, page 225
Taxi from Larache to Ksar el-Kebìr (45 mins),
then train to Rabat (2½ hrs)

Meknès and Volubilis 1 night,
pages 164 and 173
Train from Rabat (2 hrs)

Fès 4 nights, page 139
Train from Meknès (50 mins)

Chefchaouen 3 nights, page 246
Bus and shared taxi from Fès via Ouezzane
(4 hrs)

Tetouan 2 nights, page 255
Taxi from Chefchaouen (2 hrs)

Ceuta 1 night, page 261
Taxi from Tetouan (1 hr)

GOING FURTHER

Taza page 158
Train from Fès (2 hrs)

Al Hoceïma page 250
Bus or grand taxi from Chefchaouen (4 hrs)

DREAM TRIP 4
Tangier→Rabat→Chefchaouen→Ceuta

The north of the country has an extraordinary mix of everything Moroccan: Tangier's seductive seediness and cultural ghosts, Chefchaouen's picture-postcard streets, the mountain culture of the Rif, Rabat's power and Fes's spirituality.

Tangier's heyday as a haven for radical writers and thinkers may have passed but it is still the first experience many have of Africa, and the place from which many others leave, making its streets feel ripe with dreams and expectations.

Along the coast to the southwest, Asilah is a rarefied place, by Moroccan standards, its whitewashed streets home to art, music and fine dining.

A little further south, Larache feels a lot further from western Europe. Dustier and more run-down, it is, in its own way, no less attractive. Nearby Lixus has Roman ruins, overgrown but evocative, and with great views.

Reserved Rabat, the country's capital, has none of the ostentation of Casablanca but a few fascinating sights nonetheless and, across the water, an intriguingly troublesome sibling: Salé, with a pirate past.

Meknès, to the east, has more trappings of power, albeit from an earlier incarnation, and Fès is steeped in spiritual and historical significance in a setting that has changed little since medieval times.

In the foothils of the Rif mountains, Chefchaouen consumes extraordinary quantities of whitewash in order to keep its walls and streets quite so sparkling. Tetouan is more multicoloured and multifaceted; less easy to love but with plenty of interest.

The Mediterranean coast winds to the east, with more beaches and Spanish influences, and, in Ceuta and Melilla, Spanish enclaves.

TANGIER

Tangier is a product of its location: the gate to the Mediterranean Sea and the meeting point of Africa and Europe. The Phoenicians and Carthaginians established trading posts here. The Romans made it a capital city. It was invaded by the Vandals and Visigoths and occupied by the Arabs. The Portuguese took the town before the Spanish arrived. From 1923 to 1956, it was an international city, and its tax-free status and raffish reputation attracted European and American writers and artists. Tangier also had fame as a gay destination in the days when homosexuality attracted severe moral opprobrium in Europe. These days, Tangier is trying to bury these ghosts and reinvent itself as a modern city with a new port, stadium and business district. Arriving by sea, it may well be your first point of contact with Morocco and, despite a certain reputation for hassle, Tangier has remained popular with travellers. The kasbah, former residence of sultans, is particularly worth visiting, as is the medina, a dense maze of houses, shops and narrow, steep streets. A day is probably enough to see the main sights; two days would give you more time to take in the atmosphere and make a side trip to the Caves of Hercules on the Atlantic coast.

→ ARRIVING IN TANGIER

GETTING THERE

Tangier's **Ibn Battouta Airport** ① *T0539-393720*, is 15 km southwest of the city on the N1 road to Rabat. Entry formalities can be slow. Catch bus 17 or 70 from the terminal to the Grand Socco (Place du 19 Avril 1947), or take a grand taxi (160dh by day, 200dh after 2000, rates displayed on wall by customs).

The train no longer stops at Tangier Ville and Port. Rather, the terminal is at **Tangier Moghougha**, a 15dh petit taxi ride from the town centre, 20dh for the port, more at night; have change ready. Taxi drivers will want to fill up their vehicles so you may have to wait.

CTM buses arrive at the terminal in Avenue des FAR, adjacent to the port gates and the former Tangier Ville railway station. Private lines arrive at the terminal at the end of Rue de Fès. There are plenty of buses to Tangier from Casablanca, Fès, Meknès and Rabat, as well as from local places, such as Asilah, Larache and Tetouan. The bus station is a short (12dh) petit taxi ride from the city centre hotels.

If you are driving into the city in the summer from the south, expect slow traffic north of Asilah after the motorway ends. The A1 from Rabat brings the driver into Tangier along Rue de Fès. The N16 from Ceuta feeds into Av Mohammed V, as does the N2 from Tetouan.

There are car/passenger ferry services from Algeciras in Spain and Gibraltar. Within the port compound, there is a rank for both kinds of taxi. Hard negotiation over prices will probably be necessary.

MOVING ON

A bus or grand taxi will take you south to Asilah in about 45 minutes. The train is a better, faster option (35 minutes), but you'll need to get a petit taxi to get to the train station.

GETTING AROUND

Tangier is quite a small place but the bus station (*mahattat el kirane*) is a good way out. You will need to get a petit taxi (15dh), which ought to be metered, or a grand taxi. A trip within the city by petit or grand taxi is 12dh. Taxis can be flagged down even when they have other passengers. If it is going in your direction, it will take you. There are handy Boughaz minibuses and grands taxis from the Grand Socco to the bus station and the Atlantic coast sights.

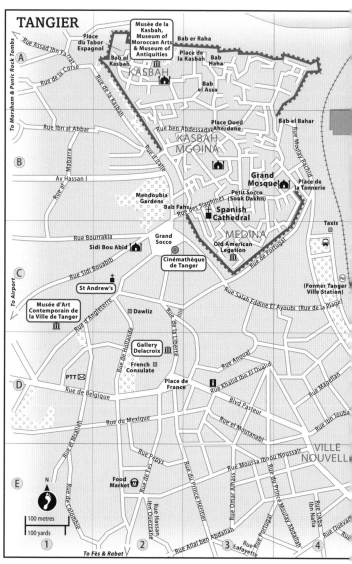

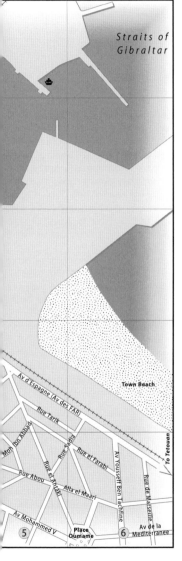

→ BACKGROUND

Perhaps the oldest city in Morocco, Tangier was active as early as 1600 BC. There was a Phoenician settlement here. Roman mythology ascribes its founding to the Greek giant Antaeus, son of Poseidon, god of the sea, and Gaia, goddess of the Earth. Antaeus challenged Hercules, but the hero killed the giant and had a child by his widow, Tingis. Hercules pulled apart Spain and Africa to give this son, Sophax, a city protected by the sea. Then, out of filial piety, King Sophax named his city Tingis.

Thanks to its location on the Straits of Gibraltar, Tangier has always been important. At one point, Rome made it capital of the empire's North African provinces, its people receiving Roman citizenship in AD 38. Rome controlled the city until AD 429. Later, the Vandals and Byzantines struggled to control the region, then the Muslim Arabs took the city in AD 706. It remained a point of conflict between major Arab and Berber dynasties, before achieving commercial importance in the Mediterranean during the 1300s.

Tangier was first conquered by the Portuguese in 1437 and subsequently reoccupied in 1471; it became Spanish in 1578 and Portuguese again in 1640. They built fine houses, Dominican and Franciscan chapels and a cathedral, and the city was part of the dowry brought by the Portuguese Catherine of Braganza when she married Charles II of England in 1661. The English succeeded in alienating the Portuguese population, forcing both religious orders and Jews out of the city, before finally departing themselves in 1684, destroying the kasbah as they left. Sultan Moulay Ismaïl rebuilt the town after they left.

In the 19th century Tangier became a popular base for European merchants, and housed a large European colony. It was also the focus of political competition between expansionist European powers. In 1923 the city became a tax-free International Zone controlled by a 30-member international committee. From then until the early 1960s, Tangier had its heyday as a hedonistic, decadent free port and the playground of an international demi-monde – thus reinforcing the truth of earlier descriptions of the city. St Francis had seen it as a centre of sin, while, in the 17th century, Samuel Pepys had described it as a latter-day Sodom.

CELEBRITY VISITORS

The streets of Tangier are full of artistic and literary memories. Among its illustrious visitors (other than Pepys and St Francis) are Camille Saint-Saëns (who drew on Issaoua trance music for his *Danse macabre*), film stars Marlene Dietrich and Errol Flynn, Oscar Wilde, author-translator Paul Bowles, Ian Fleming, Richard Hughes (*High Wind in Jamaica*) and James Leo Herlihy (*Midnight Cowboy*). Woolworth-heiress Barbara Hutton had a house here, as did the heiress to the Knoll furniture fortune, the crumbling York Castle, up in the kasbah. Winston Churchill, Ronnie Kray and the photographer Cecil Beaton all passed through. Painters who discovered light and the Orient in Tangier include Eugène Delacroix in 1832, Henri Matisse (1912), Kees Van Dongen and, more recently, Francis Bacon. The city's reputation as a haven of freedom for the likes of Tennessee Williams, Truman Capote, William Burroughs, Allen Ginsberg, Jack Kerouac, Brion Gysin and Joe Orton in the 1950s and 1960s continues to draw visitors. Today backpackers relive something of those heady days by visiting the **Tanger Inn**, Rue Magellan, a surviving fragment of Burroughs' Interzone (see box, opposite).

Though many of the city's literary sites were lost in the demolition-rebuilding of the 1990s, the romantic-minded can still find something of Tangier's artistic soul. There are plenty of decaying apartment buildings, restaurants and low-life bars. The **Grand-Hôtel Villa de France** still survives, home to Gertrude Stein and Matisse, as does the **Teatro Cervantes**. Down near the port, next to the **Hôtel Cecil** (a favourite with Roland Barthes), is the **Immeuble Renschaussen**, where Burroughs and Gysin did artistic cut-ups in one of the lofts. Up at the kasbah, the **Palais Menebhi** was home to Gysin's 1001 Nights bar. Further west on the Montagne at the **Villa Mimosa**, Bowles finished *Let it Come Down*, another tale of an American adrift in the mysterious East. West of the city, the **Plage Merkala** was the setting for tales by M'rabet, Charhadi and other members of Bowles' coterie. And the heavily revamped **Salon de thé Porte** still carries a hint of a literary yesteryear.

THE END OF COSMOPOLITAN TANGIER

Tangier as a centre of easy money and loose morals was not to last, however, and the free-port was reunited with Morocco in October 1956, although its tax-free status was maintained until 1960. Since Independence, Tangier has declined in international economic importance, and its tourism was soon overshadowed by the enormous development of the industry elsewhere in the Mediterranean. Today, the city functions essentially for the Moroccan tourist and travel market. In the summer, up to two million migrant workers and their families pass through the port, and Tangier is their first contact with their homeland. In the 1980s, the green cliff tops of La Montagne, west of the city, came to be favoured by Gulf emirs as the ideal place for a holiday home. Soon, vast palaces in the neo-Kuwaiti style appeared like UFOs in the pine and eucalyptus woods around the city.

ON THE ROAD
With William Burroughs in Interzone

William Burroughs got interested in Tangier after reading a couple of Paul Bowles novels. In 1953, just after the publication of *Junkie*, he left New York for anywhere – and wound up in Tangier. Disappointment was quick to set in; the city's literary coterie was hostile and Burroughs wrote in a 1954 letter to Alan Ginsberg: "There is an end-of-the-world feeling in Tangier, with its glut of nylon shirts, Swiss watches, Scotch and sex and opiates sold across the counter. Something sinister in complete laissez-faire. And the new police chief up there on the hill accumulating dossiers. I suspect him of unspeakable fetishistic practices with his files." Paul Bowles proved hostile and manipulative, too. A moment of vengeance came, however, when the the city's senior writer was set upon by enraged baboons in the countryside and forced to flee for his life. Wrote Burroughs: "They got vicious purple-assed baboons in the mountains a few miles out of town … I intend to organize baboon sticks from motorcycles. A sport geared to modern times."

The exotic splendours of Tangier left Burroughs unmoved. As he put it in another letter to Ginsberg: "Don't ever fall of this inscrutable oriental shit like Bowles puts down." There was no adoration of the mysterious East here.

As Burroughs' life in the city gradually decayed into a drugged-up blur, he was dubbed the 'Invisible Man'. Rarely emerging from his hotel in the Petit Socco, he divided his time between writing, 'delicious afternoon sleeps in a darkened room', and the half-light of the Bar Mar Chica, whose denizens included fellow addicts and his lover Kiki. A cure at the Hôpital Benchimol produced meagre results, "the philosophic serenity conveyed by an empty scrotum" was not enough to break the opium habit. Eventually, Burroughs left for England for further treatment. He returned to take up residence at the Villa Mouniria and, in 1957, finished the manuscript which was to become *The Naked Lunch*. The 'International Zone of Tangier' features here as 'Interzone' (the book's first title), a place of shady deals and narcotic visions. Over time, however, Burroughs' idea of the city changed, and he came to find it had 'a wild beauty'.

For more on the Tangerine atmosphere of the 1950s, look out for the Bowles' novels *Let it come down* (1952) and *The Sheltering Sky* (1949), both republished in paperback. *The Letters of William S Burroughs* (1983) give a frank view of the writer's tribulations in Tangier.

CONTEMPORARY TANGIER

Tangier has always been through highs and lows, and the 1990s were in many ways the trough of a low period. A building boom, in part financed by the profits of the kif trade, meant masses of new development as profits were recycled in. Many historic buildings were torn down, replaced by blocks of concrete-brutalist ugliness. And then came the late king's 'clean up public life' campaign. Corruption scandals and court cases hit the city, various local figures disappeared behind bars or overseas, all to the good many would say. But the big change came with Mohammed VI's accession to the throne in July 1999. The new king made the northwest the first region he visited outside the capital. Tangier was ecstatic. The long-ignored Palais Marshan was dusted down; there seemed to be some hope for a region too long forgotten by the powers that be.

A feisty local press have kept things moving along; associations have been set up to do something for street kids, to support the unemployed and illiterate, to save the kasbah and the Teatro Cervantes. The general environment has improved too, with new management for city services and an awareness that not everything old should be pulled down. Tangier's appeal for creative types has also remained intact; the **Cinema Rif** on the Grand Socco has been renovated and reborn as the **Cinémathèque de Tangier**, an important centre for the arts in the heart of the city.

THE FUTURE OF TANGIER

With a population that has quadrupled from 250,000 in 1982 to a million, Tangier continues to sprawl ever further inland, its growth fuelled by rural in-migration and high unemployment. In times of pressure, the frustration of the deprived spills over in riots in the poor areas on the city edge. But things are better than they were, and many of the *bidonville* inhabitants are being rehoused. Work is expected to start soon on a rail tunnel between Spain and Morocco, though it is unlikely to be completed before 2025, and the city's future development will certainly be interesting to watch as Morocco moves closer to the European Union.

With its special history, Tangier is an endearing place, a town of past cosmopolitan glories. Some say it is best remembered from a vantage point, perhaps a cliff-top café, overlooking the Straits and the distant Iberian coast across the choppy sea, but no doubt it will remain a place of legend. As Mohammed Choukri put it, "In Tangier, any capable storyteller can invent a story and be sure to convince listeners of its truth."

→ PLACES IN TANGIER

Tangier is more of an atmosphere than a city with numerous unmissable sights. If you manage to avoid hasslers and hustlers, then it is a city for the flâneur, for strolling, with steep streets and stairways as well as boulevards. Yet there are minor galleries, out-of-the-way cafés and semi-sights for you to put together a wander with a purpose. The main attraction is the views: over the Straits to Spain, from Ville Nouvelle to the medina, down alleys which could twist on forever or end in a sticky situation.

Of the ancient city nothing remains. Descriptions are full of 'it is possible that' and 'probably be' and the few antique pieces that have been unearthed are disappointing from a dating and workmanship point of view. The limits of the city have been defined, using the position of necropolises. It extended west to Mendoubia, south to Bou Kachkach and northwest to Marshan Plateau, where there are Punic or maybe Roman tombs hollowed out of the rock, overlooking the Straits.

GRAND SOCCO

The Grand Socco is where the medina begins. Tangier's answer to Jemaâ el Fna in Marrakech, the square has been spruced up, apparently on suggestion of the king, and it now has fountains and seats and tiled pedestrian areas. At the top of the square the **Cinémathèque de Tangier** ① *T0539-934683, www.cinemathequedetanger.com*, has become one of Morocco's most significant arts venues, showing Moroccan and international arts films and documentaries. Formerly the Cinema Rif, it is the centrepoint of a cultural renaissance in the city and stages premieres, seasons and themed cycles and also has a good café with free Wi-Fi. Note the tiled minaret of the **Sidi Bou Abid Mosque** (1917) on the corner of the Grand Socco and Rue Sidi Bou Abid.

On Thursday and Sunday Rifi Berber women sell all sorts of wares in Rue de la Plage (Rue Salah Eddine el Ayoubi). Along Rue d'Angleterre they also sell woven blankets. On the

Rue Bourrakia side of the Grand Socco, the arch with Arabic on it leads into the **Mendoubia Gardens**, a quiet, tree-filled place in the heart of Tangier. These gardens were formerly part of the residence of the Mendoub and contain 30 bronze cannons, remnants of old French and British warships. The Mendoubia Palace is the former residence of the sultan's representatives on the International Commission.

KASBAH

In Tangier, the kasbah is constructed on the highest point of the medina. It was fortified back in Roman days and it was the traditional residence in Tangier of the sultan and his harem. It was burnt to the ground by the English as they left in 1684. More recently, during the heyday of Tangier as an international city, the kasbah was considered a fashionable address for people such as the novelist Richard Hughes (who lived at 'Numéro Zero, La Kasbah, Tangier'). Today, parts of the kasbah are threatened by landslips: after particularly heavy rains, the locals hold their breath and wait to see whether a section of the cliffs will slither down towards the sea. Especially at risk is **York Castle**, 17th-century home of English governor, the Duke of York.

To get to the kasbah from the Grand Socco, head downhill across the square, aiming for the horseshoe-arched entrance gate and follow down Rue d'Italie and then up Rue de la Kasbah and enter by Bab el Kasbah. From the medina, follow Rue des Chrétiens from the Petit Socco, and then Rue Sidi Ben Rassouli to Bab el Assa.

Musée de la Kasbah ① *T0539-932097, Sat-Mon, Wed and Thu 0900-1600, Fri 0900-1130, 1330-1600, 10dh*, is in the former palace of the kasbah, the Dar Al Makhzen, and includes Moroccan arts and antiquities. The palace was built by the Sultan Moulay Ismaïl in the 18th century, and was used as the Sultan's palace up until 1912, when Sultan Moulay Hafid, exiled to Tangier, lived there. The palace is itself worth seeing, with an impressive central courtyard. A museum since 1922, it has had a recent overhaul, with projections, video, large maps and music all illuminating the exhibits from Tangier and the surrounding region. The hub of the museum is seven rooms around a large central courtyard with pale marble columns. This is truly a magnificent setting for the displays. Exhibits range from prehistoric bone tools to decorated ostrich eggs. The collection of ceramics is especially strong and there is also a mosaic from Roman Volubilis. Pick up an explanatory leaflet in English on your way in.

The garden of the palace, a beautiful mature Andalucían arrangement with fragrant plants and a marble fountain, is also worth exploring. As you leave the palace, stop at **Café Le Detroit** – if it's open – for a drink and pastries. In front of the palace is the **Place de la Kasbah**, where criminals were once punished or executed. In the sea wall a gate leads out onto a belvedere with excellent views across to Spain. Nearby is **Villa Sidi Hosni**, former residence of Barbara Hutton, the American heiress who was famous for her parties, among other things (read all about it in Iain Finlayson's *Tangier, City of the Dream*).

MEDINA

Lying below the kasbah and running from the Grand Socco (Place de 19 Avril, 1947) down to the port, the medina is focused on the **Petit Socco**, and is full of narrow, twisting streets and old houses, many of which are now shops, hotels or restaurants catering for tourists. It is a quarter that has captured the imagination of numerous European and American writers, the stories of Paul Bowles being among the most evocative. Tangier medina has the advantage over many others of a slope, which aids one's sense of direction a little: generally you go down to the Petit Socco and up to the kasbah. If you really don't have time to get lost, get an official guide, but avoid the advances of the unofficial ones.

Rue Siaghine, the old silversmiths' street, running from the Grand Socco to the Petit Socco, is still an important commercial area of the medina and the easiest route by which to enter the main area of the medina. To the right of Rue Siaghine, is the **mellah**, the Jewish quarter. You also pass the **Spanish Cathedral**, now boarded up.

The **Petit Socco**, the belly of the medina, was once bigger, but now seems strangely cramped. It is surrounded by a number of famous but primitive *pensiones* and the **Café Central**, formerly a café-bar attracting the likes of William Burroughs, Allen Ginsberg and Jack Kerouac. However, today, with no alcohol sold in the medina, it is a fairly ordinary café with a terrace from which to watch life pass by.

Below the Petit Socco, the **Grand Mosque** lies in between Rue de la Marine and Rue des Postes. This is built on the site of a Portuguese cathedral, although that had been predated by a mosque and, probably, a Roman temple. Opposite is a 14th-century *medersa*. Also on Rue des Postes (Rue Mokhtar Ahardan) is the **Pensión Palace**, where Bertolucci filmed scenes for *The Sheltering Sky*, based on the Paul Bowles novel.

The **Old American Legation** ① *8 Zankat Amerika, T0539-935317, www.legation.org, 0930-1200 and 1600-1830, free,* is America's oldest diplomatic property. It was given to the US by the Moroccan sultan in 1821 and used as a Consulate until 1961. It has the distinction of being the only historical monument to have remained in US possession since the birth of the American Nation. Now a museum and study centre, on display here is a letter from George Washington to Moulay Abdallah and a collection of mirrors, as well as a good collection of prints, including works by Lecouteux and Ben Ali Rbati, an early Moroccan naïve painter.

VILLE NOUVELLE

Tangier's Ville Nouvelle is a veritable catalogue of late 19th and early 20th-century architectural styles. **Place de France** (Place de Faro) has a good view of the bay, with the famous **Café de France** alongside, where wartime agents met and made deals. Next to it is the **Terrasse des Paresseux**, where would-be emigrants can see across the Straits to Spain and shoe-shine boys and Polaroid-snappers harass the tourists. **Boulevard Pasteur** (becoming Avenue Mohammed V further down) is the main shopping and business street of the new town. Find time to explore the area behind here; look out for the 1940s cinemas, have tea at **Pâtisserie Porte**, then drop in at the Librairie des Colonnes back on the main boulevard. You could then wander medina-wards again down Rue de la Liberté, stopping off for contemporary art, photography and video art at the **Galerie Delacroix** ① *1100-1300, 1600-2030, free,* if there is an exhibition on.

NEAR THE GRAND SOCCO

At 50 Rue d'Angleterre, is the Anglican **Church of St Andrew's** consecrated in 1905. The churchyard gate is discreet, in a low white-washed wall, just left of some bird-sellers' stalls, at the top side of the Grand Socco. Inside, the church hides in luxuriant vegetation. The key is kept by the groundsman, who will unlock the church and give you a guided tour. Architecture and internal decoration are modelled on Moorish Granada. Note the Arabic inscriptions of the Lord's Prayer and Gloria at the altar end. Memorials and graves, both inside and outside, feature a number of important former residents of Morocco, including

19th-century British consul Sir John Drummond Hay, early 20th-century *Times* correspondent Walter Harris, Caïd Sir Harry McLean, Scottish adviser to Sultan Moulay Abd al Aziz, and Emily Keane, 19th-century wife of the Cherif of Ouezzane. Turn right out of the churchyard gate, follow the wall uphill and you will come to the former British Consulate, now the **Musée d'Art Contemporain de la Ville de Tanger** ① *52 Rue d'Angleterre, T0539-938436, 10dh*. Here there is a small but fine selection of late 20th-century Moroccan painters. There are a couple of wacky pictures by wild woman Chaïbia Tallal, plus early works by the likes of Farid Belkahia, founder of the Casablanca École des Beaux Arts, Saâd Hassani and others.

MARSHAN

Marshan is a neighbourhood of 20th-century villas up on the Marshan plateau, west of the kasbah. **Café Hafa**, the cliff-top café, lies down a narrow street near Rue Shakespeare. Crowded at weekends with local youth, it is the place for a sticky, Polo-mint tasting tea, flavoured in season with orange-blossom. The **Punic rock tombs**, little more than large coffin-sized shapes hollowed out of the soft rock, are nearby. The closest cliff-top viewing place near the poorer parts of the city, it is popular with local women and kids on weekend afternoons.

BEACHES

Back in the centre, the town beach and the clubs alongside it (which still offer a range of drinking, eating and dancing opportunities) were previously an expat zone where anything was permissible and a good time easily available. In its heyday, this beach was said to be the third most beautiful in the world, after Rio de Janeiro and Miami. Jack Kerouac and Joe Orton were among the habitués. Roland Barthes enjoyed Las Tres Caravelas beach. More recently, Mario Testino photographed the local wildlife. During the day, the locals are out playing football. Work is continuing to clean it up, but it may still be wise to avoid the beach itself after dark. There are more relaxing, less crowded and cleaner beaches east along the coast – possibly on the stretch south of Ceuta. Nearer Tangier, there is bathing at **Playa Blanca** and **Sidi Kankouch**, also further on at **Plage Dahlia** (11 km after Ksar Es Seghir). Beaches west of Tangier such as **Plage Merkala** can be dangerous for swimming but have the advantage of being sunny until the early evening.

ATLANTIC COAST WEST OF TANGIER

An excursion west is a rewarding experience, with a dramatic drive en route. The coast of Southern Spain can be easily seen on a clear day, and from the coast road to the north of the town, there is a special viewpoint. The options are to negotiate a round-trip price with a grand taxi driver in Rue d'Angleterre, take a Boughaz minibus from the port gates, or, in your own transport, follow Rue Sidi Bou Abid and Rue Sidi Amar on to the S701. This goes up into the **Montagne**, an exclusive suburb of royal palaces and villas, past discreet gates with plaques bearing names like Siddartha. In places, the road and woods would not be out of place in Devon (except for a few palm trees). You may see pines sculpted by the Chergui wind. After dense eucalyptus woods, the landscape opens up, with views of the ocean and fine stands of parasol pine.

Some 11 km from Tangier, the extreme northwestern corner of Africa is reached. Coming from Tangier, bear right for the **Cap Spartel lighthouse**, with its Café-Bar Sol. Going left, rocky coastline is followed by the wild Atlantic and **Robinson Beach**. This is a dramatic place, and swimmers should exercise caution (there are drownings every year and very little the coastguard can do). In spring, there are plenty of wild flowers, while in summer, tiny temporary cafés with cane awnings spring up among the rocks above the crashing surf.

South of Cap Spartel, the **Caves of Hercules** ① *1000 to sunset, nominal charge*, are natural formations which were extended by quarries for millstones up to the 1920s. Later, prostitutes worked here and Tangier's rich and famous held parties. From a window shaped like Africa, which overlooks the sea, there is an impressive view.

After the Caves of Hercules take a rough farm track off the road to Roman **Cotta**, a small site centred around a factory for *garum* (anchovy paste) and the remains of a temple.

COAST EAST OF TANGIER

① *Bus 15 from Grand Socco, Tangier, serves this route, which is busy on a Sun and very busy in summer. Out of season many places are closed.*

From Tangier, 10 km east along the S704 road takes you around **Cap Malabata**, where tourist developments, including the **Hotel/Casino Mövenpick** complex, numerous cafés, as well as some excellent beaches, are used by the people from Tangier. Cap Malabata is where the Atlantic and the Mediterranean meet, and it is said the waters (with a little imagination) can be seen as two different colours. The views are certainly magnificent. The Victorian pile on the hill is the **Château Malabata**, a Gothic folly inhabited by a family.

Ksar es Seghir is a small seaside town 37 km east of Tangier, dominated by the ruined Portuguese castle. The town was named Ksar Masmuda under the Almohads and Ksar al Majaz under the Merinids, who added walls and gates in 1287. The Portuguese took the town in 1458. The floor of the town's hammam, the mosque and the intact sea gate arch should be noted. There are other cafés and restaurants, including the recommended **Restaurant Caribou**, **Café Dakhla** to the west of the town, **Café Dahlia** to the east and **Café Lachiri** on the bridge (seafood). There are possibilities for camping, and a splendid beach. Onwards, between Ksar es Seghir and Ceuta, is a string of beautiful and deserted beaches.

TANGIER LISTINGS

WHERE TO STAY

The best places to stay in the medina are mostly clustered at its northwestern tip, in or near the Kasbah.

€€€€ Nord-Pinus Tanger, 11 Rue Riad Sultan, La Kasbah, T0661-228140, www.hotel-nord-pinus-tanger.com. Tangier's most sophisticated hotel, the attractive **Nord-Pinus** has an extraordinary position at the very top of the kasbah, looking over the sea to Spain, or down into the gardens of the palace. Opened in 2007, the hotel merges traditional Moroccan design elements (such as zellige tiles, embroidery and rugs) with strikingly bold contemporary artwork and decorative pieces, managing to create a sense of timeless elegance and luxury. It's a wonderful place to stay and soak up the atmosphere of Tangier; sit on the terrace reading one of the many beautiful books lying around and listen to the birdsong in the palace gardens below. The restaurant, serving high-quality French and Moroccan cuisine, is also open to non-guests; ring to reserve.

€€€ La Tangerina, 19 Rue Riad Sultan, La Kasbah, T0539-947731, www.latangerina.com. Lower key (and also lower in price) than the **Pinus** next door, this is still a very elegant place to stay. There are cosy communal areas with antique touches and a lovely outdoor terrace filled with pot plants, shaded seating and hosting gorgeous seafront vistas. Rooms are stylish and contemporary and feature horseshoe arches. The best rooms have geranium-fringed private terraces with sea views. There's also a hammam.

€€€ Riad Tanja, Rue du Portugal, Escalier Américain, T0539-333538, www.riadtanja.com. Big, stylish bedrooms have ornate wooden furniture, red rugs, large pouffes and views over the market; the couple of smaller rooms without external windows are less desirable. The restaurant is a popular destination in its own right.

€€ Dar Nour, 20 Rue Gourna, La Kasbah, T0662-112724, www.darnour.com. Not for those partial to swinging cats, this is nevertheless a stylish, romantic place. The merging of several houses in the narrow backstreets of the kasbah has created lots of cosy nooks and crannies. If all this makes you feel a little claustrophobic, you can escape to the roof terrace, where there's a spectacular 360° view. It's a quiet spot too, away from the bustle of the medina. Old furniture and fresh flowers set off the Moroccan fabrics and lights to fine effect. Traditional Moroccan meals cooked to order. 10 rooms.

€€ Hotel Continental, 36 Rue Dar Baroud, T0539-931024, hcontinental@iam.net.ma. This old-timer hotel was used by Bertolucci in the film *The Sheltering Sky*. Faded glory in abundance, it has saggy furniture, beautiful old-but-chipped tiling, antique radios and timeworn rugs. Rooms are kept clean and some have fabulous views over the seafront. It's at the eastern end of the medina, directly above the port.

€€ Hotel el Djenina, 8 Rue el Antaki (Rue Grotius), just off Av d'Espagne, T0539-942244, eldjenina@menara.ma. 40 well renovated, airy rooms with en suite bathrooms. The hotel is clean and simple – not especially full of character or style but reliable and modern, which makes it stand out in Tangier.

€€ Hotel Rembrandt, Av Mohammed V, T0539-937870/2. Conveniently in the centre of the Ville Nouvelle, **Rembrandt** has a good pool, a restaurant and a popular, modern bar with views through buildings down to the sea. The 73 rooms lack much character but are double-glazed against the noise and some have good views.

€ Mamora Hotel, 19 Rue des Postes (Rue Mokhtar Ahardan), T0539-934105. This clean and good-value hotel is right in the centre of the medina. The best rooms have big views over the green-tiled roofs of the mosque to the sea beyond. The morning call to prayer will almost certainly wake you, however.

€ Pensión Palace, 2 Rue des Postes (Rue Mokhtar Ahardan), T0539-936128. There's no chance of being treated like royalty here; in fact, you may not even be treated much like a paying guest. But reasonable rooms around a lovely, plant-filled square courtyard make up for the disinterested service.

€ Hotel Muniria, Rue Magellan, T0539-935337. A friendly, family-run little place with 8 rooms and a preponderance of blue, from the hand-painted wardrobes to the bedspreads. Former clients include William Burroughs, Kerouac and Ginsberg, though the hotel makes admirably little of the fact. Some sea views.

RESTAURANTS

Nord-Pinus Tangier (see above) serves high-quality French and Moroccan cuisine, with an emphasis on seafood; ring to reserve.

€€€ Riad Tanja, Rue du Portugal, Escalier Américain, T0539-333538 (see Where to stay, above). With red rugs, brass candlesticks and dark wood tables, this cosy place is especially beautiful as the evening light streams in. Moroccan cuisine with a twist, with dishes such as monkfish *pastilla* and spicy couscous.

€€€ La Fabrique, 7 Rue de Fès, T0539-374057. Tue-Sat. Tangier's top-spot for French dining, La Fabrique has a stylish, modern and light-filled dining room, excellent service and a fabulous menu of flavour-packed French favourites.

€€ Anna e Paolo, 77 Av Prince Héretier, T0539-944617. A bit of a schlep out of the centre, this is worth the effort for good Italian food such as *melanzane alla parmigiana*, as well as pizzas and pasta.

€€ El Mesón de Pepe Ocaña, 7 Rue Jabha el Ouatania. Easily missed, a popular and authentically dark and atmospheric tapas bar down a small street behind **Hotel Rembrandt**. Attracts a smart, though very male, crowd. Pull up a bar stool, order a drink and the tapas will flow.

€€ Populaire Saveur, 2 Escalier Waller. Popular by both name and nature, this little fish place on the steps up from the market to Rue de le Liberté has good set menus in a homely atmosphere.

€€ San Rémo, 15 Rue Ahmed Chaouki, T0539-938451. Tue-Sun. Fresh pasta and other European dishes in a pretty little bistro-style place with tablecloths and serious service.

€ Agadir, 21 Rue Prince Héretier. A tiny fragment of the 1950s near the Blvd Pasteur, this small and simple licensed place behind net curtains serves good, freshly cooked Moroccan and French food with a smile. Excellent tagines and *pastilla* as well as some seafood.

Cafés and pâtisseries
Café Central, in the Petit Socco. The former artistic rendezvous where William Burroughs and Tennessee Williams used to hang out. It's lost most of its magic but it's still a good place to watch the crowds go by.

Café de France, 1 Pl de France, has a history as a meeting place for artists and intellectuals. Mixed clientele of local notables, tourists and *passeurs* looking out for potential emigrants to hustle across the Straits.

NORTH ATLANTIC COAST

With none of the hassle of Tangier, yet some of its European sophistication, it's not surprising that coastal Asilah has become a firm fixture on many tourists' itineraries. Beautifully whitewashed, its old fortified Portuguese centre makes a good spot for a peaceful couple of days by the sea. Further south, Larache is much less discovered but has some of the same architectural attractions in the winding streets of its medina and, across the estuary, some evocative ancient Roman remains at Lixus.

Outside the city, cork and eucalyptus forest, gardens and beaches stretch north along the Atlantic coast. Kénitra is an industrial and military port, while further north, Mehdiya attracts surfers to its sandy beach and other visitors to its overgrown kasbah overlooking the sea. This stretch of coast is rich in birdlife, particularly on the Lac de Sidi Bourhaba and the lagoon of Merdja Zerga. There are isolated Roman remains at Thamusida and Banasa. To the south of Rabat, spring flowers carpet the valleys of the Zaër Forest, an area of gorges and rolling hills.

→ ASILAH

Asilah, 40 km south of Tangier (and also referred to as Arzila), is a striking fishing port and coastal town of white and blue houses, surrounded by ramparts and lying alongside an extensive beach. It is the northernmost of the former Portuguese outposts (the others include Azemmour, El Jadida and Safi). A small place with a Mediterranean feel, Asilah might provide a pleasant introduction to Morocco, in spite of the extent to which tourism dominates. If you turn up in August you'll coincide with the annual influx of people for the International Festival of Asilah, which usually includes jazz and Moroccan music, and exhibitions by contemporary Moroccan artists.

ARRIVING IN ASILAH
Getting there and moving on Asilah lies off the main N1 Tangier to Rabat road. The rail station is some 2 km north of the town, and there aren't very many taxis in Asilah. Buses and taxis stop at the Place Mohammed V, close to the old town. From Asilah to Larache (see page 214) is a one-hour bus journey or 45 minutes in a shared taxi.

BACKGROUND
Modern Asilah stands on the site of the Phoenician town of Silis, or perhaps Zilis. The area was subsequently settled by Romans in Anthony's reign and by the Byzantines. In 966, the town was rebuilt by El Hakim II, ruler of Córdoba. It was the last stronghold of the Idrissid dynasty. The Portuguese occupied Asilah from 1471 and built the town's fortifications and, in 1578, King Sebastian landed there on his way to defeat at what was to become known as the Battle of the Three Kings. This defeat led to the Spanish absorption of Portugal, and thus of Asilah, but the Portuguese influence on the town is still quite discernible.

The Moroccans recovered Asilah in 1691, under Moulay Ismaïl. In 1826 Austria bombarded Asilah, then a base of piracy, as did the Spanish in 1860. In the late 19th and early 20th century Ahmed al Rasouli, the bandit chief who terrorized much of northwestern Morocco, was based in the town, as described by his one-time hostage and later friend, Walter Harris, in *Morocco That Was*. Al Rasouli built his palace in the medina and from it exercised power over much of the region, being for a time its governor. The Spanish took Asilah in 1911, as part of their protectorate of northern Morocco.

In more recent years, Asilah has played host to an international summer arts festival. The old neighbourhoods are now squeaky clean and home to weekend retreats for wealthy Casablancans. The result is pretty and whitewashed, and there are some excellent restaurants.

PLACES IN ASILAH

The medina is the main place of interest of Asilah, a quarter of predominately white and blue buildings, reflecting in their design the influence of the Portuguese. Note the modern murals on some of the houses in the medina, painted by artists during the festival. The ramparts were built by the Portuguese in the 15th century and are set with a number of important gates, including **Bab el Kasbah**, **Bab el Bahar** ('the sea gate'), **Bab Ihoumar**, a structure topped with the eroded Portuguese coat of arms, as well as **Bab el Jbel** ('the mountain gate') and **Bab Ihoumer**. At points it is possible to climb the fortifications for views of the town and along the coast. Within the medina, **Le Palais de la Culture** is a cultural centre converted from the former residence of the brigand Ahmed al Rasouli, built in 1909 right beside the sea. It is difficult to gain access except during the festival, but it is possible to visualize those who incurred al Rasouli's wrath being made to walk the plank from the palace windows over the cliff front.

The souk has a Thursday **market**, attracting farmers from the surrounding area. In addition to the sale of the usual fruit, spices and vegetables, handicrafts distinctive of the Rif region are also on display.

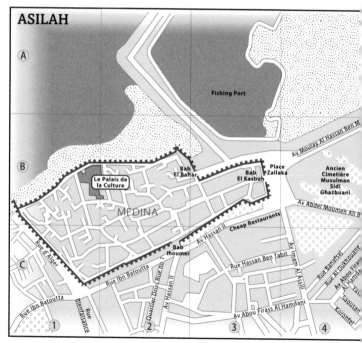

The International Festival of Asilah in August is a cultural festival which has taken place in Asilah since 1978 and involves performers and artists from all over the world. Events throughout the town attract many spectators.

The **beach** is often windy (but at times can be beautifully calm) and is frequented by bathers, men touting camel rides and fishermen. It stretches beyond the building works to the north and south of the town.

→ EL UTAD, THE STONE CIRCLE AT MZOURA

The stone circle at Mzoura makes a good excursion from Rabat or Tangier for those with plenty of time and a car. Though there are numerous prehistoric rock art sites in the High Atlas and Djebel Beni, the barrow at Mzoura is the only one of its kind in the country. The best time to visit Mzoura is in late summer when the vegetation has died back. After a rainy winter, the countryside will be at its best. This is also a good trip for birdwatchers, giving them a focus point in a rolling landscape of open fields, stands of eucalyptus and occasional corrugated-iron roofed homesteads unspoiled by industrial agriculture. It

also gives you a glimpse into the living conditions in the countryside.

The first trace of prehistoric occupation you meet are three great menhirs, lying on the ground. Look out for the scooped-out 'bowls' in one of the stones, referred to as 'cup and circle' by English archaeologists and testimony to some obscure cult after the stones had fallen. Further on, to your right, the stones of the circle once ringed a high barrow, heavily excavated by the Spanish. Most stones are only 1.5 m high and, within them, lies a sort of stone walkway – possibly the original base of the barrow. The most spectacular feature is a stone standing 4.5 m high. You can also locate a lintel in the circle, once the entrance to the barrow.

Getting there On the N1 north of Larache – a winding, busy road – there is a major roundabout near Sidi Tnine el Yamani where you should branch off for Tetouan (R417). Just under 4 km beyond the roundabout, turn left at the Somepi garage and head up the recently widened road for

Sidi Yamani. After about 3 km, in the village, you reach a Y-junction, where you need to take the left-hand fork. About 6.5 km after the village, after passing a large abandoned Spanish building on your left, you should turn off right onto a sandy track that comes after a minor cutting, with the road running slightly downhill. (If in doubt, ask a local for 'el utad', the funerary monument.) Once you turn off, the track doubles back sharply, taking you the 2.5 km to the hamlet where the circle is located. When you get to the hamlet, keep left; the track to the circle runs between the bramble hedges of the farmsteads, eventually veering round to the left.

→ LARACHE

Bigger than Asilah, and rather less bijou, Larache is a relaxed, faded seaside town, with a good beach and not too many tourists. A halfway house between Spanish and Moroccan urban life, it is a sleepy sort of place, with views over the ocean and the Loukkos estuary, plus the evocatively named 16th-century Château de la Cigogne, the Fortress of the Stork. It was at Larache that Jean Genet was to find a haven, writing his last novel here.

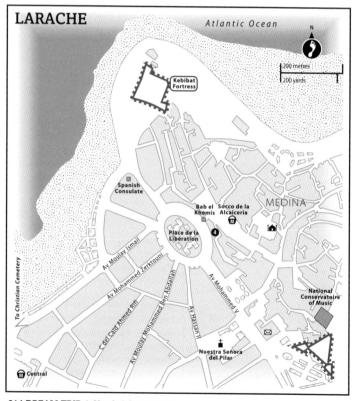

MOVING ON

When the time comes to continue the route to Rabat (see page 225) you can take a taxi to Ksar el-Kebir (45 minutes, see page 217) and then a train on to Rabat (2½ hours).

BACKGROUND

Larache (El Arayis in Arabic) is named for the vine arbours of the Beni Arous, a local tribe. The area has one of the longest histories of human occupation in Morocco, going back to Phoenician, Carthaginian and Roman times at the settlement of nearby Lixus. Larache was occupied by the Spanish from 1610 to 1689 and, as part of their protectorate, from 1911. At that time, the harbour was added and the new town was developed. Larache became the principal port of the Spanish northern zone. Today, the town draws its livelihood from the agro-food industry and fishing, although it has lost its status as a major port. Revenues from migrant workers and the building industry are important, too.

PLACES IN LARACHE

On the very edge of the old town of Larache is a large piece of Renaissance military engineering, with the usual pointy bastions, dating from the 16th century. The isolated structure, now housing the local museum of antiquities, is the **Château de la Cigogne** ① T0539-912091, Wed-Sun 0900-1200, 1500-1730. Also called Castillo de las Cigueñas or Al Fath, the museum contains a small amount of material from Lixus.

The Avenue Mohammed V is the main street of the new town. At the eastern end, heading for the central plaza, there are the fortifications and then the post office on the right and the **Iglesia de Nuestra Señora del Pilar** on the left. The circular **Place de la Libération**, with a fountain, is the heart of the town; the entrance to the medina, an arched gate, **Bab el Khemis**, is on the north side.

Exploring further, on the clifftop overlooking ocean and estuary, the 16th-century **Kebibat Fortress** was used by the Spanish as a hospital. Shamefully, it has been left to fall into ruin. The Spanish Consulate occupies a fine art deco building, and you will also easily locate the neo-Moorish central **market**, recognizable by its towers.

The medina is a poor quarter of steep and narrow streets and high walls best viewed from below or from the north side of the estuary. Just inside is the Spanish-built market square. There are a number of souks, notably **Socco de la Alcaicería**, the cloth market.

The main beach is an extensive strip of fine (though littered, in season) sand with a number of cafés nearby. To get there, see Ancient Lixus, below.

One final port of call in Larache is the tomb of writer **Jean Genet** (1910-1986), out in the old Christian cemetery near the lighthouse and prison. The cemetery has been cleaned up as, part of the works currently being financed by the regional government of Andalucía. With the views over the ocean, Genet could hardly have chosen a better final resting place.

→ ANCIENT LIXUS

① The site is just over the Oued Loukkos, on a hillside to the west of the N1. Without a car, you may have to walk or take a petit taxi (30dh) and wait by the roadside for a grand taxi with a space in order to get back again. Best option is to get the bus No 2 (3dh), which runs from the port to the beach, Plage Rimmel. Open daylight hours. The east side of the site next to the N1 is fenced in by green railings. A small site map on a metal plaque can be found next to the locked *entrance gate. After a recent incident of armed robbery here, you will be accompanied on your visit by a guard with a large wooden truncheon, which may or may not make you feel safer.*

Located on a spectacular site on the right bank of the Oued Loukkos about 4 km from the sea, Ancient Lixus is the second most important Roman site in Morocco after Volubilis. Heathland butterflies and the occasional raptor are added bonuses of a visit to the site.

Tchemich Hill, on which the town is located, 50 m above sea level, was obviously an excellent location for defensive reasons, and the views from here are beautiful, especially in the early evening, when the sun is going down over the meanders of the estuary. For some ancient writers Lixus was the location of the Garden of Hesperides, where Hercules harvested golden apples to gain his place on Mount Olympus. The first traces of settlement date from the seventh to sixth century BC, and in pre-Roman inscriptions the future Lixus is referred to as Semes. The oldest evidence of building goes back to the fourth century BC. There was a seventh-century Phoenician and later a Carthaginian settlement here. Rome annexed the town in 40 BC. Coins with Latin and neo-Punic inscriptions suggest the inhabitants had a dual culture, as was the case in so much of Roman North Africa. The town became a colony under the Emperor Claudius I, when salt, olives and fish were the main exports. Eventually reaching an area of 62 ha, Lixus prospered until the late third century AD, in part because of its strategic position on the road from Tingis (Tangier) to Sala Colonia (Rabat). It remained active and was occupied until the fifth century AD and, in Arabic historiography, re-emerges as Tohemmis. This remained a Muslim settlement until Larache was founded in the 14th century. Recent archaeological finds in the region will shed further light on the town's history.

GETTING AROUND THE SITE

The easiest way up into the site is via the track near the gate, generally closed, at the north end of the **garum** (fish salting) **basins** behind the railings on the N1 (just nip around the railings). Head uphill to find the **amphitheatre**, excavated in 1964 and, with its quality stonework, probably the most impressive ruin. Spectators would have been able to enjoy a play and superb views of the flood plain beyond at the same time. Just beyond the theatre is a small **bath complex**. There are some mosaics still in situ in the hall area, although the central mosaic of Neptune has been removed. In the circular caldarium are traces of painted plaster. Clear evidence of demolition/rebuild can be seen from the column drums inserted into a wall. After the amphitheatre, either follow the track uphill to discover the remains of **apsed temple** (crumbling half-tower) or cut across left (west) and scramble up to visit the **acropolis** area. Look out for the impressive vaulted cisterns. It is possible to make out an oratory, a small open space with a stubby column in the middle and twin semicircular niches. The layout of the colonnaded **forum** can also be seen. Dominating the highest point of the site is a rectangular, vaulted chamber some 4 m high, probably a **cistern** for feeding the nearby bath complex.

Beyond Lixus the road leads onto the **beach**, where there is a car park and camping areas. In summer, there are lifeguards and organized beach activities for the local children.

KSAR EL-KEBIR (FORMERLY ALCAZARQUIVIR)

Kasar el Kebir means the 'Great Fortress' and probably stands on the site of the Roman colony Oppidum Novum, 'new town'. Off the main N1 road, it is only a must if you have an interest in neo-Moorish Spanish colonial architecture.

The exact location of the Roman town is uncertain. Two funerary inscriptions were found here, one in Greek and one in Latin. In its favour, Ksar el Kebir is close to other ancient settlements and, if the Romans had wanted a strongpoint to guard a crossing of the Oued Loukkos, where better than here? An 11th-century settlement here was expanded and fortified by Yacoub al Mansour in the late 12th century.

But Ksar el Kebir's chief claim to fame is that it lies near the site of a great battle. Nearby, in 1578, the famous Battle of the Three Kings was fought, in which King Sebastian of Portugal, Saâdian Sultan Abd al Malek and a claimant to the throne, former Sultan el Mutawakkil, all died. The flower of Portuguese chivalry was wiped out, leading to the end of Portugal as an independent nation for some 100 years. Moulay Ismaïl destroyed much of the town in the 17th century.

The Spanish occupied Ksar el Kebir in 1911, rebuilding it, renaming it Alcazarquivir, and developing it as a military centre. There are a number of Spanish buildings in various stages of decay. Particularly fine is the Alhambra-style decoration of the former officers' mess, now housing local Ministry of Education offices. The women who work there may allow you to have a look in. In the same area, there is a flag factory with weavers using handlooms to make red cloth for flags for official buildings. The regional market is held on Sunday outside the station. There is also a much transformed Grand Mosque (an Almohad foundation) near to a Merinid *medersa*.

ARBAOUA

Arbaoua is signed to the west of the N1, and with its shady trees is a popular stopping place for Moroccan families making the journey back from Europe by car. (Note that the mosquitoes can be a nuisance.) The old frontier post between the Spanish and French zones of protectoral Morocco is at Kedhadhra, marked by a fine reinforced concrete building and lots of stalls selling pottery and wicker furniture. North of here, the first major town is Ksar el Kebir.

MOULAY BOUSSELHAM

The small beach resort of Moulay Bousselham is a relaxed summery place, increasingly popular with Fassis and others who have built second homes there. There is a fine stretch of coast but Moulay Bousselham is best known for its lagoon, Merdja Zerga ('the blue lagoon'), an important wintering site for migrating birds. Although easily reached from Souk el Arba du Gharb, only 44 km along the S216, Moulay Bousselham is bypassed by most tourists.

Background Moulay Bousselham, 'the man of the cape', is named after a 10th-century saint and mystic, who supposedly came from Egypt and converted the Atlantic coast of Morocco to Islam. The memory of Moulay Bousselham is commemorated in a *moussem* (religious festival), in July, and in a nearby *koubba* (tomb). The beach is spectacular but dangerous for swimming, although not bad for fishing. If you have a car, you could take in the nearish Roman sites of Banasa, near Souk Tlata du Gharb, and Thamusida, near Kénitra, on the way south to Rabat.

The lagoon and birdlife The lagoon, Merdja Zerga, is one of Morocco's largest, covering over 30 sq km. This and the surrounding wetlands are a designated reserve offering protection for migrating and overwintering waterbirds.

By car it is possible to approach the reserve from the south. Proceed from Souk el Arba du Gharb and, after 34 km, turn left on the 2301. After crossing the Nador Channel (Canal de Daoura), turn sharp right and park in the village, Daoura Oulad Mesbah. Access to the reserve from Moulay Bousselham is across the Oued Drade, which flows to the south of the village. Arrange a lift or hire a rowing boat (bargain firmly) and arrange for a return trip with the fisherman who ferries you across. The track down the west side of the lagoon goes through Daoura Roissia to the minor coast road, but provides ample opportunity for peaceful observation. It is estimated that half of the ducks and small waders wintering in Morocco north of latitude 30°N are found here. It will be impossible to miss the greater flamingos and spoonbills and the familiar wigeon, mallard, shoveler, shelduck and teal. Sighting a slender-billed curlew is less likely.

ANCIENT BANASA
If you need to prioritize, Banasa is the most important (in terms of visible ruins) of the ancient sites reached from the Tangier– Rabat N1 road. Like Thamusida, it is located south of the Oued Sebou, probably bridged here in ancient times. Unlike Thamusida, access is by metalled road. Banasa is awkward to get to without your own transport.

Getting there Travelling south to Rabat on the N1, you need to turn left at a minor junction south of Souk Tlata du Gharb ('Tuesday Souk in the Gharb'): look out for some abandoned farm buildings just after the turn and an avenue of eucalyptus trees on the main road. Big road signs near the turn (showing Rabat 100 km and Tangier 173 km) are parallel to the N1 and so are not easily visible. After the turn, follow the narrow road to the bridge. Here the road is being widened and follows the river to your left. At a T-junction, go left and, after about 2 km, you will find a rusty sign telling you to turn off left for Banasa. The track runs across the fields and the site is easily located by a mosque and the domed shrine of Sidi Ali Boujnoun.

The site Excavation at Banasa was not easy, as remains were buried beneath many layers of alluvium deposited by the flooding *oued*. The earliest settlement recorded here was third century BC, but the main colony was founded at the end of the first century BC by Roman Emperor Augustus. Remains include traces of houses (some indicating wealthy owners), five baths and shops. A wealth of distinctive pottery, mosaics and inscriptions has also been discovered. The alignment of the streets on a northeast-southwest grid can be seen, with a forum marking the centre of the town. Unfortunately, most of the better building material was removed and 'recycled'. The discovery here of a number of bronze inscriptions, legal texts, military diplomas and decrees of patronage, some of which are now visible in the Rabat Archaeological Museum, make this an important site.

There are also a few mosaics at the site. They include an ornamental design with the head of the ocean in the centre from one of the excavated baths; one containing fighting cocks and a bag of money; and a number with marine scenes. In one of the baths, traces of painted stucco and a very faint mural in a niche can just about be distinguished.

ANCIENT THAMUSIDA

The remains of the ancient Roman town of Thamusida can make an interesting excursion from Kénitra, though the ruins are only really feasible if you have your own transport or a lot of time. Ideally, go by car and try to cover Thamusida along with Mehdiya, the Roman site at Banasa and the stone circle at Mzoura in a long day trip.

Getting there The remains are in open agricultural land near Sidi Ali Ben Ahmed, on the left bank of the Oued Sebou, 18 km from the *oued* mouth. ToTo get there, head south on the N1 and, at the major roundabout some 10 km north of Kénitra, take the turn-off signposted Tangier 222 km, Tetouan 249 km. After passing under a railway bridge, continue northwards. The turn-off left is easily missed: look out for a pink café, some 25 m before a small Total petrol station and a mosque. Turn left at the café, and a sandy track will take you past small houses and market gardens to a sort of crossroads (go straight on, not left for another small mosque). Crossing the fields, eventually you approach the riverbank, where the track follows round to the left. Markers to look out for are the distinctive white dome, or *koubba*, of Sidi Ali Ben Ahmed, a stand of trees and, on the river, the boatmen. In the far distance, the hill of the Mehdiya kasbah is just visible.

Note that access in wet weather is problematic in a small hire car. If coming down the N1 from the north, you should look out for the roadside houses of the village of Ouled Slama, and on the right of the road, the cream-painted administrative building of the commune rurale. The Total garage and pink café are about 100 m further on.

The site Thamusida was built in an excellent position, protected from flooding (being on a flattish hillock about 12 m above sea level) but accessible from the sea by good-size boats making use of the tidal flow. The site of Roman Thamusida had been settled on and off since prehistoric times but its first recorded mention is by Ptolemy. The Roman garrison was established here under the Flavians, and monuments have been found dating from that period. So far, discoveries include the remains of a temple with three shrines beside the *oued*, the baths and some dwellings; one named the House of the Stone Floor. This **Maison du Dallage** to the east of the complex has the traditional open central courtyard with the triclinium (dining room) at the eastern end. The baths, close to the *oued*, have been altered and extended a number of times, finally covering an area of around 3000 sq m – the ground plan showing a division into separate sections for men and women. Evidence also points to the existence of fish-salting works, an iron works and shops.

The large camp to the southwest of the site was constructed by order of Marcus Aurelius. It measures 166 m by 139 m and is considered to have been large enough to house a substantial military presence. The walls of the fort had four gates, one more or less central in each wall, and 14 towers which project inwards. In the centre is the praetorium, a rectangular porticoed courtyard 45 m by 30 m with rooms on three sides. In the southwest side, one of the rooms, built on a podium and reached by four steps, is larger. On the northwest side of the praetorium, projecting into the main courtyard, are the remains of a hall constructed in the time of Septimus Severus. A wall with a number of entrance gates encloses the town on the three land sides, the fourth side being protected by the *oued*. At intervals along the wall are semicircular towers which project outwards.

Excavations began in the early 1930s. On the basis of the finds, the settlement can be assumed to have been prosperous and quite active well into the third century AD. However, it is thought that the whole area was abandoned quite suddenly between AD 274 and 280. Excavation continues sporadically, and Thamusida remains a sleepy place, the croaking of frogs and drone of irrigation pumps occasionally disturbed by flights out of the Kénitra airbase.

KENITRA

Kénitra is an industrial and military centre of importance within Morocco. It was a small military fort until 1913, when the French built a new town, as well as an artificial harbour used as a military port and to export citrus fruit and other products from the rich agricultural areas of the surrounding Gharb region. The port was developed to replace Larache, in the Spanish zone, and Tangier, in the International Zone. In 1933, Kénitra was renamed Port Lyautey by the French, after the first Resident-General of the Moroccan protectorate. US troops landed here in November 1942 as part of Operation Torch and experienced heavy casualties under fire from the port at Mehdiya. In 1947 the US returned to establish an important naval base, which they used until 1977. After independence, Port Lyautey was renamed Kénitra and it remains important as a military centre and port. It lies on the N1 from Rabat to Tangier. For the first-time visitor to Morocco, the attraction of Kénitra (beyond some early 20th-century architecture) is its potential as a base for trips to the nearby Roman site of Thamusida and to Mehdiya, with its fine kasbah, on the coast.

MEHDIYA

Mehdiya (also spelt Mehdia and Mahdia) Plage is Kénitra's one-horse beach resort, noted for windsurfing but more interesting to visit for its kasbah (some way from the town's seafront) and the nearby nature reserve around Lac de Sidi Bourhaba.

Arriving in Mehdiya Bus No 9 from Kénitra has its terminus just opposite the kasbah entrance. If you are driving from Rabat, turn left off the N1 for Mehdiya Plage as you head north at a complicated junction with the Café Bustan and petrol. The road winds over heathland to drop down to Mehdiya Plage (where there are lots of new villas). For the kasbah, head through the town. You'll note a crumbling flight of steps up to the kasbah on your right (east). Parking may be awkward. Otherwise, follow the road round and up the hillside (estuary on your left), turn right (new housing area on your right), eucalyptus wood on your left. The entrance gate to the kasbah soon comes into view.

Background Historians think that a Carthaginian trading post was established here in the sixth century BC. Around the 10th century, the site was occupied by the Berbers. Naval shipyards were established here by the Almohads. By the 16th century, a small and active commercial port visited by European merchants, Al Mamora had grown up close to the site of present day Mehdiya. The Portuguese, then expanding along the African coast after taking Ceuta in the 15th century, became interested in the area, and thus it was that King Manuel of Portugal sent out an expeditionary force, which took the little town in June 1515, renaming it São João da Mamora. The Portuguese were quickly defeated, however, and the port became a lair for pirate adventurers. By the early 17th century, along with Salé and Algiers, it was one of the leading pirate ports in North Africa and a source of irritation to the European trading nations. Like Salé (Sila in Arabic), home of a band of renegades known as the Sallee Rovers, it functioned as a sort of autonomous republic. For a while Mamora was ruled by the English adventurer Henry Mainwaring, who later continued his career in the Royal Navy before becoming a member of the English parliament (1620-1623). And it was also at Mamora that another adventurer, Saint Mandrier, was captured by Moroccan forces; this enterprising Frenchman was later to become technical adviser to the sultan on fortifications and cannon foundries.

The pirate republics of Morocco harmed European trade with the Indies. In 1614, Spanish forces took Mamora and, on a hillside overlooking the river, a new fortress was constructed. Named San Miguel de Ultramar, it forms the basis of most of the kasbah still surviving today. In May 1681, this fortress in turn fell to the advancing armies of the Alaouite Sultan Moulay Ismaïl. The victory marked the end of the Spanish *presidios*: Larache and Tangier were subsequently evacuated.

The newly taken fort was renamed El Mehdiya, 'the citadel delivered'. (Henceforth the name Mamora was to be used for the vast cork oak forests to the northeast of Salé.) Moulay Ismaïl installed a garrison, strengthened the walls and began work on a new port at the mouth of the River Sebou, ultimately abandoned in the late 18th century.

Under the French, the fortress was occupied and was the scene of clashes between US and French forces during the American Expeditionary Force landings of November 1942.

Mehdiya kasbah Uninhabited apart from a few cows, the kasbah of Mehdiya is definitely worth a visit if you are in town. There is no entrance fee, although there may be a man sitting at the gate who should be given a small tip. Within the walls, the small mosque with its whitewashed minaret is still used by local people. The smaller of the two entrance gates, **Bab el Aïn**, is of Spanish origin, while the other gate, the grander **Bab Jedid** (New Gate), flanked by two massive rectangular towers, was erected by Moulay Ismaïl. From the roof terraces there is a magnificent panorama of the river and ocean to the northwest, and over to the Sidi Bourhaba lagoon, a protected area to the south. The northwest bastion, **Borj Bab el Aïn**, is well preserved with seven cannons still in place. Below, next to the estuary, is a labyrinth of extensive storerooms, well protected by a sea wall.

The most important building, however, is the governor's house, the **Dar el Makhzen**, which, with its great mosaic patio, must have been an extremely fine residence in its day, with extensive outbuildings – close to the main entrance are the remains of a hammam and a *foundouk* (merchants' hostel). A flight of brick steps leads up to dusty overgrown terraces. Today, however, the bustle of traders and soldiers in the fortress overlooking the Sebou belongs very much to the past: goats graze on the weeds growing out of the paving, fig trees sprout from the walls, and there is no foreign army to menace the great bastions and moats. Despite the neglect, the cobbling and some other features indicate that this kasbah was restored and used under the French. Birdwatchers will find finches flitting between the crab-apple and tamarisk bushes.

The southern section of the Lac de Sidi Bourhaba and adjacent marshes are the focus of the nature reserve, popular for birdwatching. The *koubba* has a festival in August. The northern section of the lake is a pleasant area for picnicking, either by the water's edge, which can be marshy, or in the surrounding woodlands. Overwintering waterbirds are the main interest (literally thousands of ducks) and, in April, you can see spring migrants. African marsh owls are frequently reported. There is a keeper's residence on the east side.

PLAGE DES NATIONS

The Plage des Nations at Sidi Bouknadel, about 25 km northeast of Rabat, is very popular with the affluent, and more of a family beach than those of Rabat-Salé, although the currents can be dangerous. Take bus No 28 from Salé, and walk 1 km from the turning, or in summer share a grand taxi from Salé.

MAMORA FOREST

To the northeast of Rabat, the Mamora Forest is a peaceful area of cork and eucalyptus trees. Around half the cork oaks of Morocco are found here. The eucalyptus is also harvested for commercial purposes, and there are plantations of pine and acacia. More unusual is the Mamora wild pear, a tall tree, growing up to 15 m, which has white flowers in spring. There are *dayats* (shallow lakes) in the region and, in wetter years, these attract the white stork. The spotted flycatcher is a summer visitor, as is the magnificent blue roller. The turtle dove, visiting from the South, is declining in numbers as human hunting continues. Indeed, the whole area is under human pressure, as the neighbouring settlements expand and people use the forest as a source of charcoal and a place for grazing their livestock. Bissected in part by the main north–south *autoroute*, the forest can also be accessed off the Meknès road. Turn off left at Sidi Allal Bahroui. Return via the N1 and R405.

DAR BEGHAZI

ⓘ *T0537-822178, Mon-Sat, 40dh for main rooms, 100dh for whole collection.*

The Dar Beghazi is another sight close to Rabat, accessible for those with their own vehicle. Situated opposite the turn-off to the Plage des Nations, on the N1 road north of Salé, this home has been turned into a private museum to house the Beghazi family's collection of carpets, weapons and jewellery. Admission is expensive, but there is a lot to see, including a rather splendid coach.

JARDINS EXOTIQUES

ⓘ *About 15 km north of Rabat, at Bouknadel on the N1, and the No 28 bus route, 0900-1830, 5dh, children 3dh.*

These 4 ha of garden were the work of French horticulturalist and Moroccophile, M François, in the 1950s. Originally, there were over 1500 species and varieties of plants from all over the world, laid out in a network of pools, bridges and summerhouses. There was a Japanese garden with bamboo bridges and flat-stone paths, a section of Brazilian rainforest, and an area of plants from Polynesia. Unfortunately, the Moroccan pavilion is in ruins, the Middle Atlas apes look miserable in their minute cages, and the general tendency is towards Barbary jungle. However, children with a taste for adventure could have a whale of a time exploring. There are some fine palm trees and flowering datura. Things horticultural apart, the Jardins Exotiques seem to function as a minor Garden of Eden where local couples discourse in the shade, safely out of the way of prying family eyes.

NORTH ATLANTIC COAST LISTINGS

WHERE TO STAY

Asilah

Asilah is a good place to rent a private house. See the Spanish www.elbaraka.net.

€€€ Dar Zuina, Dchar el Hommar, T061-243809, www.darzuina.com. 7 km outside Asilah, this colourful, peaceful guesthouse in the countryside is surrounded by attractive gardens. The rooms are simply but stylishly furnished with a rustic feel and some have a private terrace.

€€€ Hotel Al Khaima, Km 2 Rte de Tangier, BP 101, T0539-417428. A large hotel with 113 rooms by the beach, 2 km outside town. Reasonable sized rooms come with a decent amount of wear and tear and could do with a refit. Restaurant, disco, bar, tennis courts and pool. Can be noisy though, and you don't get any of the style of Asilah.

€€ Hotel Azayla, 20 Av Ibn Rochd, T0539-416717, h.azayla@menara.ma. A modern hotel just outside the medina, Azayla is decorated with art and black and white photos, and the small rooms have wicker chairs, pine furniture, a/c and double glazing.

€€ Hotel Mansour, 49 Av Mohammed V, T0539-917390, www.hotelmansour.fr.fm. Decorated with faded photographs of scantily clad ladies in a forest with swans, this hotel doesn't go for minimalistic good taste. However the bedrooms are simple and clean. Much better value out of season.

€€ Hotel Patio de la Luna, 12 Pl Zelaka, T0539-416074, hotelpatiodelaluna@yahoo.es. Charming and whitewashed, this is Asilah's most attractive hotel. Spanish-owned, it has blue shutters and a solar-powered water heater on the roof. There's a peaceful patio with candle lamps and views over the town from the little roof terrace. Comfortable and stylish rooms have good beds. Reservations essential in summer.

€€ Hotel Zelis, 10 Av Mansour Eddahabi, T0539-417069. With 61 rooms (3rd floor ones are best) and a pool, this place is modern in a 1980s sort of way. The bright red carpets might make your eyes water but there are sea views and minibars to compensate. Exercise machines on the roof terrace facing the sea.

€ Hotel Sahara, 9 Rue Tarfaya, T0539-917185. With old tiled corridors and well-tended plants, the **Sahara** is a model budget hotel. Simple clean rooms have art and a lamp and a bed and nothing more. Some lack windows but the whole hotel is absolutely spotless and it's very friendly too. All the rooms face onto a central sunny tiled courtyard and the 5dh shared showers are good.

Larache

Reserve in summer when the town is busy.

€€ Hotel Riad, Rue (or C or Zankat) Moulay Mohammed Ben Abdallah, signed from Av Mohammed V, T0539-912626. The converted former residence of the Duchess of Guise has 24 rooms with big tiles, coloured glass and worn, loose old carpet. There's a restaurant but no bar and a small pool. The place has some vaguely stylish wrought-iron furniture, but it could do with sprucing up. In summer, karaoke in the garden may keep you awake.

€€ La Maison Haute, 6 Derb ben Thami, www.lamaisonhaute.com. Stylish and colourful, this guesthouse has bags of character in a great spot in the medina, on the corner of Socco de Alcaiceria, just behind the Pl de la Libération. There are 6 simple rooms (some without en suite) and a more expensive suite. The best rooms have good views, but all are light-filled and benefit from local textiles and homely touches. There is also a fantastic roof terrace to lounge on. Book in advance.

€ Pensión Amal, 10 Rue Abdallah Ben Yassine, T0539-912788. The closest to bus and grand taxi stations. 14 rooms, clean, quiet and better than the other rock-bottom cheapies.

RESTAURANTS

Asilah

Asilah has 2 main restaurant areas: near the old ramparts on Av Hassan II there are plenty of cheap places with seating areas under the walls, selling Moroccan food and pizzas. The more upmarket seafood restaurants are in Pl Zallaka and onto Av Moulay Al Hassan Ben Mehdi. In some of the more expensive restaurants, you will be shown a great dish of fresh fish to choose from. Your chosen fish is then weighed, and you are charged by the 100 g. If this is the case, make sure you know how much you will be charged. In the cheaper restaurants, go for grilled rather than fried fish, as the oil is sometimes used far more than it should be.

€€ Al Kazaba, T0539-417012. This restaurant and *salon de thé* has a good reputation for seafood. It's smart, with white tablecloths and incongruous all-year tinsel. The menu includes French and Moroccan cuisine; if fish isn't your thing, try the brochettes.

€€ Casa Garcia, Av Moulay Al Hassan Ben Mehdi, T0539-417465. The most feted of Asilah's restaurants, **Casa Garcia** fills up quickly with well-off Europeans. There's nothing very Moroccan about it, but the food is good enough that at least 1 person regularly flies in from France for the day just to eat here. The decor, like the food, is fishy, with crabs and lobsters suspended in nets. Turn up early or reserve, especially for the outdoor tables.

€€ La Place, 7 Av Moulay Al Hassan Ben Mehdi, T0539-417326. Simpler than most of its neighbours, **La Place** has a couple of tables outside, tagines for 50dh as well as fish dishes by weight.

€€ Le Pont, 24 Av Moulay Al Hassan Ben Mehdi. Straightforward Moroccan place, 4 plastic-covered tables facing the sea, serves seafood *pastilla*, couscous, tagines, and fish dishes, such as swordfish steak. An excellent place to try Asilah's seafood without any pretentions.

€€ Oceano Casa Pepe, Pl Zallaka, T0539-417395. Just outside the medina walls, this popular place has tables outside and smart white-jacketed waiters. Inside there are wooden beams and fake candle lamps. Good, varied seafood menu.

€€ Restaurant el Espigon, Av Moulay Hassan, T0539-417157. Famous for its paella, which must be ordered a day in advance. The roasted tomato and pepper salad is also recommended.

€ Café al Madina, just inside the medina. A good place to sit, with seats facing the square and walls. Coffee and pastries as well as snacks and Moroccan standards.

€ La Symphonie des Douceurs II, 26 Pl Zallaka, T0539-416633. Long thin café with 3D art and some pastries. Ice cream is sometimes available.

Larache

Try the fish grills down by the port for cheap fresh-out-of-the-sea seafood.

€€ Restaurant Estrella del Mar, 68 C Mohammed Zerktouni, T0539-911052. The town's best restaurant is opposite the fish market and has a suitably fishy menu. It's nicely decorated, with a carved ceiling, tablecloths and a wooden boat. *Raciones* downstairs, a bit smarter upstairs.

€€ Restaurant Larache, 18 Av Moulay Mohammed Ben Abdallah, T0539-913641. Tagines and fish – try the mixed fried seafood – in a simple place with a blackboard.

€ Restaurant Commercial, Pl de la Libération. Very cheap fish dishes served under the arches, just to the right of the gate into the medina.

RABAT

Capital only since 1913, Rabat has a long history. Behind its work-a-day façade, Morocco's second city and the country's political nerve centre bears traces of numerous civilizations. It had Roman beginnings, as Colonia Sala Junonia, a prosperous settlement. Sala gave way to Berber Chellah, and then came the Almohads, who made Rabat el Fath, the Fortress of Victory, an imperial capital. (The unfinished Tour Hassan minaret dates from this time.) In the 17th century, Rabat was rebuilt by Andalucían refugees, for a short and vivid period becoming capital of a pirate republic. Under the first Alaouite ruler, Moulay Rachid, Rabat returned to central authority. The city's Ville Nouvelle dates from the early 20th century, the land between the sultan's palace and the medina being developed as a pleasant plan of wide avenues and gardens.

→ ARRIVING IN RABAT

GETTING THERE
When coming into Rabat by bus, the principal bus terminal, for both CTM and other buses, is at Place Zerktouni, 3 km out from the centre. For the city centre, catch a No 30 bus to Avenue Hassan II, or take a petit taxi for about 20dh.

MOVING ON
From Rabat it's two hours by train to Meknès (see page 164).

GETTING AROUND
The main sites of Rabat are close enough to each other to visit on foot. In 2011, the city opened the handy Rabat–Salé tramway, with trams every four to eight minutes on two lines and 31 stops. If time is limited, you may want to get one of the blue petits taxis between monuments, say from Chellah to the Kasbah des Oudaïas; this should cost around 10dh.

TOURIST INFORMATION
National Tourist Office ① *corner of Av al Abtal and Rue Oued Fès, T0537-775171*. Office du Tourisme ① *22 Av d'Alger, T0537-730562*. Syndicat d'Initiative ① *Av Patrice Lumumba, T0537-723272*, not very useful.

→ BACKGROUND

EARLY ORIGINS
The first settlement of this area was probably outside the present city walls, on the site of the later Merinid mausoleum of Chellah. There may have been Phoenician and Carthaginian settlements, but it is with the Roman Sala Colonia that Rabat's proven urban history began. Awarded municipal privileges, Sala Colonia was the most southwesterly town of the Roman Empire for two centuries, a trading post on the Oued Bou Regreg (which has since changed course) and a defensive settlement close to the line of frontier outposts, which ran through the suburbs to the south of the present city.

Sala Colonia came under Amazigh rule from the eighth to the 10th century. However, the heretic Kharajite beliefs of the Imazighen represented a challenge to the orthodoxy of the inland Muslims. In the 10th century, the Zenata tribe built a fortified monastery, or *ribat*, on the site of the current Kasbah des Oudaïas. This functioned as a base from which to challenge the heretics on both sides of the river and their supporters, the powerful Berghouata tribe. Sala Colonia was thus eventually abandoned.

RABAT UNDER THE ALMOHADS

The *ribat* was used by the Almoravid Dynasty, but it was the Almohad Sultan Abd al Mumin who redeveloped the settlement in 1150, transforming it into a permanent fortress town, with palaces, the main mosque which still stands, reservoirs, and houses for followers, and using it as an assembly point for the large Almohad army. However, it was his grandson Yacoub al Mansour who dreamed of making Rabat one of the great imperial capitals and who, from 1184, carried out the most ambitious programme of development. He ordered an enormous city, surrounded by walls, to be built. These walls were probably completed by 1197 and ran along two sides of the city, broken by four gates, most notably the Bab er Rouah. A grid of streets, residential quarters, a covered market, public baths, hotels,

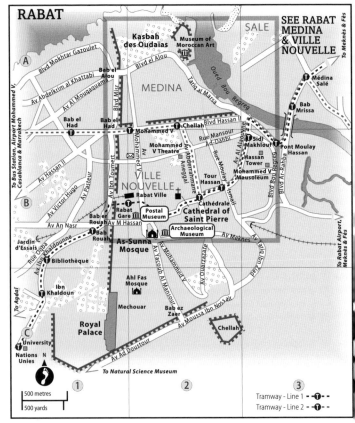

workshops and fountains were built, along with a new gateway to the medina. A bridge to Salé and its Grand Mosque, were also constructed. The most impressive monument from this period, the Hassan Mosque, was never completed, however. Projected as the largest mosque in western Islam, little more than pillars remain. The vast minaret never reached its full height and remains a stubby tower.

On Yacoub al Mansour's death in 1199 works were abandoned and Rabat then fell into decline. Parts of the city were destroyed in fighting between the Almohads and Merinids, to the point that Leo Africanus, visiting in 1500, found few inhabited neighbourhoods and very few shops. As Rabat declined under the Merinids, Salé prospered. The dynasty's most noteworthy contribution to Rabat was the funeral quarter on the Chellah site, with its impressive mausoleums, but even that eventually fell into neglect.

PIRACY AND ANDALUCIANS

Rabat's fortunes revived in the 17th century. As maritime technology advanced and the Atlantic Ocean became important to international trade, corsairing, or piracy, boomed. For a time, Rabat was the centre, with the notorious 'Sallee Rovers' more likely to have been based here than in present day Salé. (Robinson Crusoe was a fictional captive of 'a Turkish rover of Sallee'.)

Rabat also benefited from the flow of Muslims leaving Spain during the Inquisition. First rejected by Salé, the Hornacheros settled in the Rabat kasbah in 1609, and the other Andalucíans in the Rabat medina in 1610. The medina they settled in was considerably smaller than the city Yacoub al Mansour had envisaged, as indicated by the 17th-century rampart, which, when built, demarcated the extent of the settlement, and now runs between the medina and the Ville Nouvelle. The area beyond this rampart was used for farming, and most of it remained undeveloped until the French arrived. In the medina, the Andalucían influence is visible, notably in the street plan.

Fierce rivalry existed between the Hornachero and the Andalucían communities, both setting up autonomous city-states, and the period between 1610 and 1666 was marked by intermittent strife between the three towns of the Bou Regreg estuary (Rabat, Salé and the Kasbah des Oudaïas). In 1627 the three were united under the control of the Hornacheros as the Republic of the Bou Regreg, a control against which the Andalucíans frequently rebelled, most notably in 1636. The Republic lost its independence in 1638. In 1641 the three cities were again united and, in 1666 when Moulay Rachid captured the estuary, they came under the authority of the Alaouite Sultanate.

The principal background to these conflicts was the struggle for control over the profits from piracy. Rabat was especially popular with corsairs, many of whom had Mediterranean origins, because, unlike several other ports, it had not been occupied by Europeans.

ALAOUITE RABAT

Under the Alaouites, Rabat changed considerably. Trade and piracy were taken over as official functions, the profits going to the sultanate. The port declined, being replaced by Mogador (Essaouira) in the 18th century. Moulay Rachid took over the kasbah, expelling its residents, and built the Qishla fortification to overlook and control the medina. However, Sultan Moulay Ismaïl, most closely associated with Meknès, ignored Rabat, and broke the power of the corsairs.

In the late 1760s, Mohammed Ibn Abdallah had a palace built in Rabat and, since then the Alaouite sultans have maintained a palace there, making the city one of their capitals.

Increased trade with Europe in the 19th century temporarily revitalized Rabat's role as a port, but it was gradually supplanted, perhaps because of the shallow mouth of the Bou Regreg and the poor harbour facilities, but also because newer towns and cities, notably Casablanca, were more easily controlled by Europeans. In 1832 the rebellious Oudaïa tribe were settled in the abandoned kasbah, giving it its current name. The kasbah continued to be administered separately from the medina until the 20th century.

MODERN RABAT, EXPERIMENT IN URBAN PLANNING

In 1912, after complex diplomatic and military manoeuvrings, Morocco was split into two protectorates, with a large French central region and small Spanish zones in the north and the Sahara. Whereas the Moroccan sultanate had had no fixed capital, the power centre being where the sultan happened to be, the French decided that a capital was necessary for the new protectorate and Rabat was chosen in 1913. The first Resident-General, Hubert Lyautey, with his architect Henri Prost, planned and built the majority of the new capital, the Ville Nouvelle, both within and outside Yacoub al Mansour's walls, leaving the medina much as they found it, although the main thoroughfares were paved.

Efficiency and beauty were Lyautey's watchwords as he supervised the creation of the new Rabat. The European neighbourhoods were initally laid out in an area between the medina, to the northwest, and the *mechouar* or sultan's palace complex, to the southeast. A system of parks and gardens was created. The tree-lined street between the medina and the Ville Nouvelle, today's Boulevard Hassan II, a meeting place for Muslim and foreign communities, with municipal markets, bus and taxi stations and cafés.

The French planning of the new town reveals some interesting political undertones. It would have been possible, given the freedom that Lyautey had, to build the Residency General at a focal point on a new avenue, rather like Lutyens' House of the Viceroy in New Delhi. However, the new administrative buildings were built in a special area, close to the palace. With its luxuriant gardens, the Ministères neighbourhood recalls Anglo-American garden cities. The buildings, despite their importance to French rule, had simple whitewashed walls and green-tiled roofs and were linked by pergola walkways. They were kept unmonumental in scale (even the entrance to the Residency General had no obvious feature), hidden in vegetation. The French used such architectural devices to emphasize local culture, keeping the seats of power hidden in a mini garden suburb. More recent buildings, such as the new Ministry of Foreign Affairs, clash radically with this original principal. In short, in colonial Rabat, monumental buildings were only rarely used as a symbol of power. Today's Parliament Building, on the Avenue Mohammed V, is the exception, starting life as the Palais de Justice. Strongly symmetrical, with a massive colonnade, the building was probably designed to symbolize the equity and reason of French justice. Today, it is the centre of Moroccan political life.

After independence, Rabat continued to expand, its population swelled by the large number of civil servants required for the newly independent kingdom. Rabat's economy today is primarily based on its role as Morocco's administrative capital, with massive numbers of its inhabitants on the government payroll. The city has attracted large numbers of migrants from the countryside, and the formal housing market has been unable to keep up with the demand for accommodation, leading to the development of new self-built neighbourhoods like Douar Eddoum and Takaddoum. Rabat in many ways is a city of extremes, with streets of fine villas lying a stone's throw away from crowded slums (*bidonvilles*). South towards Casablanca, the new planned residential area of Hay Ryad is larger than the whole colonial city centre, while at Madinat el Irfane ('City of Knowledge'), Rabat has the country's largest concentration of faculties and university institutes. Neither Almohad sultans nor Lyautey could have imagined that a city could grow so fast in just a couple of decades.

To try to ensure the city keeps up with the pace of change, a massive infrastructure overhaul has been implemented, in an attempt to try and solve Rabat's woeful road congestion. Project Bouregreg includes the building of the Hassan II Bridge across the river and a new tram link between Rabat and Salé, both of which were opened in 2011. The project, though, isn't without controversy. Many residents' whose homes were destroyed to make way for the tramway have complained of receiving unfair compensation, while other locals point out that the high cost of tram tickets can be prohibitive. Whether Rabat's new infrastructure ends up a help or a hindrance remains to be seen.

→ PLACES IN RABAT

WALLS AND GATES

Rabat has three sets of walls: the **Almohad wall** around the kasbah, the 5 km of **Almoravid wall** around much of the city centre dating from the 12th century, and the wall now separating the medina and the Ville Nouvelle built by the Andalucíans in the early 17th century. The walls are mainly built of *pisé* or *pisé*-cement and, though considerably repaired, strengthened and adapted, they are much as they were originally. There are four gates still standing in the Almoravid wall: Bab el Alou, Bab el Had, Bab er Rouah and Bab ez Zaer. **Bab er Rouah**, south of the train station, is the most important and impressive of these. **Bab el Had**, at the intersection of Avenue Hassan II and Avenue Ibn Toumert is also worth seeing. The substantially remodelled gate has a blind arch and is flanked by two five-sided stone towers.

The scale and beauty of **Bab er Rouah**, also known as the 'Gate of the Winds', at Place An Nasr, is best seen from outside the walled city. The gate is now used as an art gallery, and is only open when exhibitions are being held. The arch of the gate is framed by a rectangular band of Kufic inscription. Between the arch and the frame there is a floral motif, with the scallop symbol on either side. The arch itself, with an entrance restored by the Alaouites with small stones, is made up of three different patterns of great simplicity, producing the overall effect of a sunburst confined within a rectangle. The entrance passage inside follows a complex double elbow. This, combined with the two flanking bastions outside, indicate that the gate was defensive as well as ceremonial.

KASBAH DES OUDAIAS

The Kasbah des Oudaïas, originally a fortified ribat, later settled by Andalucíans, is both beautiful and peaceful, and well worth a visit. It can be reached along Rue de Consuls through the medina, Boulevard el Alou along the western side of the medina, or by Tarik al Marsa, which runs along the Oued Bou Regreg. There are a number of entrances to the kasbah, but the best is via the imposing **Bab al Kasbah** gateway at the top of the hill. (There's no need to use one of the unofficial guides who may present their services; the kasbah is small and easily explored without assistance. To avoid guides altogether, you can get to the kasbah up the steps from the esplanade, which runs along the beach below the cemetery.)

ON THE ROAD

City tour

The following route takes in most of the main sites. Take a petit taxi for one of the longer hops, either from the kasbah to the Hassan Tower, or from the Chellah down to the far side of the medina. The three main sights in Rabat, namely the Kasbah des Oudaïas, the medina and the Chellah, have to be explored on foot.

Start at the kasbah then head for the Hassan Tower and the Mohammed V Mausoleum along Tarik al Marsa road, with its thundering lorries and buses. From the Tour Hassan, continue to skirt the city along Boulevard Bou Regreg, Avenue Tariq Ibn Ziad and Avenue Moussa Ibn Nossair to the fortified Chellah, clearly visible down on your left from the road. After the Chellah, head into the Ville Nouvelle by Bab ez Zaer to the As Sunna Mosque. Turn along Avenue Moulay Hassan and through Bab er Rouah to view it from the outside. Pass down Avenue Ibn Toumert, past Bab el Had to Bab el Alou, and right into the medina. Turn right down Boulevard Mohammed V and carry on through the medina to Boulevard Hassan II.

Bab al Kasbah was close to the Souk el Ghezel, the main medieval market, while the original palace was just inside. The gateway was built by Yacoub al Mansour in about 1195, inserting it into the earlier kasbah wall built by Abd al Mumin, and it did not have the same defensive role as the Bab er Rouah. The gate has a pointed horseshoe arch surrounded by a cusped, blind arch. Around this there is a wide band of geometric carving, the common *darj w ktaf*. The two corner areas between this band and the rectangular frame are composed of floral decoration, with, as in the Bab er Rouah, a scallop or palmette in each. Above this are more palmettes, a band of Koranic lettering and, on top, a wide band of geometric motifs. The entrance to the kasbah is via stairs and through two rooms, a third room being closed to the public. The inside of the gate is also decorated, though more simply.

Inside the gate, the main street, Rue al Jamaâ, runs past the **Kasbah Mosque**, the oldest in Rabat, dating from 1150, the time of Abd al Mumin. As is the case with most city mosques in Morocco, it is hard to get any real idea of the size of this building, as homes are built all around it. The minaret, complete with elaborately decorative arches, was substantially rebuilt in the 18th century. Continue along Rue al Jamaâ and you come to the **semaphore platform**, where there is a carpet factory. This gives an excellent view over surfers in the sea below, the Oued Bou Regreg, with its natural sand-bar defence, and Salé. Steps down from the platform lead to a small fort built by an English renegade, known as Ahmed el Ingliz, and the popular Kasbah beach.

Coming back from the platform take Rue Bazo, the fourth street on the left. This narrow and cobbled street winds down through the whitewashed Andalucían-style houses to the bottom of the kasbah, directly into the **Café Maure** (see page 244), alongside which is a small but beautiful garden.

The **Andalucían Garden** is supposedly formal, but it is actually the semi-abandonment and the lack of formality that make it such a dreamy, engaging place – as long as you avoid occasional tour parties. The garden was built in the early 20th century by Prosper Ricard and the Traditional Arts Department. Nettles and wild poppies spill out of flowerbeds, and cats lounge among fallen leaves and oranges, accompanied by birdsong and the tinkling of fountains.

On the other side of the garden is the **Museum of Moroccan Art** ① *0900-1600, closed Tue, 10dh, T0537-731512*, exhibiting traditional dress and jewellery from many regions of Morocco. The opulent buildings are part of the 17th-century palace that Moulay Ismaïl once used as his Rabat residence. The central building now houses the main museum collection, with arms, instruments, jewellery, pottery, musical instruments and carpets. Unfortunately, labelling in a suitable array of languages is a bit lacking in the museum. If better managed, it could provide a fine introduction to Moroccan crafts and to life in an upper-class traditional home.

MEDINA

Most of the buildings in the medina date from the arrival of the Andalucían Muslims in the 17th century, and this Andalucían character sets Rabat's medina apart from others, such as Marrakech. While the medina here is smaller and more limited in its range of markets, shops and buildings than Fès, Marrakech and Meknès, and less distinct in its way of life, its accessibility, size and the simplicity of its grid-like street pattern make it a good place to experience a Moroccan medina without getting lost. Physically close to the Ville Nouvelle, the medina is nevertheless very different in the design of its buildings and open space, and in the nature of its commerce and socialization. It is an interesting and safe place to wander, with little risk of getting lost or hassled. **Boulevard Mohammed V** is one of the major arteries.

As you enter from the Ville Nouvelle, the second right, Rue Souika, and its continuation Souk es Sebbat, are the main shopping streets, with an unusually wide range of shops and a number of traditional cafés for such a small area. **Souk es Sebbat**, originally where shoes were made, is easily recognized by its roof of woven straw and reeds. A great deal of leather work is on sale here, in particular worked leather for bags and the soft leather *babouches*. The mosque of **Moulay Slimane** at the junction of Rue Souika and Rue Sidi Fatah was constructed in 1812. The **Grand Mosque**, on Rue Souika, is a much restored Merinid building, the minaret of which is decorated with polychrome glazed earthenware tiles. Just opposite the Grand Mosque, on a side turning, is the interesting stone façade of a **fountain**, now a bookshop, but dating from the reign of the 14th-century Merinid Sultan Abu Faris Abd al Aziz.

Souk es Sebbat leads down to the river, past the mellah on the right. The **mellah** is the former Jewish area and still the poorest area of the medina, with its small, cramped houses and shops, and narrow streets. It was built in 1808 by Moulay Slimane. Originally there were 17 synagogues; those which remain today have become dwellings or storehouses. As in many Islamic cities, Jews were kept in one area, for both protection and control, and so that they would be easily accessible to the authorities when needed to carry out tasks that Muslims could not perform. There are few Jews left in the mellah, most having emigrated to Israel. There is, however, a moderately interesting *joutia*, or flea market – and some very striking poverty.

Turning left off Souk es Sebbat you can follow the **Rue des Consuls** to the kasbah. This road was where many European consuls and important merchants lived until 1912. Rue des Consuls is now lined with expensive shops selling silk embroidery, souvenirs, traditional Moroccan items in copper and leather, and carpets. The street has been enhanced by a range of roof features, including iron pillars and plexiglass vaults. There is a carpet market on the street on Tuesday and Thursday mornings. Turn right at the end

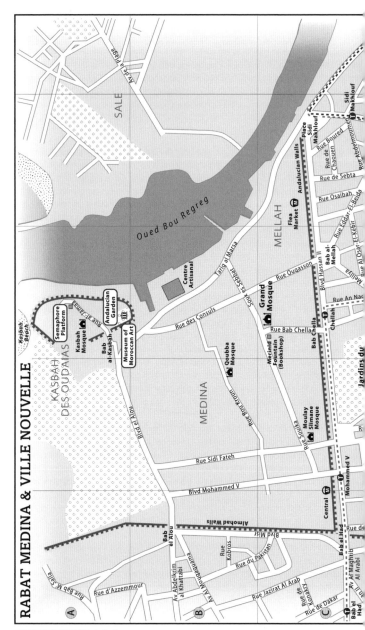

RABAT MEDINA & VILLE NOUVELLE

SALE

Ay. de la Plage

KASBAH DES OUDAIAS

Kasbah Beach

Semaphore Platform

Kasbah Mosque

Bab al-Kasbah

Museum of Moroccan Art

Andalucian Garden

Rue al-Jamaa

Centre Artisanal

Oued Bou Regreg

Tariq al Marsa

Rue des Consuls

Blvd el Alou

MEDINA

Rue Bou Krou

Rue Souika

Qoubba Mosque

Merinid Fountain (Bookshop)

Souk es-Sebat

Rue Ougasson

Grand Mosque

Moulay Slimane Mosque

Rue Bab Chella

Bab Chella

Rue Sidi Fateh

Blvd Mohammed V

Central

Almohad Walls

Bab el Alou

Blvd Misr

Rue Kobbas

Rue du Parisien

Rue d'Azzemmour

Rue Bab M.-Sella

Av Abdelkrim al Khattabi

Av A. Mouaqaouama

Rue Jazirat Al Arab

Rue de Konakry

Rue de Dakar

MELLAH

Flea Market

Andalucian Walls

Place Sidi Makhlouf

Rue de Sebta

Rue Boured

Rue de Chaouen

Sidi Makhlouf

Rue Abdelmoumen

Sidi Makhlouf

Rue Osaibah

Rue Edan-El-Beida

Rue Al Qsar-El-Kébir

Bab al-Mellah

Blvd Hassan II

Rue Mellaha

Rue An Nac

Chellah

Mohammed V

Bab el Had

Jardins du

Jardins du

R

Bab el Had

Av Maghrib Al Arabi

Bab el Had

Rue de

Tramway - Line 1 • • •
Tramway - Line 2 • • •

200 metres
200 yards

N

of Rue des Consuls and you are in Tarik al Marsa (literally, Avenue of the Port). Here you may make a death-defying dash across the street to visit the kasbah and its traditional arts museum (see above). Also on the kasbah side of the street, to your right as you look at the kasbah, is the **Centre Artisanal**. All craft products sold here have fixed prices.

HASSAN TOWER AND MOHAMMED V MAUSOLEUM
ⓘ *Daily 0830-1830, free.*

The Almohad Hassan Tower dominates the skyline of Rabat, and, even unfinished, it is an impressive building, testimony to Yacoub al Mansour's unfulfilled vision of his imperial capital. It overlooks the Oued Bou Regreg and Salé, and can be reached most easily by Boulevard Bou Regreg, or by turning right at the end of Avenue Hassan II.

The building of the mosque was abandoned on Yacoub al Mansour's death in 1199, leaving most of the minaret, but just part of the columns and walls. All the portable parts – tiles, bricks and the roofing material – have been taken for use in other buildings. The remains of the mosque were excavated and reconstructed by the French and Moroccans. The mosque would have followed a T-shape, with the main green-tiled roof section between the minaret and the modern mausoleum. The mihrab (prayer niche) would have been in the south *qibla* wall, where the mausoleum is, and therefore was not properly orientated towards Mecca. It is also unusual to find the minaret opposite the *qibla* wall.

The incomplete minaret of the Hassan Mosque stands at 45 m. When completed, it would have been 80 m, five times as high as it is wide, in keeping with the classic North African minaret style. It is decorated with geometric designs, the scale and clarity of which makes them clearly discernible from a distance. Each of the faces has a different composition, interweaving designs, arches and windows. The common Moroccan motif of *darj w ktaf*, resembling a tulip or a truncated fleur de lys, and formed by intersecting arcs with superimposed rectangles, is notable high on the north and south faces.

Adjacent to the Hassan Tower is the **Mohammed V Mausoleum**, dedicated to the first king of independent Morocco and grandfather of the current king. The building dates from 1971. The mausoleum is constructed on the site where Mohammed V, returning from his exile in 1955, gathered thousands of his people to thank God for giving independence to Morocco. The tomb chamber, but not the mausoleum's mosque, is open to non-Muslims, and features traditional Moroccan decorative motifs and techniques common in religious architecture, including a painted ceiling, the carved marble tomb, and the *zellige* (mosaic) tiles on the walls. Note the guards in their splendid uniforms.

CHELLAH
ⓘ *0830-1730, 10dh, open to non-Muslims.*

The walled ruins of Chellah, a 14th-century Merinid citadel, are reached by going past the main As Sunna Mosque in the Ville Nouvelle, and on south down Avenue Yacoub al Mansour and through the **Bab ez Zaer**. It's an impressive place: granite fragments encrusted in orange lichen, the click-clacking of large numbers of nesting storks and thick beds of clover and brambles enveloping crumbling fragments of tiles and walls. Paved paths lead between trees down to the most intact ruins, in the far corner of the site.

There are five sides to the Chellah, all different lengths, and 20 towers. Chellah was built between 1310 and 1334, approximately on the site of the Roman town of Sala Colonia. The second Merinid Sultan, Abu Yusuf Yacoub, built a mosque, and Abul Hassan, the Black

ON THE ROAD
At the top

In public buildings, offices and shops all over Morocco you will see portraits of the country's Royals, members of the ruling Alaouite dynasty which has been on the throne since the mid-17th century. Sometimes there is a triptych: a photograph of the late King Hassan II (ruled 1961-1999), flanked by the two princes, the then crown prince Sidi Mohammed and his younger brother, Moulay Rachid. On the death of Hassan II in July 1999, the crown prince came to the throne as Mohammed VI. Increasingly, his portrait as a sober-suited young technocrat is replacing that of the late king on public display. (Trendy clothes shops may have the king in ski-gear complete with woolly *gnaoua* cap.) In Hassan II's reign, shop-owners picked portraits appropriate to place: in a sports shop, there would be a picture of the king playing golf or in hunting gear, while a *crémerie* would have a picture of the king alongside a Berber milkmaid; beauty salons favoured a picture of the king and one of his daughters fully made-up for her wedding day.

Hassan II had five children. Elegant Lalla Myriem, the eldest daughter, now in her forties, was married to the son of former prime minister Abdellatif Filali. She won much admiration for her courage in getting a divorce, apparently against her father's will. She is much involved in charity work, as are the younger sisters, Lalla Esma and Lalla Hasna.

Despite the ripples from the Arab Spring reaching Morocco, with protests throughout the country calling for political reform, for the moment, Morocco's royal family remain a popular lot. The July 2011 referendum on reforming the constitution saw Mohammed VI receive a landslide victory at the polls, further demonstrating the king's popular appeal. The king is seen by many as a modernizer – an adept jet-skier with a more Euro-centric outlook than his father. Mohammed VI's public image was enhanced by his marriage to a university-educated woman of a Fassi family, now Princess Salma. The couple's first child, Prince Hassan, was born in 2003; their second, Princess Lalla Khadija, in 2007. Although Mohammed VI has attracted growing criticism in recent years for Morocco's record on human rights and freedom of speech, his popularity has managed to endure, with the majority of Moroccans willing to put their trust in the king to introduce the much-needed reforms.

Sultan, then built the enclosure wall and the gate. The Roman ruins at the lower level of the Chellah enclosure have been excavated and include a forum, baths, shops and a temple. These are not open to the public.

Bab ez Zaer is smaller and less impressive than the Almohad Bab er Rouah. It is decorated with carving, and coloured marble and tiles, with an octagonal tower on either side above which is a square platform. The entrance is on the elbow pattern; you turn right through three chambers, before walking out into a wild and lush garden. To get to the mausoleum, take the wide path to the bottom, where it stands on the right, with the Roman ruins on the left. On the far right are the tombs of local saints, surrounding a pool.

The door into the Merinid **mausoleum** (look for the date carved above the doorway), facing the Roman ruins, opens into the **mosque** of Abu Yusuf Yacoub, which consists of a small courtyard, followed by a three-aisled sanctuary. The arched doorway on the left has the remains of floral and geometric *zellige* in five colours. Entering the sanctuary, the **mihrab** is straight ahead. A door to the right leads to an area including the remains of the mosque's minaret, and a pool. From this, one enters the area of tombs, including those of

Abul Hassan and his wife Shams al Dawha. The remaining area of the mausoleum is taken up with the *zaouïa*, or mosque-monastery, of Abul Hassan. This includes a minaret, and a ruined funerary chapel, with very intricate carving, notably on the exterior of the south wall. The main part of the *zaouïa* is a rectangular courtyard with a small mosque at one end, surrounded by small cells. It had a pool surrounded by a columned arcade, the bases of the columns still discernible. The mihrab has some intricate stucco carving. The tiles on the upper portion of the minaret are perhaps recent, but the effect would have been a bright tiled structure.

VILLE NOUVELLE
The Ville Nouvelle contains some fine examples of French colonial architecture, which incorporate an element of local design tradition, particularly the main post office (PTT Centrale) and the **Bank al Maghrib**, both on **Avenue Mohammed V**. This main boulevard is wide and particularly impressive in the evening, when it is crowded with people out for a stroll. Off to the left, down a street opposite the railway station, is the Catholic **Cathedral of Saint Pierre**. Below the station is the Parliament building or **Majlis an Nuwwab**. Just past the **Hotel Terminus** is a small **postal museum** exhibiting stamps. The 18th-century (but much-restored) **As Sunna Mosque** dominates the view up Avenue Mohammed V.

The **Archaeological Museum** ① *23 Rue el Brihi, T0537-722231, Wed-Mon 0845-1630, 10dh, residents 5dh. Take the Rue Moulay Abdelaziz, opposite the As Sunna Mosque, and turn right on the Rue Brihi.* The museum houses the best archaeological collection in the country, and is worth an hour's visit. The section covering pre-history has human remains from 4000 BC. There are pieces of pottery, jewellery and metalwork from Mauritanian for bears, as well as some carved stones. Particularly fine is the Bronze Age Nkhila stela, with its concentric curves and humanoid figure.

The museum is best known, however, for its Roman pieces, displayed in the **Salle des Bronzes**, which may be closed, but should be opened on request. The Hellenistic bronzes, restored a few years ago with UNESCO assistance, are superb and include an exquisite head of Juba II (ruled 25 BC to AD 23) and a most realistic dog from Volubilis, Morocco's most spectacular Roman site (see page 173). Also from Volubilis is a portrait of Roman politician Cato the Younger (who was defeated by Julius Caesar in 46 BC at Utica, and who committed suicide by falling on his sword) and an *ephèbe* – a naked Graecian youth with ivy crown. The position of the left hand suggests that he is a doryphorous, a spear carrier. There is a fine athletic horserider, probably based on a Greek original by Polyclitus.

All around the Salle des Bronzes are a series of vitrines packed with archaeological finds. Most explanations are in French only, but you will be able to pick out candelabra, metal fittings from harnesses and furniture, a damascened trophy and a cuirass with lion and elephant heads. There are some small pieces of marble statuary, including some heads and a snoozing – or hungover – Silenus, with a jug from which water, or maybe wine, would have trickled. And there is some jewellery, brooches, odd bronze feet, minute acrobats, a gold feather and a tiny bracelet with crescent moon.

Among the most interesting pieces are those that tell something of life in the Roman garrison towns of Mauritania Tingitana. There is a display of builders' tools, including plumblines, compass and triangle from Banasa, and there is a bronze military diploma from Ceuta (Roman Ad Septem), conferring citizenship on a soldier who had completed his service in the legion.

The **Postal Museum** was opened in 1970. It belongs to the PTT, which has brought together this small and interesting collection of instruments once used by their service. The items range from a post van to an envelope and between are telegraph machines, belinographs, which reproduced photographs over long distances, and the Baudot telegraph with printer. Among the postage stamps is Morocco's first official stamp from May 1912 but the collections of more recent stamps will catch the eye. Philately is a good export earner.

To the south of the As Sunna Mosque is the **palace complex** ① *not open to the public*, where the sovereign spends part of the year. It is not possible to go beyond this point up the central avenue of the complex. Construction of the Royal Palace began in 1864. It is surrounded by a wall cut by three gates. Inside the complex is an open space known as the *mechouar*. Here stands the **Ahl Fas Mosque** where the King leads prayers each Friday when he is in the capital.

Southwest of the Ville Nouvelle is the **Natural Science Museum** ① *Ministry of Energy and Mining, Quartier administratif, Agdal, T0537-688400, Mon-Fri 0800-1200 and 1430-1830, free,* is part of the Ministry of Energy and Mining. Here there is a reconstruction of a sauropod dinosaur. The skeleton of this creature, which is almost 15 m in length, was discovered in 1979 in the Azilal region of the High Atlas.

→SALE

Historic Salé, on the north bank of the Bou Regreg estuary, was once a rival to Rabat in the days of piracy and Andalucían Muslims fleeing the expanding power of Catholic Spain. The medina of Salé has a fine medersa and a striking early Merinid gate, the Bab Mrisa. For those with enough time, Salé is worth a visit.

ARRIVING IN SALE
Getting there Salé is most easily reached from Rabat by using the tram link. If you get off at Gare Salé tram station (beside the railway station) the city centre sights are within easy walking distance. You can also come by grand taxi (from the grand taxi rank just past the Parc du Triangle de Vue, on Avenue Hassan II) or by taking bus No 6 or 12 from Avenue Hassan II. Travellers coming in from the north can get off at Salé railway station.

Once in Salé it is possible to explore most of the centre on foot, though the tramline is also useful if you don't feel like walking and the city also has its own petits taxis. If you have your own transport, go along Tarik al Marsa, Avenue Hassan II or Boulevard du Bou Regreg and cross the bridge below the Hassan Tower. It is possible to walk this route in 30 minutes.

Getting around Salé medina is small and easy to explore. Walking in any direction you are likely to arrive at the souks, the Grand Mosque and Abul Hassan Medersa, or the city walls. As elsewhere, early 20th-century French planners at Salé preserved the historic city walls and left a wide space between the medina and land for new building. If you arrive by grand taxi, you will be dropped by the gardens adjacent to the Bab Mrisa gate, one of the most unusual city gates in Morocco.

BACKGROUND
Salé, Sala or Sla in Arabic, derives from the Roman Sala Colonia. Salé was founded in the 11th century, and its Great Mosque dates from 1163-1184. The town was embellished

and fortified by the Merinids in the 13th century, becoming an important commercial centre. Great rivalry, even armed conflict, has existed between Rabat and Salé, although they were united in the Republic of the Bou Regreg. Up until the 17th century Salé enjoyed long periods as the more important of the two cities, being known for religious learning and piety. With the coming of Rabat's capital status, Salé gradually turned into a dormitory settlement for the city. New businesses and light industries, however, are gradually springing up on the road north out of Salé. While Rabat is known as the city of gardens, Salé is perhaps the city of sanctuaries. The 14th-century Medersa Abul el Hassan is well worth visiting.

BAB MRISA

Bab Mrisa, or 'Gate of the Little Harbour', was originally the sea gate of the medina, as there was once a channel running to it from the River Bou Regreg. The gate is wide, and its 11-m high horseshoe arch would have allowed the sailing boats of the day to pass within the walls for repairs. (Since medieval times, the access canal has silted up.) Although Bab Mrisa was built by the Merinid Sultan Abu Yusuf in the 1260s, in style it is closer to the

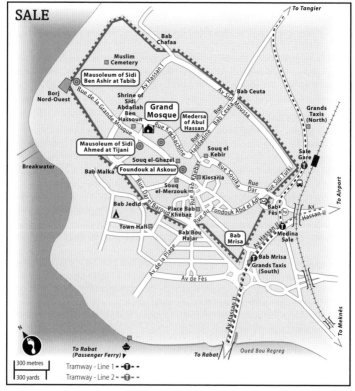

Almohad gates – the triangular space between the arch and the frame is covered with floral decoration centred on the palmette, with the use of the *darj w ktaf* motif down the sides. Originally it had a porch. Alongside the gate there are two tall defensive towers. It may be possible to get access to the top of the gate. You may be able to find a caretaker by a small door on the left, inside the gate, which gives access to a small garden leading to a round tower. From this tower walk back along the top of the rampart to the gate. There is another similar sea gate, the next gate around the wall to the left.

ABUL HASSAN MEDERSA

① 0800-1200, 1430-1800. Open to non-Muslims.

This *medersa* (religious school) is the most important building in Salé and the only *medersa* in the region. It was built by the Merinid Sultan Abul Hassan, the Black Sultan, and was completed in 1342. To reach it follow the city walls around to the left from Bab Mrisa to a small square at Bab Bou Hajar, alongside a park. Just beyond this is an area where cars should be parked. Take the small lane off to the far right at the end of this area. Take the first left, then the first right. Some 200 m later, just after the lane passes under a house, turn left.

The particularly large **Grand Mosque** in front was built by the Almohad Sultan Abu Yusuf Yacoub in the late 12th century, although the minaret and door are both modern. Just beyond the mosque is the tomb of Salé's patron saint, **Sidi Abdallah Ben Hassoun**. The *medersa* is to the left of the mosque.

Before you pass through the beautiful Merinid doorway, note the intricate decorations below a green-tiled roof resting on cedar lintels. The *medersa* is quite small, with a courtyard surrounded by a gallery, its columns decorated with *zellige* mosaic tiling. The walls above the columns are decorated with geometric and floral motifs, while the ceilings of the ground floor have panelled wood in geometric patterns. Both the wood carving of the prayer hall ceiling and the stucco have been restored, but much of the decoration is original and in good condition. To reach the upper floors, return to the entrance and climb the stairs. These are the students' cells, which seem tiny and ill-lit, but give an insight into the nature of *medersa* life. From the roof is a view of Salé and, beyond it, Rabat.

MAUSOLEUM OF SIDI BEN ASHIR AT TABIB

The Mausoleum of Sidi Ben Ashir at Tabib is located close to the western wall of the cemetery that lies between the medina and the sea. This 14th-century Muslim saint was famous for curing people, and the sick still visit his tomb for its curative powers. This is a very striking building, quite tall, brilliant white in contrast to the blue sky and the background of ochre of the city walls. Adjacent, in the walls, cannon still point defensively out to sea.

FOUNDOUK AL ASKOUR

The Foundouk al Askour is worth seeing for its portal. From Bab Bou Hajar follow Rue Bab al Khabbaz, and take the fourth lane on the left past the park, which is obstructed by three concrete posts. This leads to a textile souk. After 120 m the souk passes under an arch. On the right is the *foundouk* (merchants' hostel). It was originally built in about 1350 as a *medersa* by Abu Inan, son of Abul Hassan, and was later converted. The door is surrounded by a partially restored *zellige* mosaic of the *darj w ktaf* pattern. Above this

ON THE ROAD
Medersa – place of education for Islam

"Learning is a city, one of whose gates is memory, the other is comprehension."
(An Arab saying).

The *medersa* in North Africa is a college of higher education in which Islamic teachings lead the syllabus. The institution originated in Persia and developed in the Islamic West in the 13th century. The construction of places of advanced learning was a response by orthodox Sunni Islam to the growth of Shi'ite colleges, but they soon became important centres in their own right as bastions of orthodox Islamic beliefs. Subjects other than theology were taught at the *medersa*, but only in a limited form and in ways that made them adjuncts to Sunni teachings and acceptable to a very conservative religious hierarchy. Unfortunately, therefore, the *medersa* became associated with a rather uninspired and traditional academic routine in which enquiry and new concepts were often excluded. Knowledge and its transmission sadly fell into the hands of the least academic members of the theological establishment and the poor standards of science, politics, arts and ethics associated with the Arab world in the period since the 13th century has been put down to the lack of innovation and experiment in the *medersa* – a situation which has only very recently begun to break down in Sunni Islam.

The shortcomings of the *medersa* in creative teaching terms was in part compensated for by the development of the buildings themselves, however. They were mainly modelled on the Medersa Bou Inania at Fès (page 169), founded under Sultan Abu Inan (1348-1358), itself based on designs from Syria. The main courtyard *sahn* is surrounded by cloisters/galleries, separated from the *sahn* by ornate screens of wood. The mosque is to the east and the long *qibla* wall has a deeply set mihrab. The Merinids founded seven *medersa* in Fès during the 14th century.

"Let your eyelids enjoy my splendid beauty – you will find a marvellous virtue to chase away cares and sadness," reads one of the many carved inscriptions in the 16th-century Medersa Ben Youssef in Marrakech (see page 49), which is the largest *medersa* in North Africa and considered one of the finest. Originally a Merinid foundation but remodelled in the 16th century, it has an arcaded courtyard with intricate mosaic work, lace-like carved stucco, weathered to a faint rose-coloured patina, and finely worked cedar beams.

Moroccan *medersa* were, until quite recently, used for student accommodation and even for teaching, but the traditional life has now disappeared and the *medersa*, remain as intriguing monuments to an educational past where religious belief and education were tightly linked.

is a panel of *zellige* with the traditional eight-pointed star motif and, above that, a row of nine niches carved into a plaster panel. Inside there is a courtyard with two storeys of arcades.

SOUKS

In this area there are some interesting souks, which are perhaps more traditional than those of Rabat, and worth exploring. The textile market is Souk el Merzouk, while Souk el Ghezel is the wool market. There are stonemasons and carpenters in Rue Kechachine, and blacksmiths and brassworkers in Rue Haddadine. The Souk el Merzouk is noted for its jewellery and embroidery. The medina of Salé is also noted for a procession of multicoloured candles, or thick poles bearing various representations, which occurs every year on the afternoon before the Prophet's birthday, Mouloud an Nabi. This proceeds through the town, culminating at the **Tomb of Sidi Abdallah Ben Hassoun**. He is the patron saint of Salé and this is the most venerable of the sanctuaries in the city. It is also the most picturesque, with a most curious dome and an exterior gallery decorated with polychrome tiles. The seafaring past of the city is particularly visible in this event, with the men in pirate costumes.

MOVING ON

To Meknès

From Rabat it's 150 km to Meknès. See Dream Trip 3, page 164.

To Fès

From Meknès it's 70 km to Fès. See Dream Trip 3, page 139.

To Taza

A possible extension to this route could take you to Taza (see page 158), a two-hour train journey from Fès. An alternative or additional extension would be to spend a couple of days on the Mediterranean beaches around Al Hoceïma, page 250 (also reached from Chefchaouen, see page 246).

RABAT LISTINGS

WHERE TO STAY

There are plenty of reasonably priced hotels in Rabat, although in summer hotels can fill up quickly, especially in the mid-price range. The cheapest hotels in the medina, for which prices can be very flexible, are best avoided (with a few exceptions). The centre of the Ville Nouvelle provides a wide range of good hotels. If not exactly catching up with Marrakech and Fès, Rabat now has a few pleasant guesthouses in the upper price bracket.

€€€€ **Villa Mandarine**, 19 Rue Oulad Bousaa, Souissi, T0537-752077, www.villa mandarine.com. In the upmarket Souissi neighbourhood, close to the **Royal Golf Dar Es Salam**, this wonderfully peaceful small hotel is set among gardens and orange orchards. Antiques and local art abound throughout the communal areas, and the comfortable rooms all come with shady private terrace. Pool, bar, restaurant and spa.

€€€ **Hotel Asiah**, Pl Sidi Makhlouf, T0537-731091. Conveniently located at the end of Av Hassan II, overlooking the river and Salé, the **Asiah** is built around a courtyard in an approximation of a Moroccan palace. There's a pool and good facilities and services.

€€€ **Dar Al Batoul**, 7 Derb Jirari, T0537-727250, www.riadbatoul.com. This atmospheric riad has bags of artistic style. Each of the 8 rooms is individually decorated with gorgeous tiling, traditional textiles, stained glass and quirky use of colour, and they open on to a peaceful interior patio. Evening meals available.

€€€ **Riad Kasbah**, 39 Rue Zirara, T0537-702392, www.riadrabat.com. Run by the same people as the **Riad Oudaya**, this is a less pricey option, with brick floors, colourful bathrooms and cosy, if narrow, rooms. It's a peaceful spot, with palms in the courtyard. Simple rather than overly chic but very well placed in the heart of the kasbah.

€€€ **Riad Oudaya**, 46 Rue Sidi Fateh, T0537-702392, www.riadoudaya.com. With just 4 rooms, this French-run riad is an intimate and thoroughly relaxing place. The quiet courtyard is filled with plants and birdsong, and the rooms are elegantly furnished with bright textiles and antiques. Evening meals are available.

€€ **Hotel Belere Rabat**, 33 Av Moulay Youssef Rabat Maroc T0537-703897, www.belerehotels.com. Despite the grim concrete exterior, the **Belere** is a business-orientated 3-star hotel with all the trimmings: beige and burgundy interior, marble tiles, a piano bar and rooms with free minibars, satellite TV and Wi-Fi. Rooms facing the street can be noisy.

€€ **Hotel Royal**, 1 Rue Amman, T0537-721171, www.mtds.com/royalhotel. This central, rather old-fashioned hotel has large, good-value rooms. If you don't fancy an early morning wake-up with the call to prayer, it's best to steer clear of the rooms facing the park. The café opposite the hotel is nice for breakfast.

€ **Hotel des Oudaïas**,132 Blvd el Alou, near the kasbah, T0537-732371. On the far northern edge of the medina, the **Oudaïas** is convenient for sightseeing, though the rather tatty and none-too-quiet rooms don't match the promise of the palm and dark wood-filled reception. Nevertheless, it offers some of the best value in town.

€ **Hotel Dorhmi**, 313 Av Mohammed V, handily located just inside the medina on your right, T0537-723898. This is the best of the medina budget hotels, with rooms and reception all on the 1st floor up a flight of stairs. Spick-and-span rooms all face onto a central gallery, with white walls and pot plants. A great pick for the budget-conscious, though those who struggle with noise are best to look outside the medina.

€ Hotel Majestic, 121 Av Hassan II, T0537-722997, www.hotelmajestic.ma. A good-value choice at the upper-end of the budget price bracket. The **Majestic** has clean, pastel-toned rooms, boasting comfortable beds, balconies overlooking the medina and TV (no a/c). Double glazing keeps the noise levels down.

€ Hotel Splendid, 24 Rue Ghazza, T0537-7232 83. Beds are hard and pillows lumpy but the **Splendid** has a certain old-fashioned style: there are dial phones and ageing furniture in rooms and there's an ancient spiral staircase. Small balconies and a peaceful courtyard, with tiles, trees and metal animals, add to the good value, though the coffee is best avoided. Also good for solo travellers on a budget, with cheap single rooms.

RESTAURANTS

Most higher-quality restaurants are within the Ville Nouvelle. 2 areas have a good selection of mid-range restaurants: immediately behind the **Hotel Balima** and in the neighbourhood behind the train station. A range of fairly cheap restaurants is to be found throughout the city, but the budget options – small Moroccan canteens and café-restaurants doing set lunches, *harira* and brochettes – are in the medina, along Blvd Mohammed V, Rue Souika, Rue Sidi Fatah and adjacent streets. There are also plenty of crémeries doing juices, pâtisseries, snacks and sandwiches.

€€€ Dinarjat, 6 Rue Belgnaoui, close to the Kasbah des Oudaïas, T0537-704239, www.dinarjat.com. This upscale Moroccan restaurant is a dining experience of traditional costumed waiters, live Andalucían music and sumptuously restored architecture. After the specialities, such as lamb and prune tagine or almond chicken, recline on your couch amid the tiling and carved arches.

€€€ Le Ziryab, 10 Impasse Ennajar, T0537-733636, www.restaurantleziryab.com. Up a winding street in the medina, **Le Ziryab** hides a quality traditional Moroccan restaurant behind a heavy wooden door. More a gastronomic experience than just a meal, it only does a 5-course set menu which showcases Morocco's cuisine.

€€€ Le Grand Comptoir, 279 Av Mohammed V, T0537-201514, www.legrandcomptoir.ma. This Parisian-style brasserie is the dining choice for Rabat's see-and-be-seen crowd. An immaculately restored 1930s interior and live jazz add to the stylish ambience. The food is reliably excellent, with menu highlights including locally caught crayfish. Reservations recommended.

€€ La Mamma, 6 Rue Zankat Tanta (ex-Paul Tirard), T0537-707329, behind **Hotel Balima**. This old stalwart of the Rabat eating scene has an eclectic interior of candles, dark wood beams, hanging plastic vegetables and illuminated photos. The atmosphere buzzes with everyone from politicians to policemen most nights. Unfortunately the food (Italian cuisine with a large pizza menu) can be hit and miss.

€€ La Weimar, Goethe Institut, 7 Rue Sanaâ, T0537-732650. Once you've got through the metal detector at the entrance, this is a great little place for pizzas, an unusually wide selection of salads and chocolate cake, handily located in the neighbourhood behind the train station. It's international rather than particularly German, and there's a young vibe; the clientele is a mix of students and be-suited diplomats.

€€ Le Petit Beur (Dar Tajine), 8 Rue Damas, T0537-731322. One of the top places to sample the best of Moroccan cooking, **Le Petit Beur** is deservedly popular for its tasty tagines. It's a traditional restaurant, with tiles, low lighting and a rather formal ambience, so it's better for dinner rather than lunch.

€€ Tajine Wa Tanjia, 9 Rue Baghdad, T0537-729797. Closed Sun. A mix of traditional and contemporary, **Tajine Wa Tanjia**'s popularity stems from its offering great service, plus excellent tagines at good-value prices (68-86dh). This is the place to come and feast on a sumptuous banquet of Moroccan cuisine. A large mural fills one wall, and there's free Wi-Fi and live oud playing in the evenings. Licensed.

€ La Maison des Grillades, just inside the walls of the medina to the west of Av Mohammed V. One of several cheap eateries on the edge of the medina, the popular **La Maison** offers tagine or chicken with chips and salad for 20dh. Seating indoors or out.

Cafés, pâtisseries and cafés-glaciers
Au Délice–Pâtisserie Suisse, 285 Av Mohammed V, up from the Balima, opposite the Parliament. There are many good cafés, pâtisseries and *glaceries* on or near Av Mohammed V, including this one, which looks as though it hasn't changed since the late 1950s. Good cake and croissants.

Café Maure, at the bottom of Rue Bazo in the Kasbah des Oudaïas. Has a terrace overlooking the estuary. It's a standard stop on most tourist routes through the city but, if you can avoid the hordes, it's a good place to stop for a rest. It has good mint tea and specializes in *cornes de gazelle*, almond paste-filled pastries; someone will come round with a platter of these to tempt you.

La Génoise, Blvd Oued Akrech, opposite Dar Es Salam school. French cakes at reasonable prices.

BARS AND CLUBS

Bar Americain, Hotel Balima. A popular place for a beer or coffee, particularly during the evening promenade.

Lounge Bar, Hotel de la Tour Hassan. Thoroughly swish, with comfy seating, low lighting and pricey cocktails.

THE RIF AND MEDITERRANEAN

East of Tangier and Ceuta, along Morocco's northern coast, the Rif mountains rise steeply out of the Mediterranean, making access less easy and meaning that this is one of the country's less visited areas, despite its closeness to Europe. Chefchaouen is an exception to this rule – a popular traveller hangout, with good reason; it epitomizes the area's easy-going charms, not always disconnected from the region's kif (marijuana) production.

Further east along the Mediterranean coast, Al Hoceïma, a relaxed, if isolated holiday town with beaches and nearby fishing villages, is a possible extension to this route.

→ FES TO CHEFCHAOUEN

Just over halfway between Fès and Chefchaouen (four hours by bus) you can break the journey in Ouezzane, an important regional centre. Note that travelling on from Ouezzane can be awkward by bus, as a lot of buses are through services, which arrive full. You'll probably be better off getting a grand taxi on to Chefchaouen.

OUEZZANE

Ouezzane is a good-sized town, rumoured to be the centre of cannabis-resin trading since the clean-up in Tangier in the late 1990s. It is also a centre for the production of olive oil and, because of its Thursday souk, is a draw for local farmers and tradesmen. For visitors, there is little to see, though perched on the north-facing slopes of Jbel Ben Hellal, it has a dramatic hillside location. A track from the town (3 km) leads up to the peak (609 m) and gives a splendid view across towards the Rif. Just 9 km north of the town is Azjem, burial place of an important Rabbi, Amram Ben Djouane, who came from Andalucía in the 18th century. Here, again, are impressive views of the rugged Rif Mountains and the verdant valleys between.

Ouezzane was founded in 1727 by Moulay Abdallah Cherif, founder of the Tabiya Islamic order. This brotherhood achieved great national prominence from the 18th century, when the *zaouïa* in Ouezzane became the focus of extensive pilgrimage activity. Ouezzane had close links with the sultan's court, which was often dependent on the *zaouïa* and its followers for support.

A mid 19th-century cherif of Ouezzane married an Englishwoman, Emily Keane, in 1877 in an Anglican service – they had met at the house of the American consul where Keane was governess – although she later separated from him to live out her dotage in Tangier, where she is now buried in the Anglican Church (see page 206).

Ouezzane's **medina** has some of the most interesting architecture in the Rif, with picturesque tiled-roof houses along winding cobbled streets. The focus of the town is the 18th-century **zaouïa**, on Rue de la Zaouïa, a distinctive green-tiled building with an octagonal minaret. Non-Muslims should not approach too close. Nearby are old lodgings for the pilgrims and the decaying cherifian palace. **Place de l'Indépendence**, the centre of the medina, is busiest during the town souk on Thursday. To get to the craft souks, centred around **Place Bir Inzarane**, follow Rue Abdallah Ibn Lamlih up from Place de l'Indépendence. Ouezzane is known for woollen carpets woven in the weavers' souk at the top of the town. The blacksmiths' souk is along Rue Haddadine. There is a **Centre Artisanal** ① *Place de l'Indépendence, 0800-1900*, and another on Avenue Hassan II.

→ CHEFCHAOUEN

The blue and whitewashed town of Chefchaouen, sometimes called Chaouen and even spelt Xaouen (the Spanish version), is an exceptionally photogenic Andalucían town in the Rif, 60 km south of Tetouan, set above the Oued Laou valley and just below the twin peaks of the Jbel ech Chefchaouen, the 'Horned Mountain'. The town itself could be explored in a day, but with a room in the right hotel, you might want to stay to relax in one of its many cafés or explore the surrounding countryside. At 600 m up in the hills, it makes a good centre for walking, and many who come for a quick visit end up staying much longer. The town also has many sanctuaries for pilgrims and, each year, thousands of visitors are attracted to pay homage to the memory of Sidi Ben Alil, Sidi Abdallah Habti and Sidi el Hadj Cherif.

ARRIVING IN CHEFCHAOUEN

Getting there and around Chefchaouen's bus station is a 20-minute walk out of the town centre, or a short petit taxi journey. Coming in by grand taxi, you arrive close to the old town on Avenue Allal Ben Abdallah. Once you're in the old town, everything is accessible on foot.

Moving on By bus or grand taxi, Tetouan (see page 255) is a couple of hours away. If you're heading further east along the spectacular N2 to Al Hoceïma (see page 250), the same transport options apply but it's around four hours.

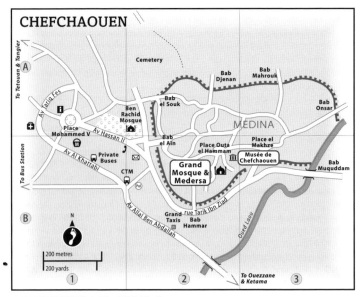

Tourist information Chaouen Rural ⓘ *Rue Machichi, T0539-987267, www.chaouen rural.org, daily 0900-1900*, is a Spanish-funded organization working with local communities and cooperatives. It organizes trips into the countryside around Chefchaouen and can also provide information on the town itself.

Note The selling of kif is big business here, the main production regions being to the east. Suitably persistent refusal should rid you of unwanted attentions, though these are almost always of the friendly-but-stoned variety, rather than aggressive.

BACKGROUND

Set in the Djeballa region, Chefchaouen was founded in 1471 by Cherif Moulay Ali Ben Rachid, a follower of Moulay Abd es Salam Ben Mchich, the patron saint of the area, in order to halt the southwards expansion of the Spanish and Portuguese. The city's population was later supplemented by Muslims and Jews expelled from Spain, particularly from Granada, and, for a time, the rulers of Chefchaouen controlled much of northern Morocco. The town also grew in importance as a pilgrimage centre.

From 1576 Chefchaouen was in conflict with, and isolated from, the surrounding area, the gates being locked each night. Prior to 1920 only three Christians had braved its forbidding walls: the Vicomte de Foucauld disguised as a rabbi in 1883; Walter Harris, *Times* correspondent and author of *Morocco That Was*, in 1889; and the American William Summers, poisoned in Chefchaouen in 1892. They found Jews still speaking 15th-century Andalucían Spanish. In 1920 the town was taken over by the Spanish as part of their protectorate. They were thrown out from 1924 to 1926, by Abd el Karim's Rif resistance movement but returned to stay until Independence in 1956.

Modern Chefchaouen has extended across the hillsides, and the old town is now ringed by a suburb of the usual three-storey family apartment buildings. Though it is now well established on tourist itineraries, both mainstream and backpacker, Chefchaouen manages to retain a village feel. Here you may have your first sighting of the distinctive garments of the women of the Rif, the red and white striped *fouta* or overskirt and the large conical straw hat with woollen bobbles.

PLACES IN CHEFCHAOUEN

There are few major sites. The centre is Place Mohammed V, with its small Andalucían garden. Avenue Hassan II leads to Bab el Aïn and the medina. The market is down some steps from Avenue Hassan II, on Avenue Al Khattabi. Normally a food market, there is a local souk on Monday and Thursday.

MEDINA

The medina of Chefchaouen is an exceptionally photogenic place and rewarding to explore. Sufficiently small not to get lost in, it has intricate Andalucían architecture, arches, arcades and porches, white- or blue-washed houses, with ochre-tiled roofs, and clean, quiet cobbled streets. In the maze of these narrow streets you run into water points, small open squares with shops and the solid ramparts of the kasbah. If driving, park the car in **Place el Makhzen** and explore the rest on foot. Approaching the medina on foot, enter by **Bab el Aïn**. From Bab el Aïn a small road leads through to **Place Outa el Hammam**. This is the main square, lively at night, and surrounded by a number of stalls and café-restaurants, popular with kif smokers.

The square is dominated by the terracotta-coloured 15th-century kasbah, now the **Musée de Chefchaouen** ① *T0539-986761, Wed-Mon 0900-1300 and 1500-1830, 0900-1700 in Ramadan, 10dh.* As a prison it housed the Rifi leader Abd el Karim from 1926, and you can visit the suitably dark and forbidding dungeon. The museum itself is not that special – it has an exhibition of local costumes, some with very delicate embroidery, tools, musical instruments, pottery, weapons and a collection of decorated wooden caskets. More interesting is the building itself; you can climb to the top of the tower for a good view of the town from the roof. There is also a peaceful Andalucían-style courtyard garden, filled with flowers and birds.

The beautiful **Grand Mosque**, with its octagonal minaret, beside the kasbah, dates from the 15th century, but was restored in the 17th and 18th. Next door is a 16th-century *medersa*, unfortunately closed. Opposite the **Restaurant Kasbah**, at No 34, is an old **caravanserai**. Further on, **Place el Makhzen**, the second square, has stalls along the top side, the **Ensemble Artisanal** at the end.

HILL WALKING
Chefchaouen has some good hill walking, with spectacular scenery and plentiful animal and birdlife. Don't be too surprised, however, if you experience suspicious questioning from the military involved in cracking down on kif cultivation, and be prepared for a long and strenuous day. Taking a guide (could set you back around 100dh) is worth considering. Look out for the natural spring, **Ras el Maa**, 3 km out of town in the direction of **Jbel Tisouka** (2050 m). You are within striking distance of the **Parc Naturel de Talassemtane**, still basically undiscovered by tourists. **El Malha**, **Beni Ahmed** and other isolated villages in this park are reached by landrover taxi from Bab Taza, 25 km to the southeast of Chefchaouen on the N2 road to Ketama (Issaguen).

→ NORTHERN RIF

The N2, the 'route of the crests' from Chefchaouen to Al Hoceïma, is one of Morocco's most dramatic journeys, a road running through a succession of small villages with stunning views over the remote valleys and towards the snow-capped Rif Mountains. Care must be taken on this narrow, hill-top road, which may be closed by snow in winter.

KETAMA
Ketama (officially called Issaguen, but referred to by just about everyone as Ketama, confusingly also the name of the area) has long had a sulphurous reputation as Morocco's capital of cannabis, a reputation not entirely undeserved. Although much money is made from kif, there is little infrastructure and few visitors stop here. The town can sometimes be snowbound in winter. The main point of interest in the area is the nearby Jbel Tidghine, the highest mountain in the Rif at 2448 m.

If you settle for a couple of minutes in a café in Ketama, someone is certain to approach you with an offer of cannabis. But the Gendarmerie royale are watching, so avoid making any purchases.

CLIMBING JBEL TIDGHINE (TIDIQUIN)
For Jbel Tidghine, you need to head for the village of **Azila**, about 5 km from Ketama. If driving, take the road south out of Ketama and turn left at the new, low angular building.

ON THE ROAD
Reefer madness

The Northern Rif has long been an area of unrest and rebellion against central authorities, notably in the Rif rebellion of Abd el Karim against the Spanish from 1921 to 1926. More recently, bandits are said to have preyed on travellers and, today, although the situation has improved, the main dilemma is how to replace one of the major sources of income for local families – cannabis cultivation. (The term 'kif' refers to the dried and chopped leaves and flowers, not the resin, and the word 'reefer' probably derives from the word 'Rif'.) Government development programmes and pressure from the EU have had little impact, simply because the cannabis plant, especially if irrigated, grows very well on the region's hillsides. If you stop over in the area, you may be invited to see the process of turning the leaves into a ball of uncut, smokeable material, the understanding being that you will buy. Do not even think of smuggling cannabis out of the country. There are links between the police and vendors, who may try to blackmail you, and the European consuls in Tangier have enough would-be smugglers to visit in the local prisons already. The police are very likely to crack down on foreigners smoking in public, even though they may turn a blind eye to locals doing the same.

Alternatively, take a local taxi. The houses of Azila are scattered around a valley below Jbel Tidghine. Follow the road through to the open 'football field', where the odd taxi parks up or, before this, turn off right by some trees on a dirt track to come out just above the mosque. You will dip down through the village, over a rough plank bridge under the walnut trees. Then, passing some quite large, concrete houses, you reach the bracken and first cedars of Tidghine's lower slopes. For the climb, there are two options: either wind slowly up the old forestry department piste, or cut straight up to intersect with the forestry track further up – a good option if you're with a local. It is said that strong 4WDs can get to within 30 minutes of the summit. Climbing time should be about 2¼ hours, the descent 1¾ hours. Remember to bring a water bottle – there is a spring where you can refill it.

The forest is truly beautiful, with butterflies in late summer, but it's under threat from locals in need of more sources of income than livestock and barely profitable cannabis cultivation. To bring the great trees down, the practice is to light the needles under the trees in summer. The resinous trunks burn easily, weakening the whole tree, which is then easy to fell in winter when the forestry wardens are less likely to make tours of inspection.

The last stretch up the mountain is shaley scree, quite easy to deal with but slow going. At the top, the views are magnificent. There are two stone-built, corrugated-iron roofed huts where you could stay the night, if you have a warm sleeping bag.

ROUTE DE L'UNITE
The R505 runs southwards from Ketama (Issaguen) to Taounate, Aïn Aicha and Fès, with views of deep valleys and forested slopes. This road, the Route de l'Unité, was built just after Independence by voluntary labour battalions to link the Spanish protectorate of the north with the former French areas. The whole region is untouched by tourism, despite its cedar woods and mountainous terrain. If driving in this region in summer, note that car accidents are frequent. Returning migrant workers out to impress in powerful cars may fail to appreciate the dangers of the winding roads.

GOING FURTHER
Al Hoceïma

Al Hoceïma has one of the most beautiful natural sites on the Moroccan Mediterranean coast. Although the town, a Spanish creation of the 1920s and 1950s, has no great monuments, there is compensation in the form of nearby beaches. Despite these coastal attractions and greenery of the surrounding hills, the difficulty of getting to Al Hoceïma by road reduces the flow of casual visitors. There is an airport, however, bringing in a few package tourists. In summer there are huge numbers of migrant workers and their families back from Europe, while the winter is very quiet. East of the town is a fertile plain enclosed on three sides by hills. And, off the Plage de Sfiha, also to the east of Al Hoceïma, is an intriguing group of islands, the **Peñón de Alhucemas**, Spanish territory since 1673, and once disputed by the French and English for their strategic position.

ARRIVING IN AL HOCEÏMA

Al Hoceïma is possibly the most isolated resort town in Morocco. You can fly there from Casablanca (in summer) or, given the distances, take an early morning bus from Chefchaouen, Fès or Taza. There are occasionally grands taxis from Taza and Fès.

Al Hoceïma is not a big place. However, you might want to take a beige-and-blue petit taxi out to one of the beaches. The beaches at Torres de Alcalá and Kalah Iris, some 60 km away to the west, can also easily be reached by public transport. Ketama and Jbel Tidghine are a feasible day trip by grand taxi from Al Hoceïma.

For tourist information, there's a **Délégation Régionale du Tourisme** ⓘ *Immeuble Cabalo, Rue Tarik Ibn Ziad, off Pl de la Marche Verte, T0539-982830, 0830-1200 and 1400-1800.*

BACKGROUND

The character of the town centre of modern Al Hoceïma is distinctly Spanish, reflecting the protectorate years. Established by the Spanish in 1926 as Villa Sanjurjo, it was built as a garrison to control the Beni Ouriaghel tribe, of which Abd el Karim was the chief, immediately after the Rif rebellion. (For those interested in colonial place names, the town was originally named Villa Sanjurjo, after one General Sanjurjo who led Spanish troops ashore here. The old part of town is still sometimes referred to by this name.) To the east of Al Hoceïma is the long and less busy beach of **Alhucemas bay**, while offshore is the Peñón de Alhucemas, a remarkable idiosyncrasy of history. This small island is owned and occupied by Spain and apparently used as a prison. It is completely dependent on Melilla for supplies and even water, and has no contact with the Moroccan mainland, off which it sits like a ship at anchor.

Today Al Hoceïma has a population of some 60,000. Off season, it has an isolated feel: Tangier lies 300 km away to the west, Melilla is 170 km to the east, Oujda some 250 km away. The image in the holiday brochures is of a villageish sort of place with low, whitewashed houses atop a cliff, surrounding a few colonial buildings. In fact, modern Al Hoceïma has streets and streets of three- and four-storey blocks, sprawling across the hillsides. This is where migrant workers put their savings. So, Al Hoceïma is turning into a big town, but one without any industry or major official functions.

Nador and Al Hoceïma are the key towns for the Ta'rifit-speaking region, and Arabic-speaking outsiders are not all that much appreciated here. Newsagents sell badges and stickers with the image of Abd el Karim, hero of the Rif War against the Spanish. Yet some cultural resistance aside, Al Hoceïma is very sleepy outside the summer season, when migrants from the Netherlands and Belgium pour in.

PLACES IN AL HOCEÏMA

Buses and taxis pull into the neighbourhood of the Place du Rif. You should thread your way over to the Avenue Mohammed V (banks and cafés), which leads down to the wide expanse of **Place Mohammed VI**. The well-maintained colonial building at the bottom is the Spanish school. The cafés on your right as you head down are worth a pause, with their views over the horseshoe bay. At the **Hotel Mohammed V**, the road curves down to the main beach. The **port** is worth a look, if you have time, and there are a handful of restaurants here. A stroll round the town will reveal various other remnants of Spanish times.

Just before the **Hotel Mohammed V**, there is a steep flight of steps that leads down to the **Hotel Quemado** complex and the **beach**. This gets pretty crowded in summer, although the sand is cleaned and raked every morning. There are pedalos and rowing boats for hire and jet skis. There is a rock to swim out to, and lots of enthusiastic playing of beach tennis.

BEACHES EAST OF TOWN

Kalah Bonita beach is just within the urban area (campsite, café-restaurant and crowds in summer, also sewage smells from the creek around the cliff). Further east are Isri, Sfiha, Souani and Tayda. The beach at **Isri** has gravelly sand and, being below a brick factory, receives a certain amount of rubble. The left turn-off for Isri beach, coming from town, is 50 m after the **Centre de visite technique**, a large white building. The gravelly beach also has the rock where Abd el Karim el Khattabi made a famous speech in 1926, urging his resistance fighters to give up their arms and accept a form of autonomous government under Spanish rule. The tribes rejected this proposal and subsequently took a pounding from the Spanish airforce. Note that city taxis do not run this far out.

The beach at **Souani** ('the orchards') is rather better. The turn-off left is signed. There is a 2-km drive down to the car park next to the beach. Take care on the looping road, and don't get distracted by the superb views over to Peñon de Alhucemas. (Without a car, Souani is accessible by grand taxi, 7dh a place; get out at Sfiha, then walk along the beach.) The sand is dark and fine, and there are few seasonal beach cafés, showers and the **Restaurant Yasmine**. In summer, for a modicum of quiet, you will need to walk along the beach towards the forest and **Tayda**, where there is an exclusive **Club Med**.

AROUND AL HOCEÏMA

There are some good day trips to the tiny fishing communities west of Al Hoceïma, namely Torres de Alcalá, Kalah Iris and rather remote Badis. Without your own transport, the easiest approach is to take a grand taxi from Al Hoceïma to Beni Boufrah, via Imzouren. **Beni Boufrah** is a small rural community about 7 km from Torres. Here you change for a local share taxi. (There is also occasional transport from Beni Boufrah to Targuist.)

Torres de Alcalá has a pebbly beach and seasonal café. Just behind the beach is a campsite among the eucalyptus trees (practically no facilities). Up on the hill are the remains of the fortress, that gives the village its name: 'the towers of the citadel', Alcalá being a Spanish word derived from the Arabic for citadel.

More interesting than Torres is **Badis**, a tiny fishing settlement about 90 minutes' walk along a good piste to the east. The track starts just behind the two-storey houses of Torres village. You could drive (and there is another, more direct, piste off the Imzouren to Beni

Boufrah road), but note that, in summer, Badis is off-limits to all outside vehicles as there is a royal campsite here. Princess Lalla Amina, Hassan II's sister, takes her annual holidays on the beach at Badis, which is unofficially off-limits to all but locals. The track runs along the clifftop and makes a good walk. You have to scramble down the last 100 m or so to reach the beach. Behind the beach, a wide valley runs inland. There is no accommodation. You can buy a few basic things at the tiny shop in the settlement about 300 m from the sea, behind the royal camping area. In summer, one of the royal security guards will probably come and have a chat.

You could make the long scramble up to what is said to be a ruined windmill high above the beach, and have a look at the tiny shrine to Abou Yacoub al Badis, born around 1260, hidden in the trees. As the Mediterranean port for Fès, Badis was once an important settlement. It was destroyed by earthquake in 1564. The Spanish-held **Peñón de Vélez de la Gomera**, generally described in the press as an islet but in fact attached to the beach at Badis by a pebbly spit, may have some fortifications which go back to Merinid times.

Kalah Iris, 60 km west of Al Hoceïma and 9 km from Beni Boufrah, has an attractive beach. Sometimes fishermen can be persuaded to run trips out to see the impressive cliffs.

WHERE TO STAY

It can be difficult to get a quiet night's sleep in Al Hoceïma in summer and practically no street names are shown.

€€€ Hotel Mohammed V, just off Pl Mohammed VI, above the beach, T0539-923314. All 30 rooms have sea views and balconies, as well as baths and tiled bathrooms. Quite plain for the money, but there is a bar and a restaurant.

€€ National, 23 Rue Tetouan, T0539-982141. Good-sized rooms with TVs and old carpets. Clean, modern bathrooms.

€ Hotel Étoile du Rif, 40 Pl du Rif (Sahat Rif), T0539-840847. A stylish pink and white Spanish building, once the town's casino, dominates the main square. Above a busy café-restaurant, it's friendly and clean and the best rooms overlook the square. Handy for bus station.

€ Hotel Nekor, 20 Rue Tahnaoute, T0539-983065. Just off Place du Rif, **Nekor** has a café downstairs and is handily placed for making an early morning getaway in a petit taxi, though the regular cries of "Nador, Nador, Nador" may wake you.

RESTAURANTS

There aren't many good options in Al Hoceïma. Try any of the cafés off Pl Mohammed VI overlooking the Playa Quemada. **Café el Nejma** and **La Belle Vue**, next to each other at the end of Rue Mohammed V, both have far-end terraces with views out over the bay.

€€ Club Náutico, fishing port, T0539-981641. A down-to-earth licensed place in the port with lots of men sitting round plastic-covered tables watching football on TV. The food is probably Al Hoceïma's best,

however; splash out on an excellent mixed plate of fried fish and don't miss the torchlit sale of the day's catch outside.

€€ La Dolce Pizza, Pl du Rif, opposite Hotel Étoile du Rif. Relatively speaking, a surprisingly atmospheric little restaurant serving up lasagne as well as pizzas.

€ Snack Maghreb el Jadied, Av Mohammed V. A friendly little snack bar next to the hotel of the same name that will rustle up brochettes or a sandwich at any hour of the day.

THE RIF AND MEDITERRANEAN LISTINGS

WHERE TO STAY

Chefchaouen

Chefchaouen is a popular place for budget travellers, as it has a good supply of clean, cheap hotels. However, note that it gets pretty cold here in winter. Light sleepers will be awakened by the heavily amplified call to prayer from the numerous mosques.

€€€ Casa Hassan, Rue Targui-Chaouen, T0539-986153, www.casahassan.com. A sophisticated place, with *tadelakt* bathrooms and big beds. Arches, painted wood ceilings, decorated chests and wood fires add interest, and there's the advantage of a/c. The place has an authentic feel, a big yellow and red hammam and a great roof terrace with views over the mountains.

€€ Barcelona, 12 Rue Al Andalous, T0539-988506. Rough wooden doors and good, simple rooms, 2 of which have a/c. Roof terrace with views and tables undercover. Coloured glass, old tiles, lots of blankets.

€€ Casa Perleta, Bab el Souk, T0539-988979, www.casaperleta.com. A highlight of Chefchaouen's riad-scene, Casa Perleta manages to sum up the simple beauty of this region's architecture. The building has been restored lovingly with the whitewashed rooms hosting hand-painted wood details, blue-painted window frames and lots of regional fabrics and crafts. Some rooms have views of the mountains and others of the street, and there's a great shaded terrace to hang out on and soak up the atmosphere. Breakfast is included, the multilingual staff are ever-helpful, and there's Wi-Fi too.

€€ Dar Mounir, T0539-988253, www. hotel-darmounir.com. Opened in 2007, **Dar Mounir** has 11 rooms, most of which are big, and the *tadelakt* bathrooms have horseshoe arches. Windows are high in the walls, which means there's not much of a view but it's all very comfortable, with good new beds, sofas and open fires.

€€ Dar Rass el Mar, Rue Rass el Maa, T0539-988080, www.chefchaouen.ch. A grand guesthouse, across the stream, under the mountain, overlooking the valley, Rass el Mar is good value for money. The garden is verdant, bedrooms are bright, bathrooms have colourful *tadelakt* and an excellent breakfast is served on the pretty terrace.

€ Andaluz, 1 Rue Sidi Salem, T0539-986034. Simple rooms are arranged around an old tiled courtyard. Single beds are on the small side but there's a wood fire downstairs and a library. Showers included.

€ Dar Terrae, Av Hassan I, T0539-987598, www.darterrae.com. Italian-run, **Dar Terrae** is a riad with style at a very reasonable price. Rooms are quite small and not all have en suite bathrooms, but the beds are comfortable, and there is an excellent multi-levelled roof terrace where you can have breakfast or relax with a mint tea. Rooms have open fires for winter, and it's also one of the friendliest places in town.

€ Hostel Gernika, 49 Onsaar, T0539-987434. Immaculately decorated in riad style, with tiles and arches, **Gernika** is a cosy hotel with a wood-burning stove and a bright seating area. Rooms have plain white walls, white curtains, good wooden furniture and views. The rooms at the top of the building have no bathroom but open up onto the 3-part roof terrace. Friendly and well run.

€ Hotel Rif, 29 Rue Tarik Ibn Ziad, T0539-986982. Friendly hotel, bar and restaurant with good views from higher rooms over the valley. A good place to get information on walking and the local area. Traveller-friendly: drummers are encouraged, you can do your own laundry, and guests are welcome to drink on the roof terrace.

RESTAURANTS

Chefchaouen

€€ Casa Aladin/La Lampe Magique, 26 Rue Targui. Though it can't seem to quite make up its mind what it's called, this is a good restaurant, where the best tables overlook the end of the square. The covered roof terrace has geraniums, while downstairs it's cosier, with elaborate window frames and red curtains. The food is reliably good Moroccan fare.

€€ Restaurant Al Kasbah, just off the square. **Al Kasbah** has lots of carved wood and cushions. There's a wide choice of tagines and couscous.

€€ Tissemlal, 22 Rue Targui, T0539-986153. Part of Casa Hassan (see Where to stay, above), this is Chefchaouen's best restaurant, an atmospheric place offering warm bread, occasional free appetizers, great salads and excellent Moroccan main dishes in a peaceful and sophisticated courtyard setting. There are comfortable seats, candles, an open fire and big metal lamps.

€ Café Snack Mounir, at the end of the square. **Mounir** offers a range of light meals, including an unusually good vegetarian selection, as well as Chefchaouen's best coffee. A good spot to sit and watch the world go by, and better than the other options in the square.

€ Café Tunssi, Bab Ansar. Just outside the medina on the slope above the stream, **Café Tunssi** has good views across to Jemaâ Buzafar, the mosque on the opposite hill, from its 3 terraced levels.

€ Chez Fouad, Rue Adarve Chabu. Metal tables, blue and white tiles, tagines, fried fish, couscous and 'pitza'. Small and cheap.

€ Jardin Ziryab, flowery gardens with tables above the far side of the stream from the centre of the town. Tea, live music and snacks and, if you really like it here, you can even stay in one of the rooms.

€ Restaurant Rincón Andaluz, just off Plaza Bab Souk. Couscous and fried fish for bargain prices at little tables on a blue-painted alleyway just outside Bab el Souk.

TETOUAN

Set between the Rif and the Mediterranean Sea, Tetouan has a dramatic beauty, the white buildings of the medina contrasting with the backdrop of the mountains. There's some impressive colonial architecture in the Spanish town, and the medina has been made a UNESCO Heritage Site. The city is an interesting place to explore, albeit with more noise and hassle than Chefchaouen to the south. Tetouan's main sites can be covered in a rather rushed half day; a full day would give you time to explore the city pretty thoroughly. Between Ceuta and Tetouan, and also further round the coast, there are a number of resorts – some fashionable, others with a more downbeat appeal – which can be visited en route or as an excursion from the city.

→ARRIVING IN TETOUAN

GETTING THERE AND AROUND
Taxis arrive in the new town, close to the bus station, about 10 minutes' walk from the medina. From the bus station, to get to the medina, head up Rue Sidi Mandri and turn third right down Avenue Mohammed V, which will bring you to Place Hassan II.

MOVING ON
A shared taxi from Tetouan to the border at Ceuta (see page 261) takes around an hour.

TOURIST INFORMATION
Office du Tourisme (ONMT) ① *30 Rue Mohammed V, T0539-961915, Mon-Fri 0830-1630.*

   Note When visiting Tetouan watch out for the various seedy characters and con artists with a keen eye for tired backpackers stumbling off a late bus. Pay attention to your belongings and avoid having any dealings with faux guides. The tourist office (below) can arrange for an official guide, should you want one, for 120dh for a half day.

→BACKGROUND

Tetouan was founded in the third century BC as Tamuda, but was destroyed by the Romans in AD 42. The Merinid ruler Sultan Abou Thabit built a kasbah at Tetouan in 1307. Sacked by Henry III of Castile in 1399 to disperse the corsairs based there, Tetouan was neglected until it was taken over by Muslims expelled from Granada in 1484. They were to bring with them the distinctive forms and traditions of Andalucían Islamic architecture, still observable in the medinas of Granada and Córdoba. Many of the Andalucíans worked as corsairs, continuing the tradition. A Jewish community was established here in the 17th century, which gave the impetus to open up trade with Europe. Trade with the West continued to boom in the 18th century during the reign of Moulay Ismaïl. In 1913 Tetouan was chosen as the capital of the Spanish protectorate over northern Morocco. The Spanish created the new town, which has remained an important regional centre in independent Morocco.

VILLE NOUVELLE

Place Hassan II, the focal point of the city and a former market, is the best place for a stroll or a sit in a café terrace during the evening. It is dominated by the **Royal Palace**, with its gleaming white walls and green tiled roof. Dating from the 17th-century, it was completely transformed under Hassan II. Looking onto the square is the **Pasha Mosque**, with its distinctive green door and green and brown tiled minaret. **Bab er Rouah**, to the southeast, has also had a facelift. The other major focus point in the Ville Nouvelle is **Place Moulay el Mehdi**, along Boulevard Mohammed V from Place Hassan II. Here there is an impressive

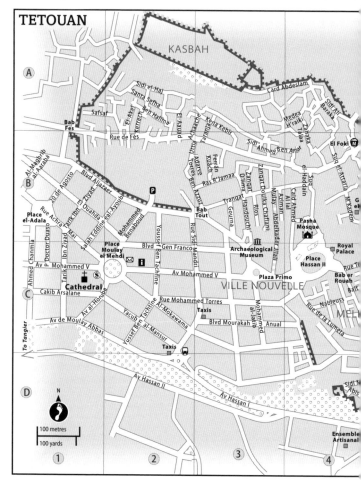

golden-yellow **cathedral** and a large fountain in the middle. **Instituto Cervantes** ⓘ *3 C Mohammed Torres, T0539-967056,* has good exhibitions and documentaries.

MEDINA

Bab er Rouah, in the corner of Place Hassan II, leads into the medina, where Andalucían influence is still apparent in the whitewashed walls and delicate wrought-iron decorations on the balconies. A typically confusing maze of streets and souks, it is well worth exploring, although, perhaps, with the assistance of an official guide. Look out for artefacts in the souks in Tetouan's favoured red colour. **Rue Terrafin** is a good route through the medina, and leads into Rue Torres and Rue Sidi el Yousti, and out at **Bab el Okla**. North of Rue Sidi el Yousti is an area with some of the larger and more impressive houses.

Souks Souk el Hout, with pottery, meat and fish, is to the left of Rue Terrafin behind the palace. Here there is a delightful leafy square; pleasant surroundings for admiring the wares. Behind the souk is a small 15th-century fortress, the **Alcazaba**, now taken over by a cooperative. Take the left hand of the two north-bound lanes from the Souk el Hout and on the right is **Guersa el Kebir**, a textile souk selling the striped, woven blankets worn by Rifi women. The red, white and blue of the fabric is particularly striking and it's sold by women dressed in the same colours. **El Foki** market can be found by following your nose – the smell of the traditional, flat, round loaves is impossible to miss. Look out too for the **L'Usaa Square**, with its white houses around a mosaic fountain and a rose garden.

Further on from this souk, leading up to Bab Sebta, are a number of specialist craft souks and shops. Running between Bab Sebta and Bab Fès is **Rue de Fès**, a more general commercial area, although with a number of souks around. From Bab Sebta the road out of the city passes through a large cemetery. Above the medina is the crumbling **kasbah** (closed to visitors), and nearby a vantage point providing stunning views over the city.

Jewish quarter On Place Hassan II, the first alleyway south of Bab er Rouah leads onto the main street of the mellah, the 19th-century Jewish quarter, where there are a number of abandoned synagogues. The original Jewish population has all but disappeared. The earliest mellah was near the Grand Mosque.

Archaeological Museum ⓘ *Blvd Aljazaer, near Pl Hassan II, T0539-967103. Mon-Fri 0830-1630. 10dh.* Built in 1943, this museum contains a small archaeological collection from the prehistoric and pre-Islamic sites of the northern region of Morocco, plus some pieces from the once-Spanish Saharan provinces and a large library. Of most interest, however, are the Roman statues and mosaics found at ancient Lixus near Larache (see page 215). The most notable mosaic portrays the Three Graces of Roman mythology – there's been some modern conservation to fill in the gaps, but it's sensitively done. Other rooms display prehistoric tools, bronzes and pottery. Of note here is the Sumerian ex-voto statuette found close to Asilah. Most of the small figures date from the first century AD. Other highlights include a scale model of the stone circle of Mzoura (see page 213), 15th-century Portugese tiles and a Latin inscription from Tamuda telling of a Roman victory over the Berbers.

Musée d'Art Marocain/Musée Ethnographique ⓘ *T0539-970505. Mon-Fri 0830-1200 and 1430-1730, Sat 0830-1200.* Housed in Bab el Okla and renovated in 2002, this small museum is definitely worth a visit. There are samples of local textiles and dress, weapons and musical instruments, plus a small Andalucían garden at the back. There is also a display of traditional tiles. Note that the technique for making tiles in Tetouan was different from the more mainstream Moroccan or Fassi *zellige* technique. The latter is a mosaic technique involving the assembling of thousands of tiny coloured ceramic pieces. The artisans of Tetouan produced tiles imitating the *zellige* mosaics by using the *cuerda seca* ('dry cord') technique, by which the different coloured glazes were separated by a pattern of geometric lines.

École de Métiers Just outside the medina, across the road from Bab el Okla, is the École de Métiers (craft school), built by the Spanish. Here craftsmen and students work on tiles, leatherwork, carpentry and pottery. The school, generally closed for holidays in August, may be open to visitors.

TAMUDA

The remains of ancient Tamuda lie to the south of the N2 road running west out of Tetouan. It was founded in the third to second centuries BC. Later, during the Roman period, in the third century AD, the original settlement disappeared under a Roman camp. So far, only remains of dwellings have been excavated, no public buildings or religious buildings. Finds from Tamuda are in the Archaeological Museum in Tetouan.

RESTINGA SMIR

From Fnideq to Tetouan, the N13 passes through a flat strip of beaches and marshes, and a number of tourist developments. Restinga Smir, 22 km from Tetouan, has a long beach and a correspondingly long line of holiday complexes, hotels, bars, restaurants, bungalows and camping areas. Until recently it was still a small fishing village, frequented only by a small number of local visitors. Now it enjoys an international reputation. There is, however, sufficient space on the vast beaches for the activities on offer, which include horse riding, mini-golf, tennis, underwater fishing and windsurfing. There's also the small marina/pleasure port of Marina Smir.

MDIQ

After Restinga Smir the road passes through Kabila, another beach and marina, to Mdiq, a small fishing port with some traditional boat construction. Mdiq shares the same coastline (and clientele) as Cabo Negro (below) and there is a sense of competition between the two. Mdiq is a well-established resort offering a range of modern hotels and restaurants (mainly fish of course), nightclubs, swimming pools and the usual selection of watersports on the beach. This is certainly a popular family resort, which is spreading to the north.

CABO NEGRO

After Mdiq turn for Cabo Negro (also known as Taifor or Ras Tarf), which is 3.5 km off the N13. Here the beach is more rugged, with low hills, dotted with small houses, overlooking the sea. This is a slightly less commercialized region, though the number of discos and nightclubs is growing. Riding is very popular here, with horses for hire by the hour and day. The roads through the town follow the contours and rise at various levels up the hill.

MARTIL

Martil, Tetouan's former port, and one-time pirate base, stands at the mouth of the Oued Martil. It is now another popular resort, with over 10 km of sandy beach. Once it was the resort of people from Tetouan who established holiday homes here on the coast but now Martil welcomes visitors from far afield.

OUED LAOU AND THE COASTAL ROAD SOUTH OF TETOUAN

Oued Laou is 44 km southeast of Tetouan along the spectacular coastal road, the S608. It is a relaxed fishing village with an excellent beach but only basic facilities. The road continues from here along the coast through the villages of Targa, Steha, Bou Hamed, and Dar M'Ter. Possibly a more convenient place to stop is the fishing village of **El Jebha** (souk Tuesday), which is served by buses from Tetouan and Chefchaouen. A tortuous mountain road, the 8500, takes the intrepid traveller from El Jebha to meet the N2 west of Ketama.

TETOUAN LISTINGS

WHERE TO STAY

€€€ Blanco Riad Hotel, Zawya Kadiria 25, T0539-704202, www.blancoriad.com. All graceful arches and columns with lashings of Arabesque design, this riad is a special place to stay. With just 8 light-filled rooms, all individually decorated with intricate tiled floors, wood inlay, lanterns and *masharabeyya* details, **Blanco Riad** manages to ooze exclusivity without ever feeling stuffy. The roof terrace has incredible views over the town, and there is a lovely secluded inner courtyard. The house used to belong to the Spanish consulate and has been lovingly restored but with a fresh, contemporary edge.

€€ El Reducto, Zanqat Zawya 38, T0539-968120, www.riadtetouan.com. This little riad, well signposted just off the plaza at the end of Mohammed V, used to belong to the prime minister under the Spanish protectorate and has been given a thorough overhaul by its current Spanish owner, who may be able to get you a good guide to the medina. Set around a rectangular courtyard, the 4 rooms range from the fairly small to a huge space with spectacular carved wood and an enormous bath. All have luxurious fabrics, drapes and antique tiles. Price includes breakfast. Half board also available.

€€ Panorama Vista, Av My el Abbas, T0539-964970. If you don't fancy staying in a riad, this is far and away Tetouan's best mid-range hotel option. The aptly (if tautologically) named **Panorama Vista** has enormous views across the valley to the Rif mountains. Rooms are modern and comfortable with TVs and good bathrooms. There's a popular café downstairs for breakfast, too.

€€ Riad Dalia, 25 Rue Ouessaa, Souika, T0539-964318, www.riad-dalia.com. At the heart of the medina (call when you arrive and they'll come and meet you), the **Dalia** offers a riad experience at bargain prices. The cheapest rooms are small, dark and without en suite but still atmospheric and are a snip. Other rooms are grander and en suite). There are stunning 360° views from the roof terrace. Popular with students and young Spaniards, who canoodle in dark corners and smoke the hookah pipes. The building was once the house of the Dutch consul, whose bedroom was in what is now the café on the top floor. The other guest rooms were apparently used by his several wives.

RESTAURANTS

€€ Blanco Riad, Zawya Kadiria 25, T0539-704202, www.blancoriad.com. Specializing in Moroccan dishes with a modern twist, **Blanco Riad** (see Where to stay, above) is a wonderful place to sample a contemporary version of the nation's cuisine. Eat outside on the patio on a balmy evening to top off a perfect day of sightseeing in Tetouan.

€€ El Reducto, Zanqat Zawya 38, T0539-968120. In a great setting (see Where to stay, above), **El Reducto** does very reasonable food, mainly traditional Moroccan, but with a few Spanish touches, such as a decent gazpacho. The quality of the food doesn't quite match that of the rarefied surroundings but there's some good wine.

€ Pâtisserie Rahmouni, 10 Rue Youssef Ben Tachfine. Whether you like your pastries creamy, nutty or flaky, you'll find an enormous selection here. There's a good savoury counter at the back, and they serve excellent coffee, too.

CEUTA

Ceuta is an odd sort of place, an enclave of provincial Spain, an African equivalent of Great Britain's Gibraltar. However, unlike Gibraltar, Ceuta has not established itself as a minor tourist attraction. Instead, it gives the impression that it would like to be a Mediterranean Hong Kong: it has the right sort of location, between two continents, developed Europe and upcoming Africa. But the Gibraltar-Spain frontier was opened in 1985, and in many ways Ceuta has been sidelined into becoming a passenger transit port. The chaotic Ceuta-Fnideq frontier may well be your first or last point of contact with Morocco.

→ ARRIVING IN CEUTA

GETTING THERE
The Fnideq-Ceuta frontier is reached most easily from Tetouan by grand taxi. The taxis leave Tetouan from opposite the main bus station, expect to pay around 25dh a place. There are also occasional buses from Tetouan to Fnideq. Note that border formalities can be slow. Passports have to be checked and stamped by Moroccan officials both ways. Vehicles have to be registered and papers, including insurance, registration and licence, checked. Cash can be exchanged on the Moroccan side of the frontier at the Banque populaire booth. Driving up to Ceuta from Tetouan you can take the direct route or take the scenic route via Martil, which takes around 45 minutes.

MOVING ON
There are nearly 20 ferries a day from Ceuta to Algeciras on the Spanish mainland, next to Gibraltar. Journey time ranges from 30 minutes to one hour.

GETTING AROUND
Unless you intend to stay the night, you will need to get from the port to the Moroccan border at Fnideq, 3 km away. There is a bus from Ceuta city centre, leaving from Plaza de la Constitución. To get there, turn left as you leave the ferry terminal, and follow round along Paseo de las Palmeras (a 15-minute walk, maximum). You can spend both pesetas and dirhams in Ceuta in restaurants and shops. Like mainland Spain, the enclave has a long afternoon siesta with shops closed 1300-1600. Sunday is very much a day of rest.

TOURIST INFORMATION
Patronata Municipal de Turismo ① *at the exit from the ferry port, Mon-Fri 0830-2030, Sat and Sun 1000-2000*, is helpful and has maps and leaflets. See also www.ceuta.es.

→ BACKGROUND

Ceuta (Sebta in Arabic) is a Spanish enclave on the Moroccan coast, which since 1995 has had the status of 'autonomous town', putting it somewhere between the Spanish autonomous regions and the municipalities. Ceuta has an excellent strategic position on the Strait of Gibraltar and was occupied by the Carthaginians, Greeks and Romans. After being taken in the Arab conquest, the site was captured by the Portuguese in 1415 but, on the union of Spain and Portugal, was transferred to Spain in 1581, under whose control it has remained ever since as little more than a military prison. Its later fame arose from its importance as a supplying fortress for Spanish forces during a series of 19th-century sieges of the northern *presidios*. Fighting near Ceuta in 1859 nearly led to the total loss of the enclave. In 1860 a Spanish military force invaded Morocco from Ceuta. In the 20th century Spain once again became embroiled in a bloody war in northern Morocco in which it badly lost important battles at Anoual in 1921 and in the Chefchaouen-Tetouan campaign in late 1924. Ceuta ultimately survived this episode thanks largely to Abdelkarim's internal political difficulties and the improved Spanish generalship under Franco. And it was from Ceuta that the future *caudillo* launched his forces to impose his form of law and order on mainland Spain in 1936.

Ceuta and Melilla, to the east, remain potential friction points between Morocco and Spain. Morocco regards both as occupied territory and, in 2002, things came to a head when Moroccan soldiers occupied a tiny rocky islet, Isla Perejil, just northwest of Ceuta. Though the island was inhabited only by goats at the time, the action was called the first

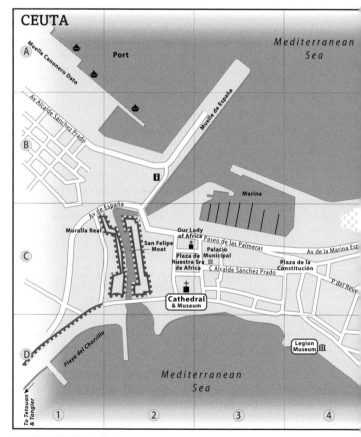

military invasion of Western European soil since the Second World War. Spain eventually reclaimed the island (though it's not entirely clear that anyone had actually taken enough notice of it before to know whether it was in fact part of Morocco or Spain), and relations between the two countries have since improved. Indeed, both would seem to have much more to lose by hostility than by a maintenance of the mutually advantageous status quo.

→ PLACES IN CEUTA

Ceuta harbour lies tucked into a bay on the north of the peninsula, with the town largely packed onto a narrow isthmus lying between Monte Hacho (204 m) in the east and the Sierra Cimera hills adjacent to the frontier with Morocco in the west. The town is Spanish in character, with a heavy military presence – armed forces occupy most of the larger and older buildings including the fortress areas. The shopping streets, such as Paseo del Revellin and Calle Real, concentrate heavily on duty-free luxury goods and electronic equipment. To the east of the town is a tree-covered hill, which is a pleasant place for a stroll. At the far eastern edge is an old Portuguese fort, or stop off at the Ermitada de San Antonio, a convent rebuilt in the 1960s, from where there is a good view of the town.

PLAZA DE AFRICA

A visit to Ceuta should probably start on **Plaza de Africa**, home to two large Catholic places of worship. The **Cathedral Museum** ① *south of Plaza de Africa, open afternoons only*, is situated in the side wall of the cathedral itself, off Plaza de Africa, and has ecclesiastical items in its collection, including the highly decorated montage of the Virgen Capitana. The **Cathedral** stands on the site of a pre-Muslim church and a mosque from the Arab period. The present building dates principally from the 17th century, though there were large-scale renovations in 1949-1958.

The **Sanctuario de Nuestra Señora de África** (Church of Our Lady of Africa) dates from the 15th century with many later additions, the largest in the 18th century, and is also on the site of a former mosque. Long seen as important as a great Christian monument in Islamic North Africa, it has a spectacular baroque altarpiece. The **Palacio**

ON THE ROAD
EU in Africa: immigration policies

It is estimated that in the year 2000, around 10,000 Africans tried illegally to cross the border into Ceuta. The reaction of the EU was to build a £200 million barrier along the border. It is made up of two 3-m razor wire fences with a patrol road between them. The fence is illuminated by spotlights, and cameras detect and record any movement. However, it has not been enough to deter some, who camp out in the hills on the Moroccan side of the border waiting for the chance to cut their way through, or to summon up the courage for the dangerous swim around the coast – one that claims the lives of many every year. Smoke from the camp fires of those wanting to cross drifts across the border post, which can have the feel of a war zone, albeit one that Europeans can stroll through unhindered.

Municipal (town hall) is an interesting modern building dating from 1926 and containing some fine panelling and frescoes by Bertucci. The centre of the Plaza de Africa is taken up with a large monument to those Spaniards who fell in the country's African wars (1859-1860). Note the bronze reliefs of battle scenes by Susillo.

MUSEO DE CEUTA (ARCHEOLOGY SECTION)
ⓘ *30 Paseo del Revellin, Mon-Sat 1000-1400 and 1700-2000 (1000-1400 and 1900-2100 Jun-Sep), Sun 1000-1400, free.*

The Municipal Museum on Paseo del Revellin is well laid out and attractive. Rooms I and II have some fine Punic and Roman amphorae and display the activities of Ceuta and the sea, including the salt-making pans on the ancient site of what is now the Parador and the Plaza de Africa. Room III has items relating to underwater archaeology, with some well-preserved and decorated amphorae and pots, a corn-grinding wheel and a lead depth sounder. Other rooms (IV and V) display medieval crafts of Hispanic-Islamic origins. Rooms VII and VIII are given over to scenes, artefacts and written sources of the Spanish-Moroccan war (1859-1860). Nearby, the **Church of San Francisco** stands in Plaza de los Reyes, which reputedly contains the bones of the Portuguese King Sebastian.

LEGION MUSEUM
ⓘ *Av Dean Navarro Acuña 6, Mon-Sat 0900-1300, free.*

Celebrating the founding and activities of the Spanish Legion, there is a variety of armaments, uniforms and military memorabilia on display here.

CITY WALLS
Forming an impressive ring around the city, these Portuguese-built fortifications are at their best adjacent to the San Felipe moat and the Muralla Real. The exterior fortifications are also impressive – **Fort Desnarigado** and **Fortaleza del Hacho** (the latter, still occupied by the military, is closed to the public). Fortaleza del Hacho is probably Byzantine in origin but was strengthened under the Ommayyad dynasty. It was reconstructed by the Portuguese and redeveloped by the Spanish in the 18th and 19th centuries. In the west of the town above the Ramparts Pedro La Mata are the impressive **Merinid Walls**, a 14th-century construction on earlier buildings. Of the original 2 km of walls, there now remains only a 500-m section, interesting nevertheless, including the old **Fès Gate**. Adjacent to

Plaza de la Paz on Paseo Marina are the ruins of the **Arab baths**, heavily reconstructed but accessible and a useful reminder of the high urban forms of the Arab period.

MUSEO DE CEUTA (FINE ARTS SECTION)

ⓘ *Revellín de San Ignaciao courtyard, Mon-Sat 1000-1400 and 1700-2000 (Jun-Sep 1000-1400 and 1900-2100), Sun 1000-1400, free.*

Inside the city walls, the city museum's fine arts gallery is an excellent contemporary art space, with white angular walls and some interesting temporary exhibitions of Spanish art.

CEUTA LISTINGS

WHERE TO STAY

If you will arrive late in the day, make sure that you reserve your hotel room in advance.

€€€ **Hotel Plaza Ruiz**, 3 Pl Teniente Ruiz, T(+34)956-516733, hostalesceuta@ hotmail.com. One of Ceuta's more desirable small hotels, it has 17 a/c rooms with small bathrooms and pine furniture on a little square just off the main street.

€€€ **Hotel Ulises**, T(+34)956-514540, www.hotelulises.com. By far the swishest hotel in Ceuta. The 124 stylish rooms have dark wood furniture and floors, flatscreen TVs and are decorated using lots of neutral tones, black and white photos and modern art. There's Wi-Fi on the 1st floor but the top-floor rooms have the best views. There's also a pool.

€€ **Bohemia**, C Cameons, T(+34)956-510615. A central place with a degree of old style, **Bohemia** has good rooms, 3 of which have balconies. Shared bathrooms, plants and lots of photos of Marilyn Monroe.

€€ **Hostal Real**, 1 C Real, T(+34)956-511449, www.hostalreal.net. Bang in the centre of town, a good budget option, with clean if not overly bright rooms. Book ahead.

RESTAURANTS

The so-called fisherman's village (actually a modern area where nobody seems to live), just to the east of the marina, has several restaurants; try **Riad Ahlam**, **La Cantina** and **La Peña**.

€€ **Gran Muralla**, Pl de la Constitución, T(+34)956-517625. A proper Chinese restaurant overlooking the square with views and an interior genuine enough to make it seem like a Chinese enclave in a Spanish enclave.

€€ **La Marina**, 4 Alférez Bayton, T(+34)956-514007. Posh but friendly, Marina does paella and a wide range of other fish dishes. Popular.

€€ **Trattoria Pizzería Firenze**, 3 Alférez Bayton, T(+34)956-512088. Wed-Sun. Genuine Italian food; try the ravioli or tagliatelle with egg, spinach and porcini mushrooms or good pizzas.

€€ **Ulises Café**, next to the hotel of the same name (see above). A chic and bijou place for a fine glass of wine or a bar snack.

€ **Café Central**, 2 Millán Astray. Sophisticated café bar used by Ceuta's young professionals, with low lighting and hanging glass lamps.

€ **El Quijote**, 5 Pedro de Meneses. A small, friendly tapas bar on a pedestrian street.

€ **La Bodeguilla**, C Millán Astray. Buzzing tapas bar with a good range of *tostadas*.

€ **La Jota**, 6 Méndez Núñez, T(+34)956-515365. Excellently priced and tasty meals, as well as snacks, sandwiches, cakes and ice cream in a real local-feel restaurant. A great place to hang out and it won't break the bank. They usually have a daily special for under €10.

SHOPPING

There are numerous shops selling duty-free electronic goods, though nothing seems cheaper than a web search would turn up in Europe. Spirits and fuel are cheaper here than in Morocco, or Spain, come to that, given Ceuta's tax status.

PRACTICALITIES

INS AND OUTS

→ BEST TIME TO VISIT MOROCCO

Morocco is a good destination all year round, although January and February can be a bit cold and miserable in the north; Tangier and Fès are not much fun in heavy rain. However, after a wet winter, spring is green and sprinkled with flowers in northern and central Morocco. Routes from Tangier are busy in summer with returning migrant workers from Europe in overloaded cars and are best avoided. Urban sightseeing is fine all year round, although in Marrakech and Fès the heat can be oppressive during the day from July to late September. If you are going to do the southern routes, such as the Dadès and Draâ valleys, February and March are magnificent. Blossom fills the valleys, the days are bright and you won't suffer too much on public transport or driving.

Summer and autumn are good for walking and climbing in the High Atlas; spring can be too, though lingering snow often makes higher routes difficult unless you have good equipment. The Jbel Saghro (see page 191), south of the High Atlas, is a winter walking destination, as are the Anti-Atlas. Windsurfers and surfers will find winds on the Atlantic coast are stronger in summer, but the swell is bigger in winter.

Desert and pre-desert areas are mostly dry and hot but, from December to February, are also extremely cold at night. On the other hand, mountain areas can get quite hot during the summer days. Occasional but heavy showers occur, turning dry riverbeds into dangerous flash floods, while snow blocks the passes of the High Atlas in winter.

Some of the major cities, in particular Casablanca, have high pollution levels, which can make life unpleasant, especially in summer.

→ GETTING TO MOROCCO

AIR

The main international airports in Morocco are **Aéroport Marrakech Menara**, page 35; **Aéroport Casablanca Mohammed V**, page 97, **Aéroport Agadir Al Massira**, page 113 and **Aéroport Tangier Ibn Battouta**, page 199. There are also some international flights to **Aéroport Les Angads**, 15 km from Oujda; **Aéroport Charif Al Idrissi**, Al Hoceïma; **Aéroport Fès Saïss**, Fès; **Aéroport Hassan I**, Laayoune; **Aéroport Taourirt**, Ouarzazate, and **Aéroport Rabat-Salé**, 10 km from Rabat. All these airports are well connected by buses or grands taxis.

Major European airlines run frequent scheduled flights to Morocco's main airports at Casablanca-Mohammed V, Marrakech and Agadir, with most flights operating from France and Spain. National carrier **Royal Air Maroc (RAM)** is reliable. Prices are similar to **Air France** and **British Airways**. The cheapest flights are usually with budget airlines **EasyJet, Ryanair** and **Atlas Blue**. Charter flights are another possible cheap option; run by package holiday companies, they fly mainly to Agadir.

From the UK and the rest of Europe EasyJet (www.easyjet.com) flies daily from London Gatwick to Marrakech. Ryanair (www.ryanair.com) flies a few times a week from London Luton, also to Marrakech, and to Fès from London Stansted on Thursdays and Sundays.

Budget airlines aside, options from the UK to Morocco include **Royal Air Maroc** (www. royalairmaroc.com), which flies daily from Heathrow to Casablanca. RAM also flies out of main western European airports. **Air France** (www.airfrance.com) flies out of Paris to Casablanca and Rabat.

It is possible to get a flight to Gibraltar, Almería or Málaga, and then continue by boat to Ceuta or Tangier in northwest Morocco, or Melilla or Nador further east (see Ferry, below).

From North America RAM flies to Casablanca from Montreal and New York. Flight time from New York to Casablanca is six hours 40 minutes.

FERRY

The shortest ferry crossings from Europe to Morocco are from Tarifa, Algeciras or Gibraltar to Tangier or Ceuta. Longer crossings run from Almería (Spain) and Sète (France), to Melilla and Nador. Ceuta and Melilla are Spanish enclaves so you cross a land border in Africa. Algeciras to Ceuta is fast but the advantage is lost at the Fnideq land border crossing into Morocco. Algeciras to Tangier is the most convenient crossing, Tangier being the northernmost point on the Moroccan rail network and (almost) the starting point of the autoroute down to Casa–Rabat. In the summer months, those with cars will find ferries booked solid months in advance, as Moroccans working in Europe return home to visit family.

When you leave Spain for Morocco, your passport is checked by the Spanish authorities before boarding. Moroccan border formalities are undertaken on board: you fill in a disembarkation form and have your passport stamped at a *guichet*, generally as you get on board. Leaving Morocco, you fill in an embarkation form and departure card, which are stamped by the port police before getting on the boat. (Various people will offer to sell you the police *fiches* but you can pick one up for nothing when you check in.) When you travel from Spain to Spanish enclaves Ceuta and Melilla, this does not apply.

Websites providing details of services (boats and hydrofoils) include **www.tras mediterranea.es** and **www.frs.es**.

TRAIN

Train travel to Morocco is a relatively cheap option and a convenient way to tie in a visit to Morocco with a short stay in Europe, though Interrail tickets are no longer valid in the country. **ONCF** Moroccan rail services can be checked on www.oncf.ma.

→TRANSPORT IN MOROCCO

When planning a trip in Morocco, remember that the distances are great and that long trips on buses can be tiring. Bus journeys are often excruciatingly slow, even over relatively short distances. To make maximum use of your time, especially if you don't mind dozing on a bus, take night buses to cover the longer distances. If you have sufficient funds, then there is always the option of internal flights – although these may not always fit in with your schedule. Public transport is reasonably priced, and the train network is good and being heavily invested in, although it doesn't cover the whole country. Car hire can be expensive; although you may be able to get a small car for 1800-2500dh a week, you still have petrol or diesel costs on top of this. In many places, however, a car enables you to reach places which are otherwise inaccessible.

AIR

Royal Air Maroc (www.royalairmaroc.com) operates domestic flights, most routed via Casablanca and requiring waits in the airport. Cities served include Tangier, Marrakech, Agadir and Ouarzazate. There are limited direct flights between Marrakech and Fès.

For RAM enquiries, call T089-000 0800. All major towns have RAM agencies, generally on the main boulevard.

ROAD

Bicycles and motorcycles Mountain bikes, mopeds and sometimes small motorcycles can be hired in tourist towns. There is no shortage of mechanics to fix bikes and mopeds. Trains, buses and even grands taxis will take bikes for a small fee. Some European companies now run cycling holidays, with bikes being carried on vans on the longer stretches. Off-road biking is popular near Tafraoute in the Anti-Atlas and the Gorges du Dadès.

If you go touring with a bike or motorcycle, beware of the sun. Wear gloves and cover those bits of exposed skin between helmet and T-shirt. For motorcyclists, helmets are complusory, and *gendarmes* will be happy to remind you of the fact.

Riding a motorbike in Morocco is even more testing than driving a car. Watch out for stray pedestrians and note that vehicle drivers will not show you much respect. Where flocks of animals are straying across the road, try not to drive between a single animal and the rest of the flock, as it may well try to charge back to join the rest. Use your horn. If you are going to go off-road, wear boots and make sure your tyres are in tiptop condition.

Theft from bicycle paniers is a problem. Anything loosely attached to your bike will disappear when you are being besieged by a horde of children in an isolated village.

Bus Domestic bus services are plentiful. Price variations are small, while the quality of service varies enormously. On long-distance buses you will find that there is a man who helps stow luggage on the roof or in the hold, so have a couple of dirham coins handy for him. Broadly speaking, if the train, a **Supratours** bus or a grand taxi run to your destination, don't bother with the small bus companies. For early-morning services it's worth getting your ticket in advance, also at peak times when many Moroccans are travelling, such as the end of Ramadan and around Aïd el Kebir (two months after the end of Ramadan).

In southern Morocco, the safest and most comfortable service is also with **Supratours**. Next best is the **CTM**, **Compagnie de Transport Marocain** (white buses with blue and red stripes). Often (but not always) their services run from stations away from the main *gare routière* (inter-city bus station). This is the case in Casablanca, Fès and Marrakech, for example. For Tangier, the CTM station is just outside the port zone gates. For information (*renseignements*) on CTM services, try T0522-458881 or www.ctm.ma. Both Supratours and CTM buses usually run on time. As an example of prices, a single from Marrakech to Essaouira costs 65dh with Supratours.

Most towns have city buses which provide great opportunities for local pickpockets when crowded. Casablanca buses are terrible, so have 20dh notes ready for short red-taxi runs. The orange **Alsa** buses in Marrakech are fine.

Car hire As distances are great, having a car makes a huge difference to the amount of ground you can cover. All the main hire car companies are represented and there are numerous small companies, which vary hugely in reliability. The Peugeot 205 is felt to be a more reliable small car, with slightly higher clearance and better road holding. A good deal would give you a Fiat Uno for 500dh a day with unlimited mileage, although some Marrakech agencies can be cheaper. 4WDs available in Morocco include the Suzuki Gemini (two people) and the Vitara (four people), at around 800dh per day; long-base Mitsubishi Pajeros (six people) are hired at 900-1000dh per day. Toyotas are said to be the best desert 4WDs. Landrovers are very uncomfortable for long cross-country runs on road, especially in summer without air conditioning. There is huge demand for hire cars during the Christmas and Easter breaks. Always try to have the mobile phone number of an agency representative in case of emergency. Always drive more slowly than you would in Europe.

Regarding insurance, the best agencies will provide all risk insurance. Check for scratches and especially tyre condition (this includes spare tyre), presence of jack and warning triangle, working lights and safety belts. When hiring an all-terrain vehicle, try to ascertain that the agency you are hiring from has a reliable, well-maintained fleet. Make sure that the vehicle will go into four-wheel drive easily.

Driving: Speeds are limited to 120 kph on the autoroute, 100 kph on main roads, 60 kph on approaches to urban areas and 40 kph in urban areas. The wearing of seat belts is compulsory outside the cities, and the gendarmes will be watching to see you're wearing them. Note that the police are empowered to levy fairly hefty on-the-spot fines for contravention of traffic regulations.

Petrol: Hire cars in Morocco generally run on petrol (super) rather than diesel. Lead-free petrol is *sans plomb*. In remote areas, remember to fill up whenever possible, preferably at one of the larger petrol stations; new-looking service stations in towns are best.

Safety: There are a number of dangerous stretches of road which you may have to deal with in your hire car. Much concentration is needed on the four-hour drive on the winding, mountainous N9, Marrakech to Ouarzazate, via the Tizi n'Tichka. Fog and icy surfaces are possible in winter. The new N11, the Casablanca to Marrakech motorway, has much improved road transport between the two cities but care must be taken on the Rabat to Fès N1, especially as there are few crash barriers. In the Middle and High Atlas barriers are put across the road on routes to Azrou, Ifrane, Midelt and over the Tizi n'Tichka and Tizi-n-Test when snow blocks roads.

If you are driving into remote areas, always travel with two vehicles. If you are unused to off-road vehicles, employ the services of a driver (around 300dh a day). Remember that progress will be slow, and that distances tend to be measured in hours rather than in kilometres. When you park your vehicle at night, it is essential to leave it in a place where there is a night watchman (*le gardien de nuit*). All good hotels and streets with restaurants will have such a figure who will keep an eye out.

In the case of accidents, you have to get a *constat de police* (a police report), which is a document drawn up by the police, stating whose fault the accident is. Depending on the type of insurance, the client pays a percentage of the cost of repairs. If you have a *sans franchise* (rental contract) you will have nothing to pay.

Taxi Long-distance grands taxis, generally Mercedes 200 saloon cars, run over fixed routes between cities, or within urban areas between the centre and outlying suburbs. There is a fixed price for each route and passengers pay for a place, six in a Mercedes, nine in a Peugeot 504 estate car. Taxis wait until they are full.

Between towns, grands taxis are quicker than trains or buses and, normally, only a little more expensive. Each town has a rank for grands taxis, generally, although not always, next to the main bus station. The drivers cry out the name of their destination and, as you near the taxi station, you may be approached by touts eager to help you find a taxi.

In mountain areas, the same system applies, although the vehicles are Mercedes transit vans (where there is tarmac) or Landrovers, which have two people next to the driver and 10 in the back.

Petits taxis are used within towns and are generally Fiat Unos and Palios. They are colour-coded by town (blue for Rabat, red for Casa, khaki for Marrakech, tasteful pistachio green in Mohammedia). Officially they are metered, with an initial minimum fare, followed by increments of time and distance. There is a 50% surcharge after 2100. A petit taxi may take up to three passengers. In Marrakech, Rabat and Casablanca, drivers generally use the meters; in Tangier they try to charge what they like. In some cities (notably Rabat and Casablanca, where taxis are in short supply) drivers allow themselves to pick up other passengers en route if they are going the same way, thus earning a double fee for part of the route. Taxi drivers welcome a tip – many of them are not driving their own vehicles and make little more than 100dh a day. In terms of price, a short run between old and new town in Marrakech will set you back 12dh.

TRAIN

The ONCF (Office National des Chemins de Fer) runs an efficient though generally slowish service between major cities. There is 1900 km of railway line, the central node being at the railway town of Sidi Kacem, some 46 km north of Meknès. Coming into Casablanca airport, you can take the blue Bidhaoui shuttle train to Casa-Voyageurs station on the main north–south line. This line runs from Tangier to Marrakech, with significant stations being Kénitra, Sidi Kacem, Salé, Rabat, Casa-Voyageurs, Settat and Benguerir. The ONCF's main west–east route does Casa-Voyageurs to Oujda, the main stations on this route being Rabat, Sidi Kacem, Meknès and Fès. A new fast double-decker service connects Casablanca with Fès in three hours 20 minutes. There are also frequent trains from Marrakech to Fès. ONCF timetables are available at all main stations and can be accessed at www.oncf.ma.

Prices and journey times Prices are reasonable. A first-class single ticket, Marrakech to Fès, is 276dh, or 180dh in second class. Services between Casablanca and Rabat, depending on station and class, range form 32dh to 55dh. Casa-Voyageurs to Tangier is 175dh first class. In terms of time, Casablanca to Marrakech generally takes three hours; Casablanca to Rabat just under one hour; Rabat to Fès nearly four hours; Rabat to Tangier is 4¾ hours; Marrakech to Fès is around seven hours.

Train-bus link Supratours run buses to connect with trains from a number of stations. From outside Marrakech station, Supratours has connecting buses to Ouarzazate, Essaouira and Agadir. Sample prices as follows: Marrakech to Agadir 95dh, Marrakech to Ouarzazate 80dh.

Train classes On the trains, first-class compartments are spacious and generally quieter than second class. Second-class rail fares are slightly more expensive than the CTM buses. You gain, however, in time saved, reliability and safety. Trains normally have a snack trolley.

Morocco has a good range of accommodation to suit all budgets. There are several well-appointed business hotels in the main cities, luxurious places for the discerning visitor and clean basic hotels to suit those with limited funds. Independent travellers appreciate the growing number of *maisons d'hôte* or guesthouses (generally referred to as riads, see box, page 41), some very swish indeed, while, in the mountain areas, walkers and climbers will find rooms available in local people's homes. Modern self-catering accommodation is also sometimes available.

HOTELS

At the budget end of the market are simple hotels, often close to bus or train stations. There may be a washbasin, sometimes a bidet. Loos and showers will usually be shared and you may have to pay for a hot shower. Outside the big tourist cities, such hotels have almost exclusively Moroccan customers. Although they are generally clean, it may be best to bring a sheet with you if you're planning to use them a lot. Water, especially in the southern desert towns, can be a problem. Generally, there will be a public bath (hammam) close by for you to take a shower after a long bus journey.

More expensive one-, two- and three-star type hotels are generally in the new part of town (Ville Nouvelle neighbourhoods). Showers may be en suite, breakfast (coffee, bread and jam, a croissant, orange juice) should be available, possibly at the café on the ground floor, for around 20dh. Light sleepers need to watch out for noisy, street-facing rooms. In this price bracket are a number of establishments with a personal, family-run feel.

Top hotels are generally run by international groups. They tend to be vast and brash, revamped and nouveau riche, or solid but tasteful and even discreet with a touch of old-fashioned elegance.

RIADS AND GUESTHOUSES

The big phenomenon of the past 20 years in the Moroccan tourist industry has been the development of the guesthouse. Wealthy Europeans have bought old property in the medinas of Marrakech, Fès and Essaouira as second homes. Rather than leave the property closed for much of the year, the solution was to rent it out. See box, page 41.

YOUTH HOSTELS AND MOUNTAIN ACCOMMODATION

There are 11 hostels in all affiliated to HI, located in the cities (including Casablanca, Rabat, Fès, Meknès and Marrakech) as well as Azrou (Middle Atlas) and Asni (High Atlas). Overnight charges are 20-40dh, with use of the kitchen 2dh. There is a maximum stay of three nights and priority is given to the under-30s. For information try the **Moroccan Youth Hostel Federation**, Parc de la Ligue arabe, Casablanca, T0522-220551.

In the mountains there are three main options for paid accommodation: floor space in someone's home, a gîte of some kind, or a refuge run by the CAF (Club Alpin Français, http://cafmaroc2011.ffcam.fr). The refuges are shelters with basic dormitory and kitchen facilities. Rates depend on category and season.

PRICE CODES

WHERE TO STAY

€€€€ over €140   €€€ €71-140
€€   €35-70   €   under €35
Prices are for double rooms. Singles are marginally cheaper.

RESTAURANTS

€€€ over €30   €€ €15-30   € under €15
Price codes are for a two-course meal for one person, excluding drinks or service charge.

→FOOD AND DRINK IN MOROCCO

MOROCCAN CUISINE

The finest of the Moroccan arts is possibly its cuisine. There are the basics: harira and bessera soups, kebabs, couscous, tagine and the famous *pastilla* (pigeon, egg and almonds in layers of filo pastry). And there are other dishes, less well known: gazelle's horns, coiling *m'hencha* and other fabulous pastries.

Moroccan cooking gets its characteristic flavours from a range of spices and minor ingredients. Saffron (*zaâfrane*), though expensive, is widely used, turmeric (*kurkum*) is also much in evidence. Other widely used condiments include a mixed all spice, referred to as *ra's el hanout* ('head of the shop'), cumin (*kamoun*), black pepper, oregano and rosemary (*yazir*). Prominent greens in use include broad-leaved parsley (*ma'dnous*), coriander (*kuzbur*) and, in some variations of couscous, a sort of celery called *klefs*. Preserved lemons (*bouserra*) can be found in fish and chicken tagines. Bay leaves (*warqa Sidna Moussa*, 'the leaf of our lord Moses') are also commonly employed. Almonds, much used in pâtisserie, are used in tagines too, while powdered cinnamon (*karfa*) provides the finishing touch for *pastilla*. In pâtisserie, orange-flower water and rose water (*ma ouarda*) are essential to achieve a refined taste.

Starters *Harira* is a basic Moroccan soup; ingredients vary but include chick peas, lentils, veg and a little meat. Often eaten accompanied with hard-boiled eggs. *Bissara* is a pea soup, a cheap and filling winter breakfast. *Briouat* are tiny envelopes of filo pastry, akin to the Indian samosa, with a variety of savoury fillings. They also come with an almond filling for dessert.

Snacks Cheaper restaurants serve kebabs (aka brochettes), with tiny pieces of beef, lamb and fat. Also popular is *kefta*, meatball brochettes, served in sandwiches with chips, mustard and harissa (red-pepper spicy sauce). Tiny bowls of finely chopped tomato and onion are another popular accompaniment. On Jemaâ el Fna in Marrakech, strong stomachs may want to snack on the local *babouche* (snails).

Main dishes *Seksou* (couscous) is the great North African speciality. Granules of semolina are steamed over a pot filled with a rich meat and vegetable stew. Unlike Tunisian couscous, which tends to be flavoured with a tomato sauce, Moroccan couscous is pale yellow.

Tagines are stews, the basic Moroccan dish. It is actually the term for the two-part terracotta dish (base and conical lid) in which meat or fish are cooked with a variety of vegetables, essentially, carrot, potato, onion and turnip. Tagine is everywhere in Morocco. Simmered in front of you on a *brasero* at a roadside café, it is always good and safe to eat. Out trekking and in the south, it is the staple of life.

In the better restaurants, look out for *djaj bil-hamid* (chicken with preserved lemons and olives), sweet and sour *tajine barkouk* (lamb with plums), *djaj qudra* (chicken with almonds and caramelized onion) and *tajine maqfoul*. Another tasty dish is *tajine kefta*, basically fried meatballs cooked with eggs and chopped parsley. In eateries next to food markets, delicacies such as *ra's embekhar* (steamed sheep's head) and *kourayn* (animal feet) are popular.

All over Morocco, lamb is much appreciated, and connoisseurs reckon they can tell what the sheep has been eating (rosemary, mountain pasture, straw or mixed rubbish at the vast Mediouna tip near Casablanca). Lamb is cheaper in drought years, when farmers have to reduce their flocks, expensive when the grazing is good, and is often best eaten at roadside restaurants where the lorry drivers pull in for a feed.

Desserts A limited selection of desserts is served in Moroccan restaurants. In the palace restaurants, there will be a choice between *orange à la cannelle* (slices of orange with cinnamon) or some sort of marzipan *pâtisserie* such as *cornes de gazelle* or *ghrayeb*, rather like round shortcake. *El jaouhar*, also onomatopoeically known as *tchak-tchouka*, is served as a pile of crunchy, fried filo pastry discs topped with a sweet custardy sauce and almonds. Also on offer you may find *m'hencha*, coils of almond paste wrapped in filo pastry, served crisp from the oven and sprinkled with icing sugar and cinnamon, and *bechkito*, little crackly biscuits.

In local *laiteries*, try a glass of yoghurt. Oranges (*limoun*) and mandarins (*tchina*) are cheap, as are prickly pears, sold off barrows. In winter, in the mountains, look out for kids selling tiny red arbutus berries (*sasnou*) carefully packaged in little wicker cones. Fresh hazelnuts are charmingly known as *tigerguist*.

Dishes for Ramadan At sunset the fast is broken with a rich and savoury *harira* (see above), *beghrira* (little honeycombed pancakes served with melted butter and honey) and *shebbakia* (lace-work pastry basted in oil and covered in honey). Distinctive too are the sticky pastry whorls with sesame seeds on top.

CAFES AND RESTAURANTS

Cafés offer croissant, petit-pain and cake (madeleine), occasionally soup and basic snacks. Restaurants basically divide into four types: snack eateries, in the medina and Ville Nouvelle, are generally cheap and basic. Some are modelled on international themed fast-food restaurants. Then you have the *laiteries*, which sell yoghurt and fruit juices and will make up sandwiches with processed cheese, salad and *kacher* (processed meat). Full-blown restaurants are generally found only in larger towns, and some are very good indeed. And, finally, in cities like Fès and Meknès, Marrakech and Rabat, you have the great palaces of Moroccan cuisine: restaurants set in old, often beautifully restored private homes.

Eating out cheaply If you're on a very tight budget, try the ubiquitous food stalls and open-air restaurants serving various types of soup, normally the standard broth (*harira*), snacks and grilled meat. The best place for the adventurous open-air eater is the Jemaâ el Fna square in Marrakech. Another good place is the fish market in the centre of Essaouira. There is a greater risk of food poisoning at street eateries, so go for food that is cooked as you wait, or that is on the boil. Avoid fried fish that is already cooked and is reheated when you order it.

Vegetarian food Moroccan food is not terribly interesting for vegetarians, and in many places 'vegetarian cuisine' means taking the meat off the top of the couscous or tagine. The concept is really quite alien to most Moroccans, as receiving someone well for dinner means serving them a tagine with a good chunk of meat. There are some excellent salads, however. Be prepared to eat lots of processed cheese and omelettes.

Eating in people's homes Moroccan families may eat from a communal dish, often with spoons, sometimes with the hands. If invited to a home, you may well be something of a guest of honour. Depending on your hosts, it's a good idea to take some fruit or pâtisseries along. If spoons or cutlery are not provided, you eat using bread, using your right hand, not the left hand since it is ritually unclean. If the dishes with the food are placed at floor level, keep your feet tucked under your body away from the food. In a poorer home, there will only be a small amount of meat, so wait until a share is offered. Basically, good manners are the same anywhere. Let common sense guide you.

DRINK

Tea and coffee All over Morocco the main drink apart from water is mint tea (*thé à la menthe/attay*) a cheap, refreshing drink which is made with green tea, fresh mint and masses of white sugar. The latter two ingredients predominate in the taste. If you want a reduced sugar tea, ask for *attay msous* or *bila sukar/sans sucre*). In cafés, tea is served in mini metal teapots, poured from high above the glass to generate a froth (*attay bi-rizatou*, 'tea with a turban') to use the local expression. Generally, tradition has it that you drink three glasses. To avoid burning your fingers, hold the glass with thumb under the base and index finger on rim.

Coffee is commonly drunk black and strong (*kahwa kahla/un exprès*). For a weak milky coffee, ask for a *café au lait/kahwa halib*. A stronger milky coffee is called a *café cassé/kahwa mherza*.

Wines and spirits For a Muslim country, Morocco is fairly relaxed about alcohol. In the top hotels, imported spirits are available, although at a price. The main locally made lager **beers** are Flag, Flag Spécial, Stork, Castel and Heineken. In the spring, look out for the extremely good Bière de Mars, made only in March with Fès spring water.

Morocco produces **wine**, the main growing areas being Guerrouane and Meknès. Reds tend to prevail. Celliers de Meknès (CdM) and Sincomar are the main producers. At the top of the scale are Médaillon and Beau Vallon. Another reliable red is Domaine de Sahari, Aït Yazem, a pleasant claret, best drunk chilled in summer. The whites include Coquillages and Sémillant. At the very bottom of the scale is rough and ready Rabbi Jacob, or, cheaper and still cheerful, Chaud Soleil. The local fig firewater is Mahia la Gazelle.

Morocco has a number of regional and local festivals, often focusing around a local saint or the harvest time of a particular product, and are fairly recent in origin. The *moussems*, or traditional local festivals, have on occasion been banned in recent years, the authorities giving as a reason the health risks created by gatherings of large numbers of people in places with only rudimentary sanitary facilities. The main Moroccan festivals come in three categories: firstly, the more religious festivals, the timing of which relates to the lunar Islamic year; secondly the annual semi-commercial regional or town festivals with relatively fixed dates; and thirdly, the new generation of arts and film festivals.

Religious holidays and festivals

Religious holidays are scheduled according to the Hijna calendar, a lunar-based calendar. The lunar year is shorter than the solar year, so the Muslim year moves forward by 11 days every Christian year.

1 Muharram First day of the Muslim year.

Mouloud Celebration of the Prophet Mohammed's birthday.

Ramadan A month of fasting and sexual abstinence during daylight hours.

Aïd el Fitr (the Lesser Aïd) A 2-day holiday ending the month of Ramadan.

Aïd el Kebir (the Great Aïd) A 1-day holiday that comes 70 days after Aïd el Fitr. Commemorates how God rewarded Ibrahim's faith by sending down a lamb for him to sacrifice instead of his son. When possible, every family sacrifices a sheep on this occasion.

During **Ramadan**, the whole country switches to a different rhythm. Public offices open part time, and the general pace slows down during the daytime. No Moroccan would be caught eating in public during the day, and the vast majority of cafés and restaurants, except those frequented by resident Europeans and tourists, are closed. At night, the ambience is almost palpable. There is a sense of collective effort, shared with millions of other Muslims worldwide. People who never go out all year are out visiting friends and family, strolling the streets in Ramadan. Shops stay open late, especially during the second half of the month. Ramadan is an interesting and frustrating time to visit Morocco as a tourist, but probably to be avoided if possible if you need to do business.

Regional or town festivals

Feb Festival of the Almond Blossom, Tafraoute, see page 124.

Apr Honey Festival, Immouzer des Ida Outanane, see page 119.

May Rose Festival, El Kelaâ des Mgouna, Dadès Valley, see page 193.

Moussem de Sid Ahmed Ben Mansour, Moulay Bousselham, north of Kénitra, see page 217.

Jun Cherry Festival, Sefrou, see page 157.

Moussem de Moulay Abdeslam ben M'chich, Larache, see page 214.

Moussem de Sidi Mohammed Ma El Ainin, Tan Tan, south of Sidi Ifni, see page 131.

Jul Festival of Sea Produce, Al Hoceïma, see page 250.

Aug Moussem of Moulay Abdallah, El Jadida, see page 94.

Festival des Pommes, Immouzer du Kandar, see page 179.

Moussem of Moulay Idriss Zerhoun, Moulay Idriss, see page 172.

Moussem of Setti Fatma, Setti Fatma, Ourika Valley near Marrakech, see page 67.

Moussem of Sidi Ahmed ou Moussa, Tiznit, see page 130.

Sep Marriage Festival, eastern High Atlas, near Imilchil, see page 180.

Horse Festival, Tissa near Fès, contact the tourist office, see page 140.

Moussem of Moulay Idris al Azhar, Fès, see page 142.

Oct Date Festival, Erfoud, see page 186.

Arts festivals

Feb **Salon du livre**, Casablanca. Morocco's biggest annual bookfair. Prix du Grand Atlas, literary events.

May **Les Alizés**, Essaouira. Small classical music festival in early May, www.alizesfestival.com.

Festival des Musiques Sacrées, Fès – generally late May running into Jun. Attracts a strange mixture of the spiritual, the hippy and the wealthy. Accompanied by popular music concerts open to all. See www.fesfestival.com.

Mawazine Festival, Rabat. The capital comes alive with world music and pop concerts held in various venues.

Jun **L'Boulevard**, Casablanca. Annual urban music (hip-hop, electro, fusion, rock, etc) festival, www.boulevard.ma.

Festival Gnaoua, Essaouira. One of Morocco's most successful music festivals, www.festival-gnaoua.co.ma.

Festival National des Arts Populaires, Marrakech, see page 56.

Jul **Festival Rawafid des créateurs marocains de l'étranger**, Casablanca. Focusing on work by Moroccan artists abroad. Music and film.

Aug **Arts Festival**, Asilah. Paintings of the medina, festival now in its 30th year.

Sep **Festival international du film méditerranéen**, Tetouan. Long-established but slightly erratic small film festival.

Tanjazz Tangier jazz festival, mixture of free and paying concerts, www.tanjazz.org.

Dec **Festival international du film de Marrakech**, Marrakech. Established annual film fest, www.festivalmarrakech.info.

ESSENTIALS A-Z

Accident and emergency
Police: T19. **Fire brigade**: T15. Larger towns will have an **SOS Médecins** (private doctor on-call service) and almost all towns of any size have a pharmacy on duty at night, the *pharmacie de garde*. Any large hotel should be able to give you the telephone/address of these. For most ailments, a *médecin généraliste* (GP) will be sufficient.

Dress
In coastal resorts, you can wear shorts and expose arms and shoulders. However, when wandering round medinas and going to city centres, both men and women should cover shoulders. Sandals are fine but shorts should be baggy not skimpy. Expect lots of remarks and attention if you do go wandering round the souks in your running shorts. Have some smart but cool tops with you for summer travelling. Inland, winter is cold. Night temperatures in the desert and at altitude are low all the year – a fleece is handy, even as a pillow.

Drugs
Kif or marijuana represents a good source of income for small farmers in the Rif. However, the European Union has put pressure on Morocco to stop production. There is no serious attempt to stop those Moroccans who so wish from having a gentle smoke, and *kif* is also consumed in the form of *maâjoun* cakes, a local variant of hash brownies, which have been known to lead to much merriment at otherwise staid occasions. However, as a tourist, under no circumstances do you want to be caught by the police in the possession of drugs of any kind. And anyone caught exporting the stuff will be made an example of.

Electricity
Morocco has a fairly reliable electricity supply of 220V, using continental European round 2-pin plugs. In some more remote areas, however, there is no mains electricity.

Embassies and consulates
For embassies and consulates of Morocco, see www.embassy.goabroad.com.

Health
No vaccinations are required to enter Morocco. You should be up to date with **polio**, **tetanus**, **typhoid** and **hepatitis A** protection. If you are going to be travelling in rural areas where hygiene is often a bit rough and ready, then you should consider having a **hepatitis B** and **rabies** vaccine.

Major health risks include acute **mountain sickness**, which can strike from about 3000 m upwards and, in general, is more likely to affect those who ascend rapidly and those who over-exert themselves. Acute mountain sickness takes a few hours or days to come on and presents with headache, lassitude, dizziness, loss of appetite, nausea and vomiting. When trekking to high altitude, some time spent walking at medium altitude, getting fit and acclimatizing is beneficial.

Some form of **diarrhoea** or intestinal upset is almost inevitable; the standard advice is to be careful with drinking water and ice; if you have any doubts about the water then boil it or filter and treat it. In a restaurant, buy bottled water or ask where the water has come from. Be wary of salads if you don't know whether they have been washed or not.

Malaria is not normally present in Morocco and usually prophylaxis is not advised, but check before you go.

Language

Arabic is the official language of Morocco, but nearly all Moroccans with a secondary education have enough French to communicate with, as well as a smattering of English. In the north, Spanish maintains a presence thanks to TV and radio. Outside education, however, Moroccan Arabic in the cities and Amazigh in the mountains are the languages of everyday life, and attempts to use a few words and phrases, no matter how stumblingly, will be appreciated. Moroccan Arabic is characterized by a clipped quality (the vowels just seem to disappear), and the words taken from classical Arabic are often very different from those used in the Middle East. In addition, there is the influence of the Berber languages and a mixture of French and Spanish terms, often heavily 'Moroccanized'.

Money → *US$1 = 8.4dh, UK £1 = 13.1dh, €1 = 11.1dh (Jun 2013).*
There is a fixed rate for changing notes and no commission ought to be charged for this.

ATMs

European cash and Visa cards function in Moroccan ATMs (*guichets automatiques*), in major towns it is possible to withdraw more or less exactly the amount you need on a daily basis. At weekends and during big public holidays, airport and city-centre ATMs can be temperamental. The most reliable ATMs are those of the **Wafa Bank** (green and yellow livery) and the **BMCI**.

Banks

Main banks include the **BMCE**, **Crédit du Maroc**, **Wafabank** and **Banque Populaire**; all are widespread. The **BMCE** and the **Crédit du Maroc** seem to have the best change facilities, while the **Banque Populaire** is often the only bank in southern towns. See Opening hours, below, for banking hours.

Credit cards

Credit cards are widely accepted at banks, top hotels, restaurants and big tourist shops. For restaurants, check first before splashing out. Remember to keep all credit card receipts – and, before you sign, check where the decimal marker (a comma in Morocco rather than a dot) has been placed, and that there isn't a zero too many. You don't want to be paying thousands rather than hundreds of dirhams. To reduce problems with card fraud, it makes sense to use a credit card for payments of expensive items.

Currency

The major unit of currency in Morocco is the dirham (dh). In 1 dirham there are 100 centimes. There are coins for 1 (very rare), 5, 10, 20 and 50 centimes, and for 1, 2, 5 and 10 dirhams, as well as notes for 20, 50, 100 and 200 dirhams. The coins can be a little confusing. There are 2 sorts of 5 dirham coin: the older and larger cupro-nickel ('silver coloured' version), being phased out, and the new bi-metal version, brass colour on the inside. There is a brownish 20 dirham note, easily confused with the 100 dirham note. The 50 dirham note is green, the 100 dirham is brown and sand colour, and the 200 dirham note is in shades of blue and turquoise. Currency is labelled in Arabic and French.

You can sometimes buy Moroccan dirhams at bureaux de change at the London airports but dirhams may not be taken out of Morocco. If you have excess dirhams, you can exchange them back into euros at a bank on production of exchange receipts.

Traveller's cheques

Although somewhat time-consuming to change, traveller's cheques (TCs) are still useful (though a small commission will be charged for changing them). Take TCs from a well-known bank or company, preferably in euros. Some hotels and shops will exchange TCs.

Cost of travelling

As a budget traveller, it is possible to get by in Morocco for £30-35/US$60-70 a day although £40/US$80 is more realistic. Your costs can be reduced by having yoghurt and bread and cheese for lunch and staying in an 80dh a night hotel (you can often find even cheaper options in small towns).

In top-quality hotels, restaurants, nightclubs and bars, prices are similar to Europe. Rabat, Casablanca and Agadir are the most expensive places, while manufactured goods in remote rural areas tend to cost more. Around the 200dh mark, you can get a much better meal in a restaurant than you can in Western Europe.

Opening hours

The working week for businesses is Mon to Fri, with half-day working Sat. On Fri, the lunch break tends to be longer, as the main weekly prayers with sermon are on that day. Official business takes considerably longer in Ramadan.
Banks 0830-1130 and 1430-1600 in winter; afternoons 1500-1700 in summer; 0930-1400 during Ramadan.
Museums Most close on a Tue. Hours are generally 0900-1200 and 1500-1700, although this can vary considerably.
Shops Generally 0900-1200 and 1500-1900, although this varies in the big towns.

Public holidays

1 Jan New Year's Day.
1 May Fête du Travail (Labour Day).
9 Jul Fête de la Jeunesse.
30 Jul Fête du Trône. Commemorates the present king Mohammed VI's accession.
20 Aug Anniversaire de la Révolution.
6 Nov Marche Verte/El Massira el Khadhra. Commemorates a march by Moroccan civilians to retake the Spanish-held Saharan territories of Río de Oro and Saguiet El Hamra.
18 Nov Independence Day. Commemorates independence and Mohammed V's return from exile.

Safety

Morocco is basically a very safe country, although there is occasional violent street crime in Casablanca and (very rarely) Marrakech. Travelling on public transport, you need to watch your pockets. Do not carry all your money and cards, etc, in the same place. A money belt is a good idea. Never have more money than you can afford to lose in the pockets of your jeans. Thieves operate best in crowds, getting on and off trains and at bus and taxi stations where they can quickly disappear into an anonymous mass of people.

Be aware of the skilled con-artists in operation in certain places. Hasslers of various kinds are active at the gates of Tangier port and, to a lesser extent, in Tetouan. There are all sorts of ruses used by hasslers to extract a little money from tourists. You need to be polite and confident, distant and sceptical and even a little bored by the whole thing. Learn the values of the banknotes quickly (the yellow-brown 100dh and the blue 200dh are the big ones, a red 10dh is no great loss). Keep your wits about you. Remember, you are especially vulnerable stumbling bleary-eyed off that overnight bus.

Should you be robbed, reporting it to the police will take time – but may alert them to the fact that there are thieves operating in a given place.

Young women travelling with a male friend report few difficulties, and couples with small children will find that the little ones attract a great deal of kindly attention. However, for a woman travelling alone, the hassle and stares can be extremely tiring after a while. In towns, it helps if you dress fairly smartly and modestly, look confident, busy and as though you know where you're going. Remember, a lot of importance is given to looking smart and respectable in Morocco. The plain clothes **Brigade Touristique** are in action in a number of the main holiday destinations stamping down on hassle.

Security and terrorism

The Moroccan government claims to have broken up 55 terrorist cells in the last 10 years, and there are around 1000 Islamists in the country's jails on terrorist charges. There is tight monitoring of all fundamentalist activity and zero tolerance of anything which might lead to violence. As anything Jewish is an obvious target, there are police outside most synagogues.

Telephone → *Country code 212.*

Lots of Moroccans have mobile phones but there are also phone shops or *téléboutiques*, clearly marked in distinctive blue and white livery. They stay open late in summer, are always supervised, have change available and (generally) telephone directories (*annuaires téléphoniques*). The machines are sometimes old French coin phones, and international calls are no problem. For internal calls, put in several 1dh coins and dial the region code (even if you are in the region), followed by the number (a total of 10 digits beginning with 0). For overseas calls, put in at least 3 coins of 5dh, dial 00 and wait for a musical sequence before proceeding. Calls can also be made from the *cabines téléphoniques* at the **PTT Centrale**. Give the number to the telephonist who dials it and then calls out a cabin number where the call is waiting. Note, it is significantly more expensive to phone from a hotel.

Mobile phone coverage in Morocco is reasonably good, though international roaming prices are expensive. It might be worth getting a sim card from www.sim4travel.net, which allows free incoming calls and cheaper international calls, or buying a local Moroccan sim card on arrival.

Time

Morocco follows the UK all year round, with GMT in winter and GMT+1 in summer. Ceuta and Melilla work on Spanish time.

Tipping

This can be a bit of a 'hidden cost' during your stay in Morocco. Tipping is expected in restaurants and cafés, by guides, porters and car park attendants and others who render small services. Make sure you have small change at the ready. Tipping taxi drivers is optional. Do not tip for journeys when the meter has not been used, because the negotiated price will be generous anyway. For porters in hotels, tip around 3dh, on buses 3-5dh, and 5dh on trains and in airports.

Tourist information
Moroccan tourist boards abroad
Moroccan National Tourist Board (ONMT) For locations worldwide, see www.visitmorocco.org.

Visas

No visas are required for full passport holders of the UK, USA, Canada, Australia, New Zealand/Aotearoa, Canada, Ireland and most EU countries. Benelux passport holders require visas at the present time. On the aeroplane or boat, or at the border, travellers will be required to fill in a form with standard personal and passport details, an exercise to be repeated in almost all hotels and guesthouses throughout the country. From the point of entry, travellers can stay in Morocco for 3 months.

Visa extensions These require a visit to the Immigration or Bureau des Etrangers department at the police station of a larger town, as well as considerable patience.

Weights and measures

Morocco uses the metric system.

INDEX

CREDITS

Footprint credits
Editor: Felicity Laughton
Production and layout: Emma Bryers
Maps: Kevin Feeney
Cover and colour section: Pepi Bluck

Publisher: Patrick Dawson
Advertising: Elizabeth Taylor
Sales and marketing: Kirsty Holmes

Printed in Spain by GraphyCems

Every effort has been made to ensure that the facts in this guidebook are accurate. However, travellers should still obtain advice from consulates, airlines etc about travel and visa requirements before travelling. The authors and publishers cannot accept responsibility for any loss, injury or inconvenience however caused.

Publishing information
Footprint DREAM TRIP Morocco
1st edition
© Footprint Handbooks Ltd
July 2013

ISBN: 978 1 907263 72 9
CIP DATA: A catalogue record for this book is available from the British Library

® Footprint Handbooks and the Footprint mark are a registered trademark of Footprint Handbooks Ltd

Published by Footprint
6 Riverside Court
Lower Bristol Road
Bath BA2 3DZ, UK
T +44 (0)1225 469141
F +44 (0)1225 469461
footprinttravelguides.com

Distributed in the USA by Globe Pequot Press, Guilford, Connecticut

Photography credits

Front cover: Doug Pearson/AWL Images **Back cover**: SIERPINSKI Jacques/hemis.fr; Frank Chang/Shutterstock.com; Isabella Pfenningers/Shutterstock.com
Inside front flap: zeber/Shutterstock.com; Andrey Plis/Shutterstock.com; Gigi Peis/Shutterstock.com; kataleewan intarachote/Shutterstock.com

Colour pages: title page: zoryanchik/Shutterstock.com. **p2**: Florin Stana/Shutterstock.com, Anibal Trejo/Shutterstock.com. **p3**: OPIS Zagreb/Shutterstock.com, Rechitan Sorin/Shutterstock.com. **p4**: Vladimir Melnik/Shutterstock.com, Andre Viegas/Shutterstock.com. **p8**: Jonathan Noden-Wilkinson/Shutterstock.com. **p9**: Andy Sutton/Alamy, Kogen_Hansen/Shutterstock.com. **p10**: Florin Stana/Shutterstock.com, cdrin/Shutterstock.com, Rechitan Sorin/Shutterstock.com. **p11**: foto360/Shutterstock.com. **p12**: Alex Andrei/Shutterstock.com. **p13**: David Varga/Shutterstock.com, BonnieBC/Shutterstock.com.

p14: Inc/Shutterstock.com, amskad/Shutterstock.com, Martin Lindsa/Alamy. **p15**: Ana del Castillo/Shutterstock.com, Julius Honnor. **p16**: Ppictures/Shutterstock.com, Radu Razvan/Shutterstock.com, silver-john/Shutterstock.com. **p17**: WILDLIFE GmbH/Alamy, Rechitan Sorin/Shutterstock.com. **p18**: Julius Honnor. **p19**: Javarman/Dreamstime.com, Florin Stana/Shutterstock.com. **p20**: Curioso/Shutterstock.com. **p21**: Rechitan Sorin/Shutterstock.com, Curioso/Shutterstock.com, Anibal Trejo/Shutterstock.com. **p22**: Wolf Winte/age fotostock/SuperStock, Biosphoto/SuperStock. **p23**: Rechitan Sorin/Shutterstock.com, Virginija Valatkiene/Shutterstock.com, Curioso/Shutterstock.com. **p24**: OPIS Zagreb/Shutterstock.com. **p25**: OPIS Zagreb/Shutterstock.com. **p26**: Nico Tondini/Robert Harding Picture Library/SuperStock. **p27**: Yadid Levy/Alamy, Rechitan Sorin/Shutterstock.com. **p28**: Luisa Puccini/Shutterstock.com, Rechitan Sorin/Shutterstock.com. **p29**: Iconotec/Alamy. **p30**: John Copland/Shutterstock.com, Veronika Trofer/Shutterstock.com. **p31**: Boris Stroujko/Shutterstock.com. **p32**: Chantal de Bruijne/Shutterstock.com.